FROM FIRE TO LIGHT

FROM FIRE TO LIGHT

REREADING THE MANUSMṚTI

ARVIND SHARMA

HarperCollins *Publishers* India

First published in India by HarperCollins *Publishers* 2024
4th Floor, Tower A, Building No. 10, DLF Cyber City,
DLF Phase II, Gurugram, Haryana – 122002
www.harpercollins.co.in

2 4 6 8 10 9 7 5 3 1

P-ISBN: 978-93-5699-776-9
E-ISBN: 978-93-9440-737-4

Typeset in 11/14.2 Minion Pro at
Manipal Technologies Limited, Manipal

Printed and bound at
Replika Press Pvt. Ltd.

FSC www.fsc.org
MIX
Paper | Supporting responsible forestry
FSC™ C016779

This book is produced from independently certified FSC® paper to ensure
responsible forest management.

For

Professor Bharat Gupt

Contents

Preface xi

Part I

1. Introduction 3
2. *Manusmṛti*: The Historical Context 14

Part II

3. Sources of *Dharma* in the *Manusmṛti* 35
4. The Doctrine of *Varṇas* in the *Manusmṛti* 55
5. The Position of the *Śūdras* in the *Manusmṛti* 73
6. The Doctrine of *Āśramas* in the *Manusmṛti* 95
7. Women in the *Manusmṛti* 105

Part III

8. Legal Discrimination in the *Manusmṛti* 133
9. The Political System of the *Manusmṛti* 150
10. Foreign Policy in the *Manusmṛti* 163
11. The *Manusmṛti* on Hinduism as a Missionary Religion 182

Part IV

12. Karma and Rebirth in the *Manusmṛti* 199

13. The Doctrine of the *Yugas* in the *Manusmṛti* 221

14. The Hermeneutics of Suspicion and the *Manusmṛti* 233

15. Conclusions 251

APPENDICES

Appendix I Dalits in the Manusmṛti 273

Appendix II Clusters of Verses 279

Appendix III Is Hinduism Brahmanical? 281

Bibliography 289

Notes 299

Index 347

FROM FIRE TO LIGHT

Preface

I

To write on the *Manusmṛti* is to play with fire! This statement is not merely metaphorical; the *Manusmṛti* has a history of being literally torched.[1] But where there is fire, there is also the possibility of light.

I encountered the *Manusmṛti* in two distinct stages: during my early life in India, the land of my birth, and then later during my prolonged sojourn in the West as an academic. That I encountered it in India is nothing unusual; even Mahatma Gandhi refers to reading the *Manusmṛti* during his early life in India, which curiously enough inclined him towards atheism.[2] The general impression I formed about the book while in India was that it helped inculcate virtuous living. I remember one reference in particular, which was cited in a biographical account of Netaji Subhas Chandra Bose; Netaji is the title by which he was and is popularly revered.[3] A few words about him may not be out of place as modern Indian history, as it is currently written, has a way of passing him by. He formed the Indian National Army (INA) from among the almost 90,000 Indian prisoners captured by the Japanese in the Far Eastern theatre of the Second World War. About 45,000 of these prisoners quit the British army to join the INA. With the formation of the INA, the nightmare of the Mutiny of 1857–58—when of 139,000 sepoys, 'all but 7,795 turned against their

British masters'[4]—returned to haunt the British dream of empire. The INA's formation played a major role—not often acknowledged in history books but openly acknowledged by British Prime Minister Attlee—in prompting the British to leave India after the end of the war.

While in Germany, where he was on a mission similar to that which was to take him to Japan, Netaji married his Austrian secretary. This marriage caused some adverse reaction in India and is a delicate point in the biography of this Indian hero, who after all did such a European thing as marrying one's secretary, when almost any young woman in Bengal would have been proud of that honour. It was in an attempt to justify this marriage that the hagiographical account of Netaji's life I was reading quoted the *Manusmṛti* (2.238). The quote suggested that one could marry a 'splendid woman even from a bad family' and was meant to imply that this was what Netaji had done. Incidentally, *Manusmṛti* 2.240 may have been a better choice as it states that a woman from anywhere may be accepted in marriage. Moreover, in one reading of this verse, it could mean that a splendid woman from anywhere may be accepted. In this way, the fair name of the family of his Austrian wife would not be rendered questionable. The reader can readily see that the allusion to the *Manusmṛti* here had a positive implication.

I remember another occasion where my fellow students at school were upset by an admonishment in the *Manusmṛti* (2.215) that one should not sit in private even with one's mother, sister or daughter. Their criticism was how could anyone even think of this (the thought that such proximity might lead to unseemly thoughts or action)? But this reference only confirmed my view that the *Manusmṛti* was a book on morals—and high morals, though it could overstate its point. In my view this reference was not derogatory to women, as it emphasizes male weakness. I heard a third verse from the *Manusmṛti* at a public speech. The verse I heard this time recommended women be revered (3.56): 'Where women are revered, there the gods rejoice; but where they are not, no rite bears any fruit.'[5] While in India, I was therefore left with a positive impression of the *Manusmṛti* overall.

During the course of my stay in the West, however, I gradually discovered that allusions to the text were almost wholly negative. Massively so. And this difference in due course generated massive cognitive dissonance in me! Sometimes I would check the text to assure myself that it had been cited accurately, or that I had understood the text correctly.

As I now approach the end of my academic career and even that of life itself, I have decided to examine the text in a somewhat comprehensive way in order to understand it. Manu's name, in modern times, at least in some circles, has become a byword for oppression and regression, while even the Buddhist tradition in Burma does not hesitate to regard Manu as a great lawgiver! How are these opposing perceptions to be understood?

It has also become clear to me that as Patrick Olivelle notes, the *Manusmṛti* 'was for better or for worse the lens through which most European scholars viewed India's past.'[6] I had discovered that they continued to view India's present through this very same lens, labouring under the belief that India's social reality had not changed much over the centuries, especially where caste was concerned. An argument could be made that what they saw through this lens 'for better or worse', veered towards the worse. If *The Oxford History of India* (1958) is to be believed, 'the early Sanskritists unduly exalted the authority of the *Laws of Manu*', and even if now we know better, 'the old errors still exert a baneful influence in many directions.'[7]

One such baneful influence—verses, not complimentary to the lower castes and women, but quoted all the time in the West—perhaps could be identified as lying at the root of my cognitive dissonance. These verses had been largely absent from my exposure to the text in India in the early stages of my life. For a while I wondered whether it was just to avoid embarrassment that these verses were avoided in India, for some of them sound quite outrageous in a contemporary context and were thus not bandied around the way they are in the West. But the more I studied the subject the more apparent it became to me that there could be another reason underlying it: *that these verses were considered obsolete by the tradition itself.*

Let us take the 'caste system' for instance, which is spelled out in considerable detail in the *Manusmṛti*. Already Yudhiṣṭhira, in the *Mahābhārata* (period of composition c. 400 BCE–400 CE, thus straddling the *Manusmṛti*),[8] suggests that the mixture of castes had reached such proportions that birth could not be relied upon to determine caste. In fact, Yudhiṣṭhira cites verses putatively from the *Manusmṛti* itself to establish that caste should be determined by conduct and not birth.[9] Kumārila, in the seventh century, recognizes that rulers in India have come from all 'castes',[10] Śaṅkara, around the eighth century, remarks in his commentary on the *Brahmasūtra* 3.33 that contemporary reality in relation to caste does not conform to the textual account.[11] Udayana (c. 1000 CE), does not allude to caste but to domestic rituals as holding the tradition together,[12] and Tirrukōneri Dāsyai, in the fourteenth century, displays a degree of familiarity with the Upaniṣads which is inconsistent with the *Manusmṛti*,[13] for she was a woman who was not supposed to know that. Lakṣmīdevī, again a woman, surprisingly wrote a commentary in the eighteenth century on the *Mitākṣarā*, which is a commentary on the *Yājñavalkya Smṛti* (rather than on the *Manusmṛti*)[14] by Vijñāneśvara, who lived in the eleventh century. Interestingly, 'On matters of women's rights of inheritance and the right to hold property, status of Śūdras, and criminal penalty, Yājñavalkya is more liberal than Manu.'[15]

Moreover, there is the general impression abroad that the 'caste system'—which is believed to have characterized Hindu society ever since it was allegedly cast in that mould by the *Manusmṛti*—remained a negative factor so far as India's economic development was concerned, until loosened up by the forces of modernity released during British rule. But new data seriously challenges this view. According to a magisterial survey of world economic history by Angus Maddison, India had the largest share of global output from 100 CE to 1500 CE. In 1600 it lost that position to China but regained it in 1700. Then during the British rule, it gradually shrank to its lowest ever share.[16]

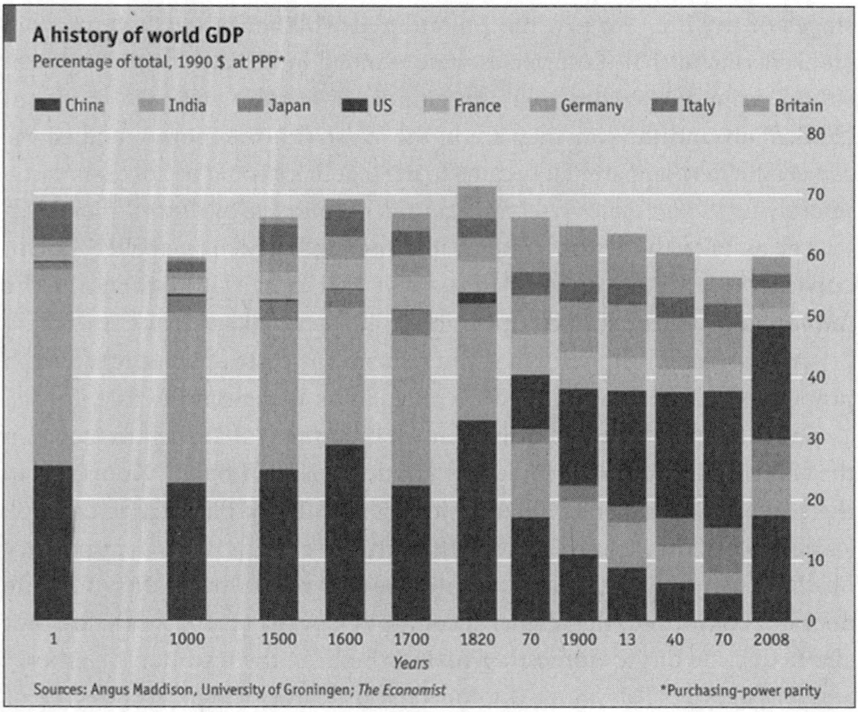

These figures are fascinating, because the *Manusmṛti* is usually placed in the second century CE, which broadly coincides with the chronology of the historical account presented above and thus creates serious problems for conventional wisdom in this regard. When the influence of the *Manusmṛti* is supposed to be the most detrimental, India has prospered, and when its influence declines, as in modern times, India heads into poverty![17]

This could mean several things. (1) That the influence of the *Manusmṛti* was not as pervasive as made out to be, and that first the Jaina and Buddhist movements and then the Bhakti movement and other reform movements kept its influence in check. (2) That the Indian share of global output would have been even higher but for the economic drag caused by the *Manusmṛti*'s baneful influence. (3) That foreign rule—first by the Indo-Bactrians, the Indo-Parthians, the Scythians and the Kuṣāṇas from around 200 BCE to 200 CE, and then by the Arabs and later by the Ghaznivids, then sustained Muslim rule from around the thirteenth to the eighteenth centuries—had a tonic effect on the economy. (4) That somehow *Manusmṛti*'s caste system secured economic benefits but only for the upper castes and classes, just as Greek and Roman slaves supported their elites. (5) Could it just be that the effect of the *Manusmṛti* was not as negative as it is usually portrayed to be? That it actually produced a template of society which promoted prosperity. In fact, the *Manusmṛti spells out prosperity as a justification of the 'caste system'* (*Manusmṛti* 1.31).

At the very least, if the explanation of India's poverty is to be found either in Hinduism or imperialism, and if the *Manusmṛti* is used as a synecdoche for Hinduism, then the data provided by Angus Maddison complicates the picture.

It thus becomes clear that the *Manusmṛti* calls for a closer examination.

II

The *Manusmṛti* is a highly contested site and will remain so after the appearance of this book, but the issue needs to be addressed in more detail.

There are several contesting perspectives from which it has been studied. Some of these approaches may be contrasted and listed as: (1) an advocacy versus critical analysis approach; (2) an emic versus etic approach; and (3) a traditional versus pathological approach.

The advocacy versus critical analysis approach presents a contrast between those for whom the *Manusmṛti* is a text, which has either to be advocated for as a blueprint of a state and society based on Hindu values *or* to be railed against as a text that is opposed to modern constitutional values. The contrast is between *Manusmṛti* serving as the basis of a 'Brahmanical' utopia or a modern dystopia. For such students of the text, the text is not so important for what it says as what it could be said to stand for or be made to stand for. Both attitudes differ from that of a student who is interested in knowing and understanding what the text says rather than what it can be made to stand for or how it could be linked to modern ideologies. In terms of such an approach, this book is about critical analysis rather than advocacy.

The student interested in approaching the text in the spirit of analysis rather than advocacy, may choose to study the text from either an emic or an etic perspective.[18] As is well known, the emic approach corresponds to that of the insider, and the etic that of the outsider. The significance of this difference would perhaps become clear if we reverted to the questions posed by the economic history of the world as laid out by Angus Maddison.

Is it entirely due to chance that the contrast between a social narrative of India based on the *Manusmṛti* and an economic narrative on India based on recent findings is being identified for contrast by an Indian and not a Western scholar? This is not to suggest that one group of scholars is less scholarly than the other; it is to suggest that while both may cherish objectivity, it may yet make a difference whether the matter is being approached from an emic or an etic perspective, and that both these perspectives can be espoused by both Indian and Western scholars.

Emic and etic approaches can produce different, even opposite, results. For instance, the sections of the *Manusmṛti* emphasized by one approach may not be considered important by another. I notice, for instance, that parts of the *Manusmṛti* which insiders (that is, Hindus in India), usually refer to are the early chapters, which tell us about the way one is supposed to lead one's life, while most outsiders (Westerners and Western scholars) focus on those concerned with caste and gender discrimination, as if that is also the current state of affairs. I have so far noticed little discussion on the fact that—in the context of caste and gender discrimination—India has had the largest affirmative action programme in the world in place for the past seventy years; a point once again more likely to be made by an Indian than a Western observer. There also seems to be greater acceptance of such programmes in India than in the United States, where one often hears it said that 'I do not own slaves, my forefathers did'. In India there seems to be a greater willingness to accept responsibility for historical wrongs, which may owe something to the principles such as that of karma laid down in the *Manusmṛti* itself.

I have associated Indians or Hindus with the emic approach and Westerners with the etic approach because Hindus naturally fall in the position of insiders and Westerners, outsiders, and because it makes the contrast between the two approaches so obvious. But the two positions are not just tied to geographical locations. For instance, an Indian can adopt the position of the outsider and thus adopt an etic approach. Similarly, an outsider to the tradition can also adopt the position of the insider and adopt the emic approach. These positions are not tied to geography, but to mentality, to the attitude adopted.

It might be helpful to illustrate the difference the approach adopted makes, with an actual example. The etic approach regards the *Manusmṛti* as the charter of the infamous caste system, but there are two Sanskrit words, *varṇa* and *jāti*, that are translated into English as caste—and the difference between the two is important. As A.L. Basham explains:

> All ancient Indian sources make a sharp distinction between the two terms; *varṇa* is often referred to but *jāti* very little, and when it does appear in literature it does not always imply the comparatively rigid and exclusive social groups of later times. If caste is defined as a system of groups within the class, which are normally endogamous, commensal, and craft-exclusive, we have no real evidence of this until comparatively late times.[19]

The crux of the matter is that *varṇa* refers to class and *jāti* to caste proper, which is to say, to the endogamous, commensal and craft-exclusive groups which the etic descriptions have in mind. Let us now introduce the emic perspective to see what happens. Hinduism describes itself as '*varṇāśrāma dharma*', especially when it distinguishes itself from other religions of Indian origin which might also use the word *dharma* for themselves—such as Buddhism, Jainism and Sikhism. Hinduism self-consciously describes itself as *varṇāśrāma dharma* in contrast to these.

The point to note is that it does *not* describe itself as upholding *jāti*, but rather *varṇa*. Thus, while the etic approach considers the *Manusmṛti* as sanctifying the formulation of the caste (*jāti*) system, the emic perspective considers it as doing so in terms of the *varṇa* system. In that sense, from the emic point of view, the etic perspective misses a vital point. This difference is not merely nominal; if we recognize the *distinction* between *varṇa* and *jāti*, then it is hard to dimiss it as superficial.

What makes this point especially interesting from an anthropological perspective is the fact that other than Hinduism, all the three religions mentioned earlier, namely Buddhism, Jainism and Sikhism, also exhibit the phenomenon of caste as a social reality. They have *jāti* as a social fact but reject *varṇa* as doctrinal fact. This makes it possible to suggest that the phenomenon of caste could perhaps be viewed as a *South Asian phenomenon* to which all the religions of Indian origin had to adjust in due course, as distinguished from considering caste as a *Hindu phenomenon*. In that case, Hinduism's decision to align itself with *varṇa* and not *jāti* takes on added significance.

This book utilizes both the approaches, depending on which of the two sheds more or better light on the matter under investigation.

III

We have so far discussed the significance of the distinction between analysis and advocacy, and the difference that the adoption of an emic or an etic approach makes in the context of a contested site such as the *Manusmṛti*. It remains to be explored how the difference between a traditional approach and a pathological approach plays out in this context. What connects this point with the previous one is that the etic approach tends to arrive at toxic conclusions about Hinduism based on the *Manusmṛti*: the social system envisaged in the *Manusmṛti* is nothing more than a pathology; and a society based on it—which it claims the Hindu society is—is also nothing more than that.

Although such an approach has been associated with the West for a long time, it was not always so. When the *Manusmṛti* was first translated into English by Sir William Jones and published posthumously in 1794 under the title *Institutes of Hindu Law*, its purpose was to assist the British, who had just begun to govern parts of India, in administering justice to the people. It was treated as a source of Hindu law to be consulted when necessary. The British were finding their feet in India politically during this period, which was a time when the so-called Orientalists were in the ascendant (as compared to those who would later be called Anglicists). When the British had to decide on the language of instruction in public education around 1835, some members of this group even espoused the cause of the classical Indian languages as a preferred medium of instruction, rather than English.

The pathologization of the *Manusmṛti* can be traced back to James Mill (1773–1836), who published his magnum opus *The History of British India* in 1818, when the British had just established themselves as the major power in India after their humble beginnings in 1757. The change in British fortunes was also reflected in a change in their attitude towards the natives, who now began to appear to them as increasingly uncivilized. In fact, James Mill especially targeted the Orientalists because of their positive attitude towards indigenous culture.

James Mill never visited India and felt no need to do so to produce an authoritative account of it. He considered the European accounts of India, which he had access to, more dependable than native sources. Mill also thought that as 'the manners, institutions, and attainments of the Hindus have been stationary for many ages', an ancient text such as the *Manusmṛti* could be used to depict their present condition. He then presented the material found in the *Manusmṛti* to prove that the Hindus had always lived in a dismal state. This trend continued thereafter and was used to justify the civilizing mission that is now associated with British rule. It was also supported by missionaries as it seemed to justify their need to convert Hindus to Christianity. The Mutiny of 1857–58 required renewed justification of the Raj, while the position of women came to be regarded as the index of a culture's civilized status. Manu's treatment of women was then singled out, placing India quite low on the scale of civilization and thus justifying the continued British presence. Modern Indian reformers also targeted the *Manusmṛti*, with Dr B.R. Ambedkar being a particularly trenchant critic of it.

The *Manusmṛti* was also used by both capitalists and communists in India to bolster their own positions. The capitalists wanted to destroy the 'rotten society' based on the *Manusmṛti* by releasing economic forces to overcome it, and the communists saw it as the system which their revolution would wipe away. Thus, both had (and have) a certain picture of Hindu society based on the *Manusmṛti,* although committed to two opposing, and even antagonistic, economic systems.

Thus, stereotypes based on a particular reading of the *Manusmṛti* have enjoyed remarkable longevity right down to our own times. An illustration of how this operates may be helpful here. Earlier in this preface I mentioned how during my adolescence I picked up verse 3.56 from the *Manusmṛti* quoted by a speaker in India who wanted to indicate how well Hinduism thought of women: 'Where women are revered, there the gods rejoice; but where they are not, no rite bears fruit.'[20] Mill used this, and similar verses, to establish *not* that the Hindus had a positive estimate of women but that they had only risen a little above sheer barbarism. I quote him now:

> The Hindus were, notwithstanding, so far advanced in civilization, except in the mountainous and most barbarous tracts of the country, as to have improved in some degree upon the manner of savage tribes. They have some general precepts, recommending indulgence and humanity in favour of the weaker sex ... When particulars indeed are explained, the indulgences recommended are not very extensive. It is added, 'Let those women, therefore, be continually supplied with ornaments, apparel, and food, at festivals, and at jubilees, by men desirous of wealth.' When it is commanded by law; as an extraordinary extension of liberality, to give them ornaments, and even apparel and food, at festivals and jubilees; this is rather a proof of habitual degradation than of general respect and tenderness.[21]

The traditional view of the *Manusmṛti* stands in sharp contrast. It is seen as a text in the Hindu legal tradition, which is rooted in the Vedas and which tries to give legal and moral shape to the teachings of the Vedas, or the *Śruti,* in a situation contemporaneous with the text. This legal tradition reflects the constant endeavour of 'Hinduism' to render the perennial Vedic tradition relevant to its times, as exemplified by the existence of forty-six such texts.[22] This endeavour is itself part of a larger effort which embraces other genres of legal literature as well, such as the *Dharma Sūtras,* which precede the *Smṛtis,* and the *Nibandhas,* which follow it. The period assigned to the *sūtras* extends roughly from the fourth century BCE to the second century CE, and that of the *Nibandhas,* from tenth century CE to the eighteenth.

The *Smṛti* genre of this literature, which, like the rest constantly relates the Vedas to the contemporary reality, covers the period extending roughly from the second to the tenth century CE. The grammarian Bhartṛhari contrasts the roles of the *Śruti* and the *Smṛti* in a famous verse: 'The *Śruti* represents the eternal tradition which has no author, and which remains unbroken through the ages, while *Smṛti* also represents an unbroken tradition because it is constantly composed by the learned scholars of the *Śruti.*' (*Vākyapadīya*: 1.136) Thus *Śruti* stands for the kind of eternity which never changes, while *Smṛti* denotes the kind of eternity which ever changes—changes all the time in its effort to keep *Śruti* relevant.[23]

In this verse, the word *Smṛti* appears to possess a wider connotation than the one we have ascribed to it so far. The word *Smṛti* has two meanings: the more limited meaning refers to the law books, so called (which in the main belong to the period stretching from the second century CE to the tenth), and the wider meaning refers to all the sacred literature of Hinduism other than the revealed texts in Hinduism, namely, the Vedas or *Śruti.* The wider meaning of the word naturally includes the narrower meaning.

The purpose of the *Smṛti* literature, in both these contexts, is to present the Vedic lore in a contemporary context. This role of *Smṛti* literature, in its narrower sense as law books, is clarified by T.M.P. Mahadevan as follows:

> The works which are expressly called *Smṛti* are law-books *dharma-śāstras*. Their purpose is to lay down the laws which should guide individuals and communities in their daily conduct and to apply the eternal truths of the Veda to the changing conditions of time and clime. And thereby preserve the integrity and ensure the progress of Hindu society. From time to time a great law-giver would arise, codify the existing laws, eliminate those which had become obsolete, and see to it that the ways of the Hindus are in a manner consistent with the spirit of the Veda. Of such law-givers the names of three have become immortal—Manu, Yājñavalkya and Parāśara. And the *Smṛtis* are named after them. Manu is the oldest giver of law. His work is called '*Mānava-dharmaśāstra*', the Laws of man or the Institutes of Manu. Here as well as in other *Smṛti*s we find instruction to all classes of people regarding their duties in life.[24]

The tendency to compose new *Smṛtis* may be considered a classical phenomenon; nevertheless, some spokespersons of modern Hinduism have also called for a new *Smṛti*, perhaps because of the singular importance attached to the *Manusmṛti* in our times. Modern Hinduism—when the term is used to refer to the form of Hinduism which evolved during the encounter of Hindu tradition with modernity from c. 1800 onwards—produced a series of spokespersons ranging all the way from Rammohun Roy (1772/4–1833) to S. Radhakrishnan (1888–1975). In this remarkable roster, historians tend to accord pride of place to the figures of Swami Vivekananda (1863–1902) and Mahatma Gandhi (1868–1948). It is noteworthy that the desire for some such work can be traced in the writings of both of them.

The following dialogue is recorded as having occurred in 1899 between Swami Vivekananda and a disciple, while Belur Math was under construction.

> Disciple: Please give me some advice in brief about social reform.
>
> Swamiji: Why, I have given you advice enough; now put at least something in practice. Let the world see that your reading of the scriptures and listening to me has been a success. The codes of Manu and lots of other books that you have read—what is their basis and underlying purpose? Keeping that basis intact, compile in the manner of the ancient Rishis the essential truths of them and supplement them with thoughts that are suited to the times; only take care that all races and all sects throughout India be really benefitted by following these rules. Just write out a Smriti like that; I shall revise it.
>
> Disciple: Sir, it is not an easy task; and even if such a Smriti be written, will it be accepted?
>
> Swamiji: Why not? Just write it out. '*Kālo hyam niravadhir vipulā ca pṛthvī*—Time is infinite, and the world is vast.' If you write it in the proper way, there must come a day when it will be accepted. Have faith in yourself. You people were once the Vedic Rishis. Only, you have come in different forms, that's all.[25]

In almost the same vein, Mahatma Gandhi wrote in the *Harijan* (28 November 1936):

> I have already suggested often enough in these columns that all that is printed in the name of scriptures need not be taken as the word of God or the inspired word. But every one cannot decide what is good and authentic and what is bad and interpolated. There should therefore be some authoritative body that would revise all that passes under the name of scriptures, expurgate all the texts that have no moral value or are contrary to the fundamentals of religion and morality, and present such an edition for the guidance of Hindus. The certainty that the whole mass of Hindus and the persons accepted as religious leaders will not accept the validity of such authority need not interfere with the sacred enterprise. Work done sincerely and in the spirit of service will have its effect on all in the long run and will most assuredly help those who are badly in need of such assistance.[26]

Madhu Kishwar, the editor of the well-known Indian 'feminist' journal *Manushi*, once spoke of replacing *Manusmṛti* with a *Madhusmṛti*. This suggestion, which perhaps outraged some people, may sound egotistical, but is not illogical, if we realize that different *Smṛtis* might be appropriate for different times.

IV

It would perhaps be useful to illustrate how widely the interpretation of the *Manusmṛti* and its verses can diverge in terms of the pathological and traditional approaches. A good example of this is provided by the following verses of the *Manusmṛti* (8.104–06):

> When telling the truth will result in the execution of a Śūdra, Vaiśya, Kṣatriya, or a Brahmin, a man may tell a lie; for that is far better than the truth.
>
> Such persons, performing the highest expiation for the sin of false testimony, should offer to goddess Sarasvatī oblations of milk-rice dedicated to the goddess Speech.
>
> Alternatively, such a person may offer an oblation of ghee in fire according to the rule, reciting the Kūṣmāṇḍa formulas, the verse to Varuṇa: 'Untie Varuṇa...' or the three formulas addressed to water.[27]

The substance of these verses is rather straightforward. The *Manusmṛti* recommends, notwithstanding the general desirability of telling the truth, that one could lie to save the life of a human being irrespective of the *varṇa* to which the person belongs; but that one should undertake an expiation for having done so.

Now let us see what the pathological approach does with this. Here is what James Mill has to say about these verses:

> Though there is no ground on which the infirmities of the human mind are more glaring, and more tenacious of existence, than that of law, it is probable that the annals of legislative absurdity can present nothing which will match a law for the *direct* encouragement of perjury. 'Whenever', says the ordinance of Menu, 'the death of a man who has been a grievous offender, either of the servile, the commercial, the military, or the sacerdotal class, would be occasioned by true evidence, from the known rigour of the king, even though the fault arose from inadvertence or error, falsehood may be spoken: it is even preferable to truth'. What a state of justice it is, in which the king may condemn a man to death, for inadvertence or error, and no better remedy is found than the perjury of witness?[28]

So, according to Mill, this provision further confirms the dubious nature of a text as one which even encourages perjury. He completely misses the humanistic dimension of the verse. Perhaps a more sympathetic modern mind will see in it a plea for the abolition of capital punishment; not in the ringing tones one finds in the *Dao De Ching* (chapter 74), but very much there, if in more prosaic terms. Mill also completely misses a startling implication of this verse: that one could tell a lie to save the life of a *śūdra*, about whom it is often averred, on the basis of the *Manusmṛti*, that his life has little value! The pathological approach sees only pathology in verses which could easily be valued instead for their humanism. This is such a glaring example of orientalism à la Said, that it will surface again later in the book.

Now what does the traditional approach to these verses look like?

These verses serve as a window to some basic ideas of Hindu ethics. Hindu ethics differs from the kind of ethics associated in the West with rationalism and fideism. Rationalism is the belief that all moral dilemmas could be resolved if we only had enough reason. Fideism is the belief that, similarly, all moral dilemmas could be resolved if only one had enough faith. Hindu ethics, however, accepts the reality of genuine moral dilemmas. It operates on the assumption that rarely are moral issues so clear cut as to involve a choice between black and white. It accepts that most of moral life will belong to a grey area, where one virtue may conflict with another.

In terms of human rights discourse, one may say that Hindu ethics is acutely aware that different human rights may clash with one another. Given this complexity of moral decision making, one should be prepared for situations that may require exceptions to be made to the prevailing general rule. This leads one to suggest another way in which Hindu ethics differs from the Western. Western ethics is universalistic in accordance with Kant's famous criterion of universalizability of moral principles. Hindu ethics, by contrast, is often accused of being only particularistic, à la Weber. But the fact is that while Western ethics is only universalistic, Hindu ethics is *both* universalistic and particularistic, rather then only particularistic.

Anyone familiar with the Hindu concepts of *varṇāśrama dharmas* (or *viśeṣa dharmas*) and *sāmānya* or *sādhāraṇa dharmas* would probably arrive at the same conclusion. A word, however, about these terms before we proceed. *Viśeṣa dharmas* or *pṛthag dharmas* denote particular duties, such as those associated with a station in life (*varṇa*), or with a stage in life (*āśrama*), and so on. *Sāmānya* or *sādhāraṇa dharmas* are duties incumbent on us as human beings, irrespective of such considerations as station or stage in life. The distinction is important in Hinduism. But what is even more significant is that Hindu ethics recognizes that *viśeṣa dharmas* and *sāmānya dharmas* could also come into conflict. Yet another feature of Hindu ethics is that moral issues have to be resolved case by case. There is no magic ethical bullet which can resolve all such issues. The danger that such an open attitude poses is that of moral relativism. Hindu ethics guards against this by insisting that if the operation of a general moral law has to be broken or suspended on account of a particular situation, then one must voluntarily undergo expiation for having broken it. The purpose of this practice is to preserve the sanctity of the general principle in a situation when it had to be violated on account of countervailing circumstances.

We discover, once we recognize this, that some acts attributed by the tradition to its characters make more sense. There is an episode in the *Mahābhārata* for instance, when Arjuna needed to fight off robbers but his famous bow, the Gāṇḍīva, was in a room in which Draupadī and Yudhiṣṭhira were conversing in private. There was a rule among the five brothers that, married as they were to the same woman, no brother could approach Draupadī if another was conversing with her in private. Arjuna would have to break this rule if he wanted to perform his public duty. He rushed in, fetched the bow and went on to take care of the robbery. When he came back everyone agreed that he has done the right thing by disregarding the rule under the circumstances and therefore the violation did not count. Nevertheless, Arjuna insisted on voluntarily undergoing the punishment agreed upon for violating the rule.

Some law books declare the person of a woman to be inviolable but allow her to be killed if she is guilty of treason, but in that case the king has to fast for three days to atone for the sin of causing a woman's death. Kumārila, often considered a senior contemporary of the famous philosopher Śaṅkara, is said to have burnt himself to death for committing the sin of betraying one's *guru*, or *gurudroha*. This was so because he had learnt the principles of Buddhism by becoming the student of Buddhist teachers, so that he could understand Buddhist doctrines. But then he had to defend Hinduism by refuting these doctrines. He had to do this to defend *sanātana dharma*, but in doing so he also committed *gurudroha*, so he atoned for it by immolating himself towards the end of his life. The verses from the *Manusmṛti* alluded to earlier, before this digression, embody this traditional Hindu perspective.

This book challenges the blanket disparagement of the text involved in the pathological view of it and sees some merit in giving more play to the traditional perspective in trying to understand the meaning and motivation of the text.

V

This book is about analysis rather than advocacy. During this analysis, it will use both the emic and the etic points of view to determine which offers a better explanation of the point under examination, and it will draw upon both the pathological and the traditional approaches with the same end in mind.

As I close, I would like to thank Shrinivas Tilak for his valuable comments on the manuscript of this book from which I benefitted immensely. I would like to thank Sanjay Kumar for helping me with Appendix 2. And I would also like to thank Faye Sutherland for preparing the manuscript for publication. My gratitude to her is beyond words.

Any errors that remain are my own.

PART I

1

Introduction

I

The *Manusmṛti* is a primary text in the study of Hinduism, both in its traditional and modern context. Many other well-known texts of Hinduism, sacred as well as secular, cite Manu as an authority. Some other *Smṛtis* are modelled on the *Manusmṛti* within the Hindu legal tradition itself. The *Mahābhārata* sometimes states 'so said Manu', as if to clinch the issue.[1] The secular *Pañcatantra* does the same,[2] as well as the *Bṛhajjātaka* of Varāhamihira.[3] The reference, however, is usually in terms of 'so said Manu', rather than 'so says the *Manusmṛti*', which creates room for suggesting that some other work of Manu is alluded to, such as a *Mānava Dharma Sūtra*. The existence of such a text is, however, far from certain.[4] It is nevertheless true that some verses cited in other sources and said to be by Manu are not found in the *Manusmṛti* as we know it. This, to a certain extent at least on the face of it, might seem to compromise the importance of the *Manusmṛti*. From another point of view, however, it could be read as magnifying its significance. It could indicate that the *Manusmṛti* was held in such high esteem that verses were attributed to its name to provide them with an air of authority. However, while the status enjoyed by the *Manusmṛti* might be subject to such occasional doubts, the status enjoyed by Manu cannot be gainsaid.

'Manu said so' seems to have had the same force in tradition as a ruling of the Supreme Court does in a modern legislative setting. This is confirmed by the curious fact of self-quotation—'Manu has said so'—in some of the verses (e.g., 10.63) within the *Manusmṛti* itself. The fact that the name of Manu is attached to the *Smṛti* itself thus confers a certain status on it. The importance attached to the text was not merely a fact in the religious, social and legal milieu but also spilled into the political arena. This is clear from the fact that 'in AD 751 King Droṇasingh of Valabhī adopted Manu as binding authority.'[5] Moreover, according to a ninth-century inscription in the Kuruattur Viṣṇu Temple, King Rajashekhara of Mahodaya Pura, who belonged to the Chera dynasty, 'never deviated one word from the laws of Manu.'

The importance of the *Manusmṛti* in the modern context is also clear: It was among the earliest Sanskrit texts to be translated into English and continues to occupy a central position in the depiction of Hindu society in Indological circles.

It has sometimes been suggested that *Manusmṛti's* significance has been overrated.[6] This is possible, but two considerations need to be borne in mind. Its importance could have been exaggerated, but its importance can hardly be denied. Besides, the fact that its significance *was* exaggerated means that its footprint in the modern study of Hinduism cannot be overlooked for that very reason. In modern times also its significance has not remained confined to the religious, social and legal milieu but has been visible in the public arena. In a well-known incident that took place on 25 December 1927 at 9 a.m. in Mahad in (then) Bombay Presidency's Colaba District, Dr B.R. Ambedkar had certain verses of the *Manusmṛti* copied and consigned to flames, as a protest against the bias of the text against the lower castes.[7]

II

Writing another book on the *Manusmṛti* does, however, require some justification, as the text has already been translated into English several times and the study of the text has over two centuries of scholarly inquiry behind it. I would, therefore, like to provide the rationale for undertaking this study of the *Manusmṛti*. This rationale lies in the method I would like to bring to bear on the text, which is best described by the expression *plural intertextuality*. I use the phrase to refer to the awareness that the complex interaction between the various parts of a text, and of the text with other texts, is fundamental for the interpretation or understanding of a text.

Manusmṛti through the Lens of Plural Intertextuality

Before we embark on this exercise let me clarify that for the purposes of this book, I accept the scholarly consensus at the moment: i) the *Manusmṛti* is the work of a single author, and ii) that it may be assigned to around the second century CE.[8] It is important to clarify this because there could be divergencies of opinion on these points, although they are unlikely to affect the main argument of the book.

With that out of the way let us apply the lens of plural intertextuality to the *Manusmṛti*.

Such an approach has hitherto been applied only in a rather limited way in relation to the *Manusmṛti*, as will become clear in the course of this study. Two illustrations might help clarify the point—one to illustrate how verses within the *Manusmṛti* need to be read together, and the other to illustrate how the *Manusmṛti* needs to be read with other texts. I understand the term 'text' broadly here, to further include the commentarial material on the one hand, and the socio-economic and political context on the other. In other words, text includes context.

Illustration 1

A verse from the *Manusmṛti*, which is often cited, is presented here in translation (9.3): 'Her father guards her in her childhood, her husband guards her in her youth, and her sons guard her in her old age; a woman is not qualified to act independently.'[9] Seen alone, this verse may create the impression that a woman, by herself, could not legally own anything. But another verse (11.195) states: 'What she receives subsequent to the marriage and what her husband gives her out of affection—upon her death that property goes to her children even if her husband is alive.'[10] This clearly demonstrates that the wife could own and pass on property. Not reading the two verses together involves a serious risk of misinterpretation. In this book a number of such clusters of verses, which range across the chapters and must be read together to avoid misinterpretation, will be delineated.

When such clusters become large enough, they merit detailed thematic treatment under distinct rubrics such as: (1) the *varṇa* system; (2) the Vedas; (3) the *yugas*; (4) the *brāhmaṇas*, (5) the *śūdras*; (6) untouchability; (7) the position of women in general, and so on. An attempt has been made to carry out such a treatment, wherever required, in the various chapters.

Illustration 2

The fact that women did not possess any legal independence according to the *Manusmṛti*,[11] has sometimes been taken to mean that only sons could inherit property, which is also said to have been the case in the ṚgVedic period.[12] There was, however, a dissenting minority which favoured the daughter's right of inheritance as well. This school maintained its position on the strength of a passage in the *Nirukta* (3.4), which is attributed by Yāska to Manu. Manu, usually regarded as a denier of rights to women, is cited here as an upholder of the daughter's right to inherit! Thus, reading *Manusmṛti* intertextually with other texts sometimes creates such moments of 'cognitive dissonance'. Altekar notes, however, that this verse 'does not … occur in the present *Manusmṛti*'.[13] How are these apparent contradictions to be read or resolved? The book intends to probe such dissonances (and resonances) for the light they shed on our understanding of the *Manusmṛti* and Hindu social reality.

III

It might be worthwhile to demonstrate, in more detail, how profoundly our understanding of the text is affected by the conscious application of the method outlined above. The following two additional cases might help highlight this fact.

Case 1

The standard understanding of the caste system in Hinduism is based on the reference to the four *varṇas* in the *Puruṣa Sūkta* of the *ṚgVeda*,[14] which is also reflected in the *Manusmṛti* (1.31–87; 8.270; 10.45). There are, however, some other descriptions in the *Manusmṛti*, which do not quite square with this. Thus, the *Manusmṛti* states elsewhere (9.321–322, emphasis added):

> When a Kṣatriya becomes haughty in any way in his behavior towards Brahmins, the Brahmin himself must become their controller, for the *Kṣatriya sprang from the Brahmin.* Fire sprang from water, *Kṣatriya from Brahmin*, and metal from stone; their all-pervasive energy is quenched when confronting their own source.[15]

According to the well-known account of the origin of the *varṇas* found in the *Puruṣa Sūkta*, all the four *varṇas—brāhmaṇa*, *kṣatriya*, *vaiśya* and *śūdra*—emerged from the same primeval being called Puruṣa. The statement in the *Manusmṛti* that the *kṣatriyas* originated from the *brāhmaṇas* contradicts this, for it claims that the *kṣatriyas* emerged from the *brāhmaṇas.* How are these two accounts to be reconciled?

Būhler notes that while according to one commentator this statement is based on a Vedic passage, another 'thinks it alludes to a Paurāṇik story, according to which the Brāhmaṇas produced with the Kṣatriya females a new Kṣatriya race after the destruction of the second varṇa by Paraśurāma.'[16] Patrick Olivelle notes: '*Kṣatriya from Brahmin*: this doctrine is already articulated in *BāU* 1.4.11 which calls *brahma* (priestly power) the womb of *kṣatra* (the ruling power).'[17] Wendy Doniger and Brian K. Smith seem to combine these threads in the following remark:

> According to many Vedic texts (*Śatapatha Brāhmaṇa* 12.7.3.12; *Taittirīya Brāhmaṇa* 2.8.8.9; *Bṛhadāraṇyaka Upaniṣad* 1.4.11–13), rulers were born from priests at the original creation and, once more, when it was necessary for the priests to create a new race of rulers after Paraśurāma had exterminated them (*Mahābhārata* 1.98).[18]

These attempts to reconcile the two different sets of statements overlook the possibility that these two statements may be reflecting *two different* accounts of the emergence of the *varṇas* found within the Hindu tradition. Scholars may have become so accustomed to repeating the account of the origin of the *varṇas* found in the *Puruṣa Sūkta* that they may just have failed to recognize the full significance of the verse. The full account is found in the very reference sometimes cited by them, but its significance seems to have gone unnoticed. The alternative account of the origin of the *varṇas*, as found in the *Śatapatha Brāhmaṇa*, and also repeated in the *Bṛhadāraṇyaka Upaniṣad*, is presented here:

11. In the beginning this world was only *Brahman*, only one. Because it was only one, *Brahman* had not fully developed. It then created the ruling power, a form superior to and surpassing itself, that is, the ruling powers among the gods—Indra, Varuṇa, Soma, Rudra, Parjanya, Yama, Mṛtyu, and Īśāna. Hence there is nothing higher than the ruling power. Accordingly, at a royal anointing a Brahmin pays homage to a Kṣatriya by prostrating himself. He extends this honor only to the ruling power. Now, the priestly power (*Brahman*) is the womb of the ruling power. Therefore, even if a king should rise to the summit of power, it is to the priestly power that he returns in the end as to his own womb. So, one who hurts the latter harms his own womb and becomes so much the worse for harming someone better than him.

12. *Brahman* still did not become fully developed. So it created the Vaiśya class, that is, the types of gods who are listed in groups—Vasus, Rudras, Ādityas, All-gods, and Maruts.

13. It still did not become fully developed. So it created the Śūdra class, that is, Pūṣan. Now, Pūṣan is this very earth, for it nourishes this whole world, it nourishes all that exists.

14. It still did not become fully developed. So it created the Law (*dharma*), a form superior to and surpassing itself. And the Law is here the ruling power standing above the ruling power. Hence there is nothing higher than the Law. Therefore, a weaker man makes demands of a stronger man by appealing to the Law, just as one does by appealing to a king. Now, the Law is nothing but the truth. Therefore, when a man speaks the truth, people say that he speaks the Law; and when a man speaks the Law, people say that he speaks the truth. They are really the same thing.

15. So there came to be the priestly power, the ruling power, the Vaiśya class, and the Śūdra class. Among the gods the priestly power (*Brahman*) came into being only in the form of fire, and among humans as a Brahmin; it further became a Kṣatriya in the form of a Kṣatriya, a Vaiśya in the form of a Vaiśya, and a Śūdra in the form of a Śūdra. In the fire, therefore, people seek to find a world for themselves among the gods, and in the Brahmin a world among humans, for *Brahman* came into being in these two forms.[19]

It could be objected that this account, while it does state that one *varṇa* is created *after* another, does not say that one is created *from* the other. However, the following passage from the *Mahābhārata* indicates that this is how it came to be understood, as is evident from the common initial statement in the various accounts. The passage from the *Mahābhārata* runs as follows:

> There is no difference of castes: this world, having been at first created by Brahmā entirely Brāhmanic, became afterwards separated into castes in consequence of works. Those Brahmins, who were fond of sensual pleasure, fiery, irascible, prone to violence, who had forsaken their duty, and were red-limbed, fell into the condition of the Kṣatriyas. Those Brahmins, who derived their livelihood from kine, who were yellow, who subsisted by agriculture, and who neglected to practise their duties, entered into the state of Vaiśyas. Those Brahmins, who were addicted to mischief and falsehood, who were covetous, who lived by all kinds of work, who were black and had fallen from purity, sank into the condition of Śūdras. Being separated from each other by these works, the Brahmins became divided into different castes. Duty and the rites of sacrifice have not been always forbidden to any of them. Such are the four classes for whom the Brāhmanic Sarasvatī was at first designed by Brahmā, but who through their cupidity fell into ignorance.[20]

Intertextuality thus comes to our aid here in two ways: in clarifying the relationship between the statements made within the same text; and in clarifying the relationship of statements made within it and those found in other texts. As an example of the first, consider now the following verses of the *Manusmṛti* (2.17–20):

> The land created by the gods and lying between the divine rivers Sarasvatī and Dṛṣadvatī is called 'Brahmāvarta'—the region of Brahman. The conduct handed down from generation to generation among the social classes and the intermediate classes of that land is called the 'conduct of good people'.

Kurukṣetra and the lands of the Matsyas, Pañcālas and Śūrasenakas constitute the 'land of Brahmin seers', which borders on the Brahmāvarta.

All the people on earth should learn their respective practices from a Brahmin born in that land.[21]

One needs to focus on the last line. The word used for *brāhmaṇa* in the text is *agrajanmā* or first-born. It is explained traditionally as: (1) first to be born among the *varṇas*; or (2) as meaning the leading limb (*agra*), the mouth; the *brāhmaṇa* is so called because the *brāhmaṇa* was born from the mouth.[22]

It seems, however, that we have here the same phenomenon noted earlier at work, that the regnant paradigm of the origin of the *varṇas*, based on the *Puruṣa Sūkta*, is being forced upon a datum, which is more cogently explained as invoking a different account of the origin of the *varṇas*. The *Puruṣa Sūkta* does not explicitly say that the *brāhmaṇa* was created *first*, rather it could be plausibly argued that the emergence of the *varṇas* was simultaneous, and the impression created by the fact that the *brāhmaṇa* is mentioned first and therefore was created first could be misleading. Tradition itself seems to recognize the weakness of this argument by providing an alternative argument from within the same paradigm. The fact that the *brāhmaṇa* is *mentioned* first in the *Puruṣa Sūkta* thus does not necessarily mean that this *varṇa* was created first. If something breaks up into parts, as India did at Partition, then saying that British India broke up into India and Pakistan cannot ipso facto mean that India was formed before Pakistan. The point then is that although attempts can be made to justify the statement in terms of the regnant account, the view that the text is here reflecting another paradigm helps provide a far more cogent explanation.

The overall significance of such a position in promoting a new understanding of the *Manusmṛti* should now be obvious. The *Manusmṛti* can now be seen as a text which participates in the plurality of the religious tradition of which it is a part, instead of reading it as if it were straitjacketing the tradition.

Case 2

The kind of image the mention of the word *Manusmṛti* conjures up at the moment, in terms of who determines what the tradition is going to be, is an elitist one. The elite in this case is represented by the male members of the three higher *varṇas*. This position within the *Manusmṛti* represents a position well acknowledged within the tradition. If, however, one approaches the issue with intertextuality in mind, then once again a remarkable and unlikely result ensues.

The *Manusmṛti* is a text of *dharma*, of determining the right thing to do. It emphasizes four determinants of *dharma* in a frequently cited verse (2.6):

> The root of the Law is the entire Veda; the tradition and practice of those who know the Veda; the conduct of good people, and what is pleasing to oneself.[23]

The following verse is also often invoked in the same context (2.12):

> Veda, tradition, the conduct of good people, and what is pleasing to oneself—these, they say, are the four visible marks of the Law.[24]

These sources of *dharma* are usually read as representing a hierarchy, with the pride of place going to the Veda. In the same *Manusmṛti*, however, one also finds the following verse (4.176):

> He should abandon any activity relating to Wealth or Pleasure that is in violation of Law and even activities sanctioned by Law when they will result in future unhappiness or are repugnant to the world.[25]

Patrick Olivelle here provides a reference to another verse (2.224) which he translates as follows:

> Some say that Law and Wealth are conducive to welfare; others, Pleasure and Wealth, and still others, Law alone or Wealth alone. But the settled rule is this: the entire triple set is conducive to welfare.[26]

This second verse is of some use here, for it refers to the three goals of life—*dharma*, *artha* and *kāma*—but once again a point of considerable significance seems to have been missed. It comes to light when an intertextual approach is adopted towards the main verse under discussion. The task of reclaiming it in an intertextual context is unfortunately rendered difficult by the exigencies of translation. The word 'Law' has been used here to translate *dharma*; and the word 'world' to translate *loka*. The word *dharma*, however, possesses a cultural resonance in Hinduism barely captured by the word 'Law',[27] and the translation of the word *loka* as the 'world', we shall discover, blunts it semantically.

If the verse is examined closely it seems to be saying that *even a Vedic practice* may be set aside if: (1) it does not lead to happiness in the long run; and (2) is reviled by the *people*. This is where the use of the word 'world' to translate *loka* becomes problematic, although nominally correct. As P.V. Kane notes, the word *loka* means people in general, or the masses, specially as a counterpoint to *śiṣṭa*, which means the elite or the classes.[28] It should also be noted that the Veda is the primary source of *dharma*, and yet even such *dharma* can be set aside, if it does not lead to well-being in the long run, or is denounced by the people. That this is not mere theory is clear from the fact that the rite of *niyoga* (levirate), which possessed Vedic sanction, is no longer acceptable within the tradition, because people began to disapprove of it.

This verse has been largely overlooked as just another verse of the text. Its true significance emerges through an intertextual approach. In terms of the text itself, once the role of people (*loka*) in determining the Law is recognized, then some other verses of the *Manusmṛti*, which too have been neglected, assume new significance. Once we recognize that the word *loka*, as people, means 'all the people' and that this blunts the elitist edge of the text, then the presence of such a verse as the following (2.223) will no longer surprise us:

> If he sees a woman or a low-born doing something conducive to welfare, he should do all of that diligently, or anything else he is fond of.[29]

In other words, the *verse is asking the high-born to emulate the virtuous behaviour of women and low-born people*. But if *dharma* is to be connected with *loka* on the one side and well-being on the other,[30] then obviously such a sentiment is not out of place.

If now we view this verse in the context of verses found in other texts then once again as in Case 1, a new vista opens up, which suggests the existence of an alternative paradigm in the tradition and how it might also be reflected in the *Manusmṛti* in these verses. To see this connection, one only needs to refer to that famous verse of the *Mahābhārata*, which appears in the context of the equally famous dialogue between Yakṣa and Yudhiṣṭhira. This verse is extremely popular although it is not included in the critical text.[31] When Yakṣa asks Yudhiṣṭhira: 'What is the way to go?' Yudhiṣṭhira replies:

> [The Vedas], as well as the *smṛtis*, are in conflict with each other, there is no single sage whose opinion is held to be authoritative by all, the truth about dharma is enveloped in a cave (i.e. it cannot be easily discerned). Therefore, the path (to be followed) is the one followed by the great mass of people.[32]

The word *mahājana*, which occurs in the last line of the Sanskrit original (*mahājano yena gataḥ sa panthāḥ*), in its semantic ambiguity epitomizes the two paradigms within the tradition for determining *dharma*. It has been rendered by P.V. Kane as the great mass of people, but the word can be taken to mean the *great personages* in society; just as it can also mean *the masses*.[33] So who decides ultimately what *dharma* is—which way to go? Two paradigms can be identified within the tradition on this point. The elite is one option—often advocated in the *Manusmṛti*, but here, in the verse under consideration, the *Manusmṛti* seems to be *also* connecting with the second option in the tradition—the people at large. And these *two* options are mentioned as such in the last two *sūtras* of the *Āpastamba Dharma Sūtra*.[34] These *sūtras* or aphorisms deal with the question of how issues of *dharma*, which have not been covered hitherto, are to be resolved. The first option proposed is that the views of the distinguished male members of the three higher *varṇas*, namely the *dvijas*, may be ascertained.[35] The last *sūtra* states, however, that, in the opinion of some, 'one should learn the remaining Laws from women and people of all classes.'[36]

It is widely accepted that Hinduism is a plural tradition. If this is so, then such pluralism will also be reflected in its legal tradition. It therefore makes more sense to study the *Manusmṛti* as reflecting the diverse strands in the tradition and blending them in its own way, than to view it as advocating only a single perspective on an issue. The point is important because it helps account for the difference between this book on the *Manusmṛti* and the many others which have preceded it. Even where other scholars and students have tried to understand the *Manusmṛti* in relation to other similar or related works and have tried to take its historical context into account, they may not have been sufficiently sensitive to its plural character in doing so.

2

Manusmṛti: The Historical Context

I

We begin this intertextual study of the *Manusmṛti* by addressing its historical context, for context also, as noted earlier, can serve as a text. By the word 'history' one normally refers to the events preceding or simultaneous with the text, in this case the *Manusmṛti*. It is, therefore, important to recognize that the *Manusmṛti* may be placed 'between the first century BCE and the second CE',[1] and perhaps 'closer to the second century CE'.[2] Hence the centuries *preceding* it will naturally have to be investigated to arrive at a proper understanding of the *Manusmṛti*. However, we will discover that what happens in the centuries *succeeding* the *Manusmṛti* will also be helpful in understanding its role—perhaps somewhat to our surprise.

II

Of the major historical developments which preceded the compilation of the *Manusmṛti*, if the date assigned to it above is correct, the chief would be the founding of the Mauryan Empire in the fourth century BCE, which is usually referred to as India's first historical empire. This dynasty lasted from c. 324 to c. 186 BCE. The circumstances of its founding will prove important for furthering our understanding of the *Manusmṛti*, for it arose in the wake of Alexander's invasion of India in 326 BCE, which provides a parallel with the *Manusmṛti*, which was also composed in the wake of foreign invasions. The founder of this dynasty, Candragupta Maurya, began by subduing north-west India and driving out the Greek garrisons.[3] Equally significant is the fact that Candragupta was assisted in this and other conquests by a *brāhmaṇa* (who is variously referred to as Kauṭilya, Cāṇakya and Viṣṇugupta) according to 'all Indian traditions'.[4] These traditions are also unanimous in ascribing to him the composition of a text on statecraft called the *Arthaśāstra*, a major treatise which has survived to this day and is considered a valuable source of knowledge on political and allied matters. Although the present text of the *Arthaśāstra* is dated to a period after the Mauryan Age, it is generally admitted that it 'contains genuine Mauryan reminiscences'.[5] This text has proved to be an important source for furthering our understanding of the *Manusmṛti*.

The next major fact of consequence for our study is the reign and figure of King Aśoka (r. 269–232 BCE), who converted to Buddhism. Although he did not formally make it a state religion, he devoted the resources of his mighty empire both to the propagation of Buddhism inside and outside India, as well as to what he called *dhamma/dharma*, which was more ecumenical and moral in its orientation. Details of his propagation of Buddhism are largely provided by Buddhist chronicles, and of the *dhamma/dharma* by the numerous inscriptions found all over his empire, which included Afghanistan and the rest of India, except for the far south (ruled by the Keraḷas, Coḷas and Pāṇḍyas), but among whom he also sent his missionaries, as he did to the Hellenistic kings of his time.

The 'special relationship between the political power and the religious establishment represented by the Brahmins was broken'[6] by these activities of Aśoka—a fact that has a special bearing on our understanding of the *Manusmṛti*; as also the fact that as a result of his pacific policies, those who succeeded Aśoka could not protect India militarily against foreign invasions from about c. 200 BCE to c. 200 CE (although Aśoka's direct culpability in this matter is a matter of debate). These foreign invasions of India, which provide the immediate backdrop of the *Manusmṛti*, occurred in four waves, represented by first the Bactrian Greeks (or the Yavanas), then the Scythians (or Śakas), then Parthians (or the Pahlavas) and finally the Yüeh-chih (or the Kuṣāṇas).[7]

In the midst of the turmoil caused by these invasions, the last king of the Mauryan dynasty was slain by his *brāhmaṇa* commander-in-chief Puṣyamitra Śuṅga in c. 186 BCE. The Śuṅga dynasty that succeeded the Mauryan was however short-lived and some indigenous or indigenized rulers began to emerge. Two deserve mention: Rudradāman (c.150) from Kathiāwar, a Śaka ruler who recorded a panegyric in Sanskrit, and Gautamīputra Śātakarṇi also from around the same time in the Deccan, who belonged to a *brāhmaṇa* dynasty.[8] In the Nasik record, Gautamīputra Śātakarṇi's mother tells us that 'her son destroyed the Śakas (Scythians), Yavanas (Greeks) and Pahḷavas (Parthians)'.[9] Both of these rulers, Rudradāman and Gautamīputra Śātakarṇi were significant supporters of the *varṇa* order.[10]

Order was restored over north India by the Gupta dynasty, which came to power around 320 CE and was also founded by a Candragupta. His son, Samudragupta (c. 335–c. 376), carved out an empire which matched the one Aśoka had inherited. The Gupta period is often referred to as the golden age of ancient India, and we pause our historical narrative at this point, to explore the four nodal connections of the historical period that preceded the *Manusmṛti,* and of the period in which the *Manusmṛti* was written. These were: (1) Candragupta and Cāṇakya; (2) Aśoka; (3) the chaos of the foreign invasions; (4) the emerging indigenous rulers.

III

As the *Manusmṛti*, in the reckoning adopted here, belongs to a period when north India was just beginning to emerge from a period of invasions, it would naturally look back upon the time of the founding of the Mauryan Empire as a reference point, as it represented consolidation in the wake of the Macedonian invasion. The template for the politics and administration of this dynasty was provided by the *Arthaśāstra* of Kauṭilya, and it is therefore not surprising that the *Manusmṛti* would try to draw upon this heritage to accomplish a similar task. In fact, according to Patrick Olivelle, 'The *Manusmṛti* represented a watershed in the development of the expert tradition of *dharma*; it co-opted material it would have viewed as belonging to the expert tradition of *Arthaśāstra*.'[11]

The strands in this argument need to be disentangled. There were two distinct traditions in India, one concerned with statecraft, as represented by the *arthaśāstra* tradition in general (as distinguished from a specific work of that name), and a tradition concerned with 'society craft' known as the *dharmaśāstra* tradition in general (as distinguished from specific works that go by that name). In the crisis represented by north India in the second century, with the old native kingdoms dead and new ones struggling to be born, the compiler of the *Manusmṛti* perhaps felt the need to incorporate elements of the *arthaśāstra* into the *dharmaśāstra*. This is one aspect of the situation—that the *dharma* tradition felt the need to go political and incorporate elements of *artha* within it, as if compelled to provide a credible alternative in the new situation. This is one sense in which the *dharmaśāstra* tradition proved receptive to the *arthaśāstra* tradition.

Such intellectual incorporation provided one level of interaction; a second is to be identified at the textual level. At this level, too, Patrick Olivelle notes that, 'there is a clear connection between some verses of Manu and the extant *Arthaśāstra*',[12] and cites the following pieces of evidence: *Manusmṛti* 8.52–57 and *Arthaśāstra* 3.1.19; *Manusmṛti* 7.102 and *Arthaśāstra* 1.4.5; *Manusmṛti* 7.105 and *Arthaśāstra* 1.15.60; and *Manusmṛti* 9.280 and *Arthaśāstra* 14.11.7.[13] It is important to mention the caveat here that these parallels are between the *Manusmṛti* and the *extant Arthaśāstra*, which may not be identical with the original *Arthaśāstra*. As Patrick Olivelle explains: 'It is impossible to determine, on the basis of their parallels whether Manu is borrowing from the extant *Arthaśāstra* or whether both texts are dependent on earlier texts of this tradition.'[14] Nevertheless, the connection is hard to deny: 'There is also a close parallel between the technical vocabularies of Manu and the *Arthaśāstra*.'[15] Olivelle feels, in relation to the 'grounds for litigation' as found in chapters 8 and 9 of the *Manusmṛti*, that 'Manu probably borrowed this classificatory system, as well as the material presented within it, from the *Arthaśāstra* tradition. The systems in Manu and the extant *Arthaśāstra*, however, are so different from each other that it is unlikely that the former borrowed directly from the latter.'[16]

The main point should not be lost sight of in the minutiae—that the *Manusmṛti's* author may have felt the need to accommodate material from the *arthaśāstra* tradition or a text within it, as a response to the crisis north India was facing. In other words, the crisis compelled the *dharmaśāstra* tradition to take over the function of the *arthaśāstra* tradition as well.

IV

The next nodal point is provided by the reign of Aśoka and its consequences, and the period of turbulence which followed the end of his rule. The crucial question we need to ask ourselves is: What was the situation that the author of the *Manusmṛti* faced when he set about compiling it in the second century, committed as he was to responding to the situation in terms of the Vedic heritage?

The attempt to answer this question brings us to a very crucial point: the assessment of the place of Aśoka in Hindu history; not in Indian history, not in world history, but in Hindu history. So far as Aśoka's role in world history is concerned, there is the famous and oft-cited tribute of H.G. Wells. After noting that 'he is the only military monarch on record who abandoned warfare after victory,'[17] Wells went on to say:

> Amidst the tens of thousands of names of monarchs that crowd the columns of history, their majesties and graciousness and serenities and royal highnesses and the like, the name of Asoka shines, and shines almost alone, a star. From the Volga to Japan his name is still honoured. China, Tibet, and even India, though it has left his doctrine, preserve the tradition of his greatness. More living men cherish his memory to-day than have ever heard the names of Constantine or Charlemagne.[18]

His place in India's history is considered equally illustrious, though it has to be defended against the charge that his policies contributed to the decline of the Mauryan Empire. The conclusion offered by R.C. Majumdar, after taking this charge into account, provides a fairly good indication of his standing in Indian history. Majumdar writes:

> Even if Aśoka's policy brought about the downfall of the Mauryan Empire, India has no cause to regret this fact. The empire would have fallen to pieces sooner or later, even if Aśoka had followed the policy of blood and iron of his grandfather. But the moral ascendancy of Indian culture over a large part of the civilized world, which Aśoka was mainly instrumental in bringing about, remained for centuries as a monument to her glory, and has not altogether vanished even now after the lapse of more than two thousand years.[19]

The assessment of his role in Hindu history differs radically from these. It is indicated by the fact he was almost a forgotten name in India until the recovery of India's past in the last few centuries. As Benjamin Walker notes:

> India did not preserve his tradition. In spite of his magnanimity towards all sects, in spite of the fact that he advocated 'reverence and liberality to ascetics and brāhmins', he was regarded by them as a hated Buddhist and a despised śūdra. According to Rhys Davids, 'The brāhmin records completely ignore him until the time when, ten or twelve centuries afterwards, all danger of his influence had passed definitely away'. Information about Aśoka is derived mainly from his famous rock edicts and from the Ceylon chronicles, and present knowledge of his is due solely to Western research. K.M. Panikkar reminds us that Aśoka, 'whose name seems to have been expunged from Indian history', was restored to honour and 'today holds a position in the minds of Indians higher than that of any monarch—the result not of Indian researches, but the work of European scholars'.[20]

There are two levels at which this silence regarding Aśoka could be understood. Patrick Olivelle identifies one such level. According to him, 'the historical reality and especially the historical memory of two or three centuries later of the Maurya state and especially of the Aśokan political, social, and religious reforms' constitutes 'the major element' among the socio-political movements which provide the background for the composition of the *Manusmṛti*.[21] He goes on to say: 'One thing that his reforms did was to displace the Brahmin from his privileged position within the social structure. The special relationship between the political power and the religious establishment represented by the Brahmin was broken.'[22] Furthermore, the Mauryas were considered *śūdras* and according to brahmanical thinking 'the usurpation of Kṣatriya royal privileges by Śūdras and the ensuing suppression of the Brahmins are presented as the sure signals of the corrupt times of the Kali age.'[23] Finally, 'there were the foreign invasions first in the border regions of the north-west and then within the heartland that established foreign rule. Many of the rulers, especially the Bactrians and the Kuṣāṇas, were partial to Buddhism.'[24]

The combined force of these factors would make Aśoka the *bête noire* of the brahmanical world, a fact which would suffice to explain why his name was forgotten in certain circles. This is one level at which this silence could be understood.

Another level at which the silence regarding Aśoka could be understood is at a broader national level, by connecting the first factor mentioned by Patrick Olivelle with the third; that is, by holding Aśoka's policies responsible for the foreign invasions that devastated the country. The well-known historian of ancient India, Hemachandra Raychaudhuri, writes thus of Aśoka's various reforms:

> The statesman who turned civil administrators into religious propagandists, abolished hunting and jousts of arms, entrusted the fierce tribesmen on the North-West Frontier and in the wilds of the Deccan to the tender care of 'superintendents of piety' and did not rest till the sound of the kettle-drum was completely hushed and the only sound that was heard was that of moral teaching, certainly pursued a policy at which Chandragupta Maurya would have looked askance. Dark clouds were looming in the north-western horizon. India needed men of the calibre of Puru and Chandragupta to ensure her protection against the Yavana menace. She got a dreamer. Magadha after the Kaliṅga War frittered away her conquering energy in attempting a religious revolution, as Egypt did under the guidance of Ikhnaton. The result was politically disastrous as will be shown in the next section. Aśoka's attempt to end war met with the same fate as the similar endeavour of President Wilson.[25]

With the fall of the Mauryan Empire, north India experienced a major political upheaval in the form of numerous invasions. As Altekar notes:

> The period of 500 years between 200 BC and 300 AD was a very dark and dismal one for Northern India. The fertile plains of the Punjab and the Gangetic valley were subjected during this period to one foreign invasion after another. First came the Greeks, who under Demetrius and Menander (c. 190–150 BC) were able to penetrate right up to Patna in Bihar. Then came Scythians and the Parthians (c. 100 BC to

> 50 AD). These ... were followed by the Kushāṇas, who succeeded in overrunning practically the whole of northern India by the middle of the 2nd century AD.[26]

The *Gārgīsaṃhitā* section of the *Yuga Purāṇa* assesses the damage caused by the invasion of Śakas (Scythians) as follows: *caturbhāgaṃ tu śastreṇa nāśayiṣyanti prāṇinām/ śakāḥ śeṣaṃ hariṣyanti caturbhāgaṃ svakaṃ puraṃ. Vinaṣṭe śakarājye tu śūnyā pṛthvī bhaviṣyati.* In other words, these wars of conquest reduced the population of north India by 'one half, 25 per cent being killed and 25 per cent being enslaved and carried away'.[27] The *Yuga Purāṇa* further informs us that during this period even women took to ploughing, presumably as a result of the decimation.[28] Indian opinion at the time seemed to blame Aśoka's pacifism for this disaster, for the same *Gārgīsaṃhitā* declares: 'the fool established the so-called conquest of dharma' (*sthāpayiṣyati mohātmā vijayaṃ nāma dhārmikam*),[29] though it does not refer to Aśoka by name.

Even more telling is the fact that his favourite title 'beloved of the gods' (*devānāmpiya*) became a synonym for a 'fool' in classical Sanskrit.[30]

From this point of view, the fact that the famous *praśasti* or panegyric of Samudragupta by the Jaina Hariṣeṇa is inscribed on an *Aśokan* pillar is of more than mere archaeological interest. It may possess a historical dimension, as if the Hindu reaction had come full circle. An Indian empire had now once again emerged, after an earlier one had been virtually destroyed by the policies of Aśoka. It was now carving an account of its martial exploits on Aśoka's pillar as if to say that is what emperors do, rather than converting arsenals into monasteries. Rama Shanker Tripathi notes that:

> [W]ith his ideal of war and aggrandisement, Samudragupta was the very antithesis of Aśoka, who stood for peace and piety. The former's achievements formed the subject of an elaborate panegyric by the court poet Hariṣeṇa, and, *strangely enough*, Samudragupta chose to leave a permanent record of sanguinary conquests by the side of the ethical exhortations of Aśoka on one of his pillars, now inside the fort of Allahabad.[31]

Perhaps the fact is not so strange.

In the light of what we have called the Hindu view of Aśoka, this is not strange at all, but the logical culmination of its assessment of Aśoka, according to which he was a national disaster so far as the political fortunes of the country were concerned. The opposition, however, seems to have been to his *pacifism* rather than his *Buddhism*, although in Aśoka's own mind they may have been connected because later dynasties with Buddhist leanings such as the Pāla—who were not pacifists—do not seem to have aroused such a reaction. According to Upinder Singh:

> There are two diametrically opposite views of Ashoka's pacifism. One is that it irrevocably weakened the military basis of the empire, and the other is that this king's pacifism was tempered by a strong element of pragmatism and had little role to play in the decline of the Maurya Empire.[32]

It seems that historians of 'Hindu' history tend towards the former, and 'Indian' and 'World' history so to say, towards the latter.

But to revert to the *Manusmṛti*, which occupies a middle chronological position in the cycle from Aśoka to Samudragupta. One thing which had survived all these convulsions from the end of the Vedic age until the time of the *Manusmṛti* was the oral transmission of the Vedas, along with the generations of *brāhmaṇas* who specialized in it. They were the people left to deal with the crisis. The task of maintaining social cohesion, in a society coming apart at the seams, was either thrust on them or assumed by them. The leadership of a society is usually provided by the rulers, but with them gone the responsibility of maintaining the society as a community now devolved to the priests. The *brāhmaṇas* thus assumed the leadership of the community and the enormous privileges they claim in the *Manusmṛti* could be construed as a consequence of this development. They had to rely on Vedic authority in order to create a template for ordering society, as it was this authority which had survived the various vicissitudes. This may explain why the text is called the *Manusmṛti,* because Manu is embedded in Vedic lore. There is the famous Vedic statement 'What Manu has said is medicine' (*Taittirīya Saṃhitā* 2.2.10.2).[33] Manu is also the progenitor of humanity in some accounts. That Manu is invoked to confer authority on the text is clear from the structure of the text of the *Manusmṛti*, which Patrick Olivelle spells out as follows:

> We have here five layers of 'telling', 'hearing', and re-telling. At the most remote level, we have the Creator himself soon after his creative activity composing a treatise and reciting it to his son Manu (I.58). Manu is the first 'hearer'. He transmits it to Marīci and the other sages (I.58), who form the second tier of 'hearers'. At Manu's command, one of these sages, Bhṛgu, teaches the seers who had come to Manu with the mission of learning the Law. Bhṛgu's first word (I.60), significantly, is 'Listen'. This group of seers, still placed *in illo tempore*, constitutes the third tier of 'hearers'. The narrator of the entire text makes only a fleeting and implicit appearance in the very first verse of the text: 'As Manu was seated, absorbed in contemplation, the great seers came up to him, paid him homage in the proper manner, and said to him.' Here we have the voice of the narrator introducing the first group of characters; then he becomes silent except for two other fleeting appearances to introduce the seers' further request at 5.1–2 and to introduce Bhṛgu's final discourse at 12.2. Evidently the narrator himself, who at one level can be identified with the historical author of the text, heard the text presumably from the seers; or he has been eavesdropping on Bhṛgu's instruction of the seers. This narrator is the fourth 'hearer'. There is then the implied fifth 'hearer', that is, all those who listen to or read this text, including modern scholars. The last verse of the book, possibly part of an interpolated section, is directed at this audience: 'When a twice-born recites this Treatise of Manu proclaimed by Bhṛgu, he will always follow the proper conduct and obtain whatever state he desires.[34]

It may also be worth noting that Manu was not a *brāhmaṇa* but a *kṣatriya*, a king. Did this also play a role in the invocation of his authority by the *brāhmaṇas*?[35]

V

The last nodal point is provided by the indigenous dynasties which had begun to emerge in the second century. They possess a striking characteristic. Such epigraphic evidence as we possess suggests that they were supporters of the *varṇa* order.

The Śaka ruler, Rudradāman (c. 150 CE), records his support of the *varṇa* scheme in his well-known Junāgarh rock inscription (line 9).[36]

Similarly Gautamīputra Śātakarṇi (c. 106 CE–c. 130 CE) according to the Nāsik cave inscription, restored order among the four *varṇas*, significantly by reconciling the *brāhmaṇas* and the *avaras* (*śūdras*). Ram Sharan Sharma's suggestion that this 'alignment of the *varṇas* was directed by the *brāhmaṇa* ruler against the *kṣatriyas*, who perhaps belonged to foreign ruling dynasties', is worth noting here.[37]

The brahmanical reaction to the crisis around this time also seems to have taken a direct political form (*śastra*) in addition to an intellectual one such as the composition of *Manusmṛti* (*śāstra*). The Śuṅgas, the Kaṇvas and the Śātavāhanas, for instance, were brahmanical dynasties which arose during this period. Does one find an echo of this in the provision, in *Manusmṛti* 10.81, that during a crisis the person of the higher *varṇa* can take recourse to the mode of living of the next *varṇa*? Thus, in a time of crisis, *brāhmaṇas* could take up the role of *kṣatriyas*. One is surprised, however, to find no glorification of a figure like Paraśurāma within it, who represents a brahmanical *avatāra* of Viṣṇu. The fact that it incorporates a section on statecraft also points in the same direction of combining *śastra* and *sāstra*.

This argument, however, has its limits. During the first three centuries of the Christian era, there was no great political power around, excepting the Sāsānian dynasty of Persia in the extreme north-west. The rest of north India was divided into 'small tribal (with republican, oligarchical or semi-oligarchical administration), oligarchical and monarchical states.'[38] In other words, the author of the *Manusmṛti*, viewing the political scene, would perhaps *not* have been impressed by the chances of success of *direct imperial* brahmanical political intervention. Rather, he was impressed by the political fragmentation all around him, which might explain why he opted for the model of the *vijigīṣu* (conqueror) and the *maṇḍala* (circle).

There is now a greater recognition in our field of the significance of the period between the passing away of Aśoka and before the rise of the Guptas—from circa 200 BCE to 300 CE—in the history of Hinduism than had been the case earlier. In fact:

> Recent work on the *Mahābhārata*, in particular by Alf Hiltebeitel, James Fitzgerald, and Madeleine Biardeau, has resulted in an increasing consensus that India's great epic was initially composed around the Sunga period, after the fall of the Mauryas, and that it was composed

in deliberate response to the anti-Brahmanical policies of emperor Aśoka.[39]

According to Johannes Bronkhorst, this was also the period during which ideas from 'Greater Magadh' were adopted by the brahmanical mainstream and that 'this process was set in motion by foreign invasions in the north-west of the subcontinent. These invasions drove the Brahmans eastward and, together with the hostility of the Nandas and Mauryas, fostered an existentialist crisis that gave birth to the Brahmans uniquely inward-looking ideology.'[40] There is also an increasing recognition now of the role of *brāhmaṇas* in the historical processes involved. The work of Uma Chakravarti suggests that *brāhmaṇas* made up the:

> ... largest single group within both the *sangha* (i.e. monks and nuns) and the laity (i.e., those who take refuge in the Buddha, but do not ordain) which leads her to conclude that many Brahmans, due to the fact that they were already a 'religious group' were attracted to Buddhism.

The title of one of Johannes Bronkhorst's book says it all: *How the Brahmins Won: From Alexander to the Guptas*!

VI

If one takes a synchronic rather than a diachronic view of the history of India, preparatory to reviewing the *Manusmṛti*, then one is struck by the fact that the great failure of Hindu civilization in north India is political. If we review its history from the beginning of the common era we find that of the 2,000 years of this history, Hindus have been under political servitude for almost half the period. The first three centuries saw at least parts of north India go under foreign rule; and effective Muslim rule over Delhi continued virtually uninterrupted from c. 1200 until 1707, the year in which Aurangzeb died. And within half a century, the foundation of British Rule had been laid at the battle of Plassey in 1757.

In other words, the crisis to which the *Manusmṛti* was reacting was only the first of two other crises in which north India had lost political control over its destiny—when the *religious* leadership represented by the *brāhmaṇas* had to take on the role of shepherding the community after it had lost control over its political destiny. It would be useful to historically compare *subsequent* reactions with those represented by the *Manusmṛti.*

The reaction of the Hindu community to the prolonged Muslim occupation was complex, but one major strand in it does seem to follow the pattern set by the *Manusmṛti*, namely, that of tightening the social structure along hierarchical lines, the Hindu version of 'circling the wagons'. Sugata Bose and Ayesha Jalal note in this context that, compared to the Muslim *ulema*:

> The Brahmanical tradition on the Hindu side could be equally exclusivist when it could not absorb and dominate and, consequently, was averse to accommodation. One Nrisinghacharya was reputed to have told a congregation of high-caste Hindus at a Kumbha Mela—a great religious fair held at the confluence of the Ganga and the Jamuna—to adopt *karmathabritti* or the habit of a tortoise, in other words withdraw into a shell in order to be impervious to Islamic influences. Indeed, if one reads the *Dharmashastra* or Hindu law books of this period, to the exclusion of other sources, one will not even begin to suspect that there were Muslims in India.[41]

There was, however, one significant difference. The incorporation of elements of statecraft in the *Manusmṛti* suggests that the possibility of regaining control over the state, which had been lost to foreigners, was a live option in the minds of those who formulated their response to the foreign invasions preceding the second century. Perhaps the prolonged nature of Muslim rule made this only a dim prospect in the eyes of the medieval successors who were caught in the same bind in which the author of the *Manusmṛti* found himself. Therefore, the medieval Hindus had to project a 'mythical' figure, that of Rāma,[42] as the restorer of the political sovereignty that had been lost, at least until the arrival of Śivājī (1627–80) on the scene.

British rule presented a similar crisis but again with significant differences. To the extent that British rule represented the replacement of one foreign rule by another, the blow was less severe. And to some extent the British rule was seen as less zealous in general than Muslim rule in promoting proselytization. The British did try to proselytize in earnest from around 1818 until 1857 but gave up after the Mutiny as it represented too much of a risk. British rule nevertheless did create a crisis, and the response again came primarily, though not solely, from brahmanical leaders. This becomes obvious as one surveys the list of the major figures of modern Hinduism: Rammohun Roy (1772/4–1833); Devendranath Tagore (1817–1905); Keshub Chunder Sen (1838–84); Rāmakṛṣṇa Paramahaṃsa (1836–86); Swami Vivekananda (1863–1902); Dayānanda Sarasvatī (1824–83); Jyotirao Phule (1827–90); Mahadev Govind Ranade (1842–1901); Gopal Krishna Gokhale (1866–1915); Bal Gangadhar Tilak (1856–1920); Sree Narayana Guru (1856–1928); Rabindranath Tagore (1861–1941); Mahatma Gandhi (1869–1943); Aurobindo Ghose (1872–1950); V.D. Savarkar (1883–1966); Sarvepalli Radhakrishnan (1888–1975), Jiddu Krishnamurti (1895–1986) and, to a certain extent, Dr. B.R. Ambedkar (1891–1956).

Out of these just five figures are not of *brāhmaṇa* ancestry: Keshub Chunder Sen, Jyotirao Phule, Swami Vivekananda, Mahatma Gandhi and Aurobindo Ghose. It is worth noting, though, that two of the most influential people in this list—Swami Vivekananda and Mahatma Gandhi—were non-*brāhmaṇas*. British rule was also different from Muslim rule inasmuch as the British claimed to be in India only temporarily (despite developing an illusion of permanence in the heyday of British imperialism), which also rendered the crisis less severe, as also their willingness to govern Hindus broadly in accordance with the legal tradition of the Hindus—of which the *Manusmṛti*, already available in an English translation in 1794, was considered an integral part.

VII

The historical context of the *Manusmṛti*, as constituted by the major events of the centuries preceding it, has already been examined. It was followed by an examination of historical contexts comparable to the one which gave rise to the *Manusmṛti*. This enabled us to view the *Manusmṛti* as a response to a situation that the Hindu community was again destined to face in the future. This section will bring a comparative lens to bear on the issue.

A hint of this approach is offered by the historian K.M. Panikkar when he writes:

> The service which a small priestly class rendered to a whole people at the time of the destruction of their political power is paralleled only by the action of the Jewish rabbis when the Temple was destroyed and Jews dispersed by the Romans. At the time when the Jewish people sank into despair, a group of learned men under Johanan ben Zakkai established the great academy at Jabneh in the heart of Roman Palestine itself and guarded zealously the doctrine of Judaism. It sent its messages to the Jewish people dispersed all over the world and thus saved Judaism for the future. That is what the Brahmins did in the 13th and the 14th centuries in the Gangetic Valley.[43]

Panikkar is referring here to the *second* crisis created by the loss of political power that the Hindu community had to face under Muslim rule, but he drops a hint which might prove helpful for us as we investigate the *first* crisis, to which the *Manusmṛti* constituted a response.

It so happens that the Jewish community also faced a crisis caused by the loss of political power in the first century, when the Romans destroyed its Temple in Jerusalem. Panikkar, in the passage cited earlier, refers to this incident and as to how the community was saved at this moment by the creation of Rabbinic Judaism, which was centred not on worship in the Temple, but in following Jewish Law as collected in the *Mishnah*, a compendium of oral law which was compiled through the efforts of Rabbi Yohanan Ben Zakkai. The fact that the *Manusmṛti* was similarly compiled around the same time provides an interesting parallel. This was especially so as its goal was also to save a community which had lost political power, by placing its focus on what we might call 'social power' as a counterblast to it—a society so well regulated by its own inner laws as to become impervious to the political vicissitudes it underwent.

VIII

Did the Hindus possess enough of a sense of history[44] to render an interpretation of the sort presented in the preceding pages credible? We noted earlier how, after the collapse of the Mauryan Empire after Aśoka, political unity was restored in north India under the Guptas. One famous piece of art which belongs to this period is the depiction of Viṣṇu's incarnation as the boar (*varāhāvatāra*) in the Udayagiri cave in central India. Three interpretations of this depiction are presented below. The reader will notice that they become more 'historical' in nature, in proportion to the sense of history granted by the scholar to the Hindus. And the reader will I hope forgive the length of the citations involved, without which the point could not be made. The first interpretation is that by A.L. Basham. He writes:

> Perhaps the most immediately impressive of all Guptan sculptures is the Great Boar, carved in relief at the entrance of a cave at Udayagiri near Bhīlsā. The body of the god Viṣṇu, who became a mighty boar to rescue the earth from the cosmic ocean, conveys the impression of a great primeval power working for good against the forces of chaos and destruction, and bears a message of hope, strength and assurance. The greatness of the god in comparison with his creation is brought out by the tiny female figure of the personified earth, clinging to his tusk. The deep feeling, which inspired the carving in this figure, makes it perhaps the only theriomorphic image in the world's art, which conveys a truly religious message to modern man.[45]

There is virtually no historical element in Basham's appreciation of this piece. This emerges in the interpretation by H.C. Raychaudhuri, who writes:

> According to sacred legends Viṣṇu in the shape of a Boar had rescued the earth in the aeon of universal destruction. It is significant that the worship of the Boar Incarnation became widely popular in the Gupta-Chalukya period. The poet Viśākhadatta actually identifies the *man* in whose arms the earth found refuge when harassed by the *Mlechchhas*, who 'shook the yoke of servitude from the neck' of his country, with the *Varāhītanu* (Boar form) of the Self-Existent Being. Powerful emperors both in the north and south recalled the feats of the Great Boar, and the mightiest ruler of a dynasty that kept the Arabs at bay for centuries actually took the title of Ādivarāha or the Primeval Boar. The Boar Incarnation then symbolized the successful struggle of Indians against the devastating floods issuing from the regions outside their borders that threatened to overwhelm their country and civilization in a common ruin.[46]

The reference to the poet Viśākhadatta in the passage just cited is an allusion to the concluding verse of Viśākhadatta's drama *Mudrārākṣasa* which, while dealing with events of the time of Candragupta Maurya, refers indirectly also to Candragupta II, who was the poet's contemporary, and may have been his patron. In J.A.B. van Buitenen's translation this verse reads:

> The Self-Begotted God did once assume
> The fitting body of a mighty Boar
> And on his snout did save the troubled Earth,
> Nurse of all beings, when she was deluged:
> Now, terrified by the barbarian hordes,
> She has sought shelter in our king's strong arms:
> May Candragupta, our most gracious king,
> Whose people prosper and whose kinsmen thrive,
> For long continue to protect the land![47]

Heinrich von Stietencron goes on to say after citing these lines:

> Whether the Udayagiri image is an illustration of the poet's words, or whether the poet was in turn inspired by the image, cannot be determined with certainty, nor is it relevant in the present context. That such identification of kings and gods was not simply flattering talk of eager panegyrists, but formed part of a royal ideology of divine kingship and was proclaimed by kings in their own inscriptions is shown, among many other instances, by the Allahabad pillar inscription of Candragupta's father Samudragupta.[48]

Stietencron is more willing than either Basham or Raychaudhuri to concede a sense of history to the Hindus at this point and detects a more specific historical reference in the sculptural depiction under discussion. He writes:

> There is a special feature in the Varāha relief of Udayagiri which is repeated nowhere else. The ocean out of which the dominating image of Varāha rises with great strength is represented with meticulous care by its endless waves, and again twice in personified form as man standing

> in this ocean with a water-pot in his hands. The two river goddesses Gaṅgā and Yamunā are seen flowing towards him.
>
> Later images do not show the ocean at all. But here the ocean (Sanskrit: *samudra*) has a special meaning. A word play takes on plastic form. Just as Varāha issuing from the mighty (ocean) *samudra* rescued the earth from *asura* oppression, even so did Candragupta II, issuing from his mighty (father) *Samudragupta* rescue the earth from *asura* (i.e. Western Kṣatrapa) oppression. The person in the water pot standing in the ocean has thus a double meaning. He is the ocean in anthropomorphic form, but he is also an image of Candragupta's father Samudragupta.
>
> The ocean was dropped altogether in later representations, since it could not carry similar connotations with other donors.[49]

It is clear, therefore, that there is enough evidence of historical memory in India to render the line of investigation adopted here worth pursuing. It is true that Hindu India does not possess a sustained tradition of historiography of the kind we find in other ancient cultures such as Greece, Rome and China. Sometimes cultures exhibit such civilizational gaps. For instance, China has a long history, a history of warfare and chivalry as well, and of course a literary tradition right from Confucius onwards, but it did not produce an epic of the kind we find in Greece, Rome and India.

One reason behind this histographic gap in India could be that historical events in ancient India were recorded on stone rather than paper. This renders the facts narrated above particularly signficant, as they are cut in stone. India has more than 90,000 inscriptions, most of which are still unread.

PART II

3

Sources of *Dharma* in the *Manusmṛti*

There are two verses in the second chapter of the *Manusmṛti* which list the sources of *dharma*. According to one (2.6): 'The root of the Law is the entire Veda; the tradition and practice of those who know the Veda; the conduct of good people; and what is pleasing to oneself.'[1] According to the other (2.12): 'Veda, tradition, the conduct of good people, and what is pleasing to oneself—these, they say, are the four visible marks of Law.'[2]

If the verses are read together it is easy to see that four sources of *dharma* (for that is the word translated by the word Law in the verses cited above) can be identified, with the second verse specifying the four as follows:

1. *Śruti* or revelation
2. *Smṛti* or tradition
3. *Sadācāra* or exemplary conduct, and
4. *Ātma-tuṣṭi* or what is satisfying to oneself.[3]

I

One may begin the investigation into the issue of the source of *dharma* or *dharma-mūla* by problematizing the listing in various ways.

The first issue to raise is: Is the list exhaustive? That is, does it cover all the sources of *dharma* actually hinted at in the *Manusmṛti*? Consider, for instance, some of the provisions made in this regard in other parts of the *Manusmṛti*.

I.1

The *Manusmṛti* also contains the following provisions in chapter 12:

> [108] If it be asked: what happens in cases where specific Laws have not been laid down? What 'cultured' Brahmins state is the undisputed Law. [109] Those Brahmins who have studied the Veda together with its supplements in accordance with the Law and are knowledgeable in scripture, perception, and inference, should be recognized as 'cultured'. [110] Alternatively, when a legal assembly with a minimum of ten members, or with a minimum of three members firm in their conduct, determines a point of Law, no one must question that Law.[4]

These verses provide two ways of deciding what *dharma* is, when a doubt arises in the matter. One answer provided is: 'What "cultured" Brahmins state is the undisputed Law' (12.108cd). This conforms to the second source in 2.6 in the *Manusmṛti*: 'The tradition and practice of those who know the Veda.' However, we also meet with the statement that if a legal assembly, set up according to certain rules, 'determines a point of Law, no one must question that Law' (12.110). In effect then, another source of law has surfaced: a legal assembly. Is it to be subsumed under the second source or does it deserve the status of a separate source?

Consider another verse which follows soon thereafter (12.113): 'When even a single Brahmin who knows the Veda determines something as the Law, it should be recognized as the highest Law, and not something uttered by myriads of ignorant men.'[5] This verse raises at least two questions: (1) Is this to be treated as an independent source of *dharma*—this utterance by one *brāhmaṇa* who knows the Veda, or is this case already covered by the first source cited earlier, as knowledge of the Veda on the part of the *brāhmaṇa* may be assumed, or by the second source, as someone representing, 'The tradition and practice of those who know the Veda', or by the fourth source, as a judgement embodying the *ātma-tuṣṭi* of the Brahmin? (2) If the judgement of one learned Brahmin is contrasted with that of 'myriads of ignorant men', then does it mean that if instead of 'myriads of ignorant men' one had 'millions of educated people', then would what they said be acceptable as *dharma*?

I.2

Consider now yet another set of verses from another part of the *Manusmṛti* (2.238–40):

> [238] A man with faith should accept fine learning even from a low-caste man; the highest Law even from a man of the lowest caste; and a splendid woman even from a bad family. [239] One should take ambrosia even from poison; words of wisdom even from a child; a good example even from an enemy; and gold even from filth. [240] Women, gems, learning, Law, purification, and words of wisdom, as well as crafts of various kinds, may be accepted from anyone.[6]

The key point to note is that the Sanskrit word translated as Law in verse 240 is none other than our *dharma*. And the verse says it can be acquired from *sarvataḥ*: an expression translated as from 'anybody' by most English translators,[7] but a word which can as easily mean from 'everywhere' or 'anywhere'. Does this open up the whole globe as a resource for *dharma*? It is worth noting that the word *dharma* is not just tagged on as an isolated item in this verse but appears with such quintessentially 'Hindu' words as *vidyā* (knowledge) and *śaucam* (purity).

An even more consequential point may be involved. Is the *Manusmṛti* saying that a source of *dharma* can be found outside the Veda and the fourfold apparatus proposed by it? Although the expression in *Manusmṛti* (2.6) says that the 'entire Veda is the root of *dharma*', the statement could also be read subliminally as 'the Veda is the root of *all dharma*', in light of such eulogies of the Veda as the following in *Manusmṛti* 12.94–99:

> [94] The Veda is the eternal eyesight for ancestors, gods, and humans; for vedic teaching is beyond the powers of logic or cognition—that is the settled rule. [95] The scriptures that are outside the Veda, as well as every kind of fallacious doctrine—all these bear no fruit after death, for

> tradition takes them to be founded on Darkness. [96] All those different from the Veda that spring up and then flounder—they are false and bear no fruit, because they belong to recent times.
>
> [97] The four social classes, the three worlds, and the four orders of life, the past, the present and the future—all these are individually established by the Veda. [98] Sound, touch, visible appearance, taste, and, the fifth, smell, are established by the Veda alone; their origin is according to attribute and action. [99] The eternal vedic treatise bears on all beings; it is the means of success for these creatures; therefore I consider it supreme.[8]

It is worth recalling here that 'according to one of the greatest Vedantic teachers, Madhvācārya, God descended into the world as Vyāsa and composed the *Mahābhārata* which elaborated the entire meaning of the Veda *as well as that which though not contained in the Veda* is the object of the absolute knowledge of God.'[9]

I.3

Consider next an earlier verse in chapter 2, which has been translated as follows (2.223):

> If he sees a woman or a low-born doing something conducive to welfare, he should do all that diligently, or anything else that he is fond of.[10]

The use of the word *śreyas* in this verse translated above as 'conducive to welfare' should make us pause, because it is also a word redolent with spiritual and religious meaning, apart from indicating that which might be 'better'. The verse says that the *yukta*, that is, the diligent Vedic student, should adopt the superior way practiced by a woman or a low caste person, and also an act as he finds pleasing. This verse is found in the second chapter of the *Manusmṛti* wherein serious instructions are being imparted to the Vedic student; the verse therefore deserves to be taken seriously as well. It is difficult not to connect it with the last aphorism of the *Āpastamba Dharma Sūtra*, also referred to earlier. Towards the end of that text the question raised is how matters of *dharma* are to be settled. The first answer provided is that one should follow the way of the *śiṣṭas* or 'cultured' twice-borns. However, the last aphorism says that some are of the view that the matter may be settled by consulting women and all the *varṇas* (*strībhyaḥ sarvavarṇebyaḥ prayiyāityeke*). Does one hear in this segment of the *Manusmṛti* the echo of this option? It seems that the third source of *sadācāra* is broadened here beyond the *dvijas* or twice-borns to include women and *śūdras*. I would further argue, in the same spirit, that the Sanskrit text *yatra vāsya ramen manaḥ* is probably referring to *ātmatuṣṭi*, and, as it is being invoked without prior reference to *Śruti* or *Smṛti*, it basically refers to one's own inclination or 'conscience'. In any case, that the verse under consideration is exceptional is clear:

> The commentators strain to make sense of this extraordinary, and apparently heretical, verse in various ways. Some suggest that the woman is the wife of the teacher and that the 'lower born' (*avaraja*) is simply someone younger than the student, while others specify that nothing contrary to the teachings should ever be done, even in this instance. 'He' almost certainly means the student of the Veda, who is apparently here allowed to imitate certain of the actions of those who are not twice-born, if those actions are 'better' (śreyas—better than those prescribed for him?) or even if he simply wants to.[11]

I.4

Another problem is raised by the statement in the *Manusmṛti* that *dharmas* change in accordance with the cosmic ages (1.85): 'There is one set of Laws in the Kṛta Age, another in the Tretā, still another in the Dvāpara, and a different set in the Kali, in keeping with the progressive shortening taking place in each Age.'[12] Patrick Olivelle notes that the meaning of 'progressive shortening taking place with each Age' is 'not altogether clear. The meaning could be "in keeping with the progressive shortening of the human span in each Age". Alternatively, the "shortening" or decrease may have a broader meaning, including the Ages themselves, the human life spans, as well the feet of Law.'[13]

All these points become relevant when we ask the question: Are the Ages (*yugas*) also not a source of *dharma* in some sense, when *dharma* depends on the Age? If we limit our vision to the *Manusmṛti*, then the *yugas* seem to emphasize certain *dharmas* rather than serve as a source for them, for the very next line in the *Manusmṛti* (1.86) states: 'Ascetic toil, they say, is supreme in the Kṛta Age; knowledge in Tretā; sacrifice in Dvāpara; and gift-giving alone in Kali.'[14]

If we take the intertextual route, however, then we discover that the *Mahābhārata* also says that *dharmas* differ with the aeons. While noting this, K. Satchidananda Murty additionally notes: 'The *Manusmṛti* says exactly the same: the first three *pādas* of its I.85, and the first three of the *Mahābhārata*, XII.252.8, are identical except for one word. In the *smṛti* the last word in the third *pāda* is "nṛṇām," but in the other it is "dharma".'[15] If we go down this intertextual route further, we realize that the assignment of various *dharmas* to various *yugas* does problematize the issue in a major way, although we were able to indulge in damage-control, as it were, so far as the *Manusmṛti* itself is concerned. K. Satchidananda Murty states quite clearly:

> I will now refer to a problematic issue which the *Mahābhārata* raises in connection with Vedic authority, and solves it. The issue is posed as follows: The knowers of *śāstras* have determined the Veda as the pramāṇa (the right means of knowledge) of dharma. But there is a decrease (hrāsa) of Vedic utterances from aeon to aeon.[16]

The use of the word decrease or *hrāsa* was noted as problematic by Olivelle in the context of the *Manusmṛti*; Murty also remarks in the context of the *Mahābhārata*:

> This could mean one of these: (i) The decisions of the Veda regarding dharma change from aeon to aeon or (ii) the corpus of the Veda is infinite, but from aeon to aeon starting from the Kṛta, what is available of it to mortals becomes more and more limited, thus resulting in the virtual shrinking of it.[17]

He then goes on to summarize the discussion in the *Mahābhārata* as follows:

> Dharmas differ from aeon to aeon. The system of dharmas in each aeon seems to depend on the capacities of human beings, which change from aeon to aeon. 'What āmnāyas (traditions/sacred texts) say is true', seems to be a platitude for the propitiation of mankind.

> The Vedas are superior to āmnāyas and are projected universally. If all of them are pramāṇam then there is no pramāṇa. If pramāṇa and apramāṇa are mutually contradictory, then from where is the śāstraness of which? Such is the problematic put forward, which expressed in a simpler form would be: If dharmas are not the same from age to age and the pramāṇa for all of them, the one Veda, is also changing, can it still be the source of eternal truth? How can mutually-contradictory traditions, some of which also contain what is opposed to the Veda, together with the Veda, or each of them be pramāṇa? The *Mahābhārata* answers this through a declaration of the principal character of a story it narrates: 'I know the dharma eternal with its secret; ancient, good and friendly for all beings. To live without malice, or at least with minimum malice, towards beings is the supreme dharma'. Thus the fifth Veda in one sentence enunciates an admirable principle by conforming to which dhārmic life would be possible. It can and should be followed in all ages and situations, and is thus an eternal law.[18]

In the end then the moral norm trumps scripture in the *Mahābhārata*!

I.5

It seems that *anumāna* and *tarka*, or logical inference and reasoning, are also admitted as ways of determining *dharma*, as stated in the *Manusmṛti* (12.105–06):

> [105] Perception, inference, and treatises coming from diverse sources—a man who seeks accuracy with respect to the Law must have a complete understanding of these three. [106] The man who scrutinizes the records of the seers and the teachings of the Law by means of logical reasoning not inconsistent with the Vedic treatise—he alone knows the Law, and no one else.[19]

On the basis of the foregoing discussion it seems possible to propose that the fourfold structure of the sources of *dharma* in the *Manusmṛti* *should be taken as illustrative rather than exhaustive* in the context of the *Manusmṛti*.

II

A second question also surfaces in relation to the schema presented in the *Manusmṛti* regarding the sources of *dharma*: Is the ordering meant to be hierarchical? That is to say: If the question we have in mind in a particular situation is 'How do I decide what is the right thing for me to do (*dharma*) in this situation?' then is one meant to first consult *Śruti*; if one does not find the answer therein, then consult the *Smṛti*; and if the answer still eludes turn to *sadācāra*; and if a suitable precedent is not forthcoming, then consult one's 'conscience'?

G. Bühler translates the *Manusmṛti* (2.6) in a manner suggestive of such an interpretation:

> The whole Veda is the (first) source of the sacred law, next the tradition and the virtuous conduct of those who know the (Veda further), also the customs of holy men, and (finally) self-satisfaction.[20]

The issue I wish to raise is whether, on the basis of the evidence derived from the *Manusmṛti*, one is supposed to follow such a hierarchical order, or utilize the sources of *dharma* independently on one's own?[21] The hierarchical view of the sources of *dharma* possesses a certain natural appeal. Thus, if a young man wonders whether he should get married and raise a family or lead a single life, the convocation address in the *Taittirīya Upaniṣad* (1.2.1) clearly instructs him to get married. Thus *Śruti* serves as a source of *dharma*.

Suppose the wife loses her husband, then what is she supposed to do? Could she marry another man? If she followed *Parāṣara Smṛti* (4.28) she could, because it allows a woman to remarry if her husband has died. Parāṣara also mentions a few other conditions under which she could remarry.[22] The *Manusmṛti* (5.157–59), however, would have her lead a life of ascetic chastity for the rest of her life. This brings us to an important point regarding the *Smṛtis* as a source of *dharma*: that they may provide different options. The *Manusmṛti* recognizes that, as a source of *dharma*, the *Śruti* may provide different answers:

> When there are two contradictory [Vedic] scriptural provisions on some issue, however, tradition takes them both to be the Law with

respect to it; for wise men correctly pronounced both of them to be the Law. After sunrise, before sunrise, and at daybreak—the sacrifice takes place at any of these times, so states a Vedic scripture.[23]

The *Manusmṛti,* however, does not seem to display a similar awareness that *Smṛtis* might differ too, probably because it was the first work of this kind. However, now numerous *Smṛtis* exist, which sometimes provide different instructions. Sometimes the same *Smṛti* may take different positions on a matter within itself. If the *Manusmṛti* is the earliest *Smṛti,* then it may not yet be fully aware of what later tradition took to be the purpose of the *Smṛtis*:

> Their purpose is to lay down the laws that should guide individuals and communities in their daily conduct and to apply the eternal truths of the Veda to the changing conditions of time and clime and thereby preserve the integrity and ensure the progress of Hindu society. From time to time a great law-giver would arise, codify the existing laws, eliminate those which had become obsolete, and saw to it that the ways of the Hindus are in a manner consistent with the spirit of the Veda.[24]

But this issue emerges in the case of *Manusmṛti* not in the form of contradiction between *Smṛtis,* but in the form of contradiction within a *Smṛti.*

If, for instance, the husband dies prematurely, leaving a childless wife behind, and the wife and her family wonder how to continue the line, the *Śruti* may not have much to say directly on this but the *Smṛti* texts speak of the institution of *niyoga* or levirate. The custom is not a palatable one, and the idea that she should have a son from the brother-in-law did not appeal to everyone but was reluctantly allowed by the *Smṛtis.* The *Manusmṛti* presents an interesting example of this situation. The practice of it is condemned in some parts of it, as in chapter 9.59–63:

> [59] If the line is about to die out, a wife who is duly appointed may obtain the desired progeny through a brother-in-law or a relative belonging to the same ancestry. [60] The appointed man should smear himself with ghee, approach the widow at night in silence, and beget a single son, never a second. [61] Some who are knowledgeable in these

> matters, seeing that this leaves the purpose of the couple's appointment unfulfilled in terms of the Law, endorse begetting a second son in such women. [62] When the purpose of his appointment to the widow has been fulfilled according to rule, however, they should behave towards each other as an elder and a daughter-in-law. [63] If, on the contrary, the appointed couple disregard the rules and behave lustfully with one another, both become outcastes, he as a molester of a daughter-in-law, and she as a violator of an elder's bed.[25]

Later, however, the *Manusmṛti* expresses a different view of the matter in verses 64 and 65 of the same chapter: '[64] Twice-born men should never appoint a widowed woman to another man, for in appointing her to another man, they assail the eternal Law. [65] The nuptial formulas nowhere mention appointment, nor do injunctions relating to marriage sanction the remarriage of widows.'[26]

Patrick Olivelle notes that these two verses 'contradict the opinion on levirate' expressed earlier in verses 59–63. He goes on to say:

> I think that here also Manu may be engaging in an argument with an opponent, whose view is given first and then refuted. Manu's own view appears to be that levirate is morally reprehensible in the case of a widow; the only allowance he makes is when the husband dies after the betrothal (8.69–70).[27]

This contradiction has been noted by many including A.S. Altekar[28] and P.V. Kane[29] in our times and by earlier commentators as well.[30] Kane notes several interesting features here. He first notes that 'Manu, though he first describes *niyoga*, ultimately condemns it in the strongest terms possible (IX.64–68).'[31] However, though 'Manu condemned the ancient practice of niyoga, he had to make provision for the *kṣetrajña* son as regards partition (IX.120–21, 145), which again involves some contradiction.' Kane goes on to say:

> It should be noticed that if the interpretation of Manu IX.69–70 be accepted, the word 'vidhavā' would have to be taken in two different senses in Manu and other texts e.g. in IX.60 where Manu speaks of niyoga, the word means a girl promised to a bridegroom who died

before the marriage ceremony was gone through, while in Manu IX.64 'vidhavā' means 'a widow whose husband died after marriage was completed.' To say the least, this contravenes the canon of Mīmāṁsā interpretation that the same word in the same passage or context should have only one meaning.[32]

The *Manusmṛti* gives mixed signals, which demonstrates that these issues were the subject of moral debate. P.V. Kane notes:

> Viśvarūpa on Yāj. I.69 states several views on the point. The first is that niyoga is bad in the present age as opposed to smṛti texts (like Manu IX.64 and 68) and to the usage of the śiṣṭas (respectable people). The second view was the same as Manu IX.69 set out above. A third view was that there was an option (as niyoga was both forbidden and allowed). A fourth view (which seems to be the view of Viśvarūpa himself) was that the smṛti texts about niyoga refer to śūdras (Manu IX.64 uses the word 'dvijāti') and it was also allowed to royal families, when there was no male to succeed (and only a brāhmaṇa was to be appointed) and Viśvarūpa relies upon two verses of Vṛddhamanu and a gāthā of Vāyu. Viśvarūpa further says that the procreation of sons by Vyāsa from the queens of Vicitravīrya should be paid no heed (i.e. is not to be relied on) like the marriage of Draupadī (to the five Pāṇḍavas). The Mahābhārata probably reflects what happened owing to the incessant internecine wars among the princes of India. Whole princely houses must have been slaughtered. If niyoga was prevalent among them, the males appointed, when they had to be of the same caste, would have been ordinary soldiers (kṣatriyas). The proud princely families very likely thought it below their dignity to associate widowed queens with ordinary kṣatriyas.[33]

This incidentally explains the emergence of the vast number of *Smṛtis* because of changing moral and social norms reflecting changing historical circumstances. The *Smṛtis* provide an answer depending on one's time and age.

It is important to bear in mind, however, that the *Smṛti* is not independent of *Śruti* as a source of *dharma and* derives its validity from it.

Smṛti has to accord with *Śruti*; Tradition draws its validity from Revelation. Thus, Kullūka Bhaṭṭa, who is placed prior to 1100 CE, while explaining why *Śruti* has been called the supreme authority (*pramāṇaṃ paramam*) in *Manusmṛti* 2.13, remarks that this is so because in the event of a conflict between *Śruti* and *Smṛti*, *Śruti* trumps *Smṛti* and cites Jābāla, Jaimini and the *Bhaviṣyapurāṇa* in support.[34]

Let us examine another moral dilemma. There are rules regarding whom one can accept food from, but suppose one is starving to death: should one starve to death or overlook those rules? The answer is provided by the conduct of the virtuous in similar situations. Thus the *Manusmṛti* says:

> [104] When someone facing death eats food given by anyone at all, he remains unsullied by sin, as the sky by mud. [105] Ajīgarta, tormented by hunger, went up to his son to kill him; and he was not tainted with sin, as he was seeking to allay his hunger. [106] Vāmadeva, a man with a clear vision of what accords with and what is against the Law, finding himself in dire straits and trying to save his life, wanted to eat dog's meat, and yet remained unsullied. [107] Bharadvāja, a man of great austerities, when he and his sons were tormented by hunger in a desolate forest, accepted many cows from the carpenter Bṛbu. [108] Viśvāmitra, a man with a clear vision of what accords with and what is against the Law, when he was tormented by hunger, came to eat the rump of a dog, taking it from the hand of a Cāṇḍāla.[35]

Thus, *sadācāra* or the conduct of the virtuous is also a source of *dharma*. It is, however, not a source of *dharma* independent of *Śruti* or *Smṛti* because the examples provided are drawn both from *Śruti* and *Smṛti* lore. As Patrick Olivelle notes:

> The story of Ajīgarta is told in *Ait B* [*Aitareya Brāhmaṇa*] 7-13-16, although there the father did not intend to eat the son. The story must have changed over time. The story of Vāmadeva eating dog's meat is told in the *MBh* [*Mahābhārata*] *13.94-5.* The story of Bharadvāja is told in Sāyaṇa's commentary on *RV* [*ṚgVeda*] 6.45.31. Viśvāmitra's story is the most famous and is told in the *MBh* [*Mahābhārata*] 12.139.[36]

Finally, another moral dilemma: What should one do if one is attracted to a woman whose *varṇa* one does not know to be the same as one's own? The *Śruti*, *Smṛti* and *sadācāra* do not help one here; they only lay down the norm that one should marry in one's own *varṇa*. But what if one's inner voice says that she belongs to the right *varṇa*? The famous example of this is provided by Dusyanta in the *Abhijnānaśākuntalam* of Kālidāsa. He feels attracted to Śakuntalā on seeing her but does not know her *varṇa*. Then he says: 'Undoubtedly, she is fit to be the wife of a *kshatriya*, since my noble mind covets her. In matters of doubt, the inclinations of their mind are, to the good, an unerring guide.'[37]

Although the hero of the play, Duṣyanta, is relying here on his inner inclinations; his *ātma-tuṣṭi* or self-satisfaction is not being used here as a source of *dharma* independent of others. What his moral instincts tell him is that Śakuntalā must be a *kṣatriya* woman, the right *varṇa* for him to marry in accordance with the *Smṛtis*.

III

The above evidence would seem to suggest that the scheme of the sources of *dharma* laid out in the *Manusmṛti* is hierarchical. There are, however, pieces of evidence found in the *Manusmṛti* which seem to be in the nature of exceptions.

III.1

The Veda is no doubt hailed as the supreme source of *dharma* in the *Manusmṛti* but we also noted one verse in the *Manusmṛti* (2.240) which allowed one to accept *dharma* from everywhere (*sarvataḥ*).

Upon examining the existing translations one gets the feeling that the significance of this statement may have been missed. Patrick Olivelle translates *sarvataḥ*, along with preceding translators, as 'anyone'. He places the set of verses, in which this statement appears, under the rubric 'non-Brahmin teachers'. When looked at through such a lens, and read with the verse which follows it, it is easy to see how the statement might be taken in a very limited sense, for the next verse says: 'In a time of adversity, the rules allow a man to study the Veda under a person who is not a Brahmin ...'[38] And so one could easily construe *sarvataḥ* as anyone, and further anyone as a non-Brahmin. This kind of bottoms-up hermeneutics does seem to suggest a limited application.

If, however, one employs a top-down hermeneutics, and reads the verse as capping a series of verses which *precede* it, a very different impression is created, even in Patrick Olivelle's own translation:

> [238] A man with faith should accept fine learning even from a low-caste man; the highest Law even from a man of the lowest caste; and a splendid woman even from a bad family. [239] One should take ambrosia even from poison; words of wisdom even from a child; a good example even from an enemy; and gold even from filth. [240] Women, gems, learning, Law, purification, and words of wisdom, as well as crafts of various kinds, may be accepted from anyone.[39]

III.2

The *Smṛtis* are supposed to follow the *Śruti* according to the *Manusmṛti*, and this is also laid down as a general principle in this matter. The *Taittirīya Upaniṣad* (1.11.1) instructs one to speak the truth (*satyaṃ vada*),[40] and one would expect the *Manusmṛti* to follow the lead. In fact, it is a universal moral recommendation, and perhaps even a natural moral intuition to speak the truth.

The *Manusmṛti* (8.103–06), however, provides an exception and in so doing seems, at least on the face of it, to 'take Law into its own hands'. That context is the following:

> [103] When a man, even though he knows the truth, gives evidence in lawsuits contrary to the facts for a reason relating to the Law, he does not fall from the heavenly world; that, they say, is divine speech. [104] When telling the truth will result in the execution of a Śūdra, Vaiśya, Kṣatriya, or a Brahmin, a man may tell a lie; for that is far better than the truth. [105] Such persons, performing the highest expiation for the sin of false testimony, should offer to the goddess Sarasvatī oblations of milk-rice dedicated to the goddess Speech. [106] Alternatively, such a person may offer an oblation of ghee in the fire according to rule, reciting the Kuṣmaṇḍa formulas, the verse to Varuṇa. 'Untie, Varuṇa …' or the three formulas addressed to water.[41]

These verses are remarkable inasmuch as: (1) they allow one to tell a lie to save a life; (2) they allow one to do so even in the case of the *śūdra*; and (3) the order in which the four *varṇas* are listed in this verse is in reverse, with the *śūdras* coming first. This is perhaps the only instance of this happening in the *Manusmṛti*. Does it mean that the life of a *śūdra* is even more valuable, at least in some contexts, than that of a *brāhmaṇa*?

III.3

The third source of *dharma*, namely, the example of the virtuous, called *sadācāra*, is usually glossed in the commentaries as *śiṣṭācāra*.[42] That is to say, the virtuous conduct of the male members of the three higher *varṇas*; the *brāhmaṇas*, *kṣatriyas* and *vaiśyas* provide the gold standard. Moreover, one's *guru* should be ideally from among them and ideally a *brāhmaṇa*; a *śūdra* teacher is to be looked down upon according to the *Manusmṛti* (3.156).

At another point in the *Manusmṛti,* however, one finds an expression such as the following: that one may learn 'The highest Law even from a man of the lowest caste'.[43] This is how Patrick Olivelle translates *antyādapi paraṃ dharmam*. (*Manusmṛti* 2.238c). Wendy Doniger (with Brian Smith) renders it as 'the ultimate law even from a man of the lowest (castes)'[44] and G. Bühler translates it as 'the highest law even from the lowest'.[45]

It seems that a contrast is being set up between the highest and the lowest and yet a transmission of *dharma* is involved. The point one wishes to make here is that *Manusmṛti* is acting here independently of the provisions regarding the transmission of *dharma* elsewhere.

The Sanskrit expression *antyādapi paraṃ dharmam* leaves no doubt that one even below a *śūdra* is meant.[46] On this point there is general agreement The controversy centres on *paraṃ dharmam*. The commentary of Kullūka Bhaṭṭa on this verse is relevant here. He expresses dissatisfaction with the way Medhātithi (c. 825–900) explains this part of the verse. According to Medhātithi it is to be understood as follows: 'If even an untouchable tells you: "Don't tarry here; do not bathe in these waters" then one should heed those words. The *dharma* here pertains to mundane and *not* supramundane *dharma.*'[47]

Kullūka offers a very different interpretation of his own. According to Kullūka what is meant is that liberative knowledge may be acquired even from an untouchable. Now the question naturally arises: How could an untouchable be in possession of liberative knowledge? Kullūka anticipates this question and explains that this is possible on account of the force of yogic accomplishment of a previous life—one may have been reborn as an untouchable as a result of residual negative karma which remains to be worked out.

This statement of Kullūka is reminiscent of Śaṅkara's gloss on *Vedāntasūtra* 3.4.36, when he concedes that *śūdras* such as Vidura, Dharmavyadha and so on, were liberated beings, on account of the inevitable maturation of *jñāna* as a result of transformative knowledge acquired earlier.[48]

III.4

In the case of *ātma-tuṣṭi* we considered the example of Duṣyanta, in *Abhijñānaśākuntalam*, who exercises his 'conscience' within the context of the fourfold *varṇa* matrix, but in the *Mahābhārata*, Śakuntalā gives herself away of *her own accord* to Duṣyanta, presumably because she felt *ātma-tuṣṭi* in doing so. This aspect of the scenario is presented by Stephanie Jamison so commendably that the relevant section is worth citing in full despite its length:

> When Duḥṣanta comes to her hermitage and finds a beautiful maiden, unprotected, with her father conveniently off in the forest, he attempts to dazzle her with offers of rich baubles and, incidentally, his kingdom (MBh I.67.1–4). Then he proposes a Gāndharva marriage ('the best kind of marriage' I.67.4). She immediately counters with an appeal to conventional, parentally controlled marriage:
>
> MBh I.67.5 phalāhāro gato rājan pitā me ita āśramāt
> Taṃ muhūrtaṃ pratīkṣasva *sa māṃ tubhyaṃ pradāsyati*
> *My father has gone from the hermitage here to gather fruit, o king.*
> *Wait for him awhile.* ***He will give me to you.***
>
> Duṣyanta responds to the underlying issue in her request by assuring her that she has the right to bestow herself:

> MBh I.67.7 ātmano bandhur ātmaiva gatir ātmaiva cātmanaḥ
> Ātmanaivātmano dānaṃ kartum arhasi dharmataḥ
> *You yourself are your own relative. You yourself are your own means.*
> *You ought to make a gift of yourself by yourself according to law.*

He thus claims that she can act simultaneously as the bride and the giver of the bride, i.e. her father. He then continues with a discourse on the forms of marriage (probably meant to muddle her little mind). When she can get a word in edgewise, she displays a mind thoroughly unmuddled; she returns to the question of her right to give herself. Accepting his arguments, she then uses this role of 'giver' to set conditions on the marriage:

> MBh I.67.15 yadi dharmapathas tv eṣa yadi cātmā prabhur mama
> *Pradāne* pauravaśreṣṭha śṛṇu me samayaṃ prabho
> *If this is a legal course and if I myself am my own master,*
> *O best of the Pauravas, hear my terms of agreement in my* giving *(of myself in marriage), o lord.*

When he solemnly agrees to her stipulations, she enters the marriage. It is hardly her fault that he later reneged and needed further legal remonstrance from Śakuntalā to acknowledge the marriage.[49]

In other words, while one could argue that the four sources of *dharma* function hierarchically within the *Manusmṛti*; one could also argue that there is enough evidence of them also functioning independently as sources of *dharma* within it (as in 2.223).

IV

Pieces of evidence, which indicate that the way the scheme of the sources of *dharma* functions, possesses a certain ambiguity in the *Manusmṛti* and may also be found not only when we treat the four sources integrally, but also when we treat them independently. It also emerges in terms of the 'segmentation' of the sources of *dharma*—an expression whose meaning will become clear as we proceed.

IV.1

The verse from the *Manusmṛti* which speaks of the fourfold template for the sources of *dharma,* and is often referred to, appears in the second chapter of the *Manusmṛti* (2.12). K. Satchidananda Murty interprets this verse and the context in which it appears as follows:

> The *Manusmṛti* does not also promote Vedic exclusiveness. Even the entire Veda is not the sole source of dharma, it says, but a source along with (a) the smṛtis and (b) conduct of its knowers, as well as (c) the conduct of the good and (d) the glad satisfaction of oneself (ātmanastuṣṭi). It is important to note that in addition to the first two, it mentions two more factors, implying that the good may not be with the Veda-knowers only and that what is taken to be Vedic teaching must also appeal to and satisfy an individual. The good in the world or a country constitute a much larger number than that of the Veda-knowers; the first includes the second. This smṛti goes on to say that the character of dharma is fourfold: the Veda, smṛti, the conduct of the good and what is pleasing to oneself (priyamātmanaḥ). It goes without saying that 'the glad satisfaction of oneself' or 'what is pleasing to oneself' cannot be also the exclusive source or character of dharma. Of course, for those inquiring into dharma, it ordains, the ultimate authority is śruti.[50]

The remarks are interesting but what he says next is even more interesting and relevant to our concern at the moment:

> But, another significant thing in this connection is the chapter in which these verses occur begins with a definition of dharma which does not refer to the Veda! 'Dharma is that which the wise and the good, without attachment and aversion, always practised, and which they acknowledged heartily (*hṛdayenābhyanujñāta*) as dharma.'[51] It is difficult to think of a more enlightening and progressive definition of dharma. As this is followed by the other verses already cited, one may venture to conclude that what is cumulatively defined by all these verses is Vaidika dharma.[52]

The key point from our perspective here is that this verse seems to create a separate segment of two of the four sources: *sadācāra* and *ātma-tuṣṭi*.

IV.2

Another verse in the second chapter seems to similarly form a segment of *sadācāra* and *ātma-tuṣṭi* but this time the people involved are not highbrow *śiṣṭas* and their *ātma-tuṣṭi*; the people involved are low caste people and women and one's own *ātma-tuṣṭi*. This verse from the *Manusmṛti* (2.223) has been alluded to earlier and is cited again in translation:

> If he sees a woman or a low-born man doing something conducive to welfare, he should do all that diligently, or anything else that he is fond of.[53]

Some English translations of the last clause tend to sound casual: 'Anything else that he is fond of';[54] 'whatever his heart and mind delights in';[55] 'as well as (any permitted act) in which his heart finds pleasure'.[56] G. Bühler's parenthetical insertion above—'any permitted act'—begs the question, for what we are arguing is that these verses almost function as independent segments when it comes to their being sources of Law. In doing so, Bühler is following the commentators perhaps already committed to the hierarchical nature of the template, but Kullūka Bhaṭṭa I think strikes the right note when he comments: *mano'sya tuṣyati tadapi kuryāt* (do that too which appeals to one's mind), thereby linking it with *ātma-tuṣṭi*.

V

These matters may now be brought to a close. We started with a neat template of four sources of *dharma*. We raised some initial difficulties to indicate that the situation might be more complex than could be handled by a fixed fourfold grid. Nevertheless, we examined the grid as it is traditionally assumed to be, namely a hierarchical one, but discovered that while in some cases it functioned hierarchically, in others the sources almost functioned as independent sources on their own. We even found that some segments referring to such sources, rather than just a source by itself, also functioned in the same way, which could either support a hierarchical perspective on the four sources (inasmuch as the segments came from that template) or an independent one (inasmuch as the segments seemed to function independently).

Our task then is to conceive of a conceptual framework which could reasonably accommodate this situation. It is true that the word used for the four sources in *Manusmṛti* is *dharma-mūla* or root or source of *dharma*, and we have stuck to this usage. In the *Manusmṛti* (2.12) the expression used in this context is *dharmasya lakṣaṇam*, or 'marker of *dharma*' as it were. I suggest that our analysis would be greatly helped by using another word in this context, namely, *pramāṇa*. There are hints of such usage in the *Manusmṛti* itself. Thus in *Manusmṛti* 3.13, *Śruti* is described as a *pramāṇa*, which is translated into English as supreme or highest authority; the word *pramāṇa* is associated with *dharma* again in *Manusmṛti* 7.203, where the king is asked to make the laws commonly held among the people he has conquered, authoritative (*pramāṇani ca kurvīta ... dharmyāni*).

I would like to pursue this association of *dharma* with the word *pramāṇa* in the present context a little further. Scholars have pointed out that the word *pramāṇa could be epistemologically* used in the following three senses: (1) as a *source* of knowledge; (2) as a *means* of knowledge; and (3) as a *test* of knowledge.[57] A simple example might help explain these distinctions. Let us imagine a well with water, a pulley with a bucket that can be lowered to draw water. Once the water is drawn up one can taste it to find out whether it is potable or not. The well is a *source* of water in the first sense of *pramāṇa*; the bucket is the *means* of obtaining that water and represents the second sense of the word; the test to determine whether water is potable or not represents the third sense of *pramāṇa*.

It seems that what we have called the four sources of *dharma*: *Śruti*, *Smṛti*, *Sadācāra* and *Ātma-tuṣṭi* have been used in all of these senses at various times in the *Manusmṛti*: sometimes as a source, sometimes as a means, and sometimes as a test of *dharma*. The issue of whether they are four in number also ties up with the discussions around *pramāṇa* in Hindu thought, which has a standard list of four, though the exact number of *pramāṇas* is also a matter of debate within it. The situation regarding *dharma* as a source of knowledge about the right thing to do, appears to follow a similar pattern.

4

The Doctrine of *Varṇas* in the *Manusmṛti*

I

It is conventional wisdom to invoke the *Puruṣa Sūkta* when discussing the doctrine of *varṇas* in Hinduism. The *Manusmṛti* is no exception to this, although we will soon discover that its manner of invoking it is exceptional in some ways. The *Puruṣa Sūkta*, to which conventional wisdom harks back, is the ninetieth hymn of the tenth *maṇḍala* of the *ṚgVeda*. The twelfth verse of the *Puruṣa Sūkta* is the one directly relevant to the issue on hand. It might be wise to cite the entire hymn, not only because it needs to be looked at in its entirety, but also because references to its other verses will crop up from time to time in the chapter. The famous French Indologist, Louis Renou (1896–1966) translates it as follows:

> *The Puruṣa Sūkta* (*Hymn of Man*)
>
> A thousand heads hath Puruṣa, a thousand eyes, a thousand feet.
> On every side pervading earth he fills a space ten fingers wide.
>
> This Puruṣa is all that yet hath been and all that is to be,
> The lord of immortality which waxes greater still by food.

So mighty is his greatness; yea, greater than this is Puruṣa.
All creatures are one-fourth of him, three-fourths eternal life in heaven.

With three-fourths Puruṣa went up; one-fourth of him again was here.
Thence he strode out to every side over what eats not and what eats.

From him Virāj [the female counterpart of the male principle, Puruṣa] was born; again Puruṣa from Virāj was born.
As soon as he was born he spread eastward and westward o'er the earth.

When gods prepared the Sacrifice with Puruṣa as their offering,
Its oil was spring; the holy gift was autumn; summer was the wood.

They balmed as victim on the grass Puruṣa born in earliest time.
With him the deities and all Sādhyas and Ṛṣis [saints and prophets of old] sacrificed.

From that great general Sacrifice the dripping fat was gathered up.
He formed the creatures of the air, and animals both wild and tame.

From that great general Sacrifice Ṛcs [stanzas of the *ṚgVeda*] and Sāma-hymns [stanzas of the *SāmaVeda*] were born;
Therefrom were spells and charms produced; the Yajus [ritual formulas of the *YajurVeda*] had their birth from it.

From it were horses born, from it all cattle with two rows of teeth:
From it were gathered kine, from it the goats and sheep were born.

When they divided Puruṣa, how many portions did they make?
What do they call his mouth, his arms? What do they call his thighs and feet?

The Brâhman [the four social classes (are referred to)] was his mouth, of both his arms was the Rājanya made.
His thighs became the Vaiśya, from his feet the Śūdra was produced.

The moon was gendered from his mind, and from his eye the sun had birth;
Indra and Agni from his mouth were born, and Vāyu from his breath.

Forth from his navel came mid-air; the sky was fashioned from his head;
Earth from his feet, and from his ear the regions. Thus they formed the worlds.

Seven fencing-sticks had he, thrice seven layers of fuel were prepared,
When the gods, offering sacrifice, bound, as their victim, Puruṣa.

Gods, sacrificing, sacrificed the victim: these were the earliest holy ordinance.
The mighty ones attained the height of heaven, there where the Sādhyas, gods of old, are dwelling.[1]

Although verse twelve of this hymn is almost ritually invoked to justify the *varṇa* scheme, scholars have noted that connecting the twelfth verse of the hymn with the *varṇa* system, though it might seem immediately obvious, is not without its problems. First of all, there are other verses in the *ṚgVeda* (8.35.16–18) which mention *three varṇas* and not four as is customary; they mention *brahma*, *kṣatram* and *viśaḥ*, but not the *śūdra*.[2] This may be attributed to the fact that these verses belong to the eighth *maṇḍala* of the *ṚgVeda* which is considered chronologically anterior to the tenth *maṇḍala*.[3] The first *maṇḍala*, which is usually considered contemporaneous with the tenth *maṇḍala*, also contains a verse which seems to allude to the four *varṇas*, for it says: 'One of high sway (i.e. Brāhmaṇa), one of exalted glory (Kshatriya), one to pursue his gain (i.e. the vaiśya) and to his labour (i.e. the sūdra), all to regard their different vocations, all moving creatures hath the dawn awakened.'[4] This verse differentiates the four *varṇas* functionally; the verse in the *Puruṣa Sūkta* does so natally. A third difficulty arises when the twelfth verse of the *Puruṣa Sūkta* is taken as proof-text of the *varṇa* system, namely, that the word *varṇa* itself does not appear in the verse; in fact, it does not appear in the entire hymn. *Puruṣa Sūkta* 10.90.12 has, however, been virtually universally accepted as the proof-text of the emergence of the *varṇa* system, despite such reservations.

It might be accepted as the proof-text despite the dissonances expressed earlier if it were the only account of the origin of the *varṇas* we possessed, a point already open to contestation through *ṚgVeda* 1.113.6 as noted above. However, other accounts of the origin of the *varṇas* are found in Vedic literature as well, which are not only quite distinct from this one but also quite distinct from one another: (1) according to the *Śatapatha Brāhmaṇa* (2.1–4.11, ff), the *brāhmaṇa* was created from the word *bhūḥ*, the *kṣatriya* from the word *bhuvaḥ*; and the *vaiśya* from *svaḥ*;[5] (2) according to the *YajurVeda* (*Vājasaneyi Saṃhitā* 16.28, ff; *Taittirīya Saṃhitā* 4.3.10.1) this is how the *varṇas* came into being: 'He lauded with one (*ekayā astuvata*) —living beings were formed; ... he lauded with three,—the Brāhmaṇa was created ... he lauded with fifteen,—the Kshatra was created ... he lauded with nineteen,—and śūdra and Arya (i.e. vaiśya) were created'[6]; (3) according to other accounts, the *varṇas* were created variously 'from different Vedas; from different sets of prayers; from the gods, and the Asuras; from non-entity, and from the imperishable and other principles.'[7]

One might argue that these are more in the nature of obiter dicta, while the RgVedic verse provides a broad setting for the origin of the *varṇas* and therefore carries more conviction. There is, however, yet another account of the origin of the *varṇas* which seems quite firmly enshrined in the Vedic texts. It is found in the *Śatapatha Brāhmaṇa,* and also occurs in the *Bṛhadāraṇyaka Upaniṣad* (1.4.11–15) and was cited at length in the Introduction.[8]

All this evidence suggests a couple of conclusions. One is that during the Vedic age, especially during its early period, the four *varṇas*, particularly the last two, were in the process of achieving social definition and society was in the process of taking shape; the second is that even as this was happening, various suggestions were being made to explain the character the society was assuming or had assumed. Two such explanations achieved a wider caché than the rest.

The question then arises: given this background, which explanation or explanations for the scheme of *varṇas* did the author of the *Manusmṛti* choose, and why?

The *Manusmṛti* chose to explain the division of society into *varṇas* primarily in terms of the account found in the *Puruṣa Sūkta.* This is clear from *Manusmṛti* I.31: 'For the growth of these worlds, moreover, he produced from his mouth, arms, thighs, and feet, the brahmin, the kṣatriya, the vaiśya, and the śūdra.'[9] It is further reinforced by *Manusmṛti* I.87–91:

> [87] For the protection of this whole creation, that One of dazzling brilliance assigned separate activities for those born from the mouth, arms, thighs, and feet. [88] To Brahmins, he assigned reciting and teaching the Veda, offering and officiating at sacrifices, and receiving and giving gifts. [89] To the Kṣatriya, he allotted protecting the subjects, giving gifts, offering sacrifices, reciting the Veda, and avoiding attachment to sensory objects; [90] and to the Vaiśya, looking after animals, giving gifts, offering

> sacrifices, reciting the Veda, trade, moneylending, and agriculture. [91] A single activity did the Lord allot to the Śūdra, however: the ungrudging service of those very social classes (10.74–80).[10]

A third piece of evidence in favour of the choice of the *Puruṣa Sūkta* account is connected with the emergence of the *brāhmaṇa* from the mouth, which is used to glorify his status (I.92–95):

> [92] A man is said to be purer above the navel. Therefore, the Self-existent One has declared, the mouth is his purest part. [93] Because he arose from the loftiest part of the body, because he is the eldest, and because he retains the Veda, the Brahmin is by Law the lord of this whole creation. [94] For, in the beginning, the Self-existent One heated himself with ascetic toil and brought him forth from his own mouth to convey divine oblations and ancestral offerings and to protect this whole world. [95] What creature can surpass him through whose mouth the denizens of the triple heaven always eat their oblations, and the forefathers their offerings (7.84)?[11]

A fourth piece of evidence in favour of the choice of the *Puruṣa Sūkta* is that the fact of the *śūdra* being born from the feet (*pādaja*) is used to put the *śūdra* down. As Pandhari-Nath Prahbu notes: 'The creation of the śūdra from the foot, symbolizes the fact that the śūdra is to be the "footman", the servant of the other *varṇas*.'[12] A fifth piece of evidence is provided by *Manusmṛti* 10.45: 'All the castes in the world that are outside those born from the mouth, arms, thighs, and feet—whether they speak foreign or Aryan languages—tradition calls Dasyus.'[13]

It seems to have gone largely unnoticed, however, that the *Manusmṛti* also alludes to *another* theory of the origin of the *varṇas*, the one found in the *Bṛhadāraṇyaka Upaniṣad*, on possibly two occasions, one of which may be considered definite and the other ambigious. The definite allusion is found in *Manusmṛti* (9.321): 'Fire sprang from water, Kṣatriya from Brahmin, and metal from stone; their all-pervasive energy is quenched when confronting their own source.'[14] Patrick Olivelle provides the following note on '*Kṣatriya from Brahmin* this doctrine is articulated already in *Bāu*, 1.4.11, which calls *brahma* (the priestly power) the womb of the *kṣatra* (the ruling power).'[15] Although Olivelle provides the right reference one wonders if the right inference has been drawn, for although the *Bṛhadāraṇyaka* account mentions the *kṣatriyas* as being formed *after* the *brāhmaṇas*, there is also the interpretation that they were formed from the *brāhmaṇas*. This finds clear articulation in later literature.

The other reference is provided by *Manusmṛti* (2.20). It is translated by Olivelle as follows: 'All the people on earth should learn their respective practices from a Brahmin born in the land.'[16] The word for 'Brahmin' or *brāhmaṇa* in the original text is *agrajanmā* or the first-born. Although the *brāhmaṇa* is mentioned first in *ṚgVeda* 10.90.12, it is not stated clearly that he was born first—in fact the whole sacrifice could be viewed as occurring simultaneously. It is in the *Bṛhadāraṇyaka* account that the *brāhmaṇa* is described as the first to come into existence, *after* whom the *kṣatriyas* and others come into being.

This investigation, if we are on the right track, helps correct the oversight that the *Manusmṛti* draws upon only one account of the emergence of the *varṇas*. If the above analysis is correct, then it draws upon two accounts out of the many available—the one in the *ṚgVeda* and the one in the *Śatapatha Brāhmaṇa* and *Bṛhadāraṇyaka Upaniṣad.*

II

What then, is the significance of the *Manusmṛti* drawing upon both accounts? One obvious significance is that it lends support to the view that both the *ṚgVeda* and the *Bṛhadāraṇyaka* account had concurrent currency; a deeper significance lies in the fact that arguably the *ṚgVeda* account can be interpreted more hierarchically than the *Bṛhadāraṇyaka* account. Although an argument could be made that the *ṚgVeda* account in itself is not necessarily hierarchical,[17] tradition has interpreted the order of the four *varṇas* as embodying a hierarchy; the *Manusmṛti* clearly takes it in that sense. This interpretation may be diagrammatically represented as follows:

Varṇas
Brahmaṇa
Kṣatriya
Vaiśya
Śūdra

The account in the *Bṛhadāraṇyaka* is one of the progressive creation of the four *varṇas* and may be diagrammatically represented as follows:[18]

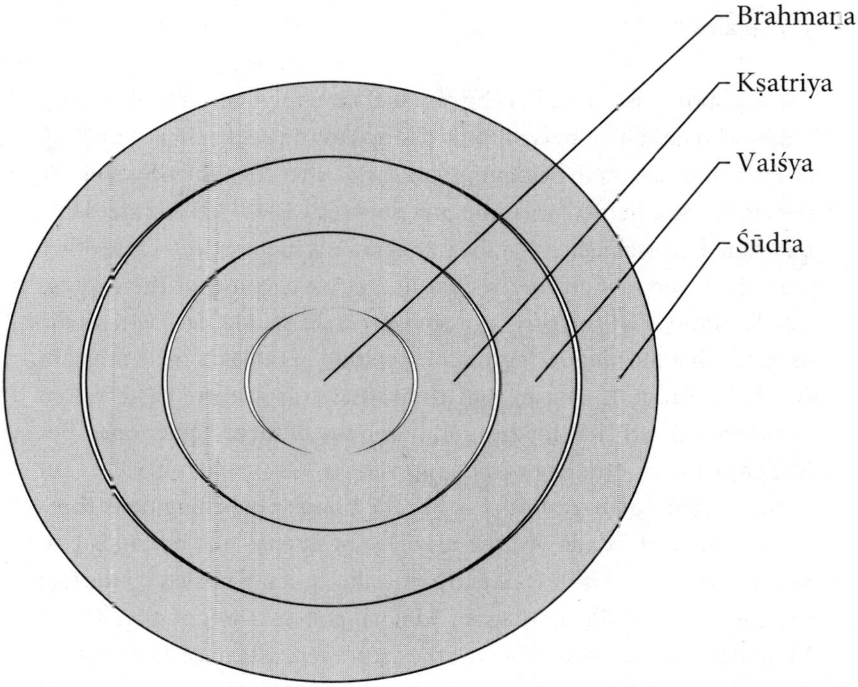

However, one discovers that the *Manusmṛti* even uses the *Bṛhadāraṇyaka* account to reinforce the hierarchy in favour of the *brāhmaṇa*!

III

Apart from the four classes or *varṇas*, Vedic society also had professions and crafts with *specific* names. Thus the *ṚgVeda* speaks of a *vaptā* or barber (10.142.4); *taṣṭā*, that is a maker of chariots (*ṚgVeda* 1.61.4, etc.); *tyaṣṭā* or a carpenter (8.102.8); a *bhiṣak* or physician (9.112.1); a *karmāra* or *kārmāra* (ironsmith) (10.72.2); and a *carmamna* or tanner (8.5.58).[19]

The *AtharvaVeda* mentions, apart from *karmāra* (3.5.6), the chariot maker or *rathakāra* (3.5.6) and the bard or *sūta* (3.5.7). These lists undergo considerable expansion in the texts of the *YajurVeda* and even more so in the *Brāhmaṇas*.[20]

What is interesting is that sometimes an attempt is made to find a place for some of these professional categories within the *varṇa* categories. The chariot maker or *ratharkāra* provides a good example of this. As P.V. Kane explains:

> The question arises whether the rathakāra is a member of three higher castes who has taken in economic distress to the profession of making chariots or is a person belonging to a caste other than the three higher varṇas. Jaimini in his Pūrvamīmāṅsā-sūtra (VI.1. 44–50) discusses this question and establishes that the rathakāra is a member of a caste other than the three higher varṇas, that he has on account of the express words in the *śruti* the privilege to consecrate sacred fires with vedic mantras, that the *mantra* for the consecration of rathakāras is 'ṛbhūṇām tvā' (Tai. Br. 1. 1. 4) and that the rathakāras are the caste called Saudhanvana which is neither śūdra nor one of three higher ones, but is slightly inferior to the three higher varṇas. Viśvarūpa (on Yāj. 1. 10) notices that in some smṛtis the rathakāra though not belonging to three higher varṇas, was allowed the privilege of upanayana, but adds that this dictum of the smṛti is due to a mistake, it being misled by the fact that he is allowed the privilege of ādhāna (consecration of sacred fire). In modern times the members of the carpenter caste in certain parts of the Deccan at least are in the habit of performing the upanayana and wearing the sacred thread.[21]

Kane provides a 'list of persons engaged in professions and crafts, which had probably become castes or were in the process of becoming castes, before the close of the Vedic period.'[22] He draws up a list of more than sixty such professional categories, some of which overlap with the professions mentioned in relation to the Vedas such as *rathakāra*, *sūta* and *karmāra*.

These professional groups emerge within the Vedic community, alongside the four *varṇas*. The case of the *rathakāra* mentioned earlier clearly establishes that the exact relationship of these groups to the four *varṇas* was an open question.

IV

In addition to these professional groups, which convoluted the *varṇa* worldview from within, were groups which originally lay outside the

Vedic world and convoluted the *varṇa* worldview from without. There is a passage in the *Aitareya Brāhmaṇa* (33.6), according to which Viśvāmitra cursed his fifty sons to the company of the lowest castes when they refused to treat Śunahśepa (Devarāta) as his son, and they became 'Andhras, Puṇḍras, Śabaras, Pulindas, and Mutibas who are among the lowest of society and are mostly composed of *dasyūs*.'[23] This passage is extremely illuminating as it illustrates both an awareness of people outside the pale of the four *varṇas*, as well as a desire to bring them into some kind of relationship with the *varṇas*.

V

Thus there are the four *varṇas* to begin with. But as various professional groups develop *within* the Vedic society, the question of their relationship to the four *varṇas* emerges. Then Vedic society comes in contact with people *outside* of itself, and the question of their relationship to the four *varṇas* also emerges. Finally, by the time of the end of the Vedic age, the four *varṇas* also begin to consist of people who were born in these classes, but otherwise did not live up to the required lifestyle of the classes. This is the context in which the word *jāti* first appears.

The 'word "*jāti*" in the sense of caste hardly even occurs in Vedic literature',[24] but it soon makes an appearance in the context of the *study* of Vedic literature, or what are called the *Vedāṅgas*. Thus in the *Nirukta* (12.13) one finds the expression '*kṛṣṇa jātīyā*' as a 'reference to a woman of the śūdra caste.'[25] Similarly, one finds a reference to '*brāhmaṇa jātīya*' in Pāṇini (5.4.9) as one 'who teaches the formation of words like "brāhmaṇajātīya" derived from words ending in "jāti" (in the sense of caste).'[26]

VI

This was the Vedic heritage the *Manusmṛti* was heir to. To recapitulate, the following elements come in play in the context of a would-be Vedic sociology: there were the four *varṇas*, and then there were the following elements complicating the neat template of the four *varṇas*: (1) professional groups arising within Vedic society; (2) new groups of people outside Vedic society pressing for inclusion in that Vedic society as it spreads to other parts of India; and (3) groups within the *varṇas*, who are so only in name or hangers-on to *varṇa* as it were.

Such was the evolving social reality, with its template of the four *varṇas* and its rough edges in Vedic times. As the Vedic age came to a close, the loose arrangement seems to have continued in an open-ended sort of way, right through the rise of Buddhism and Jainism, and to the founding of the Mauryan Empire. The *end of the Mauryan Empire*, however, was another matter. It is crucial to note here that 'the best we could do on the available evidence is to date the MDH [*Manudharmaśastra* = *Manusmṛti*] between the first century BCE and the second century CE.'[27] And that it 'may be placed closer to the second century CE.'[28]

VII

The crucial question we need to ask ourselves is: What was the situation the author of the *Manusmṛti* faced when he set about compiling it in the second century, committed as he was to responding to the situation in terms of the Vedic heritage?

How was this society—ravaged by foreign invasions—to be organized? The *brāhmaṇas* had before them the model of Vedic society, which consisted of the following elements as we saw earlier: (1) the four *varṇas*; (2) new professional groups emerging within society, in tentative relationship to the four *varṇas*; (3) new groups of people outside the Vedic society pressing for inclusion in Vedic society and (4) groups within the *varṇas* who were failing the grade.

As the *brāhmaṇas* looked around them, they found analogies to all these four elements but with their own contemporary peculiarities: (1) there were the four *varṇas* but not in as pure a state as they might have once been; (2) there were the professional groups within society, but unlike the Vedic age, these groups now consisted of *jātis*, namely, commensal, endogamous and often craft-exclusive groups of which over fifty are mentioned in the *Manusmṛti*, different from approximately the same number mentioned in the Vedic texts but analogous to them in the sense they had been encompassed within the prevailing contemporary society, just as the others had been encompassed in Vedic society; (3) there were groups outside of the existing society pressing in from the new frontiers of that society, some of them foreign groups now found in India such as the Pahlavas (Parthians), Yavanas (Greeks), Śakas (Scythians), even Cīnas (Chinese Yüeh-chih tribes) and so on, while others were already present in

India like the Dravidas, Oḍras and Pauṇḍrakas; and (4) there were groups within the *varṇas*, who had failed to live by the rules of the *varṇas*, although formally belonging to them.

The task the author of the *Manusmṛti* faced was to integrate as a *society* what had failed as a *polity* in view of the collapse of the political order after the Mauryas.

The techniques which the author of the *Manusmṛti* adopted to achieve this task had to go further than was the situation with similar groups in the Vedic age when the society was *not* in danger of collapse.

What techniques did the author of the *Manusmṛti* employ to achieve this purpose?

VIII

The author of the *Manusmṛti* had two models of the *varṇa* scheme to draw from: the one identified with the *Puruṣa Sūkta* and the one identified with the *Bṛhadāraṇyaka Upaniṣad* respectively. And, if the goal of the author was to create an 'imagined community' as will be argued later, it would seem at first sight that the *latter* model would suit his needs better. In that model, all the later *varṇas* emerge from the *brāhmaṇa* class to begin with, so they were all of the same blood, as it were. The other *jātis* could then be depicted as emerging from their further mixture. And even the *mlecchas* could be accommodated directly via a bloodline, as per the following account, for instance:

> This discussion begins by asserting that the differences between the castes were not originally present and that the existence of the three lower castes may be explained through their neglect of *dharma* and fall from the brahmanic state. Following this, reference is made to monsters and spirits (*piśāca*, *rākṣasa*, *preta*), while 'barbaric tribes' (*mlecchajāti*) are named whose knowledge and reason was lost and whose behaviour was governed solely by their desires (*svacchandācāraceṣṭita*).[29]

It will be noticed later that the *mlecchas* are accommodated in the first model as peoples who had fallen away from Brahmanical practices, and they could be brought within the pale again by resuming those practices.

The goals of the author of the *Manusmṛti* could, therefore, *also* be achieved through the second model, perhaps more easily and in an egalitarian manner. And as we saw earlier he was quite aware of the existence of this model. *Why then did he choose to adopt the one embodied in the Puruṣa Sūkta?*

The answer seems to lie at the top and the bottom. Since the *kṣatriya* leadership had faded away, the *brāhmaṇas* had to assert their leadership, and hence their primacy, in the ordering of the four *varṇas*, which they could do more effectively with the *Puruṣa Sūkta* version as interpreted by them.[30] The problem at the bottom lay in the blurring of the lower castes and the new arrivals in India from outside. Thus the *Manusmṛti* (12.43) at one point lumps the *śūdras* and the *mlecchas* together. Disturbed political and social situations, therefore, perhaps rendered the *varṇa* scheme according to the *Puruṣa Sūkta* more attractive.

This would prove to be a consequential decision. When 'Hindu' thinkers faced similar situations in the future they would tend to follow the lead of the *Manusmṛti.*

IX

The *Manusmṛti* asserts the doctrine of the four *varṇas*. It had the option of undergirding the *varṇa* system with various accounts of the origin of the *varṇas* found in the Vedas, two of which specially stood out and of which it betrays clear awareness: the account found in the *Puruṣa Sūkta* and the account found in the *Bṛhadāraṇyaka Upaniṣad*. It chose the more hierarchical of the two, as hierarchy is the simplest way to establish order. Moreover, used to crises, it made special provision for dealing with such periods through special rules for the four *varṇas* (*āpad-dharma*).

It must be borne in mind, however, that in doing so it made the four *varṇas* of one blood in the sense that the *varṇas* could rise and fall through intermarriage, as the following verses make amply clear (X.64–65):

> [64] If an offspring of a Brahmin man from a Śūdra woman were to bear children from a superior partner, within seven generations the inferior attains the superior caste; [65] a Śūdra thus attains the rank of a Brahmin, and so does a Brahmin the rank of a Śūdra—one should understand

that this rule holds good also for offspring born from a Kṣatriya or a Vaiśya man.[31]

This is important because the view is sometimes expressed that *varṇas* are like 'species' and differ among themselves as animals do. Animals, however, do not 'intermarry', so Manu's concept of the *varṇas* is quite different.[32]

The *Manusmṛti* also had to deal with the various *jātis*. We saw how, in the Vedic period, tentative efforts were made to link the professional groups with the four *varṇas*. In this case, the *Manusmṛti* chose a more radical procedure and explained the *jātis* as emerging out of the admixture of the *varṇas*. The actual statement of it makes for dull reading (*Manusmṛti* 10.8–12):

> [8] From a Brahmin man by a Vaiśya girl is born a son called Ambaṣṭha; and by a Śūdra girl, a Niṣāda, also called Pāraśava. [9] From a Kṣatriya man by a Śūdra girl is born a son called Ugra, who is cruel in his behaviour and in his dealings, a being with the physical characteristics of both a Kṣatriya and a Śūdra.
>
> [10] A Brahmin's children by the three lower classes, a Kṣatriya's by the two lower classes, and a Vaiśya's by the one lower class—tradition calls these six 'low-born' …
>
> [11] From a Kṣatriya man by a Brahmin girl is born a Sūta by caste; sons of a Vaiśya by Kṣatriya and Brahmin women are a Māgadha and a Vaideha, respectively; [12] and from a Śūdra by Vaiśya, Kṣatriya, and Brahmin women are born respectively an Āyogava, a Kṣattṛ, and a Cāṇḍāla, the worst of all men—so originates the intermixture of classes.[33]

This dense account comes to life when we realize what the *Manusmṛti* has achieved by this device: it had made all these *jātis* of one blood with the *varṇas*!

To integrate the class of people on the periphery rather than at the centre, the *Manusmṛti* uses a different device. The account of the *Aitareya Brāhmaṇa* was referred to earlier in this context. P.V. Kane notes:

> It is probably owing to this legend that the Manusmṛti (X.43–45) is prepared to regard the Pauṇḍrakas, the Oḍras, Dravidas, Kāmbojas,

> Yavanas, Śakas, Pāradas, Pahlavas, Cīnas, Kirātas, Daradas and Khaśas as being originally kṣatriya castes, but later on reduced to the position of śūdras by the non-performance of Vedic saṁskāras (like upanayana) and by the absence of contact with brāhmaṇas. Manu further adds that the various castes that are outside the (influence of the) four varṇas are all known as *dasyus* whether they speak the language of Mlecchas or of Āryas.[34]

We come now to the last class of people within the proper *varṇas* who do not live up to its ideal. This was considered most reprehensible in the case of *brāhmaṇas*. In the Vedic age they were just called so-called *brāhmaṇas* but in the *Manusmṛti* they fall to the level of the *śūdra*. Thus 8.102:

> He should treat Brahmins who are cattle-herders, traders, artisans, performers, servants, or money lenders just like Śūdras.[35]

Similarly, having compromised their status as *brāhmaṇas*, they could be excluded from the *śrāddha* ceremony.[36]

This is significant because it is not at all clear if the *śūdra* was totally barred from participation in Vedic ritual and studies in the Vedic age. But by now this rule of formal exclusion was in place and so the *brāhmaṇa,* who did not live like a *brāhmaṇa,* fell to the status of the *śūdra*.

In a sense, then, the *Manusmṛti* was trying to replace the *state system*, which had collapsed, with a '*caste system*'. Something similar was destined to happen again when the 'Hindu' state system collapsed during Muslim rule in north India, as noted earlier.[37] J. Duncan M. Derrett notes:

> Puruṣottama, minister of Rāmacandra Yādava about AD 1310, immediately before the massive incursions of Muslims from the north in the Deccan, claimed to be a student of Veda and *smṛti* and to have given separate courses of conduct to the various *varṇa-s* and *āśramas*, in other words to have administered *varṇāśrama dharma*, *dharma* in its entirety.[38]

This claim is remarkably similar to that of the *Manusmṛti*, which seems to provide the original model of how to use the *varṇa* model to save society when the state has collapsed or is about to collapse and pass into foreign hands.[39]

The *Manusmṛti* turns out to be a somewhat different document than what it is usually supposed to be, when viewed from such a historical and holistic perspective.

X

In adapting the *Puruṣa Sūkta* version of the *varṇa* system, the *Manusmṛti* did make some subtle significant changes in its presentation of it. If we go back to the *Puruṣa Sūkta* and read it in its original context, then we find that, as P.V. Kane observes:

> In the Puruṣasūkta (X. 90. 12) the brāhmaṇa, kṣatriya, vaiśya and śūdra are said to have sprung from the mouth, arms, thighs and feet of the supreme Puruṣa. In the very next verse the sun and the moon are said to have been born from the eye and mind of the Puruṣa. This shows that the composer of the hymn regarded the division of society into four classes to be very ancient and to be as natural and God-ordained as the sun and the moon.[40]

When we turn to the *Manusmṛti*, however, we find that a new feature has been introduced when the *Puruṣa Sūkta* is alluded to, in verse 31 and verses 87–91, in the very first chapter of the *Manusmṛti*. When the *Puruṣa Sūkta* is alluded to in verse 31, it is with the prefatory clause that the four *varṇas* were created *lokānām tu vivṛdyartham* or 'for the sake of the prosperity of the worlds'.[41] Similarly, when the *Puruṣa Sūkta* is again alluded to in verses 89–91 it is with the prefatory clause that the *varṇas* were created *sarvasyāsya tu sargasya guptyartham* or 'in order to protect this universe'.[42]

The *Puruṣa Sūkta* does not contain any such rider that the four *varṇas* were created for the sake of achieving a certain objective. As P.V. Kane noted, the four *varṇas* are presented as a *fact*; the *Manusmṛti* attaches *value* to this fact, by which the *varṇa* system may be judged. This is a subtle but remarkable development. What was originally just taken as given in the *ṚgVeda* as an institution, is made answerable in the *Manusmṛti* as an institution in relation to a purpose which it is meant to serve, and this purpose is the 'prosperity of the worlds' or 'the protection of the universe'. In other words, the well-being of the world.

Once such value is thus tagged to an institution, it naturally becomes an object of judgement in terms of the extent to which the role or function it was instituted to perform is being fulfilled by it. And what if that role is not being adequately fulfilled by the institution?

There is thus a disguised but dramatic change in the context in which the *varṇa* system is viewed in the *ṚgVeda* and in the *Manusmṛti*. In the *ṚgVeda* it is arguably something natural and indissoluble; in the *Manusmṛti* it has become something instituted with a purpose, and therefore dissoluble if the purpose is not served. Many factors could be responsible for this development. It could be the experience of society with the *varṇa* scheme which caused this line of thinking to emerge, or it could be the result of innovative thinking by some members of society, or both. It could be the result of social critiques, both from within the tradition as in the Upaniṣads or from without by Jainism and Buddhism. The conclusion, however, seems inescapable that something originally considered permanent had now been made contingent.

If this is so then the *Manusmṛti* should ideally reflect some awareness, in the later chapters, of the consequences of this move made within it in its first chapter. It surfaces in verse 176 of chapter 4. It is translated by Patrick Olivelle as follows: 'He should abandon any activity relating to Wealth or Pleasure that is in violation of Law, and even activities sanctioned by Law when they will result in future unhappiness or are repugnant to the world.'[43] The translation seems to dilute the meaning of the verse; the earlier translation of Bühler appears to do the same: 'Let him avoid (the acquisition of) wealth and (the gratification of his) desires, if they are opposed to the sacred law, and even lawful acts which may cause pain in the future or are offensive to men.'[44]

The trouble lies with translating the word *dharma* as Law, and for this, one may blame the English language's inadequacy or the Sanskrit language's versatility. Western civilization, right from the Greeks, has had trouble translating *dharma*, which is rendered as piety (*eu'sebeia*) in the Aśokan inscriptions and as righteousness (*diké*) in Kuṣāṇa times. The Aramaic inscriptions of Aśoka translate the word differently.[45] Modern writers also struggle with the word.[46] It might be worth turning to the verse in the original Sanskrit to assess its significance:

parityajed arthkāmau yau syātāṃ dharmavarjitau
dharmam cāpyasukhodarkam lokavikruṣṭameva ca

The sense of the first line is straightforward in a way: one should give up *artha* and *kāma* proscribed by *dharma*; it is the second line which one needs to focus on. It says that even *dharma* (itself) may be given up under two conditions: if it does not lead to well-being in the long run; and, if it is denounced by the people. The translation of *dharma* as 'sanctioned by Law' or as 'lawful acts' dilutes its meaning. In translating it as 'religion', Wendy Doniger and Brian K. Smith are closer to the mark,[47] if we take it in the following spirit:

> Translations can sometimes be quite revealing. If we try to find an Indian synonym for the term *religion* (admittedly difficult to define even within the Western tradition!), we have to choose from a variety of terms, none of which coincides precisely with our word. The most common and most general term is *dharma*, today usually translated as 'religion'.[48]

So, the verse says that one may give up something as important as even 'religion' under the two conditions spelled out. Now that we have grasped the significance of the use of the word *dharma*, let us look at its content. According to the *Manusmṛti,* the primary source of *dharma* is the Veda (2.6) so even that *dharma,* which is rooted in the Veda, may be given up under the two conditions mentioned. It is salutary to recall that the *varṇa* scheme is one such *dharma*. So even that can be given up under some conditions. We saw how in the first chapter of the *Manusmṛti* the *varṇa*-scheme was made *conditional*; in this fourth chapter it is clearly made *dispensable* under the force of the same logic.

What then are the two conditions under which even the *varṇa* scheme may be given up? One is when it does not contribute to human flourishing in the long run. And the second is when it is denounced by the people. P.V. Kane draws attention to a very important point in relation to the Sanskrit word used to describe the second condition, namely *loka-vikṛuṣṭa*; in doing so he actually refers to the verse another consideration. He writes:

> It should be noted that the word used ... is 'lokavidviṣṭa' or 'lokavikruṣṭa' (hated or reviled by the people) and not 'śiṣṭa-vidviṣṭa,'

> the idea being that even if orthodox learned *pandits* insist the people must follow what the Veda and smṛtis declare to be Dharma, common people may give up practices condemned by them or hateful to them.[49]

The significance of this distinction will become clearer in the light of the discussion in the chapter on sources of *dharma* in the *Manusmṛti* where the question raised was: Who decides what is Hinduism—the male members of the three upper *varṇas*? Or all members of the community, including women and the lower castes? Here we see the *Manusmṛti* coming out in favour of the second option for determining what *dharma* is.

Perhaps one should also return to another issue flagged earlier, which has fairly radical overtones, namely, that if people did not think the *varṇa* scheme or the 'caste system' in general contributed to their well-being in the long run and were strongly opposed to it, then could it be given up within the framework evolved by the *Manusmṛti*?

There can be little doubt that the verse allows it; what we need to consider is its radical nature, which seems to have been missed both by traditional and modern writers. A good example of the former is provided by Śaṅkara:

> Śaṁkarācārya in his bhāṣya on Vedāntasūtra 3.33 remarks that, though in his day varṇas and āśramas had become disorganized and unstable as to their dharmas, that was not the case in earlier ages, since otherwise the śāstras laying down the regulations for them would have to be deemed dysfunctional or futile.[50]

The possibility of what to do if the system itself becomes purposeless or futile in the future is not raised by him. Modern scholars such as Julius Lipner recognize that caste is dissolving in Mauritius but 'there is no reason to suppose that Mauritian Hindus will not continue to value their identity as Hindus.'[51] However, the issue of this happening within India is rarely raised from within a Hindu framework. In fact, not only the average person but even an Indian intellectual, if asked whether he or she thought Hinduism could exist without the caste system according to the *Manusmṛti*, might respond in the negative.

Yet it is quite clear from what has been said above, that the answer will have to be in the affirmative in terms of the *Manusmṛti*.

5

The Position of the *Śūdras* in the *Manusmṛti*

I

Two aspects of the *Manusmṛti* have been the foci of special criticism: its treatment of the *śūdras* and its treatment of women. It thus seems reasonable for anyone writing a book on how to read the *Manusmṛti* to devote special chapters to them. A subsequent chapter on the position of women in the *Manusmṛti* will reveal how a single verse has been so influential in this regard that the entire landscape on the subject came to be viewed through its lens and perhaps distorted. That chapter will also demonstrate how it is just not possible to develop an unbiased view on the matter until that verse is examined and the manner in which it was misinterpreted, fully identified.

The situation in relation to the position of *śūdras* in the *Manusmṛti* is similar. A verse has also been identified as representative of the abominable position of the *śūdras* in the *Manusmṛti*. The relentless focus on this verse, cited below, tends to obscure the finer points of the issue. The verse runs as follows (*Manusmṛti* 11.132):

> For killing a cat, a mongoose, a blue jay, a frog, a dog, a monitor lizard, or a crow, a man shall perform the observance of killing a śūdra.[1]

This verse has led a host of scholars to draw the conclusion regarding the *śūdra*, as A.L. Basham does, that 'little value was set to his life in law. A brāhmin killing a śūdra performed the same penance as for killing a cat or dog.'[2] Basham cites a footnote after this statement, indicating that his statement is based on *Manusmṛti* 11.132.[3] Similarly, that outstanding scholar of *dharmaśāstras*, P.V. Kane, also notes that 'the life of a śūdra was esteemed rather low' and concludes the section by citing the *Manusmṛti*: 'Manu (11.131) says "on killing a cat, an ichneumon, cāṣa, a frog, a dog, iguana, owl and crow, the prāyaścitta is the same as that of killing a śūdra".'[4] Historian Ram Sharan Sharma presents a more nuanced view but ultimately veers to the same conclusion when he writes:

> What is most shocking to the modern democratic mind is the fact that Āpastamba and Baudhāyana provide the same penance for killing a śūdra as for killing a flamingo, a *chāsa*, a peacock, a brāhmaṇī duck, a *pracalāka*, a crow, an owl, a frog, a muskrat, a dog etc. This extreme view, which attaches the same importance to the life of a śūdra as to that of an animal or a bird, may not have found universal acceptance, for the same lawgivers prescribe a wergeld of ten cows and a bull for killing a śūdra. But there is no doubt that the early brāhmanical law attached very little importance to the life of a śūdra.[5]

The reaction of Kane and Sharma to these provisions is worth comparing. P.V. Kane becomes apologetic in the face of such a verse to the extent of providing a footnote to the effect that the British attitude to Indian servants was no better:

> Those who are familiar with the cases decided in India in which Indian servants or coolies were kicked by European employers and died as a result and in which the offenders were either acquitted or let off on a small fine (on the ground that the deceased had an enlarged spleen) need not feel surprised at the above statement of affairs in India.[6]

Sharma's approach is more analytical, for he notes two features overlooked by others: (1) that the *Sāmavidhāna Brāhmaṇa* (1.7.7.)

'prescribes almost the same penance for killing a śūdra as for killing a cow';[7] and, (2) that the preceding verses in the *Manusmṛti* run as follows:

> [128] If a Brahmin kills a Kṣatriya *unintentionally*, however, he should give one thousand cows and a bull to purify himself. [129] Or, he may perform during three years the observance prescribed for killing a Brahmin, keeping himself controlled, wearing matted hair, living far away from the village, and making his home at the foot of a tree. [130] A Brahmin who kills a virtuous Vaiśya should perform the same observance for one year, or give one hundred cows along with a bull. [131] One who kills a Śūdra should perform the same vow completely for six months, or give ten white cows along with a bull to a Brahmin.[8]

Then follows the verse under discussion about killing the various animals listed earlier, as a result of which the person should observe *śūdrāhatyāvratam*, that is to say, undergo the same penance as laid down above for killing a *śūdra*. It is not the *lives* of the animals which are being equated with that of the *śūdra*; it is the standard set for penitential observance which is being equated. One may, however, still argue that even such an equation does not bode well, for the same value is attached to the life of the *śūdra*. To see the difference, we have to turn to the set of verses cited earlier, *Manusmṛti* 128–31, and note the expression with which they begin: *akāmataḥ*—without intention. Commentators, such as Kullūka Bhaṭṭa, regularly gloss the verses that follow with this in mind—that the killing has to be unintentional.[9] It is not as if the *śūdra* could be killed with impunity; *unintentional homicide* is involved; and three commentators 'expressly state the penance for the murder of a śūdra is to be performed for *intentionally* killing any one of these animals, while Medhātithi thinks that the rule holds good if one has killed all of them.'[10]

In other words, once the verse is read in the context of the other verses with which it occurs, the equation of the worth of the life of a dog with that of a *śūdra* turns out to be a caricature. The reference to the killing of a *śūdra* seems to be a reference to *accidental* homicide. When the commentarial literature is taken into account, this conclusion is only reinforced. The danger of equating disparate items in terms of value just because they are brought together within a penal or penitential provision, becomes evident when we look at a verse such as the following in the *Manusmṛti* (11.67): '… stealing grain, base metals, and livestock; sex with women who drink;

killing a woman, a śūdra, vaiśya, or a kṣatriya; and being an infidel—these are secondary sins causing loss of caste.'[11]

But there is more. If the life of a *śūdra* was considered of little value by the *Manusmṛti*, would it authorize one to save a *śūdra*'s life by telling a lie? And yet this is precisely what the *Manusmṛti* (8.104–06) asks one to do in the following verses, which have been cited earlier in another context. Let us look at them in G. Bühler's translation this time:

> 104. Whenever the death of a Śûdra, of a Vaiśya, of a Kshatriya, or of a Brâhmaṇa would be (caused) by a declaration of the truth, a falsehood may be spoken; for such (falsehood) is preferable to the truth.
>
> 105. Such (witnesses) must offer to Sarasvatî oblations of boiled rice (karu) which are sacred to the goddess of speech, (thus) performing the best penance in order to expiate the guilt of that falsehood.
>
> 106. Or such (a witness) may offer according to the rule clarified butter in the fire, reciting the Kûshmâṇḍa texts, or the *Rik*, sacred to Varuṇa, 'Untie, O Varuṇa, the uppermost fetter,' or the three verses addressed to the Waters.[12]

We are poised at a delicate stage in our investigation now. These verses occur in chapter 8 of the *Manusmṛti* and no one has so far suggested that they are not part of the text. And the *Manusmṛti* was among the earliest Hindu texts to be translated into English, so scholars have pored over it for over two centuries now. Is it possible that over all this long period even stalwarts like A.L. Basham, P.V. Kane and Ram Sharan Sharma have all overlooked the significance of these verses in assessing the value the *Manusmṛti* attached to the life of the *śūdra*, not to mention the noted Indologists who preceded them?[13] How is such a colossal oversight to be explained? Is it just an unfortunate occurrence or is there a deeper cause underlying it?

There may be a deeper cause underlying it because James Mill, in his influential *The History of British India* (1818), used these verses as proof that the Hindus encouraged perjury, with the result that these verses became further proof of the depravity of Hinduism (instead of providing evidence of its humanity) and thus got elided from the discourse about the *śūdra*. James Mill wrote:

> Though there is no ground on which the infirmities of the human mind are more glaring, and more tenacious of existence, than that of law, it is probable that the annals of legislative absurdity can present nothing which will match a law for the *direct* encouragement of perjury. 'Whenever,' says the ordinance of Menu, 'the death of a man, who had been a grievous offender, either of the servile, the commercial, the military, or the sacerdotal class, would be occasioned by true evidence, from the known rigour of the king, even though the fault arose from inadvertence or error, falsehood may be spoken: it is even preferable to truth.' What a state of justice it is, in which the king may condemn a man to death, for inadvertence or error, and no better remedy is found than the perjury of witness?[14]

A standard example of degenerate Hinduism reveals itself, upon examination, as a standard example of Saidian Orientalism!

II

We will discover in a subsequent chapter on the position of women in the *Manusmṛti* how useful it is to draw a distinction between the *Manusmṛti's* attitude towards women in the *abstract*, and the *Manusmṛti's* attitude towards women in the *concrete*—as sister, mother, wife or daughter, for example. We will also note a difference in the tone, tenor and texture of these two discourses.

It seems such an approach also sheds much light on the position of the *śūdras* as depicted in the *Manusmṛti*. When discussed as a class, the *śūdra* is at the bottom of the totem-pole, as someone to avoid, and is even equated with untruth. The main duty of this class, according to the *Manusmṛti,* is to serve the higher *varṇas*. However, while in the abstract the *śūdra* belonged to a class, in the concrete the *śūdra* was the member of the larger family unit which he served. It will, therefore, be an instructive exercise in determining the position of the *śūdra* in the *Manusmṛti,* to compare the depiction of the *śūdra* in these two roles—as the generic member of a class, and as a concrete individual related to a family.

P.V. Kane has drawn up a list of eleven disabilities to which the *śūdra* was subject in *Smṛti* literature[15] and these come in handy as a way of carrying out this exercise in relation to the position of the *śūdra* as a member of the class.

II.1 A member of the *śūdra* class was not allowed to study the Vedas

The *Manusmṛti* (4.80–81) confirms this:

> 80. Let him not give to a Śūdra advice, nor the remnants of his meal, nor food offered to the gods; nor let him explain the sacred law (to such a man), nor impose (upon him) a penance.
>
> 81. For he who explains the sacred law (to a Śūdra) or dictates to him a penance, will sink together with that (man) into the hell (called) Asaṁvṛta.[16]

So not only is the *śūdra* debarred from studying the Vedas, he is also prevented from receiving spiritual advice. In a sense this is a greater impairment of his right than not being allowed to study the Vedas, because in Hinduism scriptural or sacred exclusion does *not imply* soteriological exclusion. All those who have Vedic or sacred knowledge may be saved, but all those who will be saved need not possess Vedic or sacred knowledge. As P.V. Kane notes:

> Śaṅkarācārya on Vedāntasūtra (I.3.38) quotes Śānti. 328.49 and says that the śūdra has no *adhikāra* (eligibility) for Brahmavidyā based upon *a study of the Veda*, but that a śūdra can attain spiritual development (just as Vidura and Dharmavyādha in the Mahābhārata did) and that he may attain to *mokṣa*, the fruit of correct knowledge.[17]

Presumably spiritual advice would be needed to achieve such correct knowledge.

Another verse in the *Manusmṛti* (10.2), however, runs as follows: 'The Brāhmaṇa must know the means of subsistence (prescribed) by law for all, *instruct the others*, and himself live according to (the law).'[18] The famous ninth-century commentator, Medhātithi, points out that 'this rule provides an exception to IV.80, where it is said that a Brāhmaṇa shall not give spiritual advice to a Śūdra.'[19] I think the key to understanding why

Medhātithi would regard this as an exception lies in grasping the *Sitz im Leben* involved. The *śūdra* was a member of the household and was always serving the master, almost like a *śiśya* or disciple if not more so, so that the relationship was likely to acquire a human dimension. This humanity would tend to trump the rigidity of the law, and the master would probably not be willing to withhold spiritual advice if asked.

It should also be kept in mind that although *śūdras* were not permitted to study the Vedas, there is clear evidence that they could hear texts like the *Mahābhārata* and the *Bhāgavata Purāṇa*. The closest we come to a recognition of this in the *Manusmṛti* may be in the verse which states that the *śūdra* 'has no qualification with regard to the law, but he is not prohibited from following the law'.[20] The verses that follow are worth citing, as they highlight the fact of the *śūdra* obtaining the desired ends in this world and the next:

> 127. (Śūdras) who are desirous to gain merit, and know (their) duty, commit no sin, but gain praise, if they imitate the practice of virtuous men without reciting sacred texts.
>
> 128. The more a (Śūdra) keeping himself free from envy, imitates the behaviours of the virtuous, the more he gains without being censured, (exaltation in) this world and the next.[21]

II.2 Another disability: The *śūdra* was not authorized to consecrate sacred fires and perform solemn Vedic sacrifices

This disability can be and has been questioned by scholars on the basis of other texts,[22] but the *Manusmṛti* is not one of them. However, what the *śūdra* was authorized to perform were acts of charity or what are called *pūrtadharma*. These are spelled out in *Manusmṛti* 4.226. However, what is even more interesting, and in keeping with the argument being developed here, is that the proximity of the *śūdra* to the *brāhmaṇa* may have contributed to the development of the view that as a servant, he achieved the results of the actions performed by the master, by merely serving him. *Manusmṛti* (10.122) points in that direction when it says (in G. Bühler's translation): 'But let (a *śūdra*) serve Brāhmaṇas, either for the sake of heaven, or with a view to both (this life and the next); for he who is called the servant of a Brāhmaṇa thereby gains all his ends.'[23] However, the bond which forms between the master and the servant, to which attention was drawn earlier, comes out more clearly in the following translation by Patrick Olivelle, and even more so in his note on the verse. Olivelle's translation runs as follows: 'He should serve Brahmins for the sake of heaven or for both, for when he has the name "Brahmin" attached to him, he has done all there is to do.'[24] Olivelle then comments on the verse as follows: '*when he has the name "Brahmin" attached to him*: the meaning appears to be that when a Sūdra serves a Brahmin, that name attaches to him: e.g. "He is a Brahmin's servant". By some extension of the name, he can call himself a Brahmin!'[25]

II.3 The *śūdra* could not perform some sacraments

Various texts express various views in the matter of the performance of the sacraments (*saṃskāras*) by *śūdras*, but *Manusmṛti* 10.127 clearly permits *śūdras* to perform all religious acts which *dvijas* perform but without the Vedic mantras. Some interpret *Manusmṛti* 4.80 to restrict this provision:

> The Mit. on Yāj. III.262 explains the words of Manu IV.80 about vratas in the case of śūdras as applicable only to those śūdras who are not in attendance upon members of the three higher castes and establishes that śūdras can perform vratas (but without homa and muttering of *mantras*). Aparārka on the same verse (Manu IV.80) explains that the śūdra cannot perform vratas in person, but only through the medium of a brāhmaṇa.[26]

Within the context of the *Manusmṛti*, however, the following remarks of P.V. Kane deserve serious consideration:

> When Manu prescribes (II.32) that the śūdra should be given a name connected with service, he indicates that the śūdra could perform the ceremony of nāmakaraṇa. So when Manu (IV.80) states that he deserves no saṁskāra, what he means is that no saṁskāra with Vedic mantras was to be performed in his case. Medhātithi on Manu IV.80 says that the prohibition to give advice and impart instruction in dharma applies only when these are done for making one's livelihood, but if a śūdra is a friend of the family a brāhmaṇa's friendly advice or instruction can be given.[27]

The last sentence in this citation seems to support the suggestion that there might be a difference in the way the *śūdra* is to be treated, when the *śūdra* is considered a member of the larger family and when this is not the case.

II.4 The liability of the *śūdra* for many offences was higher than that of other *varṇas*

To cite just two examples:

> Manu VIII.366 prescribe[s] death in the course of a śūdra having intercourse with a brāhmaṇa woman whether she was willing or unwilling. On the other hand, if a brāhmaṇa committed rape on a brāhmaṇa woman he was fined a thousand and five hundred if he was guilty of adultery with her (Manu VIII.378), and, if a brāhmaṇa had intercourse with a kṣatriya, vaiśya or śūdra woman, who was not guarded, he was fined five hundred (Manu VIII.305).[28]

Similarly, in the case of slander and libel (*vākpāruṣya*):

> If a śūdra reviled a brāhmaṇa he received corporal punishment or his tongue was cut off (Manu VIII.270), but if a kṣatriya or a vaiśya did so they were respectively fined 100 or 150 (Manu VIII.267) and if a brāhmaṇa reviled a śūdra, the brāhmaṇa was fined only 12 (Manu VIII.268).[29]

There are some points worth noting here. One is that *compared* to the provisions of the *Dharmasūtras*, the *Manusmṛti* sometimes takes a more positive view of the *śūdra*. For instance, the *brāhmaṇa* is fined in the *Manusmṛti* for reviling a *śūdra* but is not fined at all in *Gautama Dharma Sūtra* 12.13.[30] In fact, 'Manu's punishment of a brāhmaṇa abusing a śūdra is significant, for in the Dharmasūtras', in general, 'the brāhmaṇa goes scot-free'.[31]

The other point is even more significant. This is the case when the *śūdra* received lighter punishment compared to the other *varṇas*. The first example is provided by the case of theft: 'with respect to theft, the liability of a Śūdra is eight times; that of a Vaiśya, sixteen times; that of a Kṣatriya, thirty-two times; and for a Brahmin, sixty-four-times, or fully hundred times, or twice sixty-four times; for he knows whether it is good or bad.'[32] As *śūdras* were meant to be servants, one would have expected higher fines against them to discourage domestic theft; but the verse seems to adopt a different line of logic. The *brāhmaṇa* was supposed to be able to distinguish between right and wrong better—hence to be held answerable to a higher standard of probity.

Curiously, the other case in which the liability was raised in the direction of the *brāhmaṇa* was in the case of beating someone. According to *Manusmṛti* 8.299–300: 'When they misbehave, a wife, son, slave, pupil, or uterine brother may be beaten with a rope or a bamboo stick on the back of their bodies and never on the head. If he beats them in any other way, his liability is the same as for theft'[33]—lowest for the *śūdra*, and highest for the *brāhmaṇa*.

The punishment for theft and beating—if we assume that one major theatre for these crimes would be the home—was more lenient in the case of *śūdras*.

II.5 A greater period of impurity was attached to the birth and death of a *śūdra*

The period of impurity associated with the birth and death of a *śūdra*, namely a month, was more than that for a *brāhmaṇa*, which was ten days. This provision appears to be counter-intuitive as one would assume that the period of impurity would be greater for someone whose person is considered more 'sacred', such as that of a *brāhmaṇa*.

As against this, however, a *śūdra* could not commit an offence causing loss of caste, as per the well-known line of *Manusmṛti* 10.126: *na śūdre pātakam kiñcit* (A *śūdra* is not affected by any sin causing loss of caste).[34]

II.6 A *śūdra* could not propound *dharma*

According to *Manusmṛti* 8.9, a learned *brāhmaṇa* should be appointed as a judge, and *Manusmṛti* 8.20 reinforces the point by saying that 'A king may appoint as his judge even a brāhmaṇa who is so by birth only (i.e., who does not perform the peculiar duties of a brāhmaṇa) but never a śūdra.'[35]

The *śūdra*, however, even if an untouchable, could apparently impart instruction leading to *mokṣa* according to *Manusmṛti* 2.238.

II.7 A *brāhmaṇa* was permitted to accept gifts from *śūdras* only under certain circumstances, according to some *Dharmasūtras*[36]

The *Manusmṛti*, however, seems to be more relaxed in the matter and allows gifts to be accepted from all, in both normal and abnormal times. For instance, according to *Manusmṛti* 4.251: 'He [the graduate] may accept a gift from anyone for the purpose of supporting his elders and dependants and honouring gods and guests; but he may not use it to gratify himself.' A verse later the *Manusmṛti* also says (4.253):[37] 'A share cropper, a friend of the family, and one's cowherd, slave, and barber—among Śūdras, these are the ones whose food is fit to be eaten, as also a person who has presented himself.'[38] This seems to allow the graduate to accept gifts even from a *śūdra*.

I find it striking that those *śūdras* whose food could be eaten were people in a personal relationship with the person involved, and in a relationship often domestic in nature. Perhaps the earlier verse on the acceptance of gifts needs to be viewed in a similar way. In any case, a more grudging acceptance of gifts is also permitted, perhaps because a time of adversity is involved, in *Manusmṛti* 10.102–03:

> [102] A Brahmin who has fallen on hard times may accept gifts from anybody; that something pure can be sullied is impossible according to the Law. [103] By teaching, officiating at the sacrifices of, and accepting gifts from, despicable individuals, Brahmins do not incur any sin, for they are like fire and water.[39]

It also needs to be noted that:

> Manu is the first writer explicitly to describe the śūdra as a sharecropper, a fact which can only be deduced from the *Arthaśāstra* of Kauṭilya. While the sharecropper (*ardhasītika*) retains only 1/5th or 1/4th portion of the produce in the *Arthaśāstra*, in Manu he seems to retain half the produce.[40]

II.8 The *brāhmaṇa* could accept food from other *varṇas*; but only from some *śūdras* under certain conditions

The rule, however, is relaxed in the *Manusmṛti* in some circumstances:

> Manu IV.211 forbade in general the food of a śūdra to a brāhmaṇa and by IV.223 he laid down that a learned brāhmaṇa should not take cooked food from a śūdra who did not perform śrāddha and the other daily rites (mahāyajñas) but that he may take from such a śūdra uncooked grain for one night, if he cannot get food from anywhere else.[41]

We saw earlier, however, that when it came to the crunch, food was accepted by *brāhmaṇas* even from untouchables (*Manusmṛti* 10.107–08). And even if sometimes the food of the *śūdra* could not be eaten, *in some cases the master could not eat one's own food until the śūdra had eaten first* (*Manusmṛti* 3.116).

II.9 The *śūdra* could not touch a *brāhmaṇa*

It seems that in due course the *śūdra* came to be looked upon as a person who could not touch a *brāhmaṇa,* but this is not the state of affairs in the *Manusmṛti. Manusmṛti* 3.156 speaks disapprovingly of *śūdra* pupils and *śūdra* teachers, but it is difficult to visualize this relationship without physical touch of some kind being involved, at least of the feet.

II.10 Sometimes it is maintained that the only *āśrama* admissible to the *śūdra* was that of the householder

P.V. Kane notes in this connection:

> In the Śāntiparva (63.12–14) it is said, 'in the case of a śūdra who performs service (of the higher classes), who has done his duty, who has raised offspring, who has only a short span of life left or is reduced to the 10th stage (i.e. is above 90 years of age), the fruits of all āśramas are laid down (as obtained by him) except of 'the fourth.' Medhātithi on Manu VI.97 explains these words as meaning that the śūdra by serving brāhmaṇas and procreating offspring as a house-holder acquires the merit of all āśramas except *mokṣa* which is the reward of the proper observance of the duties of the fourth āśrama. [42]

This comes close to reflecting the sentiments in *Manusmṛti* 10.122 cited earlier. It must be remembered, however, that although *sannyāsa* may have been denied to the *śūdra*, *mokṣa* was not denied to the *śūdra.*

II.11 It has often been alleged that little value was attached to the *śūdra*'s life

This point has been covered in the first section of the chapter, but it is striking in this context that there are references to the longevity of the *śūdras* in *Manusmṛti* 2.137 and 2.155, which seems to go against the idea that no value was attached to the *śūdra*'s life.

Yet another disability may be added to the list. According to a verse in the *Manusmṛti* (10.129), the *śūdra* is not permitted to accumulate wealth because it pains the *brāhmaṇa*. K.V. Ranga Swami Aiyangar construes 'this injunction as an exaggerated statement (*arthavāda*) addressed to the śūdra himself,'[43] but Ram Sharan Sharma thinks that 'the text does not provide any basis for such an interpretation.'[44] S.V. Ketkar compares this injunction 'to the admonition in the English prayer-book advising a poor man "therewith to be contented".'[45] Ram Sharan Sharma also offers the following explanation:

> Since the passage in question occurs in the chapter on times of distress, it may have been directed against the Buddhist monks or foreign rulers who were looked upon as no better than śūdras. At any rate it is evident from the law of inheritance that the śūdra owned property [Manusmṛti IX.157]. This can also be inferred from the old rule repeated by Manu [Manusmṛti 11.34] that the vaiśyas and śūdras should surmount their misfortunes through payment.[46]

The pattern of the family and social relations of which the *śūdra* was a part, as reflected in *Manusmṛti* 4.182–86, should not go unnoticed:

> [182] The teacher is the ruler of Brahman's world; the father, of Prajāpati's world; the officiating priests, of the world of gods; [183] the sisters, of the world of Apsarases; maternal relatives, of the world of the Viśvedevas; affinal relatives, of the world of the waters; and the mother and maternal uncles, of the earth. [184] The children, the aged, the feeble, and the sick are to be regarded as the rulers of space. His older brother is equal to his father, and his wife and son are his own body. [185] *His slaves are his own shadow*, and his daughter is the object of supreme compassion.

> When he is *assailed by any of these*, therefore, he should always bear it without losing his temper. [47]

One must also look on the other side of the ledger. P.V. Kane notes in this context:

> If the śūdra laboured under certain grave disabilities, he had certain compensating advantages. He could follow almost any profession except the few specially reserved for brāhmaṇas and kṣatriyas. Even as to the latter many śūdras became kings and Kaut. in his Arthaśāstra (IX.2) speaks of armies of śūdras … The śūdra was free from the round of countless daily rites. He was compelled to undergo no *saṃskāra* (except marriage), he could indulge in any kind of food and drink wine, he had to undergo no penances for lapses from the rules of the śāstras, he had to observe no restrictions of gotra and pravara in marriage.[48]

In addition, *śūdra* women enjoyed more freedom than their sisters. Ram Sharan Sharma explains:

> Thus it was laid down that, if the husband leaves his home, a wife of the brāhmaṇa or the kṣatriya varṇa, who has issue, shall wait for five years, a wife of the vaiśya varṇa for four years, and one of the śūdra varṇa for three years. If she has no issue, the waiting period will be cut down by one year in the case of the brāhmaṇa, and by two years each in the cases of the kṣatriya, the vaiśya and the śūdra, with the result that in such a case a wife of the śūdra varṇa will have to wait for only one year. Such a rule again implies the comparative independence of the women of the lower orders, among whom marriage ties were easily dissoluble.[49]

A similar freedom in the matter of eating was also available to the *śūdras* as mentioned earlier.

> The twice-born should perform the *cāndrāyaṇa* penance if he eats dried meat, mushrooms growing on the earth and meat about the origin of which he has no knowledge, or which had been kept in a slaughter-house. Similarly if the twice-born takes the meat of carnivorous animals, boars, camels, cocks, crows, human beings and asses, he

should perform a very difficult penance known as the *taptakṛcchra*. If in these references the dvija is taken as a member of the first three varṇas, it would imply that śūdras were free to take all varieties of meat. Commenting on a passage of Manu Kullūka states that, by eating garlic and other kinds of forbidden roots, the śūdra cannot commit an offence leading to loss of caste. This would suggest that garlic, onion and various kinds of meat were regarded as the legitimate food of the members of the lower orders.[50]

Thus the situation of the *śūdras* may not be as abject in the *Manusmṛti* as is usually portrayed, if we take the existence, even in hostility, of such elements as *śūdra śiṣyas* (3.156); *śūdra gurus* (3.156); *śūdra* kingdoms (4.61); wealthy *śūdras* (11.34) and *śūdras* who apparently even owned slaves (9.179).

III

The issue of the presence of untouchability in the *Manusmṛti* is also a good touchstone of the position of the *śūdras* in that text.

The first point to note here is that there is a tendency in some writings on untouchability to separate the untouchables as a separate social class beyond the *śūdras*, for which the term *pañcama* (fifth) is sometimes used. The position of the *Manusmṛti* (10.4) on this is very clear: there is no fifth (*nāsti tu pañcamaḥ*). As this statement is made at the beginning of the tenth chapter just prior to the discussion of the mixed classes, its importance cannot be denied. Thus P.V. Kane reflects sober scholarly opinion when he writes: 'The theory of the early smṛtis was that there were only four varṇas and there was no fifth varṇa. Vide Manu X.4 and Anuśāsanaparva 47.18. When in modern times the so-called untouchables are referred to as *pañcamas* that is something against smṛti tradition.'[51]

If any group is regularly characterized as untouchable in ancient Hindu literature, it is the *caṇḍāla,* and the following piece of evidence clearly establishes the inclusion of the *caṇḍāla* within the category of the *śūdra*:

> Pāṇ[iṇi] II.4.10 and Patañjali say that a Samāhāra-dvandva can be formed from several subdivisions of śūdras that are not *niravasita* e.g. we have the compound 'takṣyāyaskāram' meaning carpenters and

> blacksmiths, but not '*caṇḍāla-mṛtapam*', because caṇḍālas and mṛtapas are niravasita śūdras (and so the compound will be 'caṇḍālamṛtapāḥ). Therefore it follows that Pāṇ[iṇi] and Patañjali included caṇḍālas and mṛtapas among śūdras.[52]

Manusmṛti 10.41 confirms this; it declares that all *pratiloma* castes have the *dharma* of *śūdras*, and the *caṇḍāla* belongs to that class according to the *Manusmṛti* (10.12).

With this clarification in place, we may now proceed to discuss untouchability in the *Manusmṛti*. We are handicapped in this exercise, however, by the fact that the commonly used Sanskrit word for untouchable, namely *aspṛśya*, does not occur in the *Manusmṛti*. Its earliest use in this sense is probably in the *Viṣṇu Dharma Sūtra* (5.104), which is usually placed in the second century CE or later, that is, around or soon after the time of the *Manusmṛti*. Thus the institution of untouchability as we know it was perhaps beginning to crystallize around this time. That perhaps only a few groups, such as the *caṇḍāla*, are considered *aspṛśya* by the *Manusmṛti*, indicates this. P.V. Kane arrives at this conclusion as follows:

> Medhātithi in his commentary on Manu X.13 is positive *that the only pratiloma who is untouchable is the caṇḍāla* and no bath is necessary on coming in contact with other pratilomas (viz. sūta, māgadha, āyogava, vaidehika and kṣatṛ). Kullūka also says the same. Therefore it follows that in spite of the smṛti texts (notes 170, 171, 173) including the pratilomas among antyajas along with the caṇḍālas, such authoritative and comparatively early commentators as Medhātithi (about 900 A.D.) were firmly of opinion that they were not untouchable. Manu V.85 and Aṅgiras 152 prescribe a bath for coming in bodily contact with a divākīrti (a caṇḍāla), udakyā (a woman in her monthly period), patita (one outcasted for sin &c.), sūtikā (a woman after delivery), a corpse, one who has touched a corpse. *It follows therefore that the only antyaja who was aspṛśya according to Manu was the caṇḍāla.*[53]

This passage gives rise to several points which are worth probing in detail. The first is that, in later times, even the shadow of a *caṇḍāla* was considered polluting. That such was not the case in the time of the

Manusmṛti, and even more broadly during the earlier period, is established by the following considerations:

> It does not appear from the ancient smrtis that the shadow of even the caṇḍāla was deemed to be polluting. Manu V.133 (which is nearly the same as Viṣṇu Dh. S. 23, 52) declares 'flies, spray from a reservoir, the shadow (of a man), the cow, the horse, the sun's rays, dust, the earth, the wind and fire should be regarded as pure.' Yaj. I.193 is a similar verse (Mārk. Purāṇa 35.21 is almost the same). Manu IV.130 prescribes that one should not knowingly cross the shadow of the image of a deity, of one's *guru*, of the king, of a snātaka, of one's teacher, of a brown cow or of a man who has been initiated for a Vedic sacrifice. *Here no reference is made to the shadow of a caṇḍāla*. Medhātithi on Manu V.133 expressly says that 'shadow' means 'shadow of a caṇḍāla and the like'. Kullūka, however, adds on Manu IV.130 that on account of the word 'ca' in that verse the shadow of caṇḍālas was included in the injunction of that verse. Therefore it is legitimate to infer that Manu and Yāj. did not prescribe that even the shadow of a caṇḍāla was impure and caused pollution.[54]

The other point which emerges about untouchability is that it was not directed towards the *caṇḍāla* alone. Thus a person could not touch even next of kin during certain periods without risk of pollution. P.V. Kane explains:

> The ancient Hindus had a horror of uncleanliness and they desired to segregate those who followed unclean professions like those of sweepers, workers in hide, tanners, guardians of cemeteries &c. This segregation cannot be said to have been quite unjustifiable. Besides those who are not familiar with ancient or even modern Hindu notions must be warned against being carried away by the horror naturally felt at first sight when certain classes are treated as untouchable. The underlying notions of untouchability are religious and ceremonial purity and impurity. A man's nearest and dearest women relatives such as his own mother and wife or daughter are untouchable to him during their monthly periods. To him the most affectionate friend is untouchable for several days when the latter is in mourning due to

death in the latter's family. A person cannot touch his own son (whose thread ceremony has been performed) at the time of taking meals. In this latter case there is no idea of impurity and in most of these cases there is no idea of superiority or inferiority. As many professions and crafts were in ancient times hereditary, gradually the idea arose that a man who belonged to a caste pursuing certain filthy or abhorred avocations or crafts was by birth untouchable. [55]

There was, however, something which set the *caṇḍāla* apart. It was the 'only caste that is said by the most ancient dharmasūtras to be untouchable by birth.'[56] In due course, three kinds of *caṇḍālas* were identified: (1) the offspring of a *śūdra* from a *brāhmaṇa* woman; (2) the offspring of an unmarried woman; and (3) the offspring of a union with a *sagotra* girl (who has the standing of a sister in Hindu lore).[57] The three types of *caṇḍālas* were all so by the virtue of *their birth*.[58] Another category, similar to that of *caṇḍāla*, found in the *Manusmṛti* is that of the *śvapāka*;[59] both had to wear distinctive marks by the king's order according to the *Manusmṛti* (10.55). These fit the category of untouchables in the *Manusmṛti* (10.51–56):

> [51] Cāṇḍālas and Śvapacas, however, must live outside the village and they should be made Apapātras. Their property consists of dogs and donkeys. [52] Their garments are the clothes of the dead; they eat in broken vessels; their ornaments are of iron; and they constantly roam about.
>
> [53] A man who follows the Law should never seek any dealings with them. All their transactions shall be among themselves, and they must marry their own kind. [54] They depend on others for their food, and it should be given in a broken vessel. They must not go about in villages and towns at night; [55] they may go around during the day to perform some task at the command of the king, wearing distinguishing marks. They should carry away the corpses of those without relatives—that is the settled rule. [56] They should always execute those condemned to death in the manner prescribed by authoritative texts and at the command of the king; and they may take the clothes, beds, and ornaments of those condemned to death.[60]

While going into these details one should not lose sight of a basic dynamic, that 'the mixed castes and the untouchables were being absorbed as inferior śūdras, who were distinguished from the ordinary śūdras by their separate habitations, backward culture and primitive religious beliefs,'[61] for the, 'myths of their origins show that they were supposed to have śūdra blood in their veins.'[62]

IV

The only *āśrama* to which the *śūdra* was entitled seems to have been that of the householder.[63] Or as V.S. Agrawala puts it, 'Three things cannot be denied to him namely marriage, cooking of daily food in the Gṛihya fire, and Śrāddha,' on the basis of *Manusmṛti* 4.223 and 3.197.[64] There is, however, a verse in the *Manusmṛti* (10.127) which allows the *śūdras* to perform all the acts of the *dvijātis, but* without the Vedic mantras. Moreover, according to another verse (*Manusmṛti* 10.128), a *śūdra* obtains this world and the next by imitating the practices of good men without envy.

Thus a series of concessions, as it were, can be identified in the case of the *śūdra*. The *Śāntiparva* (63.12–14), however, states that a *śūdra* who has led a full life obtains the fruits of all the *āśramas*, and Medhātithi elaborates on this while explaining *Manusmṛti* 6.97 as follows: that the *śūdra*, by serving *brāhmaṇas* and living as a householder 'acquires the merit of all āśramas except *mokṣa* which is the reward of the proper observance of the duties of the fourth āśrama.'[65]

This means that the *śūdra* was barred from *sannyāsa* but two verses refer to him as obtaining 'both the ends'. Thus in 10.122 *ubhayārtha* is referred to and in 12.128 'this and that world' is indicated. The other world is identified with heaven in these cases, but elsewhere in the *Manusmṛti* the second world is identified with *mokṣa* (2.9; 8.343).

Moreover, the restriction on *sannyāsa* also needs to be analysed carefully. What is it in *sannyāsa* that leads one to liberation? *Sannyāsa* consists of a certain outward mode of life like carrying a stick but *also* conveys the idea of renouncing all actions, which is an inner state. It is generally agreed that it is the inner transformation and not outward signs which lead to *mokṣa*. Therefore Śaṅkara in his commentary on

Vedāntasūtra 1.3.34 distinguishes between the words *sannyāsa* and *nyāsa*. He uses the former to refer to the fourth *āśrama* with its appurtenances, which is restricted to the male members of the three *varṇas*. He uses *nyāsa* then to refer to inner abandonment of desire, which can be practised by women, *śūdras* and others.

The point is that it is inner detachment which leads to *mokṣa*, and not donning the outer garb. There is a distinction here to be drawn between formal and real *sannyāsa*. Real *sannyasa*, or *nyāsa*, is open to all; formal *sannyāsa* is restricted to the male members of the three higher *varṇas* but denied to *śūdras*. However, if it is *nyāsa* which really leads to *mokṣa*, then the denial of *sannyāsa*, whatever its social significance, turns out to be of no real spiritual consequence, although the social significance of such denial should not be overlooked.

Thus, our formulation seems to be justified that while various strictures are passed on *śūdras* and restrictions placed on the *śūdra* as a class, the complexion of the situation tends to change when they are dealt with as individuals. Thus although *in general* a *brahmāṇa* may not take food from the *śūdra* (*Manusmṛti* 4.211), yet, according to *Manusmṛti* 4.253, food may be accepted by a *snātaka* from 'a sharecropper, a friend of the family, one's cowherd, slave, and barber—among śūdras'.[66] Similarly, although according to *Manusmṛti* 4.80, 'he must never give a Śūdra advice, leftovers, or anything offered to the gods; teach him the law; or prescribe an observance to him',[67] yet the *brāhmaṇa,* on the other hand, is directed in general to instruct the other three *varṇas* in *Manusmṛti* 10.2: 'The Brahmin must know the means of livelihood of all according to rule, and he should both teach them to the others and follow them himself.'[68]

We see the tendency described above at work later in Medhātithi, who says in his commentary on *Mansumrti* 4.80 that 'the prohibition to give advice and impart instruction on dharma applies only when these are done for making one's livelihood, but if the śūdra is a friend of the family of a brāhmaṇa friendly advice or instruction can be given.'[69]

Finally, the *Manusmṛti* also at times demonstrates sensitivity towards the *śūdras* as when it states that people who are of low birth (*jātihīna*) should not be insulted for that reason (*Manusmṛti* 4.141) and thus anticipates some of the provisions of the Scheduled Castes and Scheduled Tribes (Prevention of Atrocities) Act of 1989, as pointed out in the appendix.

V

One reason why the *śūdra* was assigned an inferior status was based on the logic of the *Puruṣa Sūkta*: that the low status of the *śūdra* is justified because he was born from the feet of the Puruṣa. Such a reference to the *Puruṣa Sūkta* in the *Manusmṛti* is found in 8.270. The verse has been translated into English by Patrick Olivelle as follows: 'if a once-born man hurls grossly abusive words at twice-born men, his tongue shall be cut off, for he originated from the lowest part.'[70] Olivelle explains the clause 'lowest part' (*jaghanya-prabhava*) as follows:

> A once-born man is a śūdra. The implied background of this harsh punishment is the creation myth of the Puruṣasūkta (R.V. 10.90), which has become a root metaphor in the Dharma literature. The twice-born here probably refers specifically to Brahmins, who were born from the mouth (speech). When a man born from the feet uses speech to abuse a man born from the mouth, he loses his right to the tongue, the organ of speech.[71]

It is perhaps an example of the humour of history that, in the course of time, the *śūdras* were able to claim that because they came from the feet of the Puruṣa, *as did the Gaṅgā river*, they were of commendable birth as they were thereby related to her. If this point is pressed, they could even claim that because the *Gaṅgā* fell on the head of *Śiva* they could also lay claim to that place. Thus, they could even claim to be superior to the *brāhmaṇas* because the latter found a place only in the mouth of the cosmic person, whereas the *śūdras* could claim to have found a place on the top of his head by virtue of sharing their connection with the river *Gaṅgā*.

I do not know whether such a claim was actually made during the Nāyaka period in the history of south India in the late medieval period. We do have evidence that 'Nāyaka-period poets constantly praise the Śūdra origins of their kings.'[72] The *śūdra* poet, Cēmakuura Veṇkaṭakvai, revels in the *śūdra* origin of the Nāyaka kings as follows:

> Born from the feet of incarnate Hari,
> reaching the head of Hara,
> this goddess (*Gaṅgā*) is celebrated

from tip to toe:
may she, together with *her* lord,
grant perfect lordship
to King Raghunātha, son of Acyutendra,
this precious jewel of a Nāyaka,
scion of a family that shares her place of birth.[73]

From the above, it is clear that: 'Like the *Gaṅgā*, the Śūdra emerges from the feet of the god, as the Veda itself proclaims in the famous Purusha hymn (RV 10.90). The Nāyakas can thus claim *Gaṅgā* as a sister, and their genealogies never hesitate to appropriate her prestigious qualities for themselves'.[74]

Such a claim is made in the following lines:

Virtuous Cevvappa (founder of the Tanjavur line),
delight of the earth,
was born in the pure and brilliant class
(*vimalaśrīruciravarṇamunaa*)
that has *Gaṅgā* of the lotus face,
beloved of God,
for a sister.[75]

It is clear therefore that the feet can also be used to elevate the status of the *śūdra* and to imply a high rather than a low birth as happens in the *Bhīmeśvarapurāṇa.* A similar claim was also made by the earlier Kākatīya Dynasty of eastern Deccan.[76] There is, however, hardly any evidence of this happening in the *Manusmṛti.*

6

The Doctrine of *Āśramas* in the *Manusmṛti*

I

Varṇa and *āśrama* are two foundational institutions of classical Hinduism and recognized as such in the *Manusmṛti*. They are often mentioned in that order and cohere inasmuch as 'the theory of *varṇa* dealt with man as a member of the Aryan society' while the 'theory of the *āśramas* addressed itself to the individual'.[1] Of the two, the institution of the *āśramas* has not been subjected to as much adverse criticism as that of *varṇa* (and in fact has even been lauded).[2] This even prompts T.M.P. Mahadevan to remark that 'we are on safer ground when we come to consider the nature of *āśrama-dharma* (duties pertaining to the stages in life)',[3] as compared to *varṇa dharma*.

The *āśramas* are discussed in considerable detail in the *Manusmṛti*, and are enumerated in that text, as in many others, as four in number. They are meant to follow each other as one goes through one's life; a quarter of one's lifespan may be notionally allotted for each informally although considerable flexibility exists in the matter. Thus according to *Manusmṛti* 6.87: 'Student, householder, forest hermit, and ascetic'[4] are the four stages of life or what are called *āśramas*. The Sanskrit terms used for them most often are *brahmacarya āśrama*, *gṛhastha āśrama*, *vānaprastha āśrama* and *sannyāsa āśrama*.

II

One needs to be broadly familiar with the history of the institution to gauge the significance of the references to it in the *Manusmṛti*. References to the institution can be traced back to the early Vedic period.[5] Patrick Olivelle has persuasively argued that although the four *āśramas* are usually perceived as four stages of life to be successively pursued, their original conception may well be of four *optional* lifestyles. That is to say, one was free to adopt one of the four options for life: one could continue studying; become a householder; or a hermit; or remain a lifelong renunciant.[6]

Traces of such an understanding of the *āśramas* seem to surface in the *Manusmṛti*. For instance, the *Manusmṛti* states, just before embarking on a discussion of the householder's life, that after one has graduated: 'He should carry out the observance relating to the three Vedas at the teacher's house, an observance *lasting thirty-six years, or one-half or one-quarter of the time, or else until he has learnt them*.'[7] Similarly, the *Manusmṛti* seems to suggest, at the end of chapter 6, that the householder may either take *sannyāsa*, that is to say, renounce the world, or as Bühler puts it, 'become an ascetic' (*Manusmṛti* 6.94) or 'he may live at his ease under the protection of his son' (6.95).[8]

There is little doubt, however, that, on the whole, the *Manusmṛti* favours the successive model of the *āśramas* over the optional one. This would make sense in terms of the historical period of Indian history immediately preceding it, which witnessed the depopulation of the country as well as the adoption of Buddhism and Jainism, especially the former, by the very rulers whose invasions had depopulated it. This probably made renunciation, favoured by these two religions, such a viable option that the Vedic tradition felt compelled to incorporate it fully into the Vedic lifestyle. This would explain not only the adoption of the fourfold system, with each *āśrama* following the other, as a way of accommodating this new development of the renunciatory lifestyle, with the spin that it is best relegated to the last years of one's life. This might also help explain the fact that the life of the hermit receives extended treatment in the *Manusmṛti*. A major feature of this life is that, in principle, the wife could accompany one in this stage of life (*Manusmṛti* 6.8), which is not possible in the last stage of the ascetic or renunciant (6.42).

These points may be clarified by distinguishing between two forms of renunciation, eremitic—where one renounces married life but *wanders alone thereafter*, alone 'like the horn of a rhinocerous' as some texts graphically put it; and cenobitic—where one once again renounces married life but *then joins a monastic community*, and thus lives in company with other monks most of the time rather than alone. This difference between eremitic and cenobitic monasticism may shed light on the provisions of the *Manusmṛti*. The treatment of the life of the hermit, as distinguished from that of the renunciant or the ascetic, seems to suggest that the householder could incorporate renunciation into one's life as an extension of the life of the householder and one did not have to abandon the life of a householder to pursue that lifestyle if one was attracted to it. Mahatma Gandhi's conscious decision not to become a 'renunciant', and not don the ochre robe, but instead lead the life of a 'hermit' testifies to the continuing appeal of the option.[9]

This could be one way in which the *Manusmṛti* tried to respond to the challenge posed by the success of the monastic movements of Buddhism and Jainism. The other way was to provide for it within the system of the *āśramas*. We see here something quite extraordinary in the sense that the *Manusmṛti* tries to accommodate *monastic renunciation within a married setting* in the case of the third stage of *vānaprastha*! This, however, had its limitations. Renunciation is after all renunciation and in practical terms, the renunciation of married life. So that was also provided for in the final stage of life.

We perhaps need to understand more fully the formidable nature of the challenge faced by the *Manusmṛti*. If one became keen to follow a spiritual course of life in India in the centuries around the beginning of the Christian era, one faced two obstacles—the need to feed oneself and the need for a support structure in case of a crisis, such as poor health. Cenobitic monasticism of the kind that emerged in India around the sixth century BCE or even earlier, took care of both of these by creating a *community* of monks who *begged* for food. The begging took care of the food problem and the community provided the support system.

Now this by itself should not have posed a threat to Vedic society, *except for the fact that these monastic movements recruited young men and women into the Orders, which was seen as a threat to the stability of the Vedic order.* These objections to the movements remained rather hypothetical so long as Buddhism and Jainism remained marginal movements, but then a series of developments precipitated a crisis. First came Aśoka's patronage of Buddhism on a scale which ultimately changed the name of Magadha to Bihar (Bihar stems from *vihāra,* a Buddhist monastery); followed by Samprati, one of Aśoka's successors, promoting Jainism. This was followed by no less than four foreign invasions, which left north India depopulated.

This was the situation that the author of the *Manusmṛti* faced in the second century. The *Manusmṛti* responded, in the political realm, by attempting to incorporate elements of the *Arthaśāstra* into the *Dharmaśāstra*; in the socio-economic realm it tried to repopulate the country by reviving the institution of marriage by emphasizing *gṛhasta-āśrama* (the householder stage among the four *āśramas* or stages); and, in the religious realm, it tried to accommodate what it might have considered the *current fashion* for renunciation within the structure of Hinduism by accepting the stages of the hermit and the renunciant (or the ascetic) within its conception of a life cycle.

However, if it was to co-opt the renunciatory lifestyle within its own structures and not be co-opted by it, then its own version had to be distinct in some way. Hinduism did so by choosing an eremitic form of monasticism rather than the cenobitic; thus eremitic monasticism was to be *its own version* of the renunciatory lifestyle, distinguishable from renunciation in Buddhism and Jainism. Other ways of distinguishing it also emerged. For instance, although Buddhist monks could leave the Order without any penalty and could actually join or leave six times, the Hindu monk was ostracized if he reverted to normal life. Similarly, while Buddhist monks could remain in touch with their families, a Hindu monk broke all contact. And so on.

How the attempt of the *Manusmṛti* fared in history comes out in clear relief once we take into account the various positions which emerged in the tradition, in relation to the system of the *āśramas*. These positions are called *pakṣas*, and the three different *pakṣas* which emerged in this connection are called *samuccaya* (an orderly collective co-ordination), *vikalpa* (option) and *bādha* (annulment).[10] It is interesting that P.V. Kane regards 'Manu (VI.1, VI.1.33–37, 87–88) as the prime supporter of this view [of *samuccaya*] … This view does not regard marriage and sexual life as impure or inferior to asceticism and on the contrary places it on a higher plane than asceticism.'[11] As for *vikalpa,* according to this view, 'there is an option after brahmacarya i.e. a man may become a *parivrājaka* immediately after he finishes his study or immediately after the householder's way of life.'[12] The third view, namely *bādha,* holds 'that there is really only one *āśrama* viz. that of the householder (brahmacarya only being a preparation to it) and the other *āśramas* are inferior to that of the householder.'[13]

III

We saw earlier how the *Manusmṛti* supports the *samuccaya* view, which advocates that all the *āśramas* be followed in a certain order. One would suspect that Manu would have chosen *bādha* if only the depopulation issue was being addressed, but as the Buddhist and Jaina positions had to be accommodated, Manu does so by incorporating the last two *āśramas* of *vānaprastha* and *sannyāsa.* With this accommodation, Manu's position gets modified into one which praised 'the *āśrama* of householder as the highest'.[14] According to the *Manusmṛti* (6.87–90):

> [87] Student, householder, forest hermit, and ascetic: these four distinct orders have their origin in the householder. [88] All of these, when they are undertaken in their proper sequence as spelled out in the sacred texts, lead a Brahmin who acts in the prescribed manner to the highest state. [89] Among all of them, however, according to the dictates of vedic scripture, the householder is said to be the best, for he supports the other three. [90] As all rivers and rivulets ultimately end up in the ocean, so people of all orders ultimately end up in the householder.[15]

Vikalpa, or the position that one could leapfrog into *sannyāsa* after *brahmacarya,* was a significant development and tells us that Manu's efforts to stop young people from joining religious orders, while still in their youth, did not fully succeed. Thus Hinduism *had to introduce this provision* within its own system of four *āśramas*, in all probability to avoid losing its spiritually precocious and earnest young men to Buddhism and Jainism. This is how a Śaṅkarācārya could take *sannyāsa* as a young man in the eighth century, although the *Manusmṛti* does not seem to provide this option. It would be interesting to know when exactly this provision was introduced; it clearly indicates the limitations of Manu's efforts in this respect. Another development which also points to the limited success of Manu's efforts to replace cenobitic monasticism with the eremitic variety is the emergence of *maṭhas* or seminaries in Hinduism by early medieval times, and their subsequent spread. Apparently the advantages of cenobitic monasticism over eremitic were so obvious that Hinduism had to adopt the attitude of 'if you can't beat them, join them' and indulge in the sincerest form of flattery, namely imitation. If these developments took place in or after the seventh century, it could be that Hinduism had regained sufficient lost ground by then to follow in the steps of Buddhism without embarrassment. It is perhaps significant that by the seventh century we start getting epigraphic evidence of the acceptance of the Buddha as an incarnation of Viṣṇu.

IV

We sought above to connect developments represented by the *Manusmṛti,* with the historical evidence provided in the previous sections. It may not be out of place, however, to remind ourselves that cogent phenomenological explanations of these developments can be offered in terms of the key concepts of the Hindu tradition itself. Thus the four *āśramas* could be easily depicted as representing the two allied as well as opposing tendencies, represented by the terms *pravṛtti* or engagement in the world and *nivṛtti* or disengagement from the world. The first two *āśramas*, those of *brahmacarya* and *gṛhastha*, would then represent engagement in the world in the first half of one's life, and the next two *āśramas* of *vānaprastha* and *sannyāsa* would represent *nivṛtti* or disengagement from the world, with *gṛhastha* representing the acme of the former and *sannyāsa* the acme of the latter. Similarly, an attempt was made above to connect the three *pakṣas* mentioned earlier—those of *samuccaya, vikalpa* and *bādha*—with historical developments, but a phenomenological explanation of them has been offered by Sarvajña-Nārāyaṇa in his commentary on *Manusmṛti* 6.35., which is summarized by P.V. Kane as follows:

> … the view that a man may pass on to *saṃnyāsa* immediately after the period of student-hood (without being a householder) applies only

> to those men who are, owing to the impressions and effects of past lives, entirely free from desires and whose tongue, sexual appetites, belly and words are thoroughly under control; the prescriptions of Manu enjoining on men not to resort to saṁnyāsa without paying off the three debts are concerned with men whose appetites have not yet thoroughly been brought under control and the word of Gautama that there is only one *āśrama* (that of the householder) relates only to those whose appetites for worldly pleasures and pursuits are quite keen.[16]

The fact of the matter is that such phenomenological explanations are also possible for what we have tried to explain historically. Of course this does not mean that the historical explanations are not valid; it just serves to illustrate how radically diachronic and synchronic explanations could diverge.

V

To revert now to the diachronic mode: What becomes so obvious from this discussion is how closely the three traditions—of what we now call Hinduism, Buddhism and Jainism—are intertwined when one tries to study the social relations in ancient India. This fact along with the synchronic insights gained earlier are judiciously brought together in the following remarks by A.L. Basham:

> The series of the four stages is evidently an idealization of the facts, and an artificial attempt to find room for the conflicting claims of study, family life, and asceticism in a single lifetime. It is possible that the system of the *āśramas* was evolved partly as a counterblast to the unorthodox sects such as Buddhism and Jainism, which encouraged young men to take up asceticism, and by-pass family life altogether, a practice which did not receive the approval of the orthodox, though in later times provision was made for it. Despite their artificiality, however, the four stages of life were an ideal which many men in India attempted to follow, and thus they deserve our consideration. Moreover, they serve as a framework round which we can model the life of the individual.[17]

It is curious that Professor Basham begins by describing the scheme of the four *āśramas* as 'artificial', when in the end he concedes that the scheme could be naturally and universally applied. But that apart we may turn to those comments which are more directly relevant to the present discussion, which is to examine more closely a situation in which Hinduism, Buddhism and Jainism interacted so closely as to create room for wondering whether they were mutually constitutive. A recent study highlights this point in our context.

VI

Just as the author of the *Manusmṛti* had to come to terms with external developments (foreign invasions of India from the north-west after the death of Aśoka), he also had to come to terms with internal challenges posed by Buddhism and Jainism, especially Buddhism. In this context, the thesis recently developed by Nathan McGovern gains special significance. In his book titled *The Snake and the Mongoose: The Emergence of Identity in Early Indian Religion* (2019), he has argued that the popular impression that Brahminical Hinduism, Buddhism and Jainism had already achieved distinct identities during the period prior to the second century CE is mistaken.[18] According to him this was a period in which these identities were being contested around the issue of who was the true *brāhmaṇa*, and the concept of the true *brāhmaṇa*, as understood by us now as normative, only crystallized in the *Manusmṛti.* He argues that all of these three religions were contesting the ideal nature of Brahminhood along two lines: the relationship between the identity of the *brāhmaṇa* to the life of the householder as distinguished from the renunciate; and, whether Brahminhood was by birth or not.

Nathan McGovern argues that gradually the 'Hindu'argument for identifying the ideal *brāhmaṇa*, as a householder who belonged to that community by birth, won the day. So contrary to the popular impression that Brahminical Hinduism, Buddhism and Jainism had already achieved self-definition by this period; according to Nathan McGovern it is best viewed as one in which the identity of the true *brāhmaṇa* was being contested by all three parties along the lines mentioned above. Brahminical Hinduism à la Manu was the product of this contestation, rather than being a partner in it from the very beginning.

The view that these religions had already crystallized by the second century CE owes much to Patañjali who, in a famous reference, is believed to have compared the relationship between the *brāhmaṇa* and the *śramaṇa* traditions to the traditional enmity found between the snake and the mongoose. According to McGovern, however, 'Patanjali never made this comparison.'[19] The comparison—usually believed to have been made in the second century BCE—was mistakenly taken as the model for understanding the relationship between the *brāhmaṇa* and the *śramaṇa* communities, suggests McGovern, who feels that such an understanding of the relationship was seriously mistaken.

This claim by McGovern also provides the context for delving deeper into the historical context of the *Manusmṛti*. According to McGovern, 'we cannot understand śramaṇism as an offshoot of Brahmanism or as arising in opposition to it. The conflict in ancient India was not between Brahmans and *śramaṇas*. It was, rather, over Brahmanhood itself.'[20] In this contest the 'neo-Brahmans', as he calls them, 'embraced the householder lifestyle made possible by increasing urbanization.'[21] It was the:

> [...] success of the householder *Brahman* in arrogating the category *Brahman* to themselves... [which] led to a bifurcation between the categories *Brahman* and *śramaṇa*. This bifurcation, ...by no means inherent in the two categories, made it possible for Patanjali in the 2nd century BCE to list *śramaṇabrāhmana* ('*śramaṇas* and *Brahmans*') as an example of 'oppositional compound'.[22]

The way the 'neo-Brahmans' set themselves apart was by insisting that Brahmanhood was by birth and that it need not involve renunciation. One already sees this pattern in outline in the *Āpastamba Dharma Sūtra*,[23] but as per McGovern:

> Āpastamba's uncompromising assertion of householder supremacy did not last long. While the other three Dharma Sūtra authors reproduced Āpastamba's articulation of the *āśrama* system as a taxonomical tool for rejecting celibate lifestyles, Manu completely revamped the system so as to produce an accommodation with renunciation. That is, he transformed the four *āśramas* from one legitimate and three illegitimate lifelong vocations into four normative stages of life. This transformation

> allowed for the accommodation of renunciatory lifestyles, but only after the obligation to produce children had been fulfilled. It was this new formulation of *varṇāśramadharma* that became the ideological pillar of classical Hinduism, and that laid the foundation for the tension between world-affirming and world-denying practices that has defined Hinduism throughout its history.[24]

The jury is still out on how widely McGovern's new thesis is going to be accepted, but it is clearly in line with the kind of reassessment being attempted in this book.

7

Women in the *Manusmṛti*

I

It is necessary to begin by clearing the air as I proceed to discuss the status of women in the *Manusmṛti*. In certain circles the *Manusmṛti* has become a byword for the negative portrayal of women. I speak of this from personal experience. An Indian Christian, a woman, proclaimed, although declaimed might be a more appropriate word, at a panel at the Harvard Divinity School in the 1970s that, according to Manu a woman was the father's chattel in childhood, the husband's chattel in youth, and the son's chattel in old age and so it has been ever since.[1]

She had summarized the position of women in Hinduism in a single statement and had ostensibly drawn that statement from the *Manusmṛti*. One could see that it was a reference to *Manusmṛti* 9.3 through a tendentious translation. It is perhaps the most frequently cited verse from that text in the context of women. Patrick Olivelle translates that verse as follows: 'Her father guards her in her childhood, her husband guards her in her youth, and her sons guard her in her old age; a woman is not qualified to act independently.'[2] The next verse is also worth citing: 'A father is reprehensible, if he does not give her away at the proper time; a husband if he does not have sex with her at the right time; and a son, if he fails to guard his mother when her husband is dead.'[3] Patrick Olivelle helpfully cross references this verse with verses 5.147–49:

> Even in her home, a female—whether she is a child, a young woman, or an old lady—should never carry out any task independently. As a child, she must remain under her father's control; as a young woman, under her husband's; and when her husband is dead, under her son's. She must never seek to live independently. She must never want to separate herself from her father, husband, or sons, for by separating herself from them, she brings disgrace to both families.[4]

The position of women in the *Manusmṛti*, and then by extension, in Hindu society, seems quite dismal in light of these verses. Even if their description as 'chattel' may contain an element of what we might consider hyperbole, it could be considered only a slight overstatement of an otherwise thoroughly negative reality.

A ray of light, however, relieves this encircling gloom in the form of Olivelle's endnote on the three verses from chapter 5:

> 5.147 *Even in their ... independently:* this and the following verse have become a *cause célèbre* in anti-Manu rhetoric, even though these or similar provisions are encountered in numerous other legal texts: *GDh* 18.1–2; *BDh* 2.3.44–46; *VaDh* 25.13; *YDh* 1.85–86. Similar sentiments are expressed later by Manu (9.2–3). Clearly, Brahmanical law saw women as eternal minors to be guarded and protected by their male relatives. Other and more positive depictions of the role of women and their relationship to males, however, are often ignored by critics. The term *svatantra* ('independent') also has specifically legal connotations and is used with reference to a person who can act independently to enter a legally binding contract.[5]

Olivelle's heart is in the right place, but if we analyse the two sets of verses from chapter 5 and chapter 9 we notice a subtle difference between the two. The verses in chapter 5 describe the *duties of the daughter* in relation to her father, husband and son, while the verses in chapter 9 describe the *duties of the father, husband* and *son* towards her. This may seem a minor point at the moment, but it will be argued later in the chapter that paying attention to this kind of positioning is crucial to forming a proper estimate of what the *Manusmṛti* has to say about women. Anyone reading the two sets of verses with this sensitivity will not fail to notice that while in chapter 5 the *duty* of the female is described somewhat abjectly, *the duty of the father-husband-son* triad, that is, of the males, is described in terms of their responsibility.

In chapter 5 the daughter is asked to live under their control and not separate herself from them; in chapter 9 the father, husband and sons are first called upon to protect her; in each case the same verb *rakṣ*, to protect, is repeated. In the next verse, each one of them is singled out for being an object of reproach (*vācyaḥ*) if they fail in their duties—the father for failing to secure a husband, the husband for failing to fulfil his conjugal duties, and the son for not taking care of the widowed mother. A different ethos pervades the set of verses in chapter 5 compared to those in chapter 9, and we will see this happen again—that when a woman is treated by the father, husband and son, with an awareness of their respective duties to her, her place comes out in a very different light in the *Manusmṛti*. We get an inkling of that here.

But to stay the present course, what about the fact that women do not possess 'independence'? Olivelle hints at the fact that those who take this to mean denial of independence to the woman in general may be overinterpreting the statement, as the expression has 'specifically legal connotations and is used with reference to a person who can act independently to enter a legally binding contract.'[6] That it does *not* mean that she cannot own wealth on her own or act on her own will become clear from what follows. While examining such verses it is perhaps worth bearing in mind that in the West women could not independently open their own bank accounts until the 1960s (with the possible exception of France).

The concept of *strī-dhana*, or 'female wealth', is a well-known concept in Hindu law. It consisted of the property which belonged to her, typically received as gifts given by relations at the time of marriage, or subsequently, over which she had virtually absolute right to ownership.[7] For those who take the statement 'a woman is not qualified to act independently' (*na strī svātantryamarhati*) to mean more than it does may find it a useful corrective to recognize that:

> Manu is the earliest writer to give a comprehensive description of Strīdhana. According to him it consists of six varieties: (1–3) gifts

> given by the father, the mother, and the brother at any time; (4) gifts of affection given by the husband subsequent to marriage; (5–6) and presents given by anybody at the time of marriage, or at the time when the bride is taken to her new home.[8]

Thus *Manusmṛti* 9.94–95:

> Tradition presents six types of women's property: what a woman receives at the nuptial fire, what she receives when she is taken away, what she is given as a token of love, and what she receives from her brothers, mother, and father. What she receives subsequent to the marriage and what her husband gave her out of affection—upon her death the property goes to her children even if her husband is alive.[9]

So much for a woman's ability to *own wealth independently*. But did she possess the power to *act independently*?

For an answer to this question we need to look at the following three verses of the *Manusmṛti* (9.89–91):

> Even if she had reached puberty, a girl should remain at home until death; one should never give her to a man bereft of good qualities. For three years shall a girl wait after the onset of her puberty; *after that time she may find for herself a husband of equal status*. If a woman who has not been given in marriage finds a husband on her own, she does not incur any sin, and neither does the man she finds.[10]

It is clear from these verses that a young girl could seek out a husband for herself, if her father could not find her a suitor within three years after the onset of puberty and so could *act* on her own.

But did this ever happen? The story of Sāvitrī is worth examining in this context. Sāvitrī is a figure in the *Mahābhārata* who has become a part of Hindu lore. We plug into the narrative in the epic as she turns into a young woman. As the epic puts it:

> The princess grew up like goddess Lakṣmī in human form, and in due time the girl became an adolescent. When people saw her, who was like a golden statue as it were, with a slim waist and broad hips—they

> thought that they were seeing a divine maiden. She had eyes like lotus leaves and she shone forth with brilliance, but no one would marry her; they were intimidated by her brilliance.

They were so intimidated by her brilliance that the father had to ask her to *choose her own husband*, an obvious point of value inversion in terms of 'tradition'. The epic describes what happened next as follows:

> Then she fasted, washed the head ritually, worshipped the gods, made offering in the fire, and made the Brahmins recite duly on an auspicious lunar day. Then she collected the remaining flowers and approached her high-souled father, like Lakṣmī incarnate. After bowing at her father's feet and offering the remaining flowers, she stood beside her father with folded hands. The king felt sore stressed of seeing his divinely beautiful daughter in the prime of youth, yet without a suitor.
>
> The King said: My daughter! It is time to give you away in marriage, but no one listens to me. Choose a husband worthy for yourself on your own. Present to me the man you wish to marry, and, after making inquiries, I shall give you away. Choose what you want. As I have heard in the books of law recited by Brahmins, so you too, blessed one, hear from me as I spell it out: a father who does not give his daughter away in marriage, a husband who does not approach his wife, and a son who abandons the mother after her husband has died—all are reprehensible. Lose no time in searching for a husband after having heard me speak thus. Act in such a way that I may not be reproached by the gods.
>
> Mārkaṇḍeya said: Having spoken thus to the daughter, he deputed his old ministers to accompany her in her travels and urged her: 'Proceed.' She, confident but bashful, saluted her father's feet and, acknowledging her father's orders, set out without hesitation. She traveled to the attractive hermitages of the royal sages, seated on a golden chariot, surrounded by aged ministers. There she saluted the feet of all the worthies distinguished by age and went through all the forests systematically. She traveled through many a region, distributing largesse in all the holy places among the prominent Brahmins.
>
> O descendant of Bharata! Now the king of Madra was sitting in the assembly hall, conversing with the divine sage Nārada who was visiting him, when Sāvitrī returned to her father's place, along with

the ministers, after having visited all the places of pilgrimage and the hermitages. Upon seeing her father seated along with Nārada, she bowed her head at the feet of both of them.

Nārada said: Where has your daughter been, O King, and from where is she coming back? Why have you not given away the young girl to a husband in marriage?

Aśvapati [her father] said: It was for this very purpose that I had sent her and she has returned. O divine sage! Hear now what she has to say about the husband she has chosen for herself.

Mārkaṇḍeya said: She, upon being urged by her father to 'describe in detail' and after acknowledging the words of the divine sage, spoke as follows: 'There is a devout *kṣatriya* Śālva king, known as Dyumatsena, who later on turned blind. After he had lost his sight and while his son was still a child, he was deprived of his kingdom by a former enemy who was a neighbor, when he found the opportunity, so he left for the forest along with his wife, accompanied by the dear child. Residing in the great forest, he performed severe austerities, observing great vows. His former son has grown up in the hermitage. [His son] Satyavān is the right match for me. I have chosen him as my husband in my heart.'

Traditionally boys are preferred to girls, but in the earlier part of the narrative, her father's prodigious piety is rewarded by the birth of a girl, namely, Sāvitrī. Then she is given a name, which is the name of the mantra which traditionally only boys recite, and now, contrary to tradition, she *selects* a husband for herself. When sage Nārada points out that the young man she has chosen for a husband will die in a year, she does not budge and *overrules* her father:

The King said: O Sāvitrī, fair lady, go and choose someone else. This one shortcoming of his makes short work of all his virtues. As the venerable Nārada has said, who is honored even by the gods: his short life will end in a year when he will cast off his body.

Sāvitrī said: Only once is property divided, only once is a daughter given away in marriage, only once does one say 'I give,' these three acts are performed only once. I have chosen my husband once for all – be he long-lived or short-lived, with or without virtue. I shall not choose another. I have made up my mind, then expressed my resolution with words, and I shall follow it up with action. My resolute mind is my authority.

Sāvitrī, hailed as the ideal type of woman in the tradition, keeps going against tradition, like a kite rising against the wind.

Finally, as predicted, her husband Satyavān dies.

We plug back into the epic narrative at this point:

Then, thinking of the words of Nārada, the poor woman calculated the day, the hour, the time, and the moment. In a mere moment she saw a person wearing yellow, with a turban, stout of body, and effulgent like the sun. He had dark, white, and red eyes, he held a noose in his hand, and looked terrifying. He stood by the side of Satyavān looking at him. On seeing him, she rose with a start, slowly put down the head of the husband, and, with folded hands, spoke thus, with a trembling heart, feeling utterly crushed. 'I know you are a god because your body is superhuman. Tell me if you will, O divine being, who are you and what do you want?'

Yama said: O Sāvitrī, you are devoted to your husband and practice asceticism. Therefore I am going to talk to you, O good woman, I am Yama. The husband of yours, Satyavān, the prince, his life has come to an end. I will tie him up and carry him along. This is what I plan to do.

Mārkaṇḍeya said: O venerable one! The Lord of Death spoke to her in this way and then proceeded to describe in detail what he was going to do to her dear husband: He is devout, handsome, and possesses many virtues. He deserves better than to be taken by my servants; therefore I have come myself. Then Yama forcefully extracted a being of the size of a thumb with his noose from the body of Satyavān. The body then became lifeless, without breath, comatose, motionless, and repulsive to look at. Yama, tying him up, began to walk in the southern direction. The great and devout Sāvitrī, of perfect vows, followed Yama, beside herself with grief.

Yama said: Sāvitrī, go back and perform the obsequies. You have done your duty by your husband. You have gone as far as you can.

Satyavān, her husband, is dead. But although Sāvitrī belongs to the warrior caste, she does *not even think of committing Satī.*[11] Is it irrelevant that the *Manusmṛti* also nowhere mentions Satī as an option for the widow? But perhaps a more pertinent question to ask is: we can see how the independence of women transfers from the *Manusmṛti* to the *Mahābhārata*. But does it transfer to real life?

The *Pañcatantra* provides interesting evidence in this respect. We saw that, at least in theory, it seems to have been a daughter's *right*—that she could choose a man for herself if she was three years past puberty and her parents had failed to find her one. Some versions of the *Pañcatantra* contain a story in which the wife urges her husband to obtain a husband for their daughter who has reached puberty, because if he won't do so the daughter will find one on her own: 'When a girl remains in her paternal home after menstruation, it is laid down that she should offer herself to a husband, choose her husband.'[12] The following Sanskrit verse attributes this position to Manu:

> *ṛtumatyām tu tiṣṭhaṇtyāṃ svecchādānam vidhīyate*
> *tasmādudvāhayennagnām manuḥ syāyambhuvo'bravīt.*[13]

We began this chapter with this section to indicate how vulnerable the *Manusmṛti* is to misinterpretation, and how an interpretation, which made her a chattel of the father, upon analysis, turns out to lead to a conclusion that she might be anything but.

II

We may now embark on an analysis of the position assigned to women in the *Manusmṛti*, having recognized how liable it has been to misinterpretation.

A general point to note in this respect is that in 'the Mahābhārata, in the Manusmṛti, and in other smṛtis and purāṇas women are charged with serious moral lapses.'[14] Since we are dealing with the *Manusmṛti* here, let us see what it has to say on this point.

The descriptions occur in chapter 2 and chapter 9. Let us first examine the verses in chapter 2 (213–15):

> [213] It is the very nature of women here to corrupt men. On that account, prudent men are never off guard in the presence of alluring young women. [214] For an alluring young woman is capable of leading

> astray not only the ignorant but even learned men under the sway of anger and lust. [215] He must not sit alone with his mother, sister, or daughter; the array of sensory organs is powerful and overpowers even a learned man.[15]

P.V. Kane points out that *Manusmṛti* 2.213–14 parallels *Anuśāsana Parva* 48.37–38. While it is helpful to know the correspondence, connecting them creates the danger of decontextualizing the verses in the *Manusmṛti*, where these verses occur in the context of the student leading a life of celibacy. They are, therefore, perhaps to be read more in the nature of a warning to the student of the perils of his lifestyle rather than meant to stigmatize women as such.

The second set of verses occurs in a later chapter (9.14–17):

> [14] They pay no attention to beauty, they pay no heed to age; whether he is handsome or ugly, they make love to him with the single thought, 'He's a man!' [15] Lechery, fickleness of mind, and hard-heartedness are innate in them; even when they are carefully guarded in this world, therefore, they become hostile towards their husbands. [16] Recognizing thus the nature produced in them at creation by Prajāpati, a man should make the utmost effort at guarding them. [17] Bed, seat, ornaments, lust, hatred, behaviour unworthy of an Ārya, malice, and bad contact—Manu assigned these to women.[16]

There is more. The rant continues (9.18–21):

> [18] No rite is performed for women with the recitation of ritual formulas—that is well-established Law. 'Without strength or ritual formula, women are the untruth'—that is the fixed rule. [19] There are, likewise, numerous scriptural passages recited in the sacred books. Listen to a sample of these intended to expose the true character of women. [20] Here is an illustration of it: 'May my father keep from me the seed that my mother, roaming about unfaithful to her husband, craved!' [21] When a woman contemplates anything harmful to her husband in her mind, that is said to be thorough expiation of that infidelity.[17]

Here again it needs to be kept in mind that these words are uttered at the end of passages which emphasize the safeguarding of women, described in 9.6 as the 'highest duty of all castes' (the word translated as caste is *varṇa* in the original [*sarva-varṇānām*]). This general reference needs to be kept in mind, for once again the verses are set off against the protection (*rakṣā*) of women, so that, as in the earlier case, the intention may be to warn those who are doing the safeguarding of the delicacy of their task rather than to stigmatize women as such.

This might sound like special pleading unless one recognizes with P.V. Kane that:

> [...] in assessing passages disparaging the character of women one maxim of the Pūrvamīmāṁsā system must not be lost sight of. The maxim is stated by Śabara (on Jaimini II.4.21) as follows: 'the purpose of a text censuring anything is not censure pure and simple, but the purpose is to enjoin the opposite of what is censured and to praise such performance.'[18]

Perhaps one should cite the Sanskrit text, especially as the point may arouse scepticism: *na hi nindā nindyam ninditum prajujyate. Kim tarhi. Ninditāditarat prasaṃśitum. Tatra na ninditasya pratiśedho gamyate kiṃ tvitarasya vidhiḥ.*[19]

If we apply this principle to the material on hand, then the disparagement of women in the verses cited from chapter 2 is not to be taken literally but is rather meant to be taken hermeneutically as extolling *brahmacarya* or celibacy. Similarly, the verses cited from chapter 9 are not meant to be taken literally, but again rather meant to be taken hermeneutically as extolling the *rakṣā* (protection) of women. And should they be disparaged in general outside such a governing context, the intention again would not be to disparage them, but to extol *vairāgya* or detachment.

III

We can distinguish between two types of depiction of women in the *Manusmṛti*: one in the *abstract* (the woman in general) and the other in the *concrete*, as sister, mother, daughter and wife.

If we now look at the sister, she is identified as deserving of respect; especially an elder one. According to *Manusmṛti* 3.133: 'Towards a sister of his father and mother and towards his *own older sister*, he should behave as towards his own mother; but the mother is more venerable than they.'[20] That such an attitude is inculcated not only towards the elder sister but sisters in general is reflected in the fact that the student is enjoined to 'address a woman who is another man's wife and who is not a blood relative of his using the words "madam", "dear lady" or "sister".' (*Manusmṛti* 2.129).[21] One is also advised to avoid arguing with one's sister by the *Manusmṛti* (4.180).[22] Brothers and sisters—older or younger—get an equal share of the maternal estate and the same holds for new partitions (9.192–93; 212),[23] and the daughter's son can receive the *śrāddha* offerings (3.148).[24]

If the sister is treated with affection and respect, the mother is venerated. The *Manusmṛti* (2.145) states: 'The teacher is ten times greater than the tutor; the father is a hundred times greater than the teacher but the mother is a thousand times greater than the father.'[25] The word, translated in English as 'greater' is *guarava* in the Sanskrit text and Patrick Olivelle notes that:

> [T]he Sanskrit *gaurava*, literally "heaviness" or "gravitas", also refers to the state of being a *guru* (elder). At one level then, the meaning is that the mother is a thousand times more a *guru* than the father, who was presented as the *guru* par excellence in verse 142.[26]

This line of thought is taken to its logical conclusion in Tantra, wherein one's mother is specifically mentioned as the best *guru*. This is in keeping with the general tenor of the tradition and P.V. Kane is even moved to remark that 'in the midst of [the] dark and underserved condemnation of women there is one very bright spot, viz. the high eulogy of and reverence for the mother in all smṛti works.'[27] She forms the triad with the father and the teacher, and the *Manusmṛti* (2.234) states: 'When someone has attended to these three, he has attended to all his duties; should someone not attend to them, all his rites bear him no fruit.'[28] The mother must never be harmed (4.162); one should avoid argument with her as with other members of the family (4.180); she is figuratively linked to the earth (4.183).

In certain contexts the first offering is made to her (9.140) and she receives the inheritance of a childless son (9.217). The significance of another verse in the *Manusmṛti* (9.104) has sometimes been overlooked in this connection; it states: 'After the father and mother have passed on, the brothers should gather together and partition the paternal inheritance equally; for they are incompetent while those two are alive.'[29] Patrick Olivelle notes that 'the ambiguity of this expression had given rise to different interpretations. That the reference is clearly to the death of the parents is indicated by the last foot of the verse: "they are incompetent while those two are alive".'[30] A.S. Altekar, however, links it with the 'apotheosis of the mother' and remarks in relation to this verse: 'The widow could not inherit the property of her husband after his death; it passed on to his sons. Yet decorum required that they should live under the protecting care of the mother after the death of the father. They could not think of partition during her lifetime (*Manu*, 9, 104).'[31] The apotheosis, however, did have its limits: although she must never be abandoned (8.389), doing so was a secondary sin (*upapātaka*) causing loss of caste, and the king could punish the mother if she broke the law (8.335).

It should perhaps be added that if we look at the injunction—that the mother must not be abandoned—in an intertextual light, then it would mean that she could not be abandoned by the son even if guilty of serious sins. It is interesting that P.V. Kane concludes this point not with a direct citation but in terms of her general glorification in the *Manusmṛti*. He writes:

> The Āp. Dh. S. I.10.28.9 prescribes that a son must always serve his mother even if she had been an outcast (for some great sin), since the mother undertakes for her son numerous (troublesome) actions. Baud. Dh. S. (II.2.48) requires the son to maintain his mother, even though an outcast, without speaking to her. Vas. Dh. S. 13.47 says 'a father who is an outcast may be abandoned, but a mother (though *patita*) is never an outcast to the son.' 'The ācārya exceeds by his greatness ten upādhyāyas, the father exceeds a hundred ācāryas, a mother exceeds a thousand fathers' says Manu II.145 (= Vas. Dh. S. 13.48).[32]

Apart from sister and mother, the wife and daughter also now need to be considered in the light of the *Manusmṛti*. We examine the attitude recommended towards the daughter first before devoting a separate section to the wife. *Manusmṛti* (4.185) describes the daughter as 'the object of supreme compassion'.[33] Most translators use similar expressions: 'the supreme object of pity'[34] says one, 'the highest object of tenderness' says another.[35] One is instructed to avoid getting into arguments with her (4.180) and *Manusmṛti* (9.89) recommends that it is better that she remain at home until death, than be given to an unworthy suitor.

The *Manusmṛti* determinedly avoids the commodification of the daughter and rejects the concept of bride-price vehemently not at one but two places.[36] The following set of verses occurs in chapter 3 (51–54):

> [51] A learned father must never accept even the slightest bride-price for his daughter; for by greedily accepting a bride-price, a man becomes a trafficker in his offspring. [52] When relatives foolishly live off a woman's wealth—slave women, vehicles, or clothes—those evil men will descend along the downward course.
> [53] At a 'Seer's' marriage, some say, the bull and cow constitute the bride-price. This is totally false. Whether the amount is great or small, it is still a sale. [54] When women's relatives do not take the bride-price for themselves, it does not constitute a sale. It is an act of respect to women, a simple token of benevolence.[37]

The second set of verses appears in chapter 9 (98–100):

> [98] Even a Śūdra should not take a bride-price when he gives his daughter; for by accepting a bride-price, he is engaging in a covert sale of his daughter. [99] That after promising her to one man, she is then given to another—such a deed was never done by good people of ancient or recent times. [100] The covert sale of a daughter for a payment under the name 'bride-price'—we have never heard of such a thing even in former generations.[38]

Another context in which positive sentiments for the daughter surface is one involving the custom of the father declaring the daughter's son as his own son for ritual purposes, if he does not have a son of his own. This practice in Vedic times led to the view that one should not marry a woman without a brother, lest her father adopt his daughter's son as his own, as it were. The daughter was then called *putrikā*, a word Patrick Olivelle translates by the word 'female-son' with the following observation:

'female-son': the term *putrikā*, which is a feminine construction of *putra* ('son'), has generally been translated as 'appointed daughter', an institution that is also found in other Indo-European cultures. This translation is somewhat misleading, because, as Jolly (1885: 147–49) has pointed out, she is not merely the one who produces a son for her father but is actually a 'son' in her own right. Many legal texts list her immediately after the natural son and before other kinds of sons (see 8.158–60) within the context of inheritance. See also verse 130 about her right to inherit the paternal estate. Although somewhat awkward, I have opted for 'female-son' to highlight the fact that she is truly a son who is female.[39]

Thus in many ways the daughter was as good as a son, a sentiment expressed in *Manusmṛti* 9.130 as follows: 'A son is the same as one's self, and a daughter is equal to a son; while she stands there as his very self, how can someone else take his property?'[40] A.S. Altekar notes: 'It is true that in Dharmaśāstra literature, generally the son of a Putrikā is classed as a substitute for the real son; *in early times, however, in some localities the daughter herself, and not her son, was regarded as the substitute*'[41] and maintains that *Manusmṛti* 9.134 lends support to this conclusion: 'If, however, a son is born after a 'female-son' has been appointed, the division in that case is equal; for a woman has no claim to primogeniture.'[42]

This last remark brings the dream-run about the daughter to an end: the daughter did not inherit property as such.

IV

It is useful to distinguish between the familial and the legal aspects, while dealing with the wife in the *Manusmṛti*, just as in dealing with the daughter it was useful to distinguish between the sentimental and the legal aspects.

The union of the husband and the wife is celebrated in the strongest possible terms in the context of the family in *Manusmṛti* (9.45–47):

> [45] Wife, self, and offspring—that is the full extent of 'man'. Brahmins, likewise, proclaim this: 'The husband, tradition says, is the wife.' [46] Neither sale nor dismissal cuts the wife loose from her husband; this

> we consider the Law established formerly by Prajāpati. [47] Once is a partition made; once is a virgin given away; once it is said 'I give'—these three are done only once each.[43]

The *Manusmṛti* (3.60–62) also draws the following picture of cordial matrimonial relations:

> [60] Good fortune smiles incessantly on a family where the husband always finds delight in his wife, and the wife in her husband. [61] For, if the wife does not sparkle, she does not arouse her husband. And if the husband is not aroused, there will be no offspring. [62] When the wife sparkles, so does the entire household; but when she ceases to sparkle, so does the entire household.[44]

One could act as the devil's advocate and argue that the first two verses are only procreatively complimentary. Then perhaps the third is genuinely so, especially when read with such other verses of the *Manusmṛti* as the following (9.26–28):

> [26] On account of offspring, a wife is the bearer of many blessings, worthy of honour, and the light within a home; indeed, in a home no distinction at all exists between a wife (*strī*) and Śrī, the Goddess of Fortune. [27] She begets children; and when they are born, she brings them up—day in, day out, the wife, evidently, is the linchpin of domestic affairs. [28] Offspring, rites prescribed by Law, obedient service, the highest sensuous delights, and procuring heaven for oneself and one's forefathers—all this depends on the wife.[45]

And it is not just the wife who eats last. According to *Manusmṛti* (3.116–18):

> [116] Once the Brahmins, the dependants, and the servants have finished their meal, only then should the *husband and wife* eat what is left over. [117] After he has honoured the gods, seers, humans, ancestors, and the guardian deities of the house, the householder should eat what remains. [118] A man who cooks only for his own sake eats nothing but sin; for the food prescribed for good men is this—eating the leftovers of a sacrifice.[46]

The overall picture of harmony or even domestic felicity, rivalling the Confucian, is depicted in the *Manusmṛti* (4.182–85) in a passage which was cited earlier, wherein various members of the larger family are linked to celestial beings.[47]

The husband may entrust his wife to the sons, or become a hermit in her company according to *Manusmṛti* (6.3). When it is said that the householder can also live under the care of the son (6.95), both husband and wife are included. A spiritual air to the alliance is also given in *Manusmṛti* 9.95: 'A husband marries a wife given to him by gods, not from his own desire. He should always support that good woman, thereby doing what is pleasing to the gods.'[48] And if chastity for the wife is generally emphasized, a verse from the *Manusmṛti* (9.101–02) also presents a more balanced picture:

> [101] 'Fidelity to each other should be observed until death'—this should be recognized as the highest Law between husband and wife put in a nutshell. [102] A husband and wife, after they have completed the marriage rite, should always work hard so as to prevent them from being unfaithful to each other and thus being split apart.[49]

On the legal side, however, the position of the wife is, as it is likely to be in any patriarchy. Her marriage is arranged in most of the recommended forms of it (*Manusmṛti* 3.20–34) and while she cannot repudiate the husband, he can repudiate her legally under the following circumstances (9.77–84):

> [77] For one year let a husband tolerate a wife who loathes him; after one year, he should confiscate her inheritance and stop cohabiting with her. [78] If a wife commits a transgression against her husband who is deranged, drunk, or sick, deprived of her ornaments and belongings, she should be cast out for three months. [79] If a wife loathes a husband who has become insane, fallen from caste, or impotent (3.150 n.), who is without semen, or who has contracted an evil disease (3.159 n.), she must neither be abandoned nor deprived of her inheritance.
>
> [80] When a wife drinks liquor or is dishonest, cantankerous, sick, vicious, or wasteful, she may be superseded at any time by marriage to

another wife. [81] A barren wife may be superseded in the eighth year; a wife whose children die, in the tenth; a wife who bears girls, in the eleventh; but a foul-mouthed wife, at once. [82] If a wife is sickly but affectionate and rich in virtue, he may marry a wife to supersede her with her consent; she should never be treated with disrespect.

[83] If a wife who has been superseded storms out of the house incensed, however, she should be locked up immediately or repudiated in the presence of the family.

[84] If, after she is forbidden, a wife drinks liquor, albeit at festivals, or visits shows and fairs, she should be fined 6 Kṛṣṇalas.[50]

The situation is further aggravated by the fact that the husband can have more than one spouse but not her, and made even worse by the fact that she can be beaten according to *Manusmṛti* 7.299–300:

[299] When they misbehave, a *wife*, son, slave, pupil, or uterine brother may be beaten with a rope or a bamboo strip; [300] on the back of their bodies and never on the head. If he beats them in any other way, his liability is the same as for theft.[51]

The practice of beating though, is severely restricted (to only the wife, son, slave, pupil or uterine brother) and also subject to serious punishment (with liability, as for theft), if not carried out according to the rules. *The peculiarity of this liability is that the higher the* varṇa *the greater the punishment.*[52] As is clear from *Manusmṛti* 8.337–38, the husband is also liable to be beaten as a pupil or son or brother, *but not by her.*

This dire private picture is somewhat relieved by some privileges enjoyed by women in general. According to *Manusmṛti* 2.138, women had the right of way, an ancient Indian version of 'ladies first'. They also did not have to pay taxes at a ferry according to *Manusmṛti* 8.407. Kane also notes that:

According to Gaut. V.23 and Yāj. 1.05 children, the daughters and sisters who were married and yet stay with their parents or brothers, pregnant women, unmarried daughters, guests and servants are to be fed before the master and mistress of the house; while Manu III.114 and Viṣṇu DH.5.67.39 go a step further and say that freshly married

> girls of the family, unmarried girls, pregnant women are to be fed even before the guests.[53]

Although Alf Hiltebeitel feels that Manu 'dramatically reduces the opening one finds in the *Āpastamba* and the *Mahābhārata* to learn *dharma* from *śūdras*, which, as we have seen, both texts mention alongside learning *dharma* from women',[54] there is room to be less pessimistic in this respect in view of *Manusmṛti* 2.223, which calls upon one to emulate her in doing what is good.

V

The overall negative picture is further darkened by the fact that the woman's status is equated with that of a *śūdra*, because she is similarly debarred from Vedic studies and her rites are performed without Vedic *mantras*. In Puranic literature this exclusion is depicted as exemption, but the fact that it involves exclusion cannot be overlooked.

This equation of women and *śūdras* has given rise to some misunderstandings. One is that their exclusion from *sacred* knowledge, that is Vedic knowledge, has sometimes been taken to mean that it also involved soteriological exclusion—the fact that they wouldn't be saved, that is go to heaven or be liberated. However, in the *Manusmṛti* at least, scriptural exclusion does *not* imply soteriological exclusion of either the *śūdras* or women. In fact, even those excluded can be saved according to *Manusmṛti* 10.62: 'Dying without the expectation of a reward, for the sake of Brāhmaṇas and of cows, or in the defence of women and children, secures beatitude [*siddhi*] to those excluded (from the Aryan community, *vāhya*).'[55] That the *śūdras* could become liberated is clear from *Manusmṛti* 2.238, according to which even an untouchable *śūdra* could instruct people in *param dharmam*. The liberation of celibate women is also mentioned in *Manusmṛti* (5.159–60):

> Untold thousands of Brahmins who have remained celibate from their youth have gone to heaven without producing offspring to continue the family line. Just like these celibates, a good woman, though she be sonless, will go to heaven when she steadfastly adheres to the celibate life after her husband's death.[56]

With this clarification, we may press the equation of *women and śūdras* to see what it reveals about the position of women in the *Manusmṛti*. Alf Hiltebeitel pushes the equation further as follows:

> It is probably no coincidence that women and Śūdras are the two main targets of *Manu's* recommendations for spectacular punishments in public view:
>
> When a woman, arrogant because of the eminence of her relatives and her own feminine qualities (*strīguṇa*), becomes unfaithful to her husband, the king should have her devoured by dogs in a public square frequented by many. (*M* 8.371)
>
> If a man of lower class deliberately torments Brahmins, the king should kill him using graphic modes of execution that strike terror into men (*citrair vadhopāyair udvejanakarair*). (*M* 9.248)

The situations are not exactly parallel. In the first case regarding women, *Manu* is only improving on what *Gautama* has to say:

> If a woman has sex with a low-caste man, the king should have her devoured by dogs and have the man executed, or punish[him?] in the manner stated above. (G 23.14–16)
>
> *Manu* also improves on the punishment of 'the male offender', who should be 'burnt upon a heated iron bed' on a stack of logs in the same public square (*M* 8.372). In the *dharmaśāstra* tradition public spectacles for adultery seem to have preceded those recommended for the execution of criminals to instill public terror.[57]

In pressing the point that the *Manusmṛti* targets both women and *śūdras* for 'spectacular punishments', however, we run into a problem. The first is that, according to A.S. Altekar, it is only from about the eleventh century onwards that 'lapses of women began to be treated with greater sternness'.[58] By contrast:

> In the Vedic period we find that women who had gone astray, were allowed to take part even in religious service, provided they confessed their error. Early Dharmaśāstra writers also were fairly lenient; Vasishṭha, for instance, has no objection to the readmission of a

woman who had voluntarily gone astray, provided she really repented and submitted to a proper penance. Parāśara recommends that a woman should be abandoned, only if she is a confirmed sinner (X, 35). Yājñavalkya would advise this step only if adultery had resulted in conception (I, 72). The same is the view of the *Mahābhārata*, which further points out that man is usually more to blame in such offences than woman. Other writers have suggested that a woman should be driven out of the house only if her associates were a person of very low caste. Otherwise she was to be segregated in the house and excluded from religious functions and privileges.[59]

The heightened punishment for adultery in the *Manusmṛti* bucks this trend. It is true that A.S. Altekar does not refer to *Gautama Dharma Sūtra* and the *Manusmṛti* but P.V. Kane does, along with other sources, when he derives the following seven propositions regarding adultery:

(1) There is no absolute right of abandonment of wife [by] the husband on the ground of adultery; (2) adultery is ordinarily an upapātaka (a minor sin) and can be atoned for by appropriate penance undergone by the wife;[60] (3) the wife who has committed aduletry [sic] but has undergone penance is to be restored to all the ordinary rights of wives (*vide* Vas. X.xi.12, Yāj. I.62, Mit. thereon and Aparārka p. 98); (4) as long as the adulteress has not undergone penance, she is to be given in the house itself starving maintenance and to be deprived of all her rights as wife (Yāj. I.70, Śāntiparva 165.63); (5) a wife, who commits adultery with a śūdra or has had a child thereby, who is guilty of killing her foetus or of attempt to kill the husband or guilty of one of the deadly sins (mahāpātakas), is to be deprived of her right to participation in religious rites or conjugal matters and is to be kept confined in a room or in a hut near the house and to be given starving maintenance and poor apparel, even after she undergoes penance (Vas. XXI.10, Manu XI.177, Yāj. III.297–98 and Mit. thereon); (6) that wives who are not guilty of acts mentioned in Yāj. I.72, III.297–98, Vas. 21.10 or 28.7 are to be given starving maintenance and residence near the house even if they do not perform penance (*vide* Mit. on Yāj. III.298); (7) wives who are guilty of the acts mentioned in Yāj. I.72, III.297–98, if they refuse to perform penance, are to be refused even starving maintenance and residence near the husband's house (Mit. on Yāj.

III.298). The propositions about maintenance set out here are accepted as the modern Hindu law by the courts in India.[61]

The point which deserves notice is that, according to Gautama, if a woman has sex with a man from a low caste the king should have her devoured by dogs, but when this punishment is repeated in the *Manusmṛti* there is no reference to having sex with a man of low caste. *Manusmṛti* (7.371–72) runs as follows in English translation:

> When a woman, arrogant because of the eminence of her relatives and her own feminine qualities, becomes unfaithful to her husband, the king should have her devoured by dogs in a public place frequented by many. He should have the male offender burnt upon a heated iron bed; they should stack logs and burn up the villain there.[62]

There is no reference to the male offender being of a low caste or a *śūdra*. On the other hand, the penalty for the *śūdra* having sex with a twice-born woman is specified in some detail, right *after* these verses, as follows:

> [373] When a convict is accused again within a year, the fine is doubled; likewise when a man has sex with a Vrātya or a Caṇḍāla woman. [374] When a Śūdra has sex with a guarded or unguarded woman of a twice-born class—he loses a limb and all his possessions, if she was unguarded. If she was guarded, a Śūdra loses everything;[63] [that is, he loses all his property as well as his life].[64]

This is only one aspect of the situation; the other is that according to P.V. Kane, 'It has been seen how way was to be made by all for the bride and the pregnant woman and it will be shown that the general opinion was that no woman was to be killed on any account (with one or two exceptions in ancient writers).'[65] When we reach the point where P.V. Kane discusses the idea that women should not be killed on any account in more detail, he has this to say:

> It was only the king who was authorised, according to Viśvarūpa, to punish a woman to death for adultery with a man of a very low caste (vide Gaut. and Manu VIII.371...) but the king had to undergo a

slight penance for doing this (vide Yāj III.268). Manu XI.190 ordains that one who has killed a woman was not to be associated with, even after he performed the requisite penance. Manu IX.232 calls upon the king to punish with death those who murder women, children and brāhmaṇas.[66]

One wonders if scholars have been misled in relation to *Manusmṛti* 8.371 regarding which *suspicion persists that a low-born person is involved.* Thus P.V. Kane observes in a footnote: 'Vide Gaut. 23.14 and Manu VIII.371 (both prescribe that a woman should be devoured by dogs if she has intercourse with a person of a lower varṇa), Vas. Dh.S.21.1–5. Even this was modified later and only *parityāga* was allowed, vide vas. 21.10, Yāj. I.72.'[67]

The point to note is that, according to the *Vaṣiṣtha Dharma Sūtra*, the *brāhmaṇa* woman who has sex with a *śūdra* is *not* killed. The following punishment is to be meted out to her:

> If a śūdra has sex with a Brahmin woman, he should be wrapped in Vīraṇa grass and thrown into the fire. The Brahmin woman's head should be shaved and her body smeared with ghee, and she should be paraded on a highway naked and seated on a black donkey. 'In this way', it is stated, 'she becomes pure'.[68]

So, we still have her 'spectacular punishment in public view' à la Lady Godiva, *but without execution*.

Given this background, one is compelled to examine the verse (8.371) more carefully. Let us look at it this time in Bühler's translation: 'If a wife proud of the greatness of her relatives or (her own) excellence, violates the duty which she owes to her lord, the king shall cause her to be devoured by dogs in a place frequented by many.'[69]

Another question which arises at this point is: Is this statement of the *Manusmṛti* an *arthavāda*—a hyperbolic utterance to denounce the deed rather than one to be taken literally. The usage is current in Hindi even today that 'so-and-so should be killed on the street like a dog', when someone performs a vile and revolting deed which violates social norms.

I must apologize for abusing the reader's patience but it was necessary to cut through this part of the wood to arrive at a clearing which yields two conclusions: (1) at least in this case, pace Hiltebeitel, the equation of the woman with the *śūdra* may not hold, with *Manusmṛti* going soft on the woman but hard on the male offender, if a *śūdra*; (2) the possibility that Manusmṛti 8.371 may be an *arthavāda* or exaggeration needs to be carefully examined.

But there is more, for which we turn to the next section.

VI

Society is kept on the straight and narrow either out of fear of punishment, human or divine, or by adherence to a high moral code. The *Smṛtis* do not instill a fear which might be forbidding enough to freeze one from going astray. And although sometimes divine retribution is invoked, it is essentially moral suasion which is resorted to by the *Smṛtis*, in contrast to other cultures where the punishment for adultery was death. In *Smṛti* culture, the person of the woman was usually considered inviolable. Could it be that it was by the inculcation of virtue that the *Smṛtis*, such as a *Manusmṛti*, chose to preserve the integrity of married life? Once we recognize this, we might be inclined to take a more indulgent view of such passages in the *Manusmṛti* as the following, which deal with the duties of wives towards the husbands:

> [151] The man to whom her father or, with her father's consent, her brother gives her away—she should obey him when he is alive and not be unfaithful to him when he is dead. [152] The invocation of blessings and the sacrifice to Prajāpati are performed during marriage to procure her good fortune; the act of giving away is the reason for his lordship over her. [153] In season and out of season, in this world and in the next, the husband who performed the marriage consecration with ritual formulas always gives happiness to his woman.
>
> [154] Though he may be bereft of virtue, given to lust, and totally devoid of good qualities, a good woman should always worship her husband like a god. [155] For women, there is no independent sacrifice, vow, or fast; a woman will be exalted in heaven by the mere fact that she has obediently served her husband. [156] A good woman, desiring to go to the same world as her husband, should never do anything displeasing to the man who took her hand, whether he is alive or dead.

[157] After her husband is dead, she may voluntarily emaciate her body by eating pure flowers, roots, and fruits; but she must never mention even the name of another man. [158] Aspiring to that unsurpassed Law of women devoted to a single husband, she should remain patient, controlled, and celibate until her death. [159] Untold thousands of Brahmins who have remained celibate from their youth have gone to heaven without producing offspring to continue their family line. [160] Just like these celibates, a good woman, though she be sonless, will go to heaven when she steadfastly adheres to the celibate life after her husband's death. [161] When a woman is unfaithful to her husband because of her strong desire for children, she is disgraced in this world and excluded from the husband's world. [162] No recognition is given here to offspring fathered by another man or begotten on another's wife; nor is it taught anywhere that a good woman should take a second husband.

[163] When a woman abandons her own husband of lower rank and unites with a man of higher rank, she only brings disgrace upon herself in the world and is called 'a woman who has had a man before'. [164] By being unfaithful to her husband, a woman becomes disgraced in the world, takes birth in a jackal's womb, and is afflicted with evil diseases (3.159 n.).

[165] A woman who controls her mind, speech, and body and is never unfaithful to her husband attains the worlds of her husband, and virtuous people call her a 'good woman'. [166] By following this conduct, a woman who controls her mind, speech, and body obtains the highest fame in this world and the world of her husband in the next.[70]

VII

Two other aspects relating to the position of women in the *Manusmṛti* also deserve attention. One of these pertains to the view that, in the *Manusmṛti*, a woman is largely treated as a progenitrix. According to this view positive statements made in the *Manusmṛti* regarding women must be considered in this light, which of course takes their sheen away. That the *Manusmṛti* should be pro-reproduction is also in keeping with its patriarchal orientation. The additional point to take into account here is that if the *Manusmṛti* was composed at the end of a period which witnessed enormous loss of life, then such emphasis on reproduction takes on a survival aspect as well, and cannot be restricted to a patriarchal bias, though the two may not be mutually exclusive. The extensive provisions made for the protection of women in the *Manusmṛti* (8.28–29; 8.358) now appear in a new light.

The other point has to do with the fact that, along with the restrictions and disabilities associated with women in general, which are perfected in the *Manusmṛti*, women also enjoyed certain privileges. Thus P.V. Kane notes that 'women were not to be killed nor were they to be abandoned even when guilty of adultery. They also enjoyed the right of precedence on the road.'[71] They had to undergo only half of the *prāyaścitta* as men for the same lapse, and received honour according to the age of the husband irrespective of their own. Women also did not have to pay taxes (except those of *pratiloma* castes). Unmarried girls had to be fed before the master and mistress of the house, and 'in marriage the usages to be followed were to be learnt from women'.[72]

The question arises: does the *Manusmṛti* show any awareness of these privileges? We discussed earlier the question of violence against women and Manu's aversion towards it, and also noted how, in certain cases of adultery, women could not be abandoned. The relevant verses from the *Manusmṛti* (11.177–78) are worth citing because they go even beyond the usual privilege accorded to women. These verses state that in spite of cases of *repeated* adultery with a member of the same caste she cannot be abandoned, only a more arduous penance is prescribed:

> [177] The husband should keep an adulterous wife confined in a single room and make her *perform the observance prescribed for a man who has sex with another man's wife.* [178] If she commits adultery again when solicited by a man of the same caste, tradition prescribes an arduous penance (11 212) and a lunar penance (11.217) as the means of her purification.[73]

The *Manusmṛti* (2.138) confirms the woman's right of precedence on the road. According to *Manusmṛti* 8.407, women do not pay the toll at a ferry crossing; in terms of preferential dining of young women, the *Manusmṛti* steals a march over other *Smṛtis*, as along with *Viṣṇu Dharma Sūtra* it goes a step further and says, 'that freshly married girls of the family, unmarried girls [and] pregnant women are to be fed even before the guests.'[74]

In so far as the usages could be learnt from women, P.V. Kane seems to suggest that it might have been restricted to matters of marriage in the *Manusmṛti*[75] but the actual verse seems to involve a broader mandate, as should be obvious from the translation cited below:

> [223] If he sees a woman or a low-born man doing something conducive to welfare, he should do all of that diligently, or anything else that he is fond of.[76]

Finally, *Manusmṛti* 11.177 is remarkable for recommending gender-equality in punishment for adultery, although this right did not extend to wives having as many husbands as husbands could have wives.

There is no doubt that women, especially as wives, had a subordinate position in many ways in the society depicted in the *Manusmṛti,* but the abjectness of their condition, which is often portrayed in the context of the *Manusmṛti,* is clearly a gross exaggeration.

PART III

8

Legal Discrimination in the *Manusmṛti*

I

The legal provisions in the *Manusmṛti* discriminate among the four *varṇas* in relation to the punishments for various offences. This will become clear from a glance at the following table:

I: DEFAMATION		
Offender	*Victim*	*Fine*
brāhmaṇa	kṣatriya	50 paṇas
---	vaiśya	25 paṇas
---	śūdra	12 paṇas
Offender	*Victim*	*Fine*
kṣatriya	brāhmaṇa	100 paṇas
vaiśya	---	150 or 200 paṇas
śūdra	---	corporal punishment

Offender	*Victim*	*Fine*
brāhmaṇa	brāhmaṇa	12 paṇas
kṣatriya	kṣatriya	12 paṇas
vaiśya	vaiśya	12 paṇas
śūdra	śūdra	12 paṇas
II. ABUSE		
Offender	*Victim*	*Punishment*
śūdra	brāhmaṇa	loss of tongue
	kṣatriya	loss of tongue
	vaiśya	loss of tongue
If the *śūdra* is a victim, the *brāhmaṇas, kṣatriyas* and *vaiśyas* only pay a fine.		
III. ASSAULT		
Offender	*Victim*	*Punishment*
śūdra	brāhmaṇa	Loss of limb
	kṣatriya	employed in assault
	vaiśya	
IV. FORCED SEX		
Offender	*Victim*	*Punishment*
brāhmaṇa	brāhmaṇa woman	fined 1,000
kṣatriya		fined 1,000, head shaved
vaiśya		year-long imprisonment, property confiscated
śūdra		loses life and property
V. MURDER		
Offender	*Victim*	*Penance*
brāhmaṇa	kṣatriya	1/4th of slaying a brāhmaṇa
	vaiśya	1/8th of slaying a brāhmaṇa
	śūdra	1/16th of slaying a brāhmaṇa
A differential scale also characterizes penances.		

These examples make the fact of differential treatment—punitive or penitential—clear. We will henceforth focus on the legal aspect. The question arises: given this fact of differential treatment, what is the range to which it extends?

The eminent scholar of Hindu law, P.V. Kane, identifies the following areas within Hindu law which were characterized by differential treatment: (1) appointment of judges; (2) order of taking up causes of litigants; (3) punishment of perjury; (4) corporal punishment; (5) punishment for defamation; (6) punishment for abuse; (7) punishment for assault; (8) punishment for adultery;[1] (9) repayment of debts; and (10) punishment for theft.[2]

Appointment of judges:

According to *Manusmṛti* 8.9, if the king himself is not trying the case, a learned *brāhmaṇa* may be appointed to do so, but in no case should a *śūdra* be appointed (8.20–22).

Order of litigation:

According to *Manusmṛti* 8.24, the cases should be taken up in accordance with the order of the *varṇas*.

Punishment for perjury:

According to *Manusmṛti* 8.123, a 'just king shall fine *and* banish perjurers of the other *varṇas* but shall merely banish' a *brāhmaṇa*.[3]

Corporal punishment:

The *Manusmṛti* confers immunity on the *brāhmaṇa* not only from capital punishment (8.374–81), that extreme form of corporal punishment, but from corporal punishment itself (8.124). The guilty *brāhmaṇa* is to be banished rather than killed.

Punishments for defamation, abuse and assault:

The punishment, according to *Manusmṛti* 8.267–301, varies inversely with the *varṇa* of the offender and conversely with the *varṇa* of the victim; the category of *varṇas* employed being sometimes four (*brāhmaṇa*, *kṣatriya*, *vaiśya*, *śūdra*), sometimes two: *dvijāti* (*brāhmaṇa*, *kṣatriya*, *vaiśya*) and *ekajāti* (*śūdra*).[4]

Punishment for adultery, rape and fornication:

P.V. Kane notes that 'the punishment for *saṅgrahaṇa* (rape and adultery) varied according to the caste of the man or the woman, according as the woman was married or unmarried and according as she was guarded (*guptā*) or unguarded.'[5] This general statement applies to the specific case of the *Manusmṛti* (8.352–85).[6]

Repayment of debts:

In the matter of the rate on interest charged, the *Manusmṛti* states as an option that one 'may take as monthly interest according to the order of the castes',[7] i.e., 2 per cent for *brāhmaṇas*, 3 per cent for *kṣatriyas*, and so on. The *Manusmṛti* (9.229) also says that if members of other *varṇas* are unable to pay a fine they 'shall discharge the debt by labour; a Brāhmaṇa shall pay it by instalments'.[8]

Punishment for theft:

In the case of theft, the following scale applies according to the *Manusmṛti* (8.337–38):[9]

Varṇa	*Factor of Fine in Relation to Value of Stolen Goods*
brāhmaṇa	64 or 100 or 64x2
kṣatriya	32
vaiśya	16
śūdra	8

II

It seems that there are a few other areas of law, besides those enumerated by P.V. Kane, where elements of legal discrimination can be identified in the *Manusmṛti*.

Law of marriage:

According to *Manusmṛti* 3.13, a *brāhmaṇa* can have four wives, one from each *varṇa*; the *kṣatriya* three; the *vaiśya* two; and the *śūdra* only one.

Law of inheritance:

The provisions in *Manusmṛti* 9.149–57 may be summarized as follows:

> In the law of inheritance Manusmṛti upholds the old rule of giving the tenth part of the property to the śūdra son of a brāhmaṇa, even when the father has no son by wives of the higher castes. There also recurs the old idea that the śūdra son of a brāhmaṇa, a kṣatriya or a vaiśya is not entitled to any share; whatever is allotted to him by his father becomes his share; a śūdra can be regarded as a kinsman but not an heir. As regards inheritance among the śūdras, even if there be a hundred sons, their shares shall be equal. Thus, the śūdra sons of the higher caste people were not always certain of receiving shares.[10]

Distribution of discovered treasure:

The *brāhmaṇa* is favoured in the matter, according to *Manusmṛti* 8.37–39. If he found a treasure, he kept it; if the king found it he gave half of it to the *brāhmaṇas*. R.N. Dandekar has observed

> Even from the point of view of civil law, the Brāhman enjoyed certain special privileges. In connection with the treasure-trove, for instance, the *Manusmṛti* lays down (8.37) that if a Brāhman finds it he may keep the whole of it 'for he is master of everything,' whereas persons belonging to other classes may not do so. The punishments prescribed for a Brāhman offender are more lenient than those prescribed for the same offense by persons belonging to other classes. For perjury, persons of the three lower classes shall be fined and banished, but a Brāhman shall only be banished. Similarly, a Brāhman is not liable to corporal punishment (*Manusmṛti* 8.123–24).[11]

Law of escheat:

Manusmṛti 9.188–89 lays down the rule that 'the property of one dying heirless escheats to the king, but there was an exception in the case of the heirless brāhmaṇas—such property was to be distributed among śrotriyas or brāhmaṇas.'[12]

Exemptions from payments:

According to the *Manusmṛti, brāhmaṇas* had:

> [T]he right to cross rivers without paying any fare for the ferry-boat and to be conveyed (to the other bank) before other people. When engaged in trading and using a ferry boat, they shall have to pay no toll. A brāhmaṇa who is engaged in travelling, who is tired and has nothing to eat, commits no wrong by taking two canes of sugar or two esculent roots.[13]

According to *Manusmṛti* 7.133, *śrotriyas* (*brāhmaṇas*) enjoy tax-exempt status.

Right to take law into one's own hand:

According to *Manusmṛti* 11.31, 'a *brāhmaṇa* who knows the law need not bring any offence to the notice of the king; by his own power alone he can punish those men who injure him.'[14]

III

Let us now bring an intertextual perspective to bear on these provisions.

Areas of Hindu law where equality before the law is compromised were identified in the preceding two sections. We can hardly claim that the account was even comprehensive, much less exhaustive, but we do hope that a representative picture of the provisions was provided in these sections. Nevertheless, despite this limitation, it is clear that not *every* aspect of Hindu law involved inequality before the law. Thus according to *Manusmṛti* 8.63: 'Trustworthy men of all the (four) castes (varṇas) may be made witnesses in lawsuits, (men) who know (their) whole duty and are free from covetousness; but let him reject those (of an) opposite (character).'[15] Similarly, *Manusmṛti* 8.254 'does not introduce any distinctions in boundary disputes between villages: witnesses are examined in the presence of the crowd of villagers.'[16] Again, all *varṇas* are equally entitled to the restoration of stolen property (*Manusmṛti* 8.40). However, 'In Manusmṛti there are some general rules of conduct for all humans,' notes Kana Mitra, 'e.g. 8:350 suggests that any human can slay an assassin, yet punishment against adultery is different for different castes; e.g. 8:359 indicates that anyone except a brahmana should suffer death for such an offence.'[17] The first comment hints at the *sāmānya* or *sādhāraṇa dharmas*. As for the second comment, it seems that later on the *brāhmaṇa* was worse off for stealing someone's wealth than their wife, for Alberuni informs us that 'If the object is very great, the kings blind a brāhman and mutilate him, cutting off his left hand and right foot, or the right hand and left foot.'[18] The *Manusmṛti* also does not prescribe *varṇa* distinctions in relation to ordeals in verses 8.114–16.

Nevertheless, it is clear that differential legal treatment is the norm in the *Manusmṛti*. Why?

IV

It is impossible to answer this question without a survey of Hindu legal history, because the legal period to which the *Manusmṛti* belongs sits between a period prior to which equality before the law was the norm, and a subsequent period in which again equality before the law became the norm. These facts are not widely known so they need to be documented first, before we revert to the following question: What special circumstances account for the developments in the Hindu legal tradition during the period to which the *Manusmṛti* belongs?

If we use the term equality in its general modern acceptation as equality before the law, then a somewhat surprising fact emerges. From the thirteenth century onwards, according to P.V. Kane, 'differential punishments had gone out of vogue'.[19] He bases this judgement on three major medieval texts: (1) the digest called *Smṛticandrikā* of Devaṇṇa Bhaṭṭa (c. 1200) from the south;[20] (2) the digest called *Madanaratnapradīpa* or *Madanaratnadīpa*, which Kane often cites as *Madanaratna* (c. 1400–1450),[21] from the north; and (3) the sixteenth-century digest called *Sarasvatīvilāsa*, from the east of India, associated with the name of the king Pratāparudra of Orissa. Kane maintains, on the basis of these texts, that the 'discriminating provisions based on caste and the ascription of minor or grave sins had become a dead letter and were not being enforced by the kings of India by the 12th Century AD at least.'[22] It is on this basis that he states: 'The smṛtis endeavoured to reach the ideal of the rule of law and succeeded to a great extent in doing so. They held that every man, whatever his rank or condition, was subject to the ordinary law of the realm and amenable to the jurisdiction of ordinary tribunals.'[23]

The error one commits in invoking only the classical *Smṛti* texts, in the context of equality before the law in Hinduism, without taking the medieval *nibandhas* into account, is tantamount to confining oneself to the Tanakh or the Old Testament alone for identifying Jewish Law, ignoring the Talmud altogether. There is, besides, the larger question of whether discriminatory legislation was ever effectively enforced and if so when and to what extent?

In the light of the history of Hinduism, the following four phases in its legal history, in relation to discriminatory provisions, can be distinctly identified:

1. The early Vedic age (represented by the *Saṃhitā* period), when virtually no legal discrimination seems to have existed.
2. The later Vedic age (from the *Brāhmaṇa* to the *Sūtra* period), when evidence of discriminatory provisions is available, but any corresponding evidence of their enforcement is absent.
3. The *Smṛti* period, when the discriminatory provisions are in place as well as some evidence on the basis of which their implementation may be *inferred*.
4. The medieval period (after 1200), when the provisions had become a dead letter.

Evidence of at least a functional division of *varṇas*, perhaps without their names yet appearing as such, can be found in the *ṚgVeda* on the basis of:

> [...] other passages, apart from the *Purusha-Sūkta*, in which the division of society into *varṇas*, though not in the rigid form of later times, is mentioned. Thus, in Rig-Veda (8, 35, 16–18), the Brahma, Kshatram, and Viśah are mentioned; while in Rig-Veda (I, 113, 16), the four *varṇas* are referred to thus: 'One to high sway (i.e. Brāhmaṇa), one to exalted glory (i.e. the Kshatriya), one to pursue his gain (i.e. the Vaiśya) and

one to his labour (i.e. the Śūdra)—all to regard their different vocations, all moving creatures hath the Dawn awakened'.[24]

The presence of the caste system itself in the ṚgVedic period is a subject of much debate. V.M. Apte concludes as follows after examining the relevant evidence:

> On the whole, it is difficult not to agree with the views, propounded long ago by Muir, that the Brāhmaṇas (far less the Kshatriyas or Vaiśyas) did not constitute an exclusive caste or race, and that the prerogatives of composing hymns and officiating at the services of the gods were not regarded, in the age of the *Ṛigveda*, as entirely confined to men of priestly families. The same thing was equally, or perhaps more, true of the minor professions, as the hymn [...] refers to the father, mother and the son following three different vocations in life, viz. those of a poet, a grinder of corn, and a physician. The heredity of occupation was, therefore, not yet a recognized principle, far less an established fact. The utmost that can be said is that there were recognized professions like priesthood, or distinctions of nobility, and these had in many cases a tendency to become hereditary, but, as in other countries or societies, their ranks might have been recruited from all sections of the community. Of the other essential features of the Caste System viz., prohibition of interdining and intermarriage, no such restriction is even remotely hinted at in the hymns of the *Ṛigveda*.[25]

The existence of legal discrimination seems most unlikely under these circumstances, especially given a passage such as the following in the *AtharvaVeda* (8. 1. 3) in which, during the course of 'a dialogue between the primeval priest Atharvan and Varuṇa, the priest boasts: 'No dāsa by his greatness, not an Āryan may violate the law that I will establish'.[26] The statement is extremely significant as the actual use of the word *varṇa* in the *ṚgVeda* is confined to *ārya varṇa* and *dāsa varṇa*.[27] K. Satchidananda Murty offers the following fuller rendition of the text:

> O Man, I, being of the nature of truth and being unfathomable, have revealed the true Vedic knowledge; so I am he who gave birth to the Veda. I cannot be partial either to a Dāsa (slave) or an Ārya; I save all

those who behave like myself (i.e., impartially) and follow my truthful commands.[28]

Discriminatory provisions emerge during the later Vedic age. However, it is not yet clear whether they are still only a myth in the priestly author's mind or reflect reality. For instance, while the *Dharmasūtras* lay down punishment for adultery and theft based on *varṇa* distinctions, Ram Sharan Sharma concludes:

> So far as the operation of these criminal laws is concerned, a passage from the *Majjhima Nikāya* shows that in cases of adultery and theft the same punishment applied to the offender, irrespective of his varṇa. Therefore the discriminatory laws of the dharmasūtras in this regard need not be taken too seriously.[29]

There is evidence to suggest that the *Smṛti* texts formed the basis of law during the *Smṛti* period. One finds a statement in the Nasik cave inscription of Vāśiṣṭhīputra Pulumāvi,[30] on the basis of which it can be said that 'towards the end of this period the Śātavāhana ruler Gautamīputra Śātakarṇi (AD 106–30) claims to have restored order out of the confusion of the four varṇas by conciliating the brāhmaṇas and the śūdras (*avaras*)'.[31] Ram Sharan Sharma thinks that 'this alignment of the varṇas was directed by the brāhmaṇa ruler against the kṣatriyas, who perhaps belonged to foreign ruling dynasties.'[32] This alignment may have resulted in:

> [...] some improvement in the *śūdra*'s legal and political status. Manusmṛti's punishment for a brāhmaṇa abusing a śūdra is significant, for in the dharmasūtras the brāhmaṇa goes scot-free. Again, the fact that the brāhmaṇa ruler, Gautamīputra Śātakarṇi, felt it necessary to court the support of the *avaras* shows the importance that was being accorded to them in the second century AD.[33]

The other example is even more striking. Hartmut Scharfe remarks that in Hindu Law:

> Generally speaking, the king had no legislative power; nevertheless there are instances where kings created new rules, usually by recognizing

> existing customs. He also had ritual powers to create positive law, viz. in areas that were not covered by the *dharma-śāstra-s*. More radical were attempts to declare a certain text officially a code of law for the state: in AD 751 King Droṇasimha of Valabhī adopted Manusmṛti as a binding authority, and in the first quarter of the 16th century King Pratāparudra of Orissa had the Sarasvatī-vilāsa composed in order to replace all previous works—with very short-lived success.[34]

The reference in the passage to *Sarasvatī-vilāsa* brings us into the medieval period, when the most glaring discriminatory provisions tended to become obsolete.

In modern times, the British are credited with having introduced equality before the law in India but in view of what has been said, and what will be said soon, the claim needs to be viewed more critically. As P.V. Kane pointedly notes:

> Even in the first quarter of the 20th century, European British subjects and Europeans and Americans in general could claim in British India some startling privileges when charged with criminal offences which even the brāhmaṇas of over two thousand years ago did not claim. For example, under Sec. 443 of the Criminal Procedure Code of India (as it existed before 1923) they could not be tried by any Indian Magistrate (however senior and experienced) and that in serious cases like murder, even a Sessions Judge who was himself an European British subject could not sentence an European British subject to more than one year's imprisonment (Section 449). Any European or American could claim to be tried by a mixed jury of which not less than one half had to be Europeans or Americans, while an Indian offender could not claim the privilege in his own country that not less than one half of the jury that tried him must be Indians. In England even now a peer indicted for treason or felony must be tried by his peers and not by the tribunals that try ordinary men (vide Halsbury's *Laws of England*, 2nd Ed. vol. 25, p. 46).[35]

We may now be in a position to offer a tentative answer to why the *Manusmṛti* opted for a differential rather than an egalitarian approach to law. If the *Manusmṛti* was composed around the second century CE, then its author had two facts staring him in the face. The first was the historical fact of the Aśokan dispensation and its *negative outcome* according to him. The second was the mythic fact that he felt they were actually living in the Kali Yuga on the basis of the recent happenings. The evil consequences of both these developments had to be avoided and *both of these shared something in common—an egalitarian approach to law.*

Aśoka (d. 232 BCE), in his edicts (Pillar Edict 7), refers to *daṇḍa-samatā,* which involves the claim of having established equality of punishment,[36] but A.L. Basham, in our view, tries to avoid its obvious meaning when he writes that:

> [...] equality of all before the law was never admitted in ancient India, and was quite contrary to most Indian thought. If the *samatā*, which Aśoka instructed his officials to employ in their judicial deals means equality the case is unique; it is probable that the word implies no more than consistency, or perhaps mildness. It is hardly likely that even Aśoka was bold enough to introduce so drastic a change in the administration of justice—one which no other ancient lawgiver, Indian or otherwise, would have agreed to.[37]

The fact that such equality was not conceived elsewhere can hardly be an argument for it not being conceived in India; the fact that no king in the world gave up war after a victory did not prevent it from happening in India, in the case of Aśoka himself. Moreover, many primitive tribal cultures have been particularly known, even celebrated, for the egalitarianism which prevails or prevailed among them. Equality before the law, as a sophisticated form of it, may not have emerged then because they did not have law in our sense of the term, but to assert that it was something 'no other ancient lawgiver, Indian or otherwise, would have agreed to' seems to involve speculation rather than fact.

Apart from Professor Basham's modernist take, or perhaps even bias, that only modernity (and not tradition) can conceive of such equality, there is the further fact that Aśoka was a Buddhist and, as already noted, the *Majjhima Nikāya* argues from a position of equality before the law in cases of theft and adultery,[38] against the pretensions of brahmanical superiority. So if the introduction of equality before the law was associated with the Aśokan dispensation, which was perceived as a political disaster by the author of the *Manusmṛti,* then he would naturally incline towards a differentiated system of law. For him, the Aśokan model would have served as a warning rather than as an example.

The feeling of almost having gone through a Kali Yuga after the collapse of the Mauryan dynasty would have reinforced this attitude, for one of the features of the Kali Yuga is either the dissolution of the *varṇa* order or its reversal. Thus the 'puranic descriptions of the Kali age speak of śūdra kings performing the *aśvamedha* sacrifice and employing Brāhmaṇa priests. While referring to Kali rulers, the *Viṣṇu Purāṇa* states that the people of various countries will intermingle with them and follow their examples.'[39]

V

The differential approach to justice also involves a rather different approach to being just. It may be useful to draw a distinction between equality and equity here, or what we might call a uniform and a proportional approach to justice. Under the concept of equal or uniform justice, all are considered equal in duties and privileges. But let us think of a system in which, if we impose extra duties on persons, we balance it by giving them extra privileges, in order to be just. One might thus charge a group of people with the extra duty of protecting the community by putting their lives at risk, and in return give them the privilege of not having to render any other service to the king, for which other members of the community are liable. This second approach embodies equity—equality would involve everyone being given a chance to be a soldier and earn a salary equally.

If we recognize the distinction between uniform and proportional concepts of justice, or alternatively, of the distinction between equality and equity, then it becomes possible to suggest that texts such as the *Manusmṛti* can be seen as struggling to provide justice along the lines of equity—not fully and completely to be sure, but discernibly and recognizably.

There is a tendency in modern times to equate equality with justice. While this is no doubt justified to a great extent, it is not the only way in which justice may be visualized or actualized. There is a difference, for instance, between one's *equal* share and one's *fair* share. Paying the *same* amount to those who have worked for a different number of hours is unfair; and paying people by different rates for the *same* kind of work is equally unfair. However, more difficult work must be rewarded with a higher rate than less difficult work. All this is obvious to our moral intuition.

It seems that in the legal texts we are discussing, some attempt was made to match privileges with responsibilities. This becomes clear if we place the table for penalty of defamation, for instance, alongside that of theft. The ratio of the fine for defamation doubles with each *varṇa* as we go up the hierarchy, and the fine each *varṇa* has to *pay* for theft also goes up with rank! In other words, a proportional rather than a uniform concept of justice is at work.

It is true that the scheme is not entirely symmetrical, but the general picture seems to be fairly consistent. Thus, according to the *Manusmṛti*, a king may be virtually a god on earth, but his divinity comes with a price tag. According to *Manusmṛti* 8.336: 'Where another common man would be fined one *kārśāpaṇa* [penny], the king shall be fined one thousand; that is the settled rule.'[40]

There are even indications that some law books proposed a general *ratio*-nal increase in penalties for *all* crimes to balance the status hierarchy of the *varṇa* scheme. What the *Manusmṛti* (8.338–39) describes in the case of theft, that 'a vaiśya, a kṣatriya and a brāhmaṇa should respectively be fined twice, four times and eight times of the fine imposed upon a śūdra',[41] the *Smṛtis* of Kātyāyana and Vyāsa 'state as a general rule for all offences'.[42] In other words, *differential treatment does not necessarily imply preferential treatment.*

This tendency to align privileges with corresponding responsibilities is traceable beyond the legal realm, into that of general moral conduct. The impression that the discriminatory provisions of the *dharmaśāstras* are invariably negatively discriminatory is so strong that evidence to the contrary tends to be overlooked. Ram Sharan Sharma, for instance, remarks: 'Manu holds that the higher the varṇa, the greater is the crime in committing theft; the guilt of a śūdra is considered the smallest, *for the habit of stealing is thought to be more usual with him.*'[43] The remark in italics appears gratuitous. No evidence is provided in support. He seems more willing to concede our point somewhat when he remarks:

> In the case of theft, the law, as laid down by Gautama, imposes the smallest fine upon the śūdra, which increases if the offender belongs to a higher varṇa. Thus, if the śūdra is required to pay eight times the

value of the stolen property, the brāhmaṇa has to pay sixty-four times. While it may indicate the former's inability to pay higher fines, the law presupposes a higher standard of conduct on the part of the members of the higher varṇas, who were little expected to commit thefts. This is in keeping with the provision that only members of the first three varṇas should be appointed officials, one of whose chief functions was to protect the people against thieves.[44]

This point also seems to apply in the case of women. Consider the following provisions:

> If a brāhmaṇa approaches unguarded women of the three lower varṇas, he shall be fined 500 paṇas; for a similar crime against an antyaja woman the fine shall be raised to a thousand paṇas. The same fine shall be imposed on a kṣatriya or a vaiśya if he has intercourse with a guarded śūdra woman. If a brāhmaṇa dallies with a vṛṣalī for a night, he removes that sin in three years, by subsisting on alms and daily muttering sacred texts. While most of these laws are meant to preserve the purity of the brāhmaṇa by preventing moral lapses on his part, they make it clear that Manu also protects the purity of the śūdra woman. *This is in keeping with his principle that women of all the four varṇas should be protected.*[45]

Similarly, the *brāhmaṇa*, in keeping with his calling, is to abstain from the consumption of liquor (*Manusmṛti* 11.95), an abstention also recommended less forcefully for others (*Manusmṛti* 11.91–97). Although the *brāhmaṇa* in general has a higher status, in 'times of trouble' he also has a harder time. According to *Manusmṛti* 11.34, 'a *kṣatriya* shall pass through misfortunes which have befallen him through the strength of his arms; a *vaiśya* and a *śūdra* by their wealth, the chief of the twice-born by muttered prayers and burnt oblations.'[46]

In a similar fashion, it is true that the penalty for perjury is no doubt lighter for a *brāhmaṇa*, but then the member of no other *varṇa* is required to act as follows either:

> A priest who has stolen gold should go to the king, declare his own act, and say, 'Sir, punish me'. The king, seizing a club, should himself strike him once; the thief is purified by the corporal or capital punishment,

> but a priest by mere inner heat. A twice-born man who wishes to dispel by inner heat the defilement that comes from stealing gold should wear rags, go to the wilderness, and carry out the vow of a priest-killer. By means of these vows a twice-born man may dispel the evil caused by theft.[47]

Again, the right of the *brāhmaṇa* to the treasure trove found by him must be set beside the otherwise indigent existence enjoined on the *brāhmaṇa*.[48] It is clear, therefore, that while there are many provisions of a discriminatory nature in the *Manusmṛti,* it does not follow that all of them necessarily imply unjust discrimination, if the concept of equity is kept in mind along with that of equality.

VI

I would like to conclude this chapter by drawing attention to some special aspects of the *Manusmṛti* according to which members of the higher *varṇas* must pay proportionately higher penalties for theft. This exceptional provision becomes even more exceptional when other factors are kept in mind. The first is that it is used as the norm *not just for theft* but in at least three other contexts: (1) when a wife, a son, a slave, a pupil and a uterine brother is struck anywhere other than on the back (8.299–300); (2) when the property of a woman relative is appropriated (8.29); and (3) when someone is killed by the rash driving of chariots (8.296).

One obvious point to note is that higher punishment for higher *varṇas* is not limited to theft, there are other areas of life to which it applied. This strengthens the point just made about the relevance of the principle of equity, in addition to equality, to understand what is going on in the *Manusmṛti*. But beyond that, if we look at the parties involved in the extension of the norm of punishment, they belong to the family circle—wife, son and younger brother. But a pupil also was part of the larger family of the householder and so was the slave. So, when it comes to dealing within the family and dealing with female relatives, the male householder is held up to a higher norm. He can't talk back to them, he must give them priority in the matter of dining, and we discover that the punishment laid down for depriving them of their rightful property is also higher.

We must also finally note that theft was a major concern that the writers of the *Smṛti* sought to address, and yet in such a major area it is the higher *varṇas* which bore the brunt. How major a factor theft was in the imagination of the writers of *Smṛtis* may be gauged from the remarks of Ludo Rocher, who writes as follows while commenting on some references in the *Smṛtis*: 'This confirms something we also know from other sources: classical India's preoccupation with theft; of all wrongdoings, theft is, in this kind of text, invariably given the most exhaustive treatment. As a result, more than thirty types of theft are enumerated…'.[49] The centrality of theft as a concern of the *dharmaśāstras* means that differential treatment worked against the higher *varṇas* in this important area, as against the general impression that it worked for them.

9

The Political System of the *Manusmṛti*

I

If we accept the traditional dates assigned to the *Arthaśāstra* of Kauṭilya, then the concept of India as a land stretching from Kashmir to Kanyakumari and from sea to shining sea was already in place around the fourth century BCE,[1] and this territorial concept had also come close to becoming a political reality under Aśoka in third century BCE. When we look at the geographical horizon of the *Manusmṛti* however, we find that it is more restricted. Three key terms appear in this context in the *Manusmṛti*: *brahmāvarta, braharṣideśa* and *āryāvarta*. It might be worth our while to revisit these terms briefly. In relation to the first, the *Manusmṛti*:

> [...] tells us that the land between the rivers Sarasvatī and Dṛṣadvatī in Central Punjab was called *Brahmāvarta*; the traditional values valid in this area were regarded as exemplary. If the Dṛṣadvatī ran next to the Sarasvatī, as modern scholars believe, the area would have been a relatively narrow strip of land which might be referred to in Ṛgveda III 23,4 and where, according to Pañcaviṃśa-brāhmaṇa XXV 10,13 and Kātyāyana-śrautasūtra XXIV 6,6, special worship was offered.[2]

As for *Braharṣideśa*:

> [...] adjacent to *Brahmāvarta*, presumably to the south or southeast (including Kurukṣetra and the land of the Matsyas, Pañcālas and Śūrasenakas) was the *Brahmarṣi-deśa* 'Land of Brahmin sages' (Manu II 19). It may be asked if these two terms, i.e. *Brahmāvarta* and *Brahmarṣi-deśa*, ever had common currency; only *Brahmāvarta* occurs a few times in other sources.[3]

The word *āryāvarta* underwent gradual extension, unlike the other two. The word, translated by Hartmut Scharfe as the 'hub of the Āryas',[4] was 'according to "some"'[5] the land between the Yamunā and the Gaṅgā (according to the *Baudhāyana Dharmasūtra* I[1], 2, 11) but was soon applied to cover a broader geographical area:

> For these authorities *brahmāvarta* and *braharṣi-deśa* constituted the western half of Āryavarta which extended by common definition from the Himalayas in the north to the Vindhyas in the south, from the *kālaka-vana* 'black forest' (perhaps near modern Allahabad) to the point where the River Sarasvatī disappears into the Thar Desert in the west.[6]

This region is, however, called '*madhya-deśa* "central region" in the *Manusmṛti* (2.21) and according to the *Manusmṛti* "Āryāvarta denotes an even greater area: the land between the two mountain ranges from the Bay of Bengal to the Arabian Sea, i.e., the whole north Indian plain".'[7]

So far so good. Over the next verse in the *Manusmṛti*, however, there is some difference of opinion. The verse (2.22) runs as follows: 'The natural range of the black buck is to be recognized as the land fit for sacrifice; beyond that is the land of foreigners.'[8] Patrick Olivelle maintains that 'The original concept of Aryāvarta first encountered within the legal tradition … corresponds to the "middle region" of Manu (I.21) and this region coincides with the natural range of the antelope known as the "black buck".'[9] Thus, for Olivelle, verse 22 merely confirms the boundaries of verse 21. However K.A. Nilakanta Sastri argues differently, pointing out the special significance of the terms *brahmāvarta* (created by the gods), the land whose traditional usages set the model for others to follow;

and *brahmarṣideśa* (which comprised) Kurukṣetra. Others were to be instructed in their respected mores by the *brāhmaṇas* born in that region. He then goes on to say:

> Lastly, all lands where the black buck (spotted antelope) roams about naturally are fit places for the performance of the *yajña* (vedic sacrifice), i.e. places where Aryans could reside; all beyond is barbarian territory (*mlecchadeśa*) (23). Here is a conscious extension of the limits of Āryadeśa to lands other than northern India; and whether the test of the natural presence of the spotted antelope is literally fulfilled or not, there is little doubt that this last verse includes India south of the Vindhyas and is capable of application to Indonesia and Indochina as well. In this context we are forcibly reminded of the seven inscriptions from East Borneo engraved on stone *yūpas* (sacrificial posts to which animals are tied before being sacrificed), and detailing many Vedic sacrifices by name which were performed for the king Mūlavarman by Brahmins who had specially gone there for this purpose.[10]

Mūlavarman reigned in Borneo around 400 CE.

The question of whether the geographical horizon of the *Manusmṛti* was limited to north India, or went beyond it, may be important for assessing the political impact that the period immediately preceding the composition of the *Manusmṛti* (placed in the second century) had on it. For if its vision turns out to be restricted to northern India, then it would indicate that the *Manusmṛti* represents the Brahmanical tradition on the defensive as it were, which would have a bearing on its political perspective; similarly, if its vision extended beyond the north then that tradition could be seen as asserting itself, and perhaps even preparing to compete with Buddhism as a missionary religion in its own way. *Manusmṛti* 2.20, which describes the *brāhmaṇas* as beacons of proper conduct, could be read in this light. Moreover, we know that:

> [...] the name Āryāvarta is explained by the commentators as indicating that Āryas appear over and over again in this region; and Medhātithi, the earliest extant commentator (ninth century), states expressly that though the land may pass for a time under the rule of barbarians (*mlecchas*), yet it is soon restored to orthodoxy by the reappearance

of Āryas—a comment full of historical import if we consider his date falling after the first Muslim impact on North India and on the eve of the definitive Muslim conquest of the North.[11]

This more assertive approach will allow us to apply the commentary retrospectively to the text, as anticipating (or even generating) the concept of Āryāvarta as 'the land [which] may pass for a time under the rule of barbarians (*mlecchas*), [and] yet is restored to orthodoxy by the reappearance of the Aryas',[12] for north India *was* overrun by foreigners prior to the period of the *Manusmṛti*, and the indigenous tradition had just begun reasserting itself, of which the *Manusmṛti* serves both as an instrument and as an illustration.[13]

II

This provides the background to introduce the remarkable point that, unlike the *Dharmasūtras*, the *Manusmṛti* devotes much more attention to kingship, to which the whole of its chapter 7 is devoted; 'for the moment, it will suffice to say that *Manu* gives central attention to the *dharma* of kings—Brahmanical kings, Hindu kings-to-be—in ways that go far beyond anything in the *Dharmasūtras*.'[14] Alf Hiltebeitel identifies four important innovations of the *Manusmṛti* over the *Dharmasūtras* after analysing the work of previous scholars—two of form and two of content. In terms of form: (1) the *Manusmṛti* is in verse compared to the *Dharmasūtras*, which are in prose; and (2) its text is narrative and dialogical in form compared to the *Dharmasūtras*. In terms of content (3) as Patrick Olivelle puts it: 'The sections of Manu dealing with the king, statecraft, and especially judicial procedure, are either absent or poorly developed in the *Dharmasūtras*. It was Manu's innovation to include these dissertations in his treatise';[15] and (4) as R. Lingat puts it, in contrast to the *Manusmṛti*, the *Dharmasūtras* 'contain little or no philosophical speculation.'[16]

Let us begin by recognizing that a text in the *Dharmaśāstra* tradition now incorporated material dealt with in the *Arthaśāstra* tradition. The issue of the relationship between the two therefore comes to the surface. We begin by noting that, while 'works on arthaśāstra enter into great detail about the government of a country in all its aspects … dharmaśāstra works deal only with a few salient features of rājaśāstra.'[17] Those treatments are significant enough to be considered by writers on the *Arthaśāstra,* which focus on the state. As Hartmut Scharfe notes:

> The Dharma-śāstra attributed to Manu must at least be mentioned in this context since its seventh book deals exclusively with the duties of the king. There are strong similarities with the Kauṭalīya Arthaśāstra which in comparison generally looks more technical and older. The bulk of the Mānava-dharma-śāstra deals with private and legal matters and it is therefore classified by modern writers as a 'lawbook'.
>
> Conversely, while the major part of the Kauṭalīya Arthaśāstra deals with public affairs, the third book of it deals with the adjudication of private affairs.[18]

These descriptive comparisons are perhaps of less moment than an etiological issue, namely, is one tradition derived from the other, as opposed to being influenced by it? Although 'several scholars have attempted to derive *arthaśāstra* from *dharmaśāstra*', Scharfe is of the view that 'though there is considerable overlap of *arthaśāstra* and *dharma*-literature, especially in the later *dharma*-texts, neither can be derived from each other. *Arthaśāstra* claims as its founding fathers Bṛhaspati and Uśanas, the *purohita-s* of the *deva-s* and the *asura-s*.'[19]

Thus, if the *Dharmaśāstra* and *Arthaśāstra* constitute independent traditions, and are oriented respectively towards areas of concern dominated by *dharma* and *artha* respectively, then tensions can arise between them, especially if there is an overlap in their treatment of matters pertaining to the state. P.V. Kane seems to minimize the chances of this happening by insisting that not only the *Kāmasūtra* (1.2.14) but the *Arthaśāstra* (3.1) also accepts *dharma* as the highest value. He quotes the following lines in support:

> In any matter where there is a conflict between dharmaśāstra and practices or between dharmaśāstra and any secular transaction, (the king) should decide that matter by relying on dharma. If śāstra comes in conflict with any rational and equitable rule then the latter shall be the deciding factor and the (strict) letter of the text will be nowhere.[20]

It seems that this refers to *dharma-śāstric* and other practices as such, and to *dharma* and *artha* as controlling values. It is quite obvious that *dharma* is the controlling value of the *Manusmṛti*,[21] notwithstanding such a statement as found in 2.225: 'Some say that dharma and material gain [*artha*] are good, others that pleasure [*kāma*] and material gain [*artha*] are good, and still others that dharma alone or pleasure alone are good, but the correct position is that the three should coexist without harming each other.'[22]

There can be little doubt that the primary orientation of the *Manusmṛti* is *dharma* and that of Kauṭilya's *Arthaśāstra* is *artha*. The *Arthaśāstra* (1.7.3–6) is very clear on this point:

> 3 He should enjoy sensual pleasures without contravening his spiritual good and material well-being; he should not deprive himself of pleasures. 4 Or, (he should devote himself) equally to the three goals of life which are bound up with one another. 5 For, any one of (the three, viz.,) spiritual good, material well-being and sensual pleasures, (if) excessively indulged in, does harm to itself as well as to the other two. 6 'Material well-being alone is supreme,' says Kauṭilya. 7 For, spiritual good and sensual pleasures depend on material well-being.[23]

One could even argue, technically, that as the 'Dharmaśāstra went by the name of smṛti (Manu II.10) while *Arthaśāstra* was treated as an Upaveda', it should take precedence over the *Dharmaśāstra* because *Śruti* trumps *Smṛti*! The point though is a subtler one, as to how the dictates of *dharma-śāstra* and *artha-śāstra* were to be reconciled if they diverged. There is discussion of this in later commentarial literature. Here is an example involving the *Manusmṛti*:

> Manu VIII.351 (which is the same as Viṣṇu-dharmasūtra V.190 and Matsyapurāṇa 227.116–117) when dealing with vyavahāra (a subject that pre-eminently belongs to arthaśāstra) provides that in killing an ātatāyin, no fault attaches to the killer: while Manu XI.89 in the chapter on prāyaścittas (which is pre-eminently a topic of dharmaśāstra) states that no penance is prescribed (i.e., there is no prāyaścitta for removing the guilt) when a person of set purpose kills a brāhmaṇa. The result is

that the latter rule prevails and sin is incurred by killing a brāhmaṇa even if the latter be an ātatāyin (though there may be no punishment by the king).[24]

Others prefer a different example which is provided below. Although the text cited is the *Yājñavalkya Smṛti*, the *Manusmṛti* (8.335) contains a similar provision in relation to relatives: The *Arthaśāstra* declares that a king should endeavour to secure friends, since the acquisition of friends is superior to the acquisition of gold and land (as is laid down in Yāj. I.352). The rule of *Dharmaśāstra* is that a king has to dispense justice, being free from anger and avarice and in accordance with the *Dharmaśāstra*. Therefore, when a suit comes before a king he must decide it according to law, even though he may lose the friendship of a person if his decision goes against the latter.[25] P.V. Kane, however, draws attention to some suggestions in the *Arthaśāstra* (5.2), which *Manusmṛti* may have difficulty endorsing, such as depriving the temples of their wealth through the superintendent of religious endowments. In some other cases, however, we are in for a surprise. We would not *expect* the *Manusmṛti* to suggest a measure such as the following found in the *Arthaśāstra* (5.1):

> That when a king cannot openly put down the principal courtiers or chiefs who are dangerous to the kingdom, he may inflict punishment on them in secret or may induce the brother of the officer to be punished to attack the latter by promising to give him the position and wealth of the officer and then destroy the attacker with weapons or poison saying that he is guilty of fratricide.

Yet the *Manusmṛti* (9.267–69) advocates similar steps:

> [267] By means of clever former thieves who had been their associates and companions and who are adept at their various activities, he should identify and instigate them. [268] Under the pretext of attending a banquet, seeing Brahmins, or watching feats of valour, they should assemble these people in one place. [269] Those who do not gather there and those who have become suspicious of the source, the king should forcibly attack and kill, along with their friends and paternal and maternal relatives (2.132 n.).[26]

On one point, however, there is a convergence which would have surprised A.L. Basham, according to whom 'the *Arthaśāstra* says nothing about fair play in battle', a statement he makes in a paragraph in which he paints a rather grim picture of polity proposed by the *Arthaśāstra*.[27] The *Arthaśāstra*, however, does contain a passage which advocates fair play in battle (13.4.52), as is summarized by R.P. Kangle in the following words:

> It is laid down that when attacking the enemy in the open battlefield or when storming a fort, care should be taken to see that the following categories of persons are not attacked by his troops: (1) *patita*, those who have fallen down, (2) *parāṅmukha*, those who have turned their back on the flight, (3) *abhipanna*, those who surrender, (4) *muktakeśa*, those whose hair are loose (as a mark of submission), (5) *muktaśastra*, those who have abandoned their weapons, (6) *bhayavirūpa*, those whose appearance is changed through fear, and (7) *ayudhyamāna*, those who are taking no part in the fight (13.4.52).[28]

These provisions may be compared with the following found in the *Manusmṛti* (7.90–95):

> [90] When he is engaged in battle, he must never slay his enemies with weapons that are treacherous, barbed, or laced with poison, or whose tips are ablaze with fire. [91] He must never slay a man standing on the ground, an effeminate man (3.150 n.), a man with joined palms, a man with loose hair, a seated man, a man declaring 'I am yours', [92] a sleeping man, a man without his armour, a naked man, a man without his weapons, a non-fighting spectator, a man engaging someone else, [93] a man with damaged weapons, a man in distress, a badly wounded man, a frightened man, or a man who has turned tail—recalling the Law followed by good people. [94] When a man is killed in battle by the enemy as he turns tail frightened, he takes upon himself all the evil deeds committed by his master; [95] while any good deeds that a man killed as he turns tail has stored up for the hereafter, all of that his master takes from him.[29]

An analysis of this convergence allows us to suggest that the *Manusmṛti* tends to 'Dharmify', so to speak, the treatment pertaining to political organization in the process of drawing material from the works in the tradition of the *Arthaśāstra*.[30] The warrior's code no doubt finds a place in the *Arthaśāstra* but it is part of a large work devoted to politics; the *Manusmṛti* covers such material in far less detail, yet the warrior's code finds a firm place in it, spelled out in graphic detail. One could suggest that this happens because it is suggestive of *dharma-yuddha* (righteous warfare) and not *kūṭa-yuddha* (treacherous warfare), for the *Manusmṛti*, as a text on *dharma*, would be more inclined to foreground *dharma* even when adopting and adapting material on political science, a science more committed to *artha* than *dharma*. The moral aspect of kingship is thus highlighted in the *Manusmṛti* beyond the *Arthaśāstra*. R.P. Kangle notes that the *Arthaśāstra*:

> [...] in 8.3 mentions only seven *vyasanas* [vices], four springing from lust and three springing from anger, the *Manusmṛti* in 7.45–52 mentions no less than eighteen *vyasanas*, ten *kāmaja* and eight *kopaja*, though it goes on to mention the same seven *vyasanas* as the *Arthaśāstra* and to speak of their relative seriousness.[31]

Winternitz additionally points out that the *Manusmṛti*, by identifying *ānvīkṣikī* with *ātmavidyā* in 7.42 'gives to Ānvīkṣikī a theological turn',[32] as one would expect. In the same spirit, the *Manusmṛti* may be said to *Brāhmaṇize* matters just as it tries to Dharmify them. In the section dealing with how conquered territories should be treated, the *Manusmṛti* (6.201) shows the 'usual slant in favour of Brāhmaṇas when he speaks of worshipping Brāhmaṇas where the *Arthaśāstra* speaks of honouring *vidyāvākyadharmasurapuruṣas* in the conquered territory (13.5.11).'[33]

III

The role of the king in monarchical systems of government, which were the order of the day in the time of the *Manusmṛti*, naturally draws attention as one moves into the text for the discussion of its political system. A preliminary point may be helpful here. In the Abrahamic traditions, the vehicle for delivering justice is either God directly from heaven or his prophets here on the earth. In the Hindu tradition, however, with its acceptance of divine incarnation, typically God appears *himself* (or *herself*) to establish righteousness, as famously promised in the *Bhagavadgītā* (4:7.8). This realization may make one less uncomfortable with the Hindu hopes of a Rāma-rājya in earlier or modern times, and the raising of the king to god-like status in ancient times, because God embodies the ideal of justice, and the king asymptotically approached God in discharging the same role as a human being.

The state consists of seven elements, according to almost all authorities of *Dharmaśāstra* and *Arthaśāstra*. As the *Manusmṛti* (9.294) puts it: 'The king and his minister, his capital, his realm, his treasury, his army, and his ally are the seven constituent parts of a kingdom; hence a kingdom is said to have seven limbs (*aṅga*).'[34] The next statement is equally important (9.295): 'But let him know that among these seven constituent parts of the kingdom (which have been enumerated) in due order, each earlier (named) is more important and (its destruction) the greater calamity.'[35] So the king is crucial both from the point of view of *Dharma*-craft and statecraft. But there is a special reason as well for mentioning this point here. The author of the *Manusmṛti* was living in an age that followed a period in which the indigenous kings had been spectacularly replaced by foreign rulers. The response then was to focus on the figure of the king both in terms of *Dharma*-craft and statecraft.

But why have a king at all? The *Manusmṛti* (7.3) confirms the answer also provided elsewhere: 'The creator created the king for the protection of all this world when everything ran through fear hither and thither, as there was no ruler in the world.'[36] And this king was endowed with the power to punish (*daṇḍa*), for without it a state of what is called *mātsya-nyāya* will prevail. The term embodies the idea that the stronger or larger fish devours the smaller; the expression is not found in the *Manusmṛti* but alluded to in a variant version in 7.20: '... the stronger would grill the weak like fish on a spit.'[37] Perhaps it is because of the anarchy which prevailed in the period preceding the composition of the *Manusmṛti* that 'Daṇḍa is raised to the status of a divinity in Manu [VII.25].'[38]

The king had been endowed with divinity even in Vedic times,[39] but when we look at the *Manusmṛti* we find five conceptions of him. As we begin to review them, it might be useful to note that the promotion of the idea of the divinity of king in human form 'should be understood as the *Dharmaśāstra* experts' attempt to exalt the institution of kingship, rather than as a theory of the divinity of kings.'[40] In the first conception, found in *Manusmṛti* 7.3–4, the ruler is described as having been created 'by extracting external particles',[41] from the gods 'Indra, wind, Yama, sun, fire, Varuṇa, moon and the lord of wealth [Kubera]',[42] who are 'the eight guardian deities of the cardinal points, beginning with Indra in the east and ending with Kubera, the lord of wealth, in the north.'[43] In another conception, found in *Manusmṛti* 9.303–11, the ruler is asked to emulate the 'energetic activity of Indra, sun, wind, Yama, Varuṇa, moon, fire and earth'.[44]

As Patrick Olivelle notes, 'these eight guardian deities of the directions are the gods from whose particles the king was initially created (see 7.4); the only difference is that earth is here substituted for Kubera. He must, therefore, imitate their activities.'[45] Olivelle therefore sees this second conception as reinforcing the first, but P.V. Kane sees this as diluting it.[46] The third conception is found in *Manusmṛti* 7.111–12, which makes him a mortal: 'When a king in his folly oppresses his own realm indiscriminately, he is soon deprived of his kingdom and his life, along with his relatives.[47] As living beings destroy their lives by oppressing their bodies, so kings too destroy their lives by oppressing their realms.'[48] The fourth conception of the king turns on his relation to *daṇḍa*, as spelled out in *Manusmṛti* 7.24–28, wherein *daṇḍa* is translated as Punishment:

> [24] All the social classes would become corrupted, all boundaries would be breached, and all the people would revolt, as a result of blunders committed with respect to Punishment. [25] Wherever Punishment, dark-hued and red-eyed, prowls about as the slayer of evil-doers, there the subjects do not go astray—so long as its administrator ascertains correctly. [26] The proper administrator of Punishment, they say, is a king who speaks the truth, acts after careful examination (7.19 n.), is wise, and has a masterly grasp of Law, Wealth, and Pleasure. [27] When a king administers Punishment properly, he flourishes with respect to the triple set (2.224 n.); but the king who is lustful, partial, and vile is slain by that very Punishment. [28] For Punishment is immense energy, and it cannot be wielded by those with uncultivated selves. It assuredly slays a king who deviates from the Law, along with his relatives.[49]

If we look at these views in the light of the two broad theories explaining the rise of kingship, namely, that of the divine origin of kingship (to be distinguished clearly from the divine right of kings) and the social contract theory echoed in some Buddhist texts, then it is worth noting that the first two conceptions of the king conform to the divine origin or orientation of kingship, while the last two have more of an element of the social contract, in the sense that the king becomes answerable to the people, either directly through the action of the people or by finding himself at the receiving end of *daṇḍa* by not employing it properly in relation to the people. In this sense we can say that the *Manusmṛti* 'makes use of both the theories as the occasion demands'.[50]

We saw earlier how the concept of the king being constituted by the elements of the *lokapālas* is propounded in the *Manusmṛti*. But how does this model work in the case of an undesirable king? Later political thought, represented in the Śukranītī (date uncertain) propounded the view that 'a king who oppresses the subjects and causes loss of dharma is made up of the parts of *rākṣasas* or demons'.[51] Given the political scene which preceded the *Manusmṛti,* one would not have been surprised if similar views had been expressed within it. Similarly, according to the *Rājanītiprakāśa* of Mitamiśra, 'the idea of the king having in him parts of the deities applied only to the mahārāja (the sovereign ruler), while the idea of a ruler doing the functions of the five deities applied only to vassal kings.'[52] One would also not have been surprised if this concept had also been elaborated in the *Manusmṛti*, but perhaps kingship on the galactic model was not yet established, as it would be in the Gupta period within a few centuries.

IV

One remarkable feature of the *Manusmṛti* which remains to be discussed is that it does not refer to the king as *dharmarāja* or *dharmarāṭ*. The latter expression does appear in the *Manusmṛti* but only as a synonym of Yama (7.7).

This is particularly noticeable as there are parallels between the *Mahābhārata* and the *Manusmṛti* and Yudhīsṭḥira is regularly addressed as *dharmarāja* in the *Mahābhārata*.[53] In fact, at one point, Kṛṣṇa even explains therein precisely why he is so called (3.180.18). Given this background and the role of the king as the upholder of *dharma* in the *Manusmṛti*, one could reasonably expect the king to have borne the epithet of *dharmarāja* therein. Could this omission be significant, and if so, how?

That it could be potentially significant is suggested by the fact that King Aśoka is often characterized as such. While discussing Aśoka's *dhamma* D.R. Bhandarkar notes that 'Evidently Aśoka is here aspiring to be a *chakravarti dhārmika dharmarāja*'[54] as defined in the Pali *suttas.* He goes on to say: 'There can hardly be any doubt that Aśoka took his cue for *dhamma-vijaya* from Buddhist *suttas* and aspired to become a *charavarti dhārmika dharmarāja.*'[55] Archaeological evidence confirms the strong association of the word *dharmarāja* with Aśoka. Nayanjot Lahiri notes that 'the most impressive Buddhist monument in Taxila was a stupa whose name, dharmarajika, alludes to Ashoka'.[56]

It is, therefore, quite possible that the *Manusmṛti* avoids the word *dharmarāja* on account of its association with Aśoka, and its author may have had some sympathy for the following counterfactual scenario:[57]

> And if the vision of the *chakravarti dhārmika dharmarāja* had not possessed and absorbed his mind, the empire of Magadha in the first instance would have extended over the whole of this country, making India one nation and afterwards might also have spread even beyond, making Pāṭaliputra, like Rome, the capital of a world power. But in consequence of the foreign policy of *dhamma-vijaya* inaugurated by Aśoka, India was lost to nationalism and political greatness.[58]

One striking feature of the *Manusmṛti* in relation to *dharma* must not be overlooked as one concludes this chapter. It consists of the king not being above the law. Although Patrick Olivelle consigns this point to an endnote, perhaps it deserves to be highlighted. *Manusmṛti* 8.336 lays down that 'In a case where an ordinary person is fined 1 kārṣāpaṇa, the king should be fined 1,000—this is the fixed rule.'[59] The context is that of theft. Patrick Olivelle remarks that 'this is quite a significant rule. If taken at its face value, it implies that even the king is not above the law! Commentators point out that in the case of the king, the fine should be thrown into water (9.245).'[60]

The argument seems to come full circle. By declaring a king as *dharmarāja* the king is in a sense almost placed above *dharma* in the Buddhist context, whereas in the *Manusmṛti,* the king is placed under *dharma,* by being made subject to it.

10

Foreign Policy in the *Manusmṛti*

I

Hindu political thought evolved what would appear to be an elaborate set of concepts during the centuries around the Common Era, which proved in some ways a lasting legacy. To assess the extent to which foreign policy advocated by the *Manusmṛti* was influenced by these concepts requires some prior acquaintance with them.

An important concept in this set is that of the *rāja-maṇḍala* or the circle of kings. This *maṇḍala* consists of a set of twelve kings or states, but there are two distinct ways in which this figure of twelve is arrived at. According to one view the four main political units involved are: (1) the *vijigīṣu* or the king who wishes to enlarge his empire by conquest; (2) the *ari*, the enemy next door; (3) the *madhyama* or the state which territorially adjoins the kingdoms of both the *vijigīṣu* and the *ari*, but is stronger than either; and (4) the *udāsīna*, the neutral king who is more powerful than all three—the *vijigīṣu*, the *ari* and the *madhyama*. Each of these kingdoms has an ally or *mitra* as well as an ally's ally or *mitra-mitra*, which amounts to twelve kings or states. Each of these four, along with their two allies *mitra* and *mitra-mitra*, are then visualized as constituting a *maṇḍala*. These four could be considered as constituting a subsidiary *maṇḍala* or circle compared to the more elaborate system of *rāja-maṇḍala* which will be introduced next.[1]

The other more elaborate scheme of the *rāja-maṇḍala* consists of the following twelve kings or states, perhaps best visualized in concentric circles: (1) *vijigīṣu*, the king bent on conquest; (2) *ari*, the enemy whose territory is contiguous with the *vijigīṣu*; (3) *mitra*, the ally whose territory adjoins that of the *ari*; (4) *ari-mitra* or the friend of the enemy, on the principle that the neighbour's neighbour is one's friend; (5) *mitra-mitra,* or the friend's friend, whose principality is next to that of the *ari-mitra*; and (6) *ari-mitra-mitra,* or the ally of the enemy's ally, beyond the *mitra-mitra*. This covers the top half of the circle. Next we look at the bottom half of the *vijigīṣu*. This gives us: (7) the *pārṣṇi-grāha*, literally 'heel-catcher',[2] the state or kingdom situated in the rear of the *vijigīṣu;* (8) *ākranda* or the *vijigīṣu's* ally in the rear (The word literally means a 'scream');[3] (9) *pārṣṇi-grāhā-sāra*, or the ally of the heel-catcher, just beyond *ākranda*; and (10) *ākranda-sāra*, the ally of the *ākranda*. This completes the circle in a way, but we get the full complement of the circle by adding two states not directly involved but relevant to this state of affairs, namely: (11) *madhyama*, literally in the middle, whose territories border on the *vijigīṣu* and the *ari* but who is stronger than either; and finally, (12) *udāsīna*, the neutral king who is more powerful than the *vijigīṣu*, the *ari* and the *madhyama.*

It is possible that this second scheme, in which the relationship of the *vijigīṣu* and the *ari* is parsed out in greater detail, is an elaboration of an earlier less ambitious version; or that the first scheme is a contraction of the more elaborate earlier scheme. In any case, the following diagram offers a partial visualization of the scheme:

POLITICAL GEOMETRY[4]

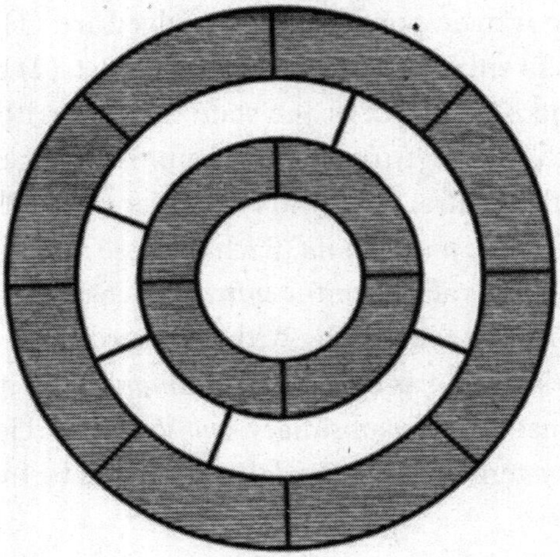

Although the diagram illustrates the idea well and the word *maṇḍala* is suggestive of a circle, it is worth noting that:

> [...] though the *maṇḍala* suggests the idea of states concentrically situated round the *vijigīṣu's* state, the actual idea is that of the states in a straight line lying one beyond the other Neither idea in its entirety might conform with the actual state of things prevailing at any time anywhere.[5]

Three additional points are worth noting before we leave this category: (1) These terms are elastic so that 'the same king may become a *pārṣṇigrāha* or an *ari* or a *mitra* or even a *vijigīṣu* in changed circumstances';[6] (2) The number twelve is not a numerical necessity for the application of the scheme, rather it suggests the pattern of possible relationships;[7] and (3) the numerous divisions seem to presuppose a number of states for the model and while this may have been the original intention, the size of states does not matter, and larger states could be involved. In fact 'the very conception of *vijigīṣu* presupposes the ideal of a large state'.[8]

Another key category, along with the *rājamaṇḍala*, is that of *prakṛti*. Every state is endowed with seven *prakṛtis* or factors, also known as the seven elements of the state (*saptāṅga*): '(1) *svāmin* (ruler or sovereign); (2) *amātya* (minister); (3) *janapada or rāṣṭra* (the territory of the state and its people); (4) *durga* (fortified city or capital); (5) *kośa* (accumulated wealth in the ruler's treasury); (6) *daṇḍa* (army) and (7) *mitra* (friends or allies).'[9] P.V. Kane points out that 'the word prakṛti in works on politics is also used for the constituents of a circle of states (of a maṇḍala).'[10] He cites *Manusmṛti* 7.156 in support. The last six are also called *dravya prakṛtis*. Thus the *rāja-maṇḍala* has 'twelve kings, (*rāja-prakṛtis*), and sixty *dravya-prakṛtis*, that is seventy-two *prakṛtis* in all',[11] according to the *Ārthaśāstra* (6.2.28) and the *Manusmṛti* (7.156).

Another important category, apart from that of *rāja-maṇḍala* and *prakṛti*, is that of *ṣāḍguṇya*, or the six measures. This formula is also associated with that of the *rāja-maṇḍala* although it does not necessarily presuppose it,[12] just as the concept of *prakṛti* is associated with that of the *rāja-maṇḍala* but does not necessarily presuppose it. This formula of *ṣāḍguṇya*:

> [...] which sums up foreign policy consists of six *guṇas* or policies: *saṃdhi*, making a treaty containing conditions or terms, that is, the

> policy of peace; *vigraha*, the policy of hostility; *āsana*, the policy of remaining quiet (and not planning to march on an expedition); *yāna*, marching on an expedition; *saṃśraya*, seeking shelter with another king or in a fort; and *dvaidhībhāva*, the double policy of *saṃdhi* with one king and *vigraha* with another at the same time.[13]

This statement is based on the *Arthaśāstra* (7.1.6–12). Its author, Kauṭilya, refers to it, only to reject it for 'a notion of only two strands (*dvaiguṇya*) e.g. treaty and conflict',[14] while another authority 'recognized three strands (*traiguṇya*) i.e., treaty, conflict and seeking shelter (KN XI.38)'.[15] Hartmut Scharfe proceeds to remark: 'If the expression *ṣadguṇya*, *traiguṇya*, and *dvaiguṇya* were taken from braiding (as seems likely), at least three strands would be appropriate (cf. the three *guṇas* of Sāṃkhya!).'[16]

If we wish to link the three concepts hitherto discussed then, as Hartmut Scharfe states, 'the "factors" (*prakṛti*) are the basis (*yoni* "womb") of the "circle" (*maṇḍala*) of the states. This circle of the states in turn is the basis of the "aggregate of six strands".'[17]

A fourth set of terms is provided by the concept of the four *upāyas*, often listed as: (1) *sāma*; (2) *dāna*; (3) *bheda*; and (4) *daṇḍa,* in terms of priorities. The key point underlying them is 'the overcoming of opposition'.[18] Opposition can be overcome by persuing a policy of conciliation, which would be *sāma*. If that fails, it could be overcome by offering financial inducements or *dāna*. If that fails, the seeds of dissension can be sown within the rival party, which would be *bheda*. Finally, force or *daṇḍa* might be used to overcome opposition. Some overlap between the *ṣadguṇas* and the *upāyas* is evident, although both sets of concepts 'may be equally old'[19] and 'the two concepts appear to have arisen independently'.[20] In both, recourse to war and use of force is only recommended as a last resort.[21] Thus there is 'something in common between *sāman* and *saṃdhi* and between *daṇḍa* and *vigraha* combined with *yāna*'.[22] However, the category of *upāyas* is capable of wider application, as it relates to the overcoming of opposition in general, 'while the *guṇas* are concerned with foreign policy only'.[23] This list of *upāyas* is enlarged in the *Mahābhārata* to include *naya* (design); *māyā* (deceitful trick); *upekṣā* (indifference), and *indrajāla* ([frightening] illusion).[24] Heinrich Zimmer omits *naya*, thereby reducing the number to seven and adds: 'These, then, are the seven ways to approach a neighbour in this unsentimental glean of fish [*mātsya-nyāya*]. I wonder whether we have textbooks in politics in the west that cover the subject with more simplicity and clarity.'[25]

These examples do not exhaust the concepts evolved by Hindu political thought, which also includes the concept of *śakti* or power, of which three are identified in the *Arthaśāstra*. The first is *utsāha* or the vigour and enthusiasm of the king, the second is *prabhāva* or the material resources at the king's command, and the third is *mantra* or counsellor diplomacy. The *Arthaśāstra* differs from its predecessors in emphasizing *mantra-śakti*. It holds might or *prabhāva* as more important than energy or *utsāha*, but to those who think 'between might and counsel, might is superior':

> 13 'No,' says Kauṭilya. 14 'The power of counsel is superior; 15 for a king, with the eyes of wisdom and science (8.2.9 n.), is able with even the slightest effort to embrace counsel and to outwit even enemies possessing energy and might through strategies such as conciliation (1.13.25 n.) and by means of secret measures (Book 5) and occult practices (Book 14).'
>
> 16 Thus, among the powers of energy, might, and counsel, it is the man who has more of each later one who outwits.[26]

The idea of *śakti* is also combined with that of *deśa* and *kāla*, or the time and place, or where and when the *śakti* or power should be exercised. The *Arthaśāstra* questions giving priority to one over the other, for according to it 'power, place, and time reinforce one another'.[27]

Another set of concepts distinguishes between various kinds of *yuddha* or battle. Battle is classified as of three types: *prakāśa-yuddha* or open warfare; *kūṭa-yuddha* or tricky warfare; and *tūṣṇīṃ-yuddha* or silent fight, or what modern psychology calls passive aggression. The concept of open battle is self-evident; and 'a fight, about the place and time of which notice has been given, is considered righteous, *dharmiṣṭha* (10.3.26)'. A curious parallel is provided here by the *non*-violent campaigns of Mahatma Gandhi, who always served advance notice to the opposite party. An example of *kūṭa-yuddha* would be to feign retreat and then attack. An example of *tūṣṇīṃ-yuddha* would be espionage and the use of agent provocateurs.

The various battle-formations yield another set of concepts called *vyūhas*. These have been summarized well by Patrick Olivelle:

> [In] the staff formation the army is arranged in a line with the field general (*balādhyakṣa*) in the front, the commander-in-chief (*senāpati*) at the rear, and the king in the middle, with the flanks protected by elephants and horses. This is used when danger is expected from all sides. In the wagon formation, used when there is a threat from the rear, the front is narrow like a needle and the rear is broad. In the boar, used when danger is perceived from the flanks, the front and the rear are narrow and the middle broad. In the crocodile, used when danger is expected from the front and the rear, the front and the rear are broad and the middle is narrow. In the needle, used when an attack is expected from the front, the army is arranged in a thin and long formation. The eagle formation is similar to the boar, except that it has longer wings extending outwards on the flanks. For a detailed discussion of these and other military formations, see *AŚ* 10.5–6.[28]

Finally, the victory secured is capable of a triple and a double classification. Thus the *Arthaśāstra* distinguishes between *dharma-vijaya*, *lobha-vijaya* and *āsura-vijaya*, in a well-known passage (12.10–16):

> 10 There are three kinds of attackers: one who conquers righteously, one who conquers out of greed, and one who conquers demoniacally. 11 Of those, one who conquers righteously is satisfied with submission. 12 He should submit to such a man; he should do so also when there is danger from enemies. 13 One who conquers out of greed is satisfied with plundering his land and property. 14 He should submit to such a man by giving money. 15 One who conquers demoniacally is satisfied with plundering his land, property, sons, wives, and life. 16 He should appease such a man with land and property and then, making himself unsusceptible to capture, take countermeasures.[29]

The other major distinction is between *dig-vijaya* and *dharma-vijaya*, which find their respective orientations in a Hindu and Buddhist context. The word *dharma-vijaya* here needs to be carefully distinguished from the same word as used in the *Arthaśāstra*, where it is a form of martial victory. King Aśoka achieved a martial victory over Kaliṅga. Incidentally, 'Kalinga also happened to be situated to the east, the direction where prospective world rulers traditionally began their conquest,'[30] which is traditionally called *dig-vijaya*. But in Rock Edict 13 'Aśoka speaks with regret about the suffering that occurred in the Kalinga war; he then goes on to praise the *dhamma-vijaya* [or *dharma-vijaya*] which has brought happiness to everybody in his own empire and abroad, for this world and the next.'[31] Thus here we have a new concept:

> In brahmanical theory *dharma-vijaya* 'conquest in accordance with righteousness' means a conquest of other countries whose rulers are reinstated in a dependent role with regional autonomy. For Aśoka, *dhamma-vijaya* 'conquest through righteousness' meant this and more: the gain of supremacy in the way of the mythical *cakkavattins* ... who rules with no blow struck.[32]

This concept of *dharma-vijaya*, although rooted in Buddhist mythos, does not seem to have much to do with the doctrinal form of Buddhism; in it there is 'no mention of *nirvāṇa* and other important dogmas, and instead several references to attainment of heaven'.[33] Thus several distinctions are involved here: (1) between *dig-vijaya* and *dharma-vijaya*; and then, (2) between the concept of *dharma* as found in Buddhist *dharma* or *dhamma*, and as found in the expression *dharma-vijaya*. Aśoka's *dhamma* in *dhamma-vijaya* should not be equated with Buddhism as such.[34] In the case of Aśoka, after the Kaliṅga war, 'the era of military conquest or *digvijaya* was over, the era of spiritual conquest or *dhamma-vijaya* was about to begin.'[35]

II

How these concepts get played out in the case of the *Manusmṛti* can potentially make a valuable contribution to our understanding of the politics in and around the time of the *Manusmṛti*.

The first point which arrests attention is that the word *cakravartī* is conspicuous by its absence, although the word had become current by the time the *Manusmṛti* was composed. The Manchapuri cave at Udayagiri belongs to the time of king Khāravela, who ruled over Kalinga around the beginning of the Christian era. In its fourth line it 'seems to describe Kharavela as the *cakavati* (that is, *cakravartin*) of Kalinga. If this reading is correct, it is the earliest epigraphic use of the epithet *cakravartin* by a historical king of ancient India.' In earlier and later literature, the word is used to signify the 'universal monarch', the universe here being coterminous with the Indian subcontinent. It is found in the *Bṛhaddevatā* (5.123) and in the *Maitrī Upaniṣad* (1.4): 'But indeed what of these? There are others, superior, great warriors, some world-rulers [*cakra-vartinaḥ*], Sudyumna, Bhūridyumna, Indradyumna, Kuvalayāśva, Yauvanāśva, Vadhryaśva, Aśvapati, Saśabindu, Hariścandra, Ambarīṣa, Anantaka, Saryāti, Yayāti, Anaraṇya, Ukṣasena …'[36] It is also found in the *Māhābhārata*,[37] and in the Purāṇas (e.g. *Vāyupurāṇa* 57.72). It is, however, absent in the *Manusmṛti,* wherein the word used most often is *vijigīṣu* or the king desirous of conquering.[38]

One reason why this omission is puzzling is that the *Manusmṛti* discusses the *rāja-maṇḍala* in some detail, and the words *maṇḍala* and *cakra* can both indicate a circle. So, the *cakravartin* could easily fit into the picture, if taken to mean the ruler who sets the whole *cakra* or circle, the *rājamaṇḍala,* in motion. No wonder then that the 'word "cakravartin" is derived by Kṣīrasvāmin as "one who wields lordship over a circle of kings" or "who makes the circle (i.e) kingdom abide by his orders".'[39] P.V. Kane traces 'one of the earliest references to the derivation of the word *cakravartin*' to a passage in the *Sāmavidhāna Brāhmaṇa* (III.5.2): 'The priest should perform the coronation with the ekavṛṣa sāman for the king whom he desires to be the sole ruler and whose circle of territory (he does not desire) to be overwhelmed (by an enemy).'[40] Thus it should not come as a surprise that H. Jacobi proposed the translation of the word *cakravartin* as '"ruler of a circle', in which *cakra* would be the forerunner of the classical *maṇḍala* "circle [of states], political system" that is found in the Arthaśāstra and in Manu.'[41] But as Hartmut Scharfe notes:

> [...] *cakra,* however, is not attested in this meaning, and one would expect to find an occasional *maṇḍalavartin*; this occurs only in the late (ninth century A.D.) Bhāgavata-Purāṇa VI 3.6 in the meaning of vassal when *maṇḍala* had acquired the meaning 'large province' as in *cola-maṇḍala.* Furthermore, the notion 'ruler of the circle' does not help us to understand the Buddhist imagery of the *cakka.*[42]

Our semantic surprise—at the absence of the word *cakravartin* in the *Manusmṛti*—is taken care of in one sense, but the reference, at the end of the previous paragraph, to the Buddhist association of the word *cakra*, opens up another area of possible explanation of the absence of the word in the *Manusmṛti*, although the etymological explanation of the word is disputed.[43]

One can distinguish between Hindu and Buddhist conceptions of the *cakravartin* around the use of *daṇḍa* or coercive force. Heinrich Zimmer offers an interesting portrayal of the Hindu version:

> Ideally, the science of government, as reviewed in the *Arthaśāstra*, stands for the daṇḍa of dharma. The king is the chief policeman of dharma within the realm that he controls, being the maintainer and staff (*daṇḍa*) of the revealed ritualistic order of civil life. Mutual good will, forbearance, and cooperation among the individuals, groups, trades, and castes are demanded within each state, just as within the fold of a family but there is no hope, according to the Indian conception, that this peaceful pattern of well-controlled, harmonious human decency should ever become transferred to the larger field of the nations.[44]

This could be contrasted with his portrayal of the Buddhist version:

> According to the Buddhist conception, the Universal Monarch is the secular counterpart of the Buddha, the 'Enlightened One', who himself is said to have 'set in motion the wheel of the sacred doctrine'. Like the Cakravartin, the Buddha is the master, not of a national or otherwise limited communion, but of the world. His wheel, the Buddhist dharma, is not reserved for the privileged castes, like the dharma of the Brāhmans, but is for the whole universe; a doctrine of release intended to bring peace to all living beings without exception. The Buddha and the Cakravartin, that is to say, manifest the same universal principle, one on the spiritual, the other on the secular plane; and both bear on their bodies, already at birth, certain characteristic auspicious signs in token of their mission: the thirty-two great marks (*mahāvyañjana*), and the numerous additional secondary marks (*anuvyañjana*).[45]

The contrast may be somewhat exaggerated but serves as a useful background for the point one wishes to make. The core point is that 'while the Hindu king is advised to keep the rod of punishment ready and visible, for it alone assures public adherence to morality and order', the 'Buddhist righteous ruler has no need of it since it is the magical wheel (*cakka*) that preserves the order, without force, supported only by the king's correct and compassionate administration of his office.'[46]

We shall revert to this contrast later. The point to note at the moment is that:

> In brahminical theory *dharma-vijaya* 'conquest in accordance with righteousness' means a conquest of other countries whose rulers are reinstated in a dependent role with regional autonomy. For Aśoka, *dhamma-vijaya* 'conquest through righteousness' meant this and more: the gain of supremacy in the way of the mythical *cakkavattin-s*, i.e., the magic wheel (*cakka-ratana*) moves ahead of the army, and as the king marches first east, then south, west and north, the other kings welcome him, submit to his rule with no blow struck, and turn to him for instruction in righteousness. Aśoka sent envoys to Ceylon, the South Indian states, and the Hellenistic states to the west (with no army following) and claimed success. Only Ceylon may have entered into some kind of dependency, but Aśoka obviously saw himself as a world leader, viewing perhaps his moral leadership only as a first step towards general acclamation. He urged his successors not to look for new conquests except 'conquests through righteousness', and if punishment could not be quite abandoned, it should be mild.[47]

It could well be that when the Mauryan dynasty collapsed in the face of the foreign invasions, *this failure came to be associated with the Buddhist ideal of the cakravartin as espoused by Aśoka*. In fairness it must be added that Aśoka did not entirely foreswear the use of force. B.N. Mukherjee notes that 'H.C. Raychaudhuri held the propagations against war and military conquest, preached by Aśoka's Dhamma, as responsible for the political disaster which later befell the empire', but adds that 'Aśoka did not altogether forbade the violence and war [*sic*]. He advised impartiality in the case of violence, and humane treatment in case of a conquest

(RE XIII). If the empire did not last long after Aśoka, it was due to the weakness and inefficiency of his successors'.[48] Aśoka also warned the Āṭavikas or forest-dwellers of the limits of his patience.[49] It is nevertheless hard to deny that:

> From the time of Bimbisāra to the Kaliṅga war the history of India was the story of the expansion of Magadha from a tiny state in South Bihār to a gigantic Empire extending from the foot of the Hindukush to the borders of the Tamil country. After the Kaliṅga war ensued a period of stagnation at the end of which the process is reversed. The empire gradually dwindled down in extent till it sank to the position from which Bimbisāra and his successors had raised it.[50]

That this collapse of the empire could be traced to Aśoka is lent credence by the following remarks of Hemachandra Raychaudhuri:

> The royal hunt and jousts of arms in *Samājas* were abolished. The army seems to have been practically inactive during the last 29 years of Aśoka's reign as the emperor himself declares with a feeling of exultation that 'the sound of the *bheri* had become the sound of the True Law, *Dharma*.' The Chinese *Hou Hanshu* (quoted by S. Konow, CII, Vol. II, p. lxvii) testifies to the fact that people of India 'practise the religion of the Buddha; it has *become a habit with them not to kill and to fight*.' The ease with which general Pushyamitra overthrew his king, in the very sight of the army, shows that unlike the earlier kings of the dynasty who took the field in person, the last of the Mauryas lost touch with his fighting forces, and ceased to command their affection. The largesses of gold lavished on the religieux must also have crippled the financial resources of the empire. The system of autonomous Rājūkas instituted by Aśoka must have let loose centrifugal forces that his successors were unable to check.[51]

The *Rājātaraṅgiṇī* tells us for instance that Jalauka, one of Aśoka's sons, made himself the independent king of Kashmir immediately after Aśoka's death.[52] We might here refer to a problem identified by Hartmut Scharfe which may provide us with a solution to *our* problem:

> The existing testimonies pose major chronological problems: the works of the Buddhist canon may be younger than the oldest parts of the epics, but are older than their late additions, and KA and Manu are both relatively late. It is puzzling that some of the first references to the *cakravartin* ideal and the 'righteous conquest' (*dharma-vijaya*) are found in Buddhist texts, though these notions were no doubt peripheral to Buddhist thought. The Buddhist king's 'wheel' is more easily explained as a fanciful abstraction from an old image of the king's chariot wheel than the other way around, and the 'righteous conquest' by moral superiority as a refinement of older notions of a victor's decency that left the vanquished foe with his life and his material possessions. Is the Buddhist rejection of *daṇḍa* conservative adherence to the old ways or a conscious rejection of the ruthless policies of the emerging state? There are signs here too that the Buddhists reacted to current ideas: the emphasis that the *cakkavatti* conquered through *dhamma* without *daṇḍa* or weapon (even though he took his army along) is an obvious polemic against the concept of the *apratihata-cakra* king who crushes his opponents through force.[53]

All these points lead to the following central point—that the *Manusmṛti* may have avoided using the word *cakravartin* because of its association with Aśoka. This reluctance to use a word connected with Aśoka can be interpreted in two ways. According to one interpretation, the aversion is essentially Brahmanical, representative of the *brāhmaṇa* community as such, because the 'one thing his [Aśoka's] reforms did was to displace the Brahmin from his privileged position within the social structure. The special relationship between the political power and the religious establishment represented by the Brahmin was broken',[54] although whether Aśoka 'was anti-brahmanical is debatable'.[55] If one pushes this line of argument further, then it would lead to the conclusion that the *Manusmṛti* avoided the word *cakravartin* because it had achieved a Buddhist reference point through the work of Aśoka.

Another point is noteworthy in this context. The message of the *dhamma-vijaya* was broadcast by Aśoka far and wide. The fact that, apart from the Prākṛta versions of Aśoka's edicts, this message also exists in the Aramaic and Greek versions, indicates how broad-based the public relations campaign of Aśoka to promote his *dhamma* was. The Greek and Aramaic versions of his edicts speak of his *dhamma* thriving 'throughout the whole world' as a result of his efforts (where the whole world meant the empire of Aśoka).[56] If we add to this Aśoka's propagation of Buddhism, the summoning of the third Buddhist council, and the missionary activity consequent thereof, then one can imagine how widespread the impact of Aśoka's policies could have been. By contrast, it is striking that the *Manusmṛti*, although a *Smṛti* and open to all in principle including *śūdras* and women, limits its audience to the *brāhmaṇas* (in *Manusmṛti* 1.103). This closed-door approach, in direct opposition to Aśoka's open to the world policy, also supports the idea of a Brahmanical reaction.

From another perspective, however, it could be urged that the collapse of the Mauryan dynasty had implications for the larger population as a whole, especially in north India. If this is true, then the reluctance of the *Manusmṛti* to use the word *cakravartin* may not be just narrowly Brahmanical, but may signify a wish to avoid reviving in the public mind any memory of the disaster that they may have come to associate with the word.

And then finally, under the Guptas, when the Hindu version of the concept of the *cakravartin* came closer to realization, the use of the word becomes acceptable once again. Heinrich Zimmer summarizes these developments well:

> The aśvamedha rite is described to the last detail in the texts of Vedic priest-lore (Brāhmaṇas and Śrauta-sūtras), and has been performed solemnly by the Hindu emperors even of comparatively recent periods—for example, by the emperors of the Gupta dynasty, who governed all of northern India from 320 to 480 AD. Samudragupta, the second of this line, ordered cut in stone a panegyric composed by his court-poet Hariṣeṇa, proclaiming that he had extended his control over an empire at least equal to that of the Mauryas under King Aśoka in the third century BC. The panegyric was cut on a pillar that already bore the edicts of King Aśoka—the point being that Samudragupta was an orthodox Hindu, whereas King Aśoka had been a Buddhist. The Hindu world-monarch (*cakravartin*), pacifying mankind by incorporating under his sole sovereignty all the kingdoms round about—the 'great king' (*mahārāja*), 'king above kings' (*rājādhirāja*; compare the Persian:

shāhānām shāh, 'shah of shahs')—was to be proclaimed equal in rank to those world-redeeming Buddhas who, through their doctrines, set in motion the wheel. Samudragupta confirmed and celebrated his position with the supreme ceremonial of the aśvamedha, the primary rite of the Vedic Hindu tradition—and this specifically was the deed that he recorded in his inscription on the stone.[57]

Aśoka never claimed the status of a *cakravartin* for himself.[58] Hartmut Scharfe suggests that this is perhaps because 'to do so openly might have appeared presumptuous'[59] but notes that he is called so in the *Divyāvadāna*.[60]

III

It is also worth examining whether the concept of *dharma-vijaya* in Hinduism is related to that of *dharma-vijaya* in Buddhism. Aśoka proclaimed himself a *dharma-vijayī* and the political part of *dharma-vijaya* seemed to have consisted in the humane treatment of enemies in the case of conquest. The word *dharma-vijaya* has this connotation in the *Arthaśāstra* (13.11), as noted earlier,[61] and also in the *Manusmṛti* (7.201–04):

> [201] After the victory, he should pay homage to gods and righteous Brahmins; grant exemptions; and issue proclamations of amnesty. [202] After ascertaining the collective wishes of them all, he should install there a relation of the enemy king and draw up a treaty; [203] make the Laws commonly held among them authoritative; and honour the new ruler, together with his chief officials, with precious gifts. [204] When carried out at the appropriate time, the unwelcome seizure of desirable property and their welcome distribution are both commendable.[62]

IV

The Hindu concept of *cakravartī* (*digvijayī*) is national, that is, largely restricted to ancient India, while the Buddhist concept seems to be global in nature. What light does the *Manusmṛti* shed on this difference?

The concept of the *āryāvarta* in the *Manusmṛti* (2.22) covers north India, so this concept in the text does not seem to embrace the whole of

India. This could be another reason why the *Manusmṛti* does not use the word *cakravartī*, as already the *Arthaśāstra*:

> [...] defines the land of the cakravartin as the territory on the earth spreading towards the north from the sea to the Himālaya, which is a thousand yojanas in extent when measured in a straight line ... Kauṭilya also employs the expression 'cāturanto rāja' (a king of the earth up to its four boundaries).[63]

Strikingly, the term *cakravartin* (universal sovereign), although 'common in ancient Indian literature, is never used in the AŚ [*Arthaśāstra*] outside of this sentence. Such a monarch is supposed not to have any opponents, which is diametrically opposed to the basic conception of the AŚ, with its circle of kings divided into allies and enemies.'[64] It is as if the ideal is laid out and then the reality is addressed.

Thus although the *Manusmṛti* does not measure up to this ideal, (which was perhaps lost sight of in the crisis which followed the collapse of the Mauryan Empire), it does make a curious contribution to this ideal through its commentators. As noted in an earlier chapter, the land of *āryāvarta* may be overrun by the *mlecchas,* but can be reclaimed as such once the *varṇāśrama* system is established there again. And this could be a continuous process. The *Manusmṛti*, by alluding to a series of people in the following verses as fallen *kṣatriyas,* and who therefore could be reinstated in the *varṇa* order, seems to indirectly acknowledge this (X.43–44): '43 By neglecting rites and by failing to visit Brahmiṇs, however, these men of Kṣatriya birth have gradually reached in the world the level of Śūdras—44 Puṇḍrakas, Coḍas, Draviḍas, Kāmbojas, Yavanas, Śakas, Pāradas, Pahlavas, Cinas, Kirātas, and Daradas.'[65]

V

Some other points also need to be highlighted in the political analysis of the *Manusmṛti*, especially as they tend to be ignored in the current discussion of the subject.

The first pertains to the meaning of the word *dharma-vijaya*. The word is used in the sense of military conquest in the *Arthaśāstra*, when it does not involve the extirpation of the defeated family. In the edicts of Aśoka, however, it is used in a sense which abjures military conquest and is redolent of Milton's famous statement about the victories of peace being more renowned than those of war. The *Manusmṛti,* however, does not echo this sense at all and the meaning of the word reverts to the sense it had in the *Arthaśāstra.*[66] This raises the question: Does this semantic retreat again signal a disillusionment in the Hindu mind with Aśoka's attempt to redefine the term?

A second point pertains to the fact that the king is never called a *dharma-rāja* in the *Manusmṛti,* despite the text incorporating the political sphere in the discourse of *dharma* through a discussion of kingship, and despite the fact that the *Mahābharata,* a text which probably influenced the *Manusmṛti,* contains the figure of Yudhiṣṭhira who is so described therein. The *Manusmṛti* thus becomes a text which explicitly deals with statecraft or *rāja-dharma,* but steers clear of the term *dharma-rāja.* Is this puzzle then also to be explained in terms of Aśoka having been considered a *dharma-rāja,* and therefore constitutes further evidence of the text's aversion to what Aśoka stood for?

A third point pertains to the absence of the term *cakravartin* in the *Manusmṛti.* That a term so well lodged in the political imagination of Hinduism should not appear in a seminal text which tries to assimilate such discourse into itself, poses another puzzle. Again, one must wonder whether the association of this word with Aśoka induced the author of the *Manusmṛti* to steer clear of it.

All of these minor points lead us to a major consideration, namely, the extent to which the negative perception of the Aśokan interlude may have influenced the vocabulary and through it the conceptualization of the role of the state in the *Manusmṛti.*

A second major point turns on the role of *dharma* in relation to the king, and this too could in a way be related to the Aśokan experience. Aśoka, as a king, stands almost above *dharma,* understood as either Buddhism or the moral norm he preached to his subjects. He clearly stood above the Buddhist order, which in fact he tried to reform and whose monks he summoned to a conference at his behest, just as Constantine would summon the bishops. Aśoka also stood above the moral norms he propagated, in the sense that they stemmed from *him.* A case could be made that in the *Manusmṛti,*[67] by contrast, the king is *not* above the law,[68] especially if we take verse 8.336 into account—as pointed out in an earlier chapter.

A third and final point concerns an expression found in the *Manusmṛti* which has virtually gone unnoticed. It occurs in the eighth chapter and forms part of the following verse (8.172): 'By taking what is due to him, by bringing together the social classes, and by protecting the weak, the king enhances his power; and he prospers here and in the hereafter.'[69]

The word involved is *varṇa-saṃsarga* which has been translated by Patrick Olivelle as 'by bringing together the social classes.' He also provides the following note on the term:

> [...] *by bringing together the social classes:* this Sanskrit expression (*varṇasaṃsargāt*) has caused enormous problems for the understanding of the verse. Commentators give diverse and contradictory explanations. Given that the two other activities are duties performed by the king, I think this also should be something that the king does. On the face of it, *varṇasaṃsarga* means confusion of classes, something the king is sworn to prevent. I think *saṃsarga* here may be used in close to its etymological meaning: combining and bringing together, not in a sexual sense which would cause the intermixing of classes, but in a broader sense. Here we can take it either as supporting the proper functioning of classes within the broader social structure, or more restrictively, as referring to the cohesiveness of each class within itself.[70]

Two points regarding this term are worth noting. The first, hinted at by Olivelle in his note, is that this term serves as a foil to another, namely, *varṇa-saṃkara*. Modern Indology may be said to be as familiar with this term as it is oblivious of the *varṇa-saṃsarga* so the point needs to be probed further. This term, *varṇa-saṃkara*, enshrines one role of the king, namely, to prevent 'confusion of classes'. As A.L. Basham explains:

> The continual injunctions to the king to ensure that 'confusion of class' (*varṇa-saṃkara*) did not take place indicate that such confusion was an ever-present danger in the mind of the orthodox brāhmaṇ. The class system was indeed a very fragile thing. In the golden age the classes were stable, but the legendary king Veṇa (p. 87), among his many

> other crimes, had encouraged miscegenation, and from this beginning confusion of class had increased, and was a special feature of the *Kali-yuga*, the last degenerate age of this aeon, which was fast nearing its close. The good king, therefore, should spare no effort to maintain the purity of the classes, and many dynasties took special pride in their efforts in this direction.[71]

This is obviously a *preventive* function of the ruler in relation to the *varṇa*. The *Manusmṛti* recognizes the phenomenon (10.24). But in the verse cited earlier, which contains the expression, *varṇa-saṃsarga* it moves further and assigns a *positive* function to the ruler, namely, that of bringing the *varṇas* together.

The significance of such a development can hardly be overstated. It clearly presents the role of the ruler as one who consciously sets out to harmonize the relations among the various *varṇas*. The identification of this role in itself amounts to a contribution to Hindu and Indic political theory. But the question remains: Is there any evidence to support that this actually happened in real life, that is, in history? After all, it could just be a theoretical flight of fancy on the part of the author of the *Manusmṛti*.

The life and actions of Guautamīputra Śātakarṇi (c. 72–95 CE) seem to provide the required evidence in support of the suggestion that such a concept is related to historical reality.[72] His reign barely precedes the period of the *Manusmṛti*, if we accept the dates now commonly assigned to that text. During his reign, the 'Śakas, Yavana, and Pahlava settlers in Western Deccan were either put to the sword or driven out',[73] and he uprooted Nahapāṇa of the Kshaharāta dynasty.[74] In the Nāsik Praśasti, he is described as *eka brāhmaṇa* or the unique *brāhmaṇa*, an expression which, 'when read with other passages, leaves no doubt that Guautamīputra Śātakarṇi not only claimed to be a Brāhmaṇa, but a Brāhmaṇa like Paraśurāma who humbled the pride of the Kshatriyas.' As a matter of fact, in the *praśasti* the king is described as 'the unique Brāhmaṇa in prowess equal to Rāma.'[75]

What is important from our point of view is the fact that in the Nāsik Praśasti:

> Gautamīputra figures not only as a conqueror but also as a social reformer, 'he crushed down the pride and conceit of the kshatriyas,

> furthered the interest of the twice-born, apparently the brāhmaṇas, as well as the lowest orders (*dvijāvarakuṭubaviyadhana*) and stopped the contamination of the four *varṇas* (castes)'.[76]

If the reference to the *kṣatriyas* above is a reference to the foreign rulers such as Śakas, Yavanas and Pahlavas, as has been suggested, then this conclusion is further strengthened. For it will explain why Gautamīputra did *not* include the *kṣatriyas* in his concord of the *varṇas,* because they were *foreigners* against whom he united the *indigenous varṇas.*

11

The *Manusmṛti* on Hinduism as a Missionary Religion

I

The student of the history of ancient Hinduism faces a paradox, because he is told that it was not possible to convert to Hinduism as it was an ethnic religion possessing a caste system based on birth.[1] However, he is also told about the spread of Hinduism to Southeast Asia.[2] If people could not convert to Hinduism, how could the people of southeast Asia become Hindus? After all, the Hindu presence there cannot be explained merely in terms of Hindu migrations.[3] It is the purpose of this chapter to resolve this dilemma with the help of the *Manusmṛti*. The dilemma has been posed by G. Coedes, the pre-eminent scholar of the Indianization of Southeast Asia, as follows: 'How can we explain this maritime drive of a people who regarded crossing the black water and contact with the *mleccha* barbarians as bringing defilement and pollution?'

How pervasive these social constructs are may be gauged, if somewhat lightheartedly, from the fact that the great Indologist, A.L. Basham, describes himself as a 'friendly *mleccha*' in the preface to his famous book.[4] The word *mleccha* is a generic Hindu term for a foreigner, often with the connotation of his or her being a non-Indian and a barbarian.[5]

II

Two hypotheses have been developed to account for the motivation underlying this eastward expansion of Hinduism. They have been called the Brahmin hypothesis and the Trader-Merchant hypothesis by Larus.[6] If the latter be referred to as the *Vaiśya* hypothesis, then one obtains a much more coherent picture of Hindu expansion in terms of Hindu social terminology. We are, however, concerned here with the view that the two have been offered as competing hypotheses: 'The first stresses the part played by Brahmins and minimizes trade and commerce; the second stresses the role of India's mercantile class and their desire to profit from the burgeoning Far East trade and downgrades the prominence of Brahmins.'[7]

The scenario, according to the Brahmin hypothesis, unfolded as follows. The political turmoil of the first few centuries of the Common Era caused by foreign invasions from the north-west, combined with the success of the heterodoxies of Buddhism and Jainism, placed the elitist and purist *brāhmaṇas* in a precarious position, impelling them to move on.

Joel Larus develops the scenario further as follows:

> The first migration of ultra-orthodox Brahmins may have left northern India to seek relief for reasons as fundamental as these. The destination of some émigrés probably was south India, the lands where the Dravidians lived. For other Brahmins, however, quitting India completely may not have been too radical a departure from tradition to reassert their cultural superiority and, hopefully, regain purity by appropriate rituals. The injunctions against sea voyages and residence abroad may not have been too great a price to pay for such opportunities. Beyond the seas and thousands of miles from the Indian subcontinent, Brahmins could both free themselves of *mleccha* pressures and also Buddhist-Jain campaigns to subvert their allegiance to Hinduism. Another complementary version of this theory maintains that Hindus were invited to settle the southeast Pacific region by native leaders who heard of 'the Brahmins' superior cultural achievements and strong religious leadership.[8]

Even in the context of the rival Trader-Merchant hypothesis, *brāhmaṇas* figure in two ways. (1) 'A few renegade Brahmins ... probably accompanied the initial waves of traders … and Brahmins followed in later periods',[9] but they are not to be 'considered as leaders or initiators of Indian colonial movements';[10] (2) the movement of the traders out of India was provoked by the movement of the *brāhmaṇas* within India.

According to Joel Larus:

> The Dravidians' conversion to Hinduism and their acceptance of its societal norms, as explained previously, took place only when Brahmins, finding in the north a continuing threat to their caste purity, re-located in the south and began to influence Dravidian behaviour. This development reached something of a climax during the centuries immediately before the Christian era. It is possible therefore that disgruntled Dravidian sailors, rejecting the Brahmin campaign against deep sea travel, could find ships going to *suvarnabhumi* and *suvarnadvipa* ready to sign them on.[11]

The words *suvarṇabhūmi* and *suvarṇadvīpa* literally mean 'golden land' and 'golden island'. The former is usually taken to refer to Burma or Malaya,[12] and the latter Sumatra in Indonesia.[13]

I maintain that both these hypotheses overlook a central element in the situation—that classical Hinduism provides an identifiable model of Hindu missionary activity, which has been virtually disregarded in this context.[14] This model may be identified in the *Manusmṛti* itself, which is usually assigned to the second century and is considered the law book par excellence of ancient Hindu culture.[15] Moreover, there is evidence that the *Manusmṛti* itself moved to Southeast Asia, perhaps as a result of the very movement for which it provided an ideology.[16] The kind of Brahmanical corps it encouraged can actually be identified in Cambodia.[17] This suggests that the *Manusmṛti* merits a much more careful examination in the context of Hindu expansion than has hitherto been the case. While it may be true that in some respects the importance of the *Manusmṛti* has been exaggerated;[18] in this respect its relevance has been unwisely ignored.

III

A cursory examination of the *Manusmṛti,* however, seems to support the opposite idea—that the Southeast Asian expansion of Hinduism may have been a flight from its rigidity, rather than an expansion fuelled by its ideology. Firstly, the *Manusmṛti* distinguishes clearly between the 'Hindus' and the 'non-Hindus' who are called Dasyus (10.45). It is noteworthy that the distinction is not based on language but on religion (10.45). All Hindus belong to the four *varṇas* and 'there is no fifth' (10.4; read again with 10.45). The picture which emerges from these passages is that of a closed system, hierarchically structured, with the *brāhmaṇas* at the top (10.3) ideally dwelling in a narrow band of land called Āryāvarta, whose dimensions are specified not with Purāṇic exaggeration but with geographical precision (2.21–25). How indeed could a religion with such a narrow vision spread beyond its own borders, not to speak of beyond India? Is it the case that there were political, social, religious and other forces at work—forces not recognized in the Law Book of Manu at all or only dimly recognized—which alone can account for the spread of Hinduism to Southeast Asia? Or does the *Manusmṛti* itself, appearances notwithstanding, provide a model of Hindu missionary expansion?

IV

But what does it mean to be missionary in Hindu terms? It is important to clarify this point before proceeding further.

Each religion has its own view of conversion. In Christianity, for instance, conversion means accepting Jesus Christ as the sole saviour and typically involves joining a church. In Islam, conversion means accepting Muḥammad as the last Prophet, along with the sole divinity of Allah, and becoming a member of the Muslim community (*ummah muslimah*).[19] In classical Hinduism, conversion meant the acceptance of the *varṇa* model. It represented the key metaphor and corresponds to the membership of a church in Christianity and of the *ummah* in Islam.[20] It also implied the acceptance of the Vedas and derivative literature in Hinduism, just as membership of the church implied the acceptance of Christian scriptures in Christianity. The acceptance of the *Sharī'ah*, which went hand in hand with becoming a Muslim, provides an interesting parallel from Islam, for similarly the acceptance of the *varṇa* was part and parcel of the process of joining the Hindu community.[21]

Each religion possesses not only its own view of conversion but also its own view about the status of the proselyte prior to conversion. In

Christianity, the non-Christian is outside the pale of salvation prior to conversion and may even be in a diabolical state. The outsider's position in Islam is more interesting and more comparable to that in classical Hinduism. According to the Qur'ān, all the people of the world have been recipients of revelation in the past—it is the final revelation which is vouchsafed to them through the Qur'ān. It is not the case that they were in a state of revelatory deprivation prior to the Qur'ān. They have *a* revelation. In the Qur'ān now they have access to *the* revelation.

Just as it is the belief of the Qur'ān that God had sent revelation to *all* the peoples of the world known to it prior to the Qur'ān (35:24, 13: 7), it is the belief of the *Manusmṛti* that all the peoples of the world were originally encompassed within the *varṇa* scheme. With the passage of time, however, the system fell in disuse among them, and they became lapsed 'Hindus', so to say. That this is clearly the case becomes apparent from a perusal of the text and commentary of *Manusmṛti* X.45: '*All the tribes of this world*, which are excluded from (the community of) those born from the mouth, the arms, the thighs and the feet (of Brahman) are called Dasyus ...'[22] The commentary of Kullūka is unambiguous on this point—that all the non-Āryan Dasyu peoples *originally* belonged to the *varṇa*-order: *brāhmaṇa-kṣatriya-vaiśya-śūdrāṇām kiryālopādinā yā jātayo bāhya jātā ... te dasyavaḥ sarve smṛtāḥ.*[23] That is to say: Dasyus comprise those peoples who were excluded on account of the disappearance of the usages of the *varṇas*.

In other words, the classical Hindu missionary position, as found in the *Manusmṛti*, can be reduced to four propositions: (1) the whole world is divisible between Āryas and Dasyus; (2) the Āryas follow the *varṇa* system; (3) the Dasyus used to observe the *varṇa* system but do not anymore, and that is what makes them Dasyus; and (4) missionary activity consists in making the Dasyus revert to the earlier practice of following the *varṇa* order. In the *Manusmṛti's* formulation of the classical Hindu position, *reversion is conversion*. Alternatively, conversion is reversion.

V

It should no longer come as a surprise, therefore, that a closer examination of the *Manusmṛti* reveals the existence of what may be called a classical

Hindu model for 'proselytization' at work which specifies both: (1) those who are to carry out this missionary activity; and (2) the people among whom this missionary activity is to be carried out.

Those who are to carry out the mission are described in *Manusmṛti* 2.17–20:

> 17. That land, created by the gods, which lies between the two divine rivers Sarasvatī and Dṛṣadvatī, the (sages) call Brahmāvarta.
>
> 18. The custom handed down in regular succession (since time immemorial) among the (four chief) castes (*varṇa*) and the mixed (races) of that country, is called the conduct of virtuous men.
>
> 19. The plain of the Kurus, the (country of the) Matsyas, Pañcālas, and Śūrasenakas, these (form) indeed, the country of the Brahmarṣis (Brahmanical sages, which ranks) immediately after Brahmāvarta.
>
> 20. From a Brāhmaṇa, born in that country, let all men on earth learn their several usages.[24]

The last verse is the key one; one might say that the tail wags the dog. The word used for *earth* is *pṛthvī* and *all the people of the earth* are referred to (*sarvamānavāḥ*). The statement is direct and unambiguous, the use of the *vidhi* form of *śikṣ* (to learn) even precludes the glib dismissal of the verse as *arthavāda* or exaggeration, by the rules of Mīmāṁsā exegesis. Nor can it be dismissed as a stray verse of little significance as it is also found in other branches of Hindu literature.[25]

In other words, the *brāhmaṇas* of Brahmarṣi-deśa are charged by the *Manusmṛti* with the universal mission which *contrasts* with the more local vision of the *brāhmaṇas* of Āryāvarta. In fact, four geographical areas are referred to by the *Manusmṛti* in 2.17–25, each wider in scope than the former. First comes Brahmāvarta, which lies between Sarasvatī and Dṛṣadvatī (difficult to identify precisely on account of changes in the course of rivers);[26] next comes Brahmarṣi (deśa) (see map); then Madhyadeśa, and finally Āryāvarta. It is the *brāhmaṇa* (*agrajanman*) of the Brahmarṣi region who is specifically charged with the universal mission. It was thus the *brāhmaṇas* of the *second* region who were charged with the responsibility of disseminating 'Hinduism' throughout the world.

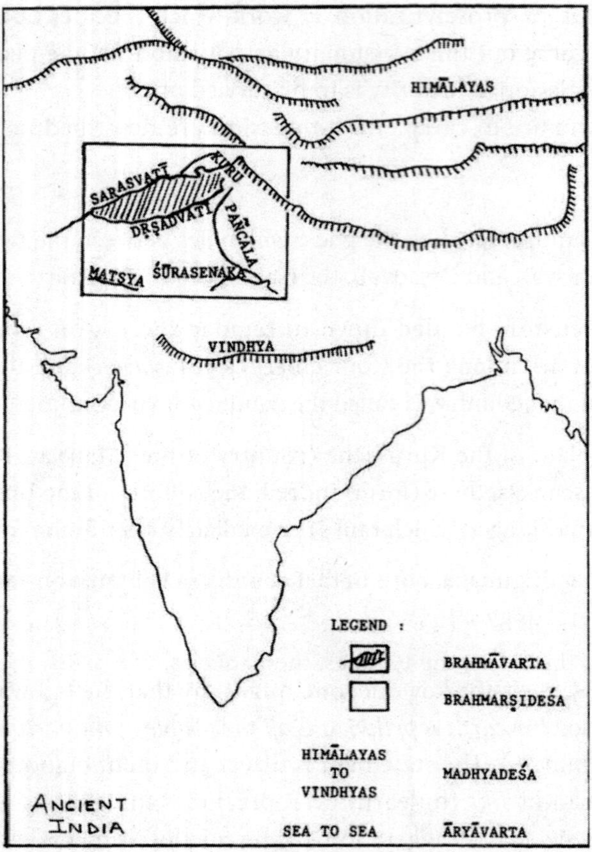

Why, it must be asked, were the *brāhmaṇas* of this region alone selected by Manu? The explanation lies in the historical circumstances of the times. The regions to the west and north of this area had been overrun by foreign invaders such as the IndoGreeks, the Śakas, the Kuṣāṇas, etc. from the second century before the Common Era onwards. Similarly, the region to the east and the south had come under the influence of Buddhism. There is evidence from the Purāṇas to suggest that the *brāhmaṇas* of these regions had become so closely associated with strictly non-orthodox practices,[27] that they could not be relied upon to champion Hinduism, in the time of Manu (second century). We will see later that the situation had changed by the time of Śaṅkara (eighth/ninth century).

But even in relation to the *brāhmaṇas* selected for missionary enterprise from this geographical region, certain questions arise: *brāhmaṇas* residing in a particular part of India, who are themselves defined in caste-specific terms, are charged with a universal mission. Moreover, the region they hail from is considered as normative in terms of the *varṇa* system, into which one can only be born (X.5). These then are the horns of the dilemma; the topmost members of the *varṇa* system are being called upon to use a birth-ascribed norm as a universalizing agent. How is this possible?

VI

The answer is provided by verses 10.43–44 of the *Manusmṛti*, wherein Manu mentions many *kṣatriya tribes* which fell from grace as a result of neglecting Vedic usages and specifies them as follows:

> 43. But in consequence of the omission of the sacred rites, and of their not consulting Brāhmaṇas, the following tribes of Kṣatriyas have gradually sunk in this world to the condition of Śūdras;
>
> 44. (Viz.) the Pauṇḍrakas, the Koḍas, the Draviḍas, the Kambojas, the Yavanas, the Śakas, the Pāradas, the Pahlavas, the Cīnas, the Kirātas, and the Daradas.[28]

One can see that many tribes inhabiting the borders of India have been included here in the list as 'fallen *kṣatriyas*', including the Chinese. The point needs to be elaborated. The tribes listed in *Manusmṛti* 10.44 could either be illustrative or exhaustive. Historical and commentarial evidence suggests that the list is illustrative. The word *bahiḥ* (outside) in the next verse could either mean (1) now excluded, or (2) excluded ab initio. J. Muir has argued on textual grounds that the former sense is meant.[29] He cites several passages from the *Mahābhārata* to show 'that the Brahmans of that age regarded the Dasyus as owing allegiance to Brahmanical institutions',[30] which clearly explains why Manu would declare that all the people of the world have to be missionized by the *brāhmaṇas*. In other words, the world is divided between the Āryas and the Dasyus; the Āryas already owe allegiance to Brahmanical institutions and the rest of the world, represented by the Dasyus, should do the same. The Dasyus constitute even a broader category compared to the *mlecchas* (*Manusmṛti* 2.23; 10.45).

One of the terms by which people, who neglect Vedic usages, are known is *vrātya*. The process of becoming a *vrātya* is described in *Manusmṛti* 2.38–40:

> 38. The (time for the) Sāvitrī (initiation) of a Brāhmaṇa does not pass until the completion of the sixteenth year (after conception), of a Kṣatriya completion of the twenty-fourth.
> 39. After those (periods men of) these three (castes) who have not received the sacrament at the proper time, become Vrātyas (outcasts), excluded from the Sāvitrī (initiation) and despised by the Āryans.
> 40. With such men, if they have not been purified according to the rule, let no Brāhmaṇa ever, even in times of distress, form a connection either through the Veda or by marriage.[31]

Verse 40 bars contact with them if '*they have not been purified according to the rule*'. The rule involved here was apparently the *vrātyastoma* referred to in the *Tāṇḍya Brāhmaṇa* (chapter 17) in Vedic times. By the time of Manu, living as a *vrātya* (11.63; also see 11.57, 11.60 and 11.66) had become an *upapātaka* or a minor offence, for which due penance was prescribed (11.125), even when it involved loss of caste (*jātībhraṃśa*). It seems then that one of the duties of the *brāhmaṇas* was to perform this rite by which people were brought within the pale of Hinduism.[32] *Manusmṛti* (10.22) actually describes the *descendants* of the *vrātya* or apostate *kṣatriyas*: 'From the Vrātya of the Kṣatriya (caste) the Jhalla, the Malla, the Licchivi, the Naṭa, the Karaṇa, the Khasa and the Draviḍa, *as well as* the descendents of apostate Brāhmaṇas and Vaiśyas.'[33]

It is clear therefore that a missionary ideology underlies the *Manusmṛti,* which can be uncovered and which helps resolve the dilemma of how a *varṇa*-oriented society could also be expansionist. According to this view, virtually people all over the world, including the *mleccha*s (11.23), that is foreigners inhabiting the rest of the world, through the convenient fiction of being 'lapsed Hindus', were candidates for conversion. This view regarded the *mleccha*s as degraded *kṣatriyas* (*Viṣṇu Purāṇa:* 2:4.3.48: *mlecchatāṃ yayuḥ*).

It is quite possible that the *Manusmṛti* model represented a Brahmanical response to the success of Buddhism as a missionary religion. *Brāhmaṇas* could perform rites of social purification and could marry, unlike the

Buddhist monks, and so the strategies the *brāhmaṇa* elite could think of would have to correspond to these facts.

VII

The question arises: Did this in fact ever happen? Did the *brāhmaṇas* of this region go forth and missionize?

One must first get a clear fix on the region itself. In order to do this, one must go right back to the period of Āryan settlement in India. A critical phase in this settlement was the Battle of the Ten Kings which is alluded to in *ṚgVeda* 7:33 and placed by Geldner in an early period. The overall situation in relation to the tribes of the *ṚgVeda*, their settlement, and the battle, is summarized by A.D. Pusalkar as follows:

> The whole of the territory known to the Vedic settlers was divided into a number of tribal principalities ruled normally by kings. The *Daśarājña* or the battle of the ten kings is an important historical event alluded to in various hymns of the *Ṛigveda*, and as many of the important tribes and personalities figured in this famous battle, it is worth while outlining the conflict. *Sudās was a Bharata king of the Tritsu family which was settled in the country which later came to be known as Brahmāvarta.* At first Viśvāmitra, a scion of the Kuśika family of the Bharatas, was the priest of Sudās, and led him to victorious campaigns on the Vipāś and Śutudri. *Viśvāmitra, however, was dismissed later by Sudās, who appointed Vasishtha as his priest*, probably on account of the superior Brahmanical knowledge of the Vasishthas.[34]

It is clear from this passage that one is dealing with the same region referred to in the *Manusmṛti*, and in Vasiṣṭha we are dealing not merely with a *brāhmaṇa* but a *purohita*, the royal priest of Sudās, to whom the whole of Book 7 of the *ṚgVeda* is ascribed. So, both the qualifications laid down in the *Manusmṛti* are fulfilled: (1) that the missionaries should be *brāhmaṇas*, who (2) hail from Braharṣi-deśa.[35]

Vasiṣṭha married Arundhatī and had many sons. One of the well-known sons was Kuṇḍina (*Vāyu Purāṇa*: 70: 80–90; *Matsya Purāṇa*: 145: 109–11). If we have read the *Manusmṛti* correctly then it was these *brāhmaṇas* who were charged with the mission to go forth in the world. The descendants of Kuṇḍina would be called *Kauṇḍinya* (*Pāṇini* 4.1.105). The movement of these *brāhmaṇas*, descendants of Kuṇḍina, must now be traced through the familiar institutions of *gotra* and *pravara* among the *brāhmaṇas*. An inscription in Mysore, belonging probably to the second century CE, mentions *brāhmaṇas* of the Kauṇḍinya *gotra*.[36] However, Chinese variants of the name Kauṇḍinya appear in Chinese texts connected with the region called Fu-nan in Southeast Asia, with the implication of local intermarriage.

It is remarkable that two phases in the process of Hinduization can be distinguished on the basis of the Chinese records, one in the first and another in the fourth century, and a Kauṇḍinya is associated with *both* of these phases. One may now refer to the *first* Kauṇḍinya, about whom 'one popular Chinese legend states that in the first century A.D., a Brahmin helped found the Fu-nan kingdom. A more reliable Chinese source of the second century A.D. notes that by this time the social and political structure of Fu-nan closely resembled a Hindu Kingdom in India.'[37] These two sentences read like a historical commentary on *Manusmṛti* 2.20 and *Manusmṛti* 2.18 respectively. A fuller account of subsequent development in this context refers to a second Kauṇḍinya:

> Towards the end of the fourth or the beginning of the fifth century A.D. the throne of Fu-nan was occupied by Kiao-chen-ju or Kauṇḍinya. The *History of the Liang Dynasty* has preserved the following story about him: 'Kauṇḍinya was a Brahman and an inhabitant of India. One day he heard a supernatural voice asking him to go and reign in Fu-nan. He reached Pan-pan to the south of Fu-nan. The people of Fu-nan cordially welcomed him and elected him king. He introduced Indian laws, manners and customs.'[38]

But Manu has also been associated with inflexibility in matters of marriage so how are the matrimonial alliances to be explained? A study of the rules of intercaste marriage in the *Manusmṛti* also reveals a feature which has virtually gone unnoticed. The text reveals a concern both with *purity* and with *purification*. Scholars have focused on the former (*Manusmṛti* 10.5) and overlooked two salient facts: (1) that a *brāhmaṇa* could marry women from the four *varṇas* and although marrying a *śūdra* woman is reprobated immediately, presumably in an Indian context (3.14–19), marriage of the *anuloma* type could raise the status of the offspring of a caste (*jāti*) 'within the seventh generation' (10.64), a phenomenon more generally known as *jātyutkarṣa*;[39] and (2) the accounts of the marriage of Kauṇḍinya with the female sovereign now take on a new meaning,[40] not to speak of other matrimonial alliances,[41] as the relationships between *brāhmaṇas* and non-Āryan women are explicitly referred to (10.56).

But still the question persists: How could the aboriginal people of a distant land be considered to be within the pale of the *varṇa* system for such marriages to take place? The name *kirāta* is typically applied to such people, especially those living in north-eastern India in mountain caves (*Vājasaneyī Saṃhitā* 30.16). The *Vāyu Purāṇa* (2.3) identifies them as a barbarous people living to the *east* of India. But the question remains: How could they be brought within the pale of the *varṇa* system? The answer is provided by verses 10.43–44 of the *Manusmṛti*, wherein Manu mentions the *kirātas* among the *kṣatriya* tribes, which fell from grace as a result of neglecting Vedic usages. There is clear evidence of 'fallen *kṣatriyas*', who are mentioned along with the *kirātas*, being accepted within the Hindu fold in India.[42] A much more direct and far less convoluted answer is also possible. The text in the *Manusmṛti* explicitly refers to the mission of the *brāhmaṇas* as extending to all human beings (*sarvāmānavāḥ*) and marriage of *brāhmaṇas* to excluded races is alluded to in *Manusmṛti* 10.28. It is not even necessary to bring the women involved within the pale of *varṇa* through pious fiction.

It is conceivable that the application of the model outside India in the distant east may have been suggested first by the partial, and then full restoration, of Hindu rule over northern India (by Gupta time), an analogy which could be intuitively extended beyond India and is explicitly extended by Medhātithi (ninth century) in his commentary on *Manusmṛti* 2.23, as pointed out by Kane:

> If a kṣatriya king of excellent conduct were to conquer the Mlecchas, establish the system of four *varṇas* (in the Mleccha country) and assign to Mlecchas a position similar to that of caṇḍālas in Āryāvarta, even that (Mleccha) country would be fit for the performance of sacrifices, since the earth is not by itself impure, but becomes impure through contact (of impure persons or things).[43]

It also appears that Manu's model was later broadened to include all *brāhmaṇas* as potential missionaries. At least by the time of Śaṅkara, when he wrote his commentary on the *Bhagavadgītā*, the shift had clearly occurred and must have been a fact of life for him to refer to it without any reservations. The fact that Śaṅkara extends to all *brāhmaṇas* the role reserved for those of Brahmarṣideśa in the *Manusmṛti* may have to do with the difference between the India of the time of Manu (second century) and that of Śaṅkara (eighth/ninth century). In his commentary on *Vedāntasūtra*, I.3.33, Śaṅkara hypothesized that although the system of *varṇa* and *āśrama* in his time was in disarray, it must have been a fact of life in an earlier age, otherwise the scriptural provisions would be meaningless.[44] It seems that, while in Manu's time all *brāhmaṇas* could not be relied upon to spread 'Hinduism' because many had become indistinguishable from Buddhists,[45] no such fears obtained in Śaṅkara's time and the mandate could be extended to all.

VIII

In his introduction to his commentary on the *Bhagavadgītā*, Śaṅkara enunciates the basic mode of the diffusion of Hindu religion and culture. He explains why God, as Kṛṣṇa, decided to preach the supreme truth through the *Bhagavadgītā*: Though he has no end to serve, out of a desire to show his grace (*bhūtānugrahajigṛkṣayā*), he taught the twofold dharma contained in the Veda once again *to Arjuna, and through him to the whole world*. Śaṅkara says that God chose Arjuna to impart his teaching, because Arjuna was in need of it, being immersed in sorrow and delusion, and because he was a good man; and the *dharma accepted and practised by good men will eventually be accepted by all.*[46] These good men were represented by the communities who practised *varṇāśramadharma* under the leadership of the *brāhmaṇas*. According to Śaṅkara, the *brāhmaṇa* model is primary. Even God incarnated himself for the sake of protecting 'earthly Brahman', a term explained by Nīlakaṇṭha to mean 'The Vedas, the Brāhmaṇas and Yajñas, or sacrifices'.[47] Moreover, Śaṅkara goes on to say that it is through the preservation of *brāhmaṇatva* that 'the Vedic religion could be preserved since thereon depend all distinctions of caste and religious order'.[48] Sastry interprets the term *brāhmaṇatva* as 'spiritual life' and while this is certainly a valid, if lofty, interpretation, the context is so clearly one of *varṇāśramadharma* that the word *brāhmaṇatva* could easily, and perhaps does, refer to the *brāhmaṇavarṇa*. As Ānandagiri explains 'kṣatriyas and others require the help of the brāhmaṇas, the spiritual class, in the performance of the sacred rites and in the study of the Scriptures.'[49]

In order to perceive the relevance and significance of these remarks, the history of the Hinduization of the region—a thread relinquished earlier—must now be picked up. After Cambodia replaced Fu-nan in dominance in the seventh century, Manu's model can be again seen in operation in Kambuja. When Jayavarman II became King of Cambodia in 802 CE he invited a *brāhmaṇa* named Hiraṇyadama from Janapada (probably in India). 'Hiraṇyadama instituted the cult of *devarāja* and initiated Śivakaivalya, the royal *guru*, into the rituals of this worship to become religiously independent of Java. The royal priesthood lasted for 250 years as evidenced by an inscription of 1052 A.D.'[50] A verse from the *Manusmṛti* is cited in an inscription about *two centuries ago*,[51] and there is evidence that the preceptor of Indravarman of Kambuja, Śivasoma by name, was a pupil of the famous Śaṅkarācārya,[52] who, as we saw earlier, espouses Manu's model in his introduction to his commentary on the *Bhagavadgītā*.

IX

It is clear, therefore, that what Larus calls the Brahman hypothesis did not operate by default. The most authoritative legal text of classical Hinduism, the *Manusmṛti*, clearly charges the *brāhmaṇas* of a particular region with the task of missionizing the world, a role which other *brāhmaṇas* also adopted. Furthermore, it also devised an appropriate myth and ritual for such expansion, as well as an appropriate sociology, and pressed the most fundamental social institution of humanity—that of marriage—into service as well. That this Brahmin model was not merely a theoretical construct but an operational reality is established by facts garnered from historical and epigraphic records of the history of Cambodia, and is supported by similar records from other parts of Southeast Asia.[53]

The conclusion of this chapter, however, requires both clarification and amplification. The conclusion contains two components: one ideological and the other historical. The historical evidence of the spread of Hinduism to Southeast Asia is too patent to be called in question. The point which readers may find more difficult to accept is the claim that Hinduism also contains an ideology for missionary activity, as distinguished from the history of its actual expansion. If one wants to *reject* the evidence of the ideology adduced here and yet wishes to *accept* the fact of widespread and undeniable evidence of Hindu beliefs and practices in Southeast Asia, then the only possible explanation of such presence seems to be Hindu migration, without involving the conversion to Hinduism by the local population.

There can be no doubt that Hindu migration was involved, but this does not negate the fact of conversion to Hinduism. For instance, 'Among the many administrative reforms taken up by Kauṇḍinya I, was the introduction of Sanskrit and [the] alphabet of North Indian origin' among 'the people of Fu-nan'.[54] The *people* existed prior to the arrival of the *individual* Kauṇḍinya and according to the Chinese accounts *they* elected him king.[55] Even if this was not the case, great caution is required in the matter. Most of the population of North America, for instance, is the result of European migration and is Christian. Are we then to conclude that Christianity is *not* a missionary religion? It is because we do not question the fact that Christianity is a missionary religion *to begin with*, that we do not draw such an erroneous conclusion.

At this stage another counter-argument against the thesis of the chapter could be adduced—that the truly missionary religion to emerge out of India is not Hinduism but Buddhism. There is little doubt that Buddhism has been a far more successful missionary religion than Hinduism.[56] However, two religions can both be missionary and yet one can be far more successful than the other. This cannot be taken to mean that the less successful religion is not missionary, only that it is less successful as such. For instance, 'In some areas where Islam and Christianity are competing for converts, Islam is gaining at a rate of ten to one.'[57] Are we to conclude from this that Islam is a missionary religion and Christianity not so? Thus there can be little doubt that ancient Hinduism was *ideologically as well as historically* a missionary religion, if we take the evidence from the *Manusmṛti* into account.

PART IV

12

Karma and Rebirth in the *Manusmṛti*

I

Karma is a key concept in Indic thought and finds an important place in the *Manusmṛti* along with the concept of rebirth, its logical corollary. This connection between karma and its effects possesses an interesting dimension in the *Manusmṛti*. The key element in the concept of karma is the invariable relationship between cause and effect, which *usually* gets linked with the process of rebirth. In one context in the *Manusmṛti*, however, it also takes a generational rather than a metempsychotic turn, as in the following verses (4.172–74):

> [172] Like the earth, practising unrighteousness does not produce instant results in this world; but turning around gradually, it cuts off its perpetrator by his roots. [173] If not himself, then his sons; if not his sons, then his grandsons—an unrighteous act once committed never fails to repay its perpetrator. [174] Through unrighteous ways a man first prospers; then he experiences good fortune; next he vanquishes his opponents; but in the end he is destroyed root and all.[1]

The Sanskrit word used in the text is *dharma* rather than *karma*; the word translated as 'unrighteousness' is *adharma*, but clearly bad action or bad karma is involved. The use of the simile of *gauḥ* is interesting because the word can mean either 'cow' or 'earth', with one set of commentators taking it in one sense and another set in the other. G. Bühler suggests, however, that 'it is not impossible that the word has to be taken both ways, and that the author wishes to give with it both a *sādharmya* and *vaidharmya dṛṣṭānta*'.[2] Patrick Olivelle elucidates this suggestion as follows:

> *Like the earth*: (*gaur iva*: lit. 'like a cow') there appears to be a double simile here, the one based on similarity and the other on dissimilarity. In the latter case, the comparison is with a cow; in the former, it is with the earth (also bearing the epithet cow). Like the earth—and unlike a cow—unrighteous conduct does not bear fruit immediately but only with the passage of time.[3]

That karma could have *familial* consequences, not merely generationally, but even in one's own time is hinted at in *Manusmṛti* 10.92: 'By selling meat, lac, or salt, a Brahmin falls immediately from his caste; by selling milk, he becomes a *śūdra* in three days.'[4] Becoming a *śūdra* here has obvious consequences for the family. P.V. Kane offers the interesting personal remark here that in his own 'boyhood some poor brāhmaṇas had begun to sell milk with the result that they were very much looked down upon by the villagers. There would be the temptation to add water to the milk to gain money.'[5]

There is a tendency sometimes to interpret the workings of karma exclusively along individualistic lines; the evidence from the *Manusmṛti* presents a more elastic concept of karma, whose effects can work down the generational chain and also affect one's family members. Similarly, there is a tendency within Hinduism to interpret the workings of karma exclusively in metempsychotic terms, but here also the *Manusmṛti* presents a more elastic picture. According to the *Manusmṛti*, karma can be shared in some situations. This is the obvious implication of *Manusmṛti* 8.304–05, 308:

> [304] A sixth portion of everyone's merits goes to the king who protects; a sixth portion of their demerits likewise goes to him when he fails

> to protect. [305] When one studies, sacrifices, gives gifts, and performs worship, the king takes a sixth portion of it as his share by providing proper protection. [308] They call a king who gathers a sixth portion as levy without providing protection 'on who gathers all the filth of the entire population.'[6]

Karma is capable of being transferred in the *Manusmṛti*, both to one and away from one. According to *Manusmṛti* 8.314–16: '[314] A wise thief, with his hair loose, should go to the king confessing his theft: "I have done this. Punish me", [315] and carrying on his shoulder a pestle, a club of Khadira wood, a spear with both ends sharpened, or an iron rod. [316] Whether he is punished or released, the thief is released from the theft; but if the king fails to punish him, he takes upon himself the thief's guilt.'[7]

An even more general pattern of karmic transference is hinted at in *Manusmṛti* 8.317: 'The murderer of a learned Brahmin rubs his sin off on the man who eats his food, an adulterous wife on her husband, a pupil and a patron of a sacrifice on the teacher, and a thief on the king.'[8]

Similarly, one could lose karmic merit just as one could acquire karmic demerit, as illustrated by the case below. According to *Manusmṛti* 3.99–101:

> [99] When a guest arrives, he [the host] should offer him a seat and water and give him food as well according to rule, after garnishing it according to his ability. [100] When a Brahmin resides without being treated with respect, he takes away all the good works of even a man who lives by gleaning ears of grain or who makes daily offerings in the five sacred fires. [101] Some straw, a place on the floor, water, and fourth, a pleasant word of welcome—at least these are never wanting in the houses of good people.[9]

The *Manusmṛti* also presents an example where karma works itself out both in this life as well as in the hereafter. This happens in the case of the wife who commits adultery. According to *Manusmṛti* 5.164: 'By being unfaithful to her husband, a woman becomes disgraced in the world, takes birth in a jackal's womb, and is afflicted with evil diseases.'[10] Could it be taken to mean that evil diseases catch up with her even in the present life? The word used in the Sanskrit text for 'evil diseases' is *pāpa-roga*, a term on which Patrick Olivelle provides the following note: 'The term *pāparoga*, which frequently occurs in Manu, does not simply refer to a serious sickness. The disease is regarded as the consequence of sins committed in previous lives (see 2.48–53). Evil diseases are generally viewed as skin diseases of various types.'[11]

The same verse also appears later literally in the *Manusmṛti* (9.30) and is translated as follows by P.V. Kane: 'By playing false to her husband (i.e. by adultery) the wife is censored in this world, she becomes (after death) a female jackal and is tormented by evil diseases (such as leprosy).'[12] According to Kane, however: 'As regards husband and wife, the Dharmaśāstra works say a good deal but all that is said should not be taken literally.'[13]

Finally, the *Manusmṛti* also seems to imply, in the following verse, that karmic sin can be dissipated within this life itself. According to *Manusmṛti* 8.318: 'When men who have committed sins are punished by kings, they go to heaven immaculate, like virtuous men who have done good deeds.'[14] P.V. Kane cites this verse in support of the belief that the 'punishment of a sinful deed (like a theft, etc.) by the king liquidated the consequences of sin, made the offender pure and enabled him to reach heaven as men of good deeds do.'[15] Thus the picture of karma which emerges in the *Manusmṛti* is of it being as something elastic, plastic and in P.V. Kane's view, occasionally bombastic.

II

Certain issues arising from the material presented above need to be faced before we venture further into karmic territory. We may not be able to resolve all the issues involved but they should be flagged. One such issue is the extent to which some of the statements made in the *Manusmṛti* regarding karma and rebirth are to be taken literally.

The point, simply put, is that the doctrine of karma and rebirth seems to have been used, at least occasionally, as a literary trope rather than as a veridical statement. It seems reasonable to ask that when the *Manusmṛti* says that if one steals bronze one becomes a ruddy goose (12.62), is it merely making a figuratively colourful connection, almost tongue in cheek, or does it intend to be taken literally and seriously? I do not mean to imply that it does not intend to convey the message that certain acts have consequences for our next lives. The point is whether, in putting matters this way, it is yielding to the temptation of indulging in a literary flourish. We know that the *Manusmṛti* indulges in wordplay as when in 9.26 it juxtaposes the words *śrī* and *strī*, or in 8.16 etymologizes the word *vṛṣala* or low-born as follows: 'Lord Justice is truly the bull (*vṛṣa*), and a man who impedes (*alam*) him the gods call a low-born (*vṛṣa-la*).'[16]

Closer to home is the way it etymologizes the Sanskrit word for meat, namely, *māṃsa*: 'Me he (*māṃ sa*) will eat in the next world, whose meat (*māṃsa*) I eat in this world—this, the wise declare, is what gave the name to and discloses the true nature of "meat" (*māṃsa*).' (*Manusmṛti* 5.55).[17] Patrick Olivelle notes:

> The belief that the food a person eats may in turn eat him appears to be old. Such sentiments are expressed in Vedic literature with reference not only to animals but also to plants and grains: JB 1.43; ŚB 12.9.1.1. Here Manu gives a phonetic etymology for the Sanskrit term for meat, *māṃsa*, the two syllables of which mean 'me' (*mām*) and 'he' (*sa*).[18]

I do not wish to be seen as deriding the *Manusmṛti* for striking an etymological blow on behalf of vegetarianism; what I am concerned with is that we may have to distinguish carefully between what it is saying *for effect* and what it is stating as *an effect* of karma.[19]

This becomes an even more delicate issue when we identify some kind of an inner logic underlying the assignments of rebirth. P.V. Kane states, for instance:

> It may be noted that some of the births assigned to those guilty of thefts of various articles have some logic or reason behind those regulations e.g. when Manu XII.62 and Yāj. III.214 prescribe that a thief of grains becomes a rat in the next birth or when Manu XII.61 prescribes that a thief of jewels, pearls and coral is born among the class of goldsmiths, one can easily appreciate this retribution as appropriate or reasonable, but the same cannot be said of all others.[20]

Could it be that a similar tongue in cheek approach underlies such apparent logic?

III

Another issue also has to do with the *Manusmṛti*'s understanding of karma. The American Council of Learned Societies sponsored two conferences on karma in 1976 and 1978. Gerald James Larson reflects thus on the papers presented on these and similar occasions:

> An interesting theoretical puzzle that has emerged from the series of conferences on the notion of karma in South Asian thought is the apparent anomaly between what might be called the 'transference of karma interpretation' and the 'non-transference of karma interpretation.' The former appears to correlate with McKim Marriott's and Ronald Inden's transactional analysis, involving giving and receiving (in the modalities of 'optimal,' 'pessimal,' 'maximal,' and 'minimal') within the context of a unified coded substance and encompassing the entire range of *varṇāśramadharma* with all of its rules and principles regarding food, pollution, marriage, work, and kinship. Textual authority for such a transactional analysis (in addition to its contextual data) includes not only Manu and other traditions of *dharma-śāstra* but also Vedic traditions of transference (e.g., the *sapiṇḍīkaraṇa*, and so forth) and more popular notions of transference found, for example, in the epics, the *Purāṇas* and later *bhakti* traditions. The 'non-transference of karma interpretation' appears to correlate with certain philosophical traditions (for example, Yoga and Vedānta), involving the notions of *liṅga*, *karmāśayas*, *vāsanās* and *saṃskāras*, in which a person's karmic heritage and karmic possibilities are construed individually with apparently no provision for transactional transference. Textual authority for such a 'non-transference perspective' is, of course, the *darśana* literature or at least those portions of *darśana* literature concerned with *mokṣa*.[21]

Larson further notes that the 'purpose of these conferences was to uncover and describe the system of karma in South Asia as an "indigenous conceptual system" and yet the two most cogent interpretations (namely, "transference" and "non-transference") appear to make that purpose unattainable.'[22] It is indeed a rather awkward outcome for a conference, designed to delineate an 'indigenous conceptual system', to find itself caught in the end on the horns of such a dilemma.

The reader will notice that the *Manusmṛti* was placed in the 'transference' category by Larson, a point on which more will be said later.

Attempts were also made to reconcile these two divergent perspectives. One such attempt was made by Karl H. Potter, whose views are summarized by Larson as follows:

> Karl H. Potter has suggested that the 'transference' orientation be designated the '*pravṛtti*-perspective' and the 'non-transference' orientation the '*nivṛtti*-perspective'. Potter has also suggested that these two perspectives may represent divergent historical traditions in South Asian thought that have coexisted with one another over many centuries and have generated various efforts at reconciliation—for example, the kind of reconciliation attempted in the *Gītā*.[23]

This resolution, however, left Larson unsatisfied:

> Why? Because it introduced the interpretive notion of 'history', a category which had no demonstrable place within any South Asian 'indigenous conceptual system' (at least prior to the middle of the nineteenth century). Quite apart from the merit or lack of merit of an historical interpretation, it appears that South Asians themselves seldom if ever used such an explanation. In other words, however, when South Asians themselves dealt with the issues of 'transference', 'non-transference', and so forth, it certainly was not from the perspective of historical interpretation, and by providing historical interpretations of South Asian thought and culture modern interpreters are more or less talking to themselves. There is nothing wrong with the latter enterprise, for at some stage in our work we as modern interpreters of South Asian culture must 'encompass' (in Dumont's sense) what South Asian culture represents in our experience. The crucial methodological issue, however, is that the 'encompassed' can never pass itself off as an adequate characterization of an indigenous interpretation. In other words, to put it directly, historical interpretation is *ours*, not *theirs!* In a South Asian environment, historical interpretation is *no* interpretation. It is a zero-category.[24]

I have cited this passage at some length because it goes to the heart of the matter in several ways. It points out that 'historical' reconciliation does not sit well with the ahistorical Hindu tradition; it also distinguishes between the emic and etic perspectives quite clearly. We are not bound to an emic perspective in this book and in fact move between the two perspectives freely, so there is nothing to prevent us from accepting the etic reconciliation. Nevertheless, Larson's problematization of the issue from an emic perspective, and his attempt to resolve it from an emic perspective, is bound to be of interest.

Larson argues that 'on the one hand we have indisputable evidence both for a "transference" and a "non-transference" perspective (and various ambiguities in between),'[25] on the other we cannot use the historical method to resolve these ambiguities as suggested by Karl Potter, 'since that approach methodologically begs the question.'[26] He then alludes to McKim Marriott's 'transactional interpretation, which nicely avoids not only unwarranted historical interpretation but a number of other methodological biases as well.' But according to Larson, if we employ an emic view, 'the acid test of a theory like Marriott's must surely be the tradition's own theoretical reflection, and yet the theory appears *not* to pass the test.' He goes on to say:

> This impasse then leads to the following dilemma: either (a) karma as an 'indigenous conceptual system' harbors an anomaly which cannot be resolved other than by going outside the indigenous tradition (in the direction of historical, structuralist, or some other non-South Asian interpretation) or (b) karma as an 'indigenous conceptual system' was never recognized as such by those theoreticians within the tradition who were responsible for creating 'indigenous conceptual systems'. Moreover, if one is tempted to suggest a third alternative, namely, that we are talking about two or more 'indigenous conceptual systems', that does not solve the anomaly, for such an alternative forces us either (a) to move back to the first part of the dilemma or (b) to argue that there is no 'indigenous conceptual system' of karma that encompasses in any important theoretical way the plurality of systems that have been uncovered. All of the possibilities, in other words, lead to the remarkable conclusion that the original question for research cannot

properly be asked—namely, what is the meaning of karma as an 'indigenous conceptual system' in South Asia? [27]

Larson, however, refused to be gored by the horns of this dilemma and tried to provide a larger conceptual framework from within the Hindu tradition to reconcile the two through the Sāṅkhya system, by invoking the following terms: (1) *liṅga*, the 'marked core' made up of *buddhi*, *ahaṃkāra*, *manas*, the five sense-capacities and the five action capacities, referred to as *trayodaśa-karaṇa* or 'thirteenfold instrument'; (2) *bhāva* or 'projecting set of predispositions' such as meritorious behaviour (*dharma*), unmeritorious behaviour (*a-dharma*), knowledge (*jñāna*), non-knowledge (*ajñāna*), absence of passion (*vairāgya*), passion (*rāga*), power (*aiśvarya*) and lack of power (*anaiśvarya*); (3) *liṅga-śarira* or 'subtle body' which is 'made of five *tanmātras* or subtle elements, and is the subtle *tāmasa*-vehicle that accompanies the *liṅga* in the process of transmigration';[28] (4) non-transmigrating *sthūla-śarira* or gross body coming from our parents; and (5) *bhautika-sarga* or manifest world which 'functions as a kind of theatre, or to use the favourite Sāṅkhya analogy, a stage…'[29] In this process the three *guṇas* play their role. Both the *liṅga* and the *bhāvas* can be predominantly *sāttvika* or *tāmasa*, with *rajas* providing the energy for either. According to such a scheme 'the term "karma" can be used appropriately both in the sense of determined "process" (namely, *liṅga*) and in the sense of determining "praxis", or purposeful human activity (namely, *bhāva*).'[30]

Larson then concludes that such a system might reconcile the 'transference' and 'non-transference' perspectives of karma because:

> …. one can describe the Sāṅkhya conceptual system of karma as a kind of interactionist social psychology in that it treats the 'individual person' as 'dividual', a product of the interacting of a 'marked core', a gross genetically inherited physical body, and a social field (*varṇāśramadharma*) wherein a continuous process/praxis unfolds. What is so strikingly different, however, is the valuation which Sāṅkhya assigns to its sociology of knowledge and its social psychology. When one inquires into what Werner Stark has called the implicit 'axiological grid' of a conceptual system, or what Max Weber has called variously

> the *Wertgesichtspunkt* (the 'value view-point'), or the *Wertbeziehung* (the 'value-relation') of a conceptual system, one encounters the remarkable conclusion that all of our 'ideas' and all of our 'social realities' are valuable only to the extent that they make us aware of that which is closest to us and yet irreducible to any intellectual or social formulation, namely, our simple presence to ourselves, our consciousness in and of itself.[31]

It may be possible to argue, however, that the *Manusmṛti* offers an existential and almost commonsensical reconciliation of these perspectives, depending on whether one is pursuing the *puruṣārthas* of *dharma, artha and kāma*, which involve a 'transference' model of karma, or *mokṣa*, which involves a 'non-transference' model of karma, for the simple reason that in pursuing the first three one mostly interacts with others and in pursuing the last, one mostly acts on one's own. One strives for other goals *with* others, one strives for *mokṣa oneself*. In any case, one is *oneself* the *key* variable in this process according to *Manusmṛti* 4.238–243:

> [238] Gradually and without hurting any creature, he should pile up merit (*dharma*) like termites an anthill, so as to secure an escort in the next world; [239] for in the next world, neither father nor mother stands by him as his escort; nor does son, wife, or relative. Only merit stands by him. [240] Alone a creature is born, and alone it dies. Alone it enjoys the fruits of its good deeds, alone also the fruits of its evil deeds. [241] While his relatives discard the dead body on earth as if it were a piece of wood or a clod of earth and depart with averted faces, his merit accompanies him. [242] To secure an escort, therefore, let him gradually pile up merit every day; for with merit as his escort, he will cross over the darkness that is difficult to cross. [243] The escort quickly leads that man, who is devoted to the Law (*dharma*) and whose sins have been erased by ascetic toil, to the next world, glittering with an ethereal body.[32]

IV

Another dimension of the issue of karma is raised when the *Manusmṛti* discusses in some detail the issue of *śrāddha* or ancestral offerings in chapter three. The following note on *śrāddha* by Bruce M. Sullivan helps us understand the concept:

> ŚRĀDDHA. Faithful; the name of a ritual performed for deceased ancestors. Rituals include the daily offering of water in memory of the deceased, as well as periodic offerings of ball of grains (Piṇḍa). Offerings are made to the father, grandfather, and great-grandfather on both the paternal and maternal sides of the family. Śrāddha rites place the deceased among the Pitṛs (Fathers, or Ancestors) who enjoy an afterlife in the celestial realm of Pitṛ Loka. Offerings of water and food provide needed sustenance for the deceased in the afterlife, without which the deceased would be a wandering, hungry ghost (Preta) who could haunt the living. Śrāddha is a ritual that was current in the Vedic era (1500 to 700 B.C.E.) and has persisted to the present despite almost universal acceptance of the idea of rebirth according to one's Karma.[33]

This description, however, does not clearly indicate an important dimension of *śrāddha* which is highlighted in its definition in the *Brahma Purāṇa*: 'whatever is given with faith to brāhmaṇas intending it to be for the (benefit of) the Pitṛs at a proper time, in a proper place, to deserving persons and in accordance with the prescribed procedure is called *śrāddha*.'[34]

We noted that the third chapter of the *Manusmṛti* deals in some detail with the rite of *śrāddha*; its twelfth chapter deals in some detail with the idea of karma and rebirth, ideas which pervade the text. The passage from Sullivan hinted at the possible contradiction between the concept of *śrāddha* and that of karma and rebirth, for if rebirth takes place according to one's karma, then how can the ancestral offerings made by others be of any consequence for the future destiny of the person? As P.V. Kane notes: 'It is difficult to reconcile the doctrine of karma and punarjanma with the system of śrāddhas in which balls of rice are offered to the three paternal ancestors of the performer of śrāddha.'[35] This logical contradiction between the practice of *śrāddha* and the concept of karma and rebirth is clearly perceived in Jainism, which categorically rejects the Hindu rite of *śrāddha* on account of its acceptance of the doctrines of karma and rebirth.[36] In the case of Hinduism, however, the situation is different, which is reflected in the *Manusmṛti*, within which both are accepted side by side, as in Hinduism in general. P.V. Kane explains:

> The offering of balls of rice to the spirits of the departed male ancestors was in vogue in the times of the Veda, probably even before the Vedas, and the theory of karma and punarjanma arose later and as people were not prepared to give up the theory of śrāddhas, they kept both.[37]

Indeed, it is remarkable that the *same* metaphor in Hindu literature has been used to illustrate the workings of both *śrāddha*, and karma and rebirth—that of a calf seeking out its mother in a herd of cows. According to the *Matsya Purāṇa*: 'Just as a calf finds its own mother among many cows that are scattered about, so the mantras repeated in the śrāddha carry the food to the Pitṛs',[38] and the 'Mahabharata says that the consequences of what a man does will seek him out later "as surely as a calf does its mother in a herd of cows".'[39]

The contradiction between the rite of *śrāddha* and the doctrine of karma and rebirth was perceived by Hindu thinkers in earlier times, and the following resolutions are attempted in the *Purāṇas*:

1. The *Agni Purāṇa* maintains that the *pitṛs*, upon being satisfied by the offerings made during *śrāddha*, confer long life, progeny, wealth, learning, heaven, *mokṣa* (final beatitude), all happiness and a kingdom[40]—a fairly impressive and comprehensive list of benefits. The point to note here is that the benefits are conferred directly by the *pitṛs*, who are presumably stationed in celestial realms from where they deliver such benefits.
2. The focus of the description in the *Matsya Purāṇa* is somewhat different and pertains to the question of *how* the benefits of *śrāddha* reach the ancestors in the *various* states they may have assumed. The answer provided is that the identification of the fathers, grandfathers and great-grandfathers with the deities Vasus, Rudras and Ādityas, in accordance with a Vedic passage, secures this. If the ancestor has become a god, the offering reaches one in the form of nectar; if an *asura* (or *daitya*), in the form of sensual enjoyments; if a beast, in the form of grass; and if a snake, in the form of wind (on which snakes are supposed to subsist).[41]

3. The *Mārkaṇḍeya Purāṇa* identifies the mechanism through which the *śrāddha* operates as follows: the superintending deities of the *śrāddha*, namely, Vasus, Rudras and Ādityas become gratified by the *śrāddha* offerings, and they in turn gratify the ancestors of human beings and confer the various benefits of longevity and so on, on the performers of the rite.[42]
4. The *Vāyu Purāṇa* offers the explanation that 'at the time of śrāddha the ancestors enter the Brahmans (invited) after assuming an aerial form and that [when] the best of Brahmans are honoured with clothes, foods (sic), gifts, eatables, liquids, cows, horses and villages Pitṛs become pleased.'[43]

There are thus fundamentally two ways of receiving the fruits of *śrāddha* by those for whom it is offered in these schemes: either through the Vedic gods in the form of Vasus, Rudras and Ādityas, or directly from the ancestors themselves.

It is worth noting that *both* these modes of reconciling *śrāddha* with the doctrine of karma and rebirth, as P.V. Kane notes,[44] are hinted at in the *Manusmṛti*. The first option is reminiscent of *Manusmṛti* 3.284: 'The fathers, they say, are the Vasus; the grandfathers are the Rudras; and the great-grandfathers are the Ādityas—this is an ancient scriptural statement.'[45] The second option is reminiscent of *Manusmṛti* 3.189: '… for the ancestors stand by those twice-born who have been invited, follow them like the wind, and sit with them as they sit.'[46]

V

The above discussion helps us transit from the discussion of karma as such to that of rebirth in the *Manusmṛti*, although obviously the two concepts are closely linked.

Ludo Rocher has observed that 'one cannot help being struck by the fact that, in the Dharmaśāstras, the construction and destruction of various systems outweigh by far the attention given to theoretical considerations and analyzing the technique of karma and rebirth.'[47] This is certainly true of the *Manusmṛti*. In view of this fact, we may first take up the various systems for investigation, and then follow up the investigation with a discussion and analysis of the technique of karma and rebirth involved in the *Manusmṛti*.

The reader may have noticed the use of the plural in the word 'systems'. Ludo Rocher explains the need for the plural form as follows:

> Manu 12.1–82 exhibits a strange mixture of general considerations on karma and *saṃsāra*, on the one hand, and different systems of reincarnation, on the other. One gets the impression that passages which originally belonged to a variety of sources—or were independent units—have been collected by the compiler of the *Manusmṛti* and put together in succession, often without the slightest transition. This procedure, which is not unknown elsewhere in Manu—and in other Dharmaśāstras—should be a warning to us when we try to describe *the* theory of karma and rebirth as it emerges from Dharmaśāstra literature. To be sure, there are a number of general underlying ideas and concepts. Yet these have been used to elaborate several very different systems, which are mutually independent but all equally within the range of *dharma*. I shall first describe the systems and then discuss some of the general ideas.[48]

Ludo Rocher then proceeds to identify five such systems of karma and rebirth in the *Manusmṛti*.

First System

Manusmṛti 12.3 introduces a threefold classification of the origins of karma, in terms of mind (*manas*), speech (*vāc*) and body (*deha*). The first system of rebirth turns on this distinction, in which examples of the three types of karma are provided by Ludo Rocher as follows:

Mental action:
- coveting the property of others
- thinking in one's heart of what is undesirable
- adherence to false (doctrines)

Verbal action:
- abusing (others)
- (speaking) untruth

detracting from the merits of all men
talking idly

Bodily action:

taking what has not been given
injuring (creatures) without the sanction of the law
holding criminal intercourse with another man's wife [49]

It is noteworthy that in this system only negative karmas are specified, and although forms of karma are specified as ten, Rocher notes that only three karmic destinies are predicted:

> Each of the three types of karma uniformly leads to a specific form of rebirth:
> (sinful) mental action → a low caste
> (evil) verbal action → a bird or a beast
> (wicked) bodily action → something inanimate'[50]

Although only negative karmas are enumerated, overcoming them through control of mind, speech and body, which qualifies one as a *tridaṇdin* or the holder of the triple staff, leads one to *siddhi* or '"complete success" which is normally interpreted as synonymous with mokṣa',[51] in accordance with *Manusmṛti* 12.10–11.

Second System

The second system in the *Manusmṛti* (12.34) uses the three *guṇas*, the constituents or qualities of matter known as *sattva*, *rajas* and *tamas* (or goodness, passion and darkness), and each of these categories leads to a specific type of rebirth, as in the first system:

sattva → the state of gods
rajas → the state of men
tamas → the state of beasts

One could possess these qualities in three degrees, so one ends up with nine subtypes, each with their own outcomes as follows:

The Realm of Goodness		
First	*Second*	*Highest*
Ascetics	Sacrificers	Brahmās
Mendicants	Seers	All-creators
Priests	Gods	Dharma
Hosts in heavenly chariots	Vedas	The great
Constellations	Lights	The unmanifest
Demons	Years	
	Ancestors	
	Realized ones	

The Realm of Passion		
Low	*Middle*	*High*
Prize-fighters	Kings	Celestial musicians
Wrestlers	Nobles	Goblins
Dancers	Preceptors of kings	Spirits of fertility
Men who make their living with weapons	Those best in wars of words	Followers of the Gods
Those addicted to gambling and drinking		Celestial nymphs

The Realm of Darkness		
Low	*Middle*	*High*
Immovable (beings)	Elephants	Actors
Worms and insects	Horses	Birds
Fish	Servants	Men who cheat
Snakes	Despised foreigners	Murderous demons
Tortoises	Lions	Flesh-eating demons
Domestic beasts	Tigers	
Wild beasts	Boars[52]	

Third System

The third system is covered in verses 52–53 of chapter 12 of the *Manusmṛti*. It starts with a very general statement, which could serve as an introduction to any treatment of karma and rebirth, and focuses on the results of negative karmas:

> In consequence of attachment to (the objects of) the senses, and in consequence of the non-performance of their duties, fools, and the lowest of men, reach the vilest births.
>
> What wombs this individual soul enters in this world and in consequence of what actions—learn the particulars of that at length and in due order.[53]

The account, however, then turns into something very specific and deals with the karmic fate of those who commit the four 'mortal sins' as it were, called *mahāpātakas*:

1. killing a brāhmaṇa
2. drinking (the spirituous liquor called) surā
3. stealing (the gold of a brāhmaṇa)
4. adultery with a *guru*'s wife[54]

Then there are those who could be 'guilty of offenses which are 'equal to' each of the four mortal sins', such as the following according to the *Manusmṛti* (11.56–59):

> [56] A lie concerning one's superiority, a slander that reaches the king's ear, and false accusations against an elder are equal to killing a Brahmin. [57] Abandoning the Veda, reviling the Veda, giving false testimony, killing a friend, eating unfit food or forbidden food—these six are equal to drinking liquor. [58] Stealing deposits, men, horses, silver, land, diamonds, or gems, tradition tells us, is equal to stealing gold. [59] Sexual intercourse with uterine sisters, unmarried girls, lowest-born women, and the wives of a friend or son, they say, is equal to sex with an elder's wife.[55]

It seems the rules for the four *mahāpātakas* 'also apply to those "associated with such offenders" (M. 11.55).'[56]

The fate of those tainted by the *mahāpātakas* is described as follows (in *Manusmṛti* 12.54): 'Those who commit grievous sins causing loss of caste first go to dreadful hells during large spans of years; upon the expiration of that they reach the following transmigratory states.'[57] Ludo Rocher also includes the comparable rebirths listed in the *Yājñavalkya Smṛti* in a parallel column.

Mortal Sinners Type	*Form after Rebirth*	
	Manu	*Yājñavalkya*
Brahmin-killer	Dog	Deer
	Pig	Dog
	Donkey	Pig
	Camel	Camel
	Cow	
	Goat	
	Sheep	
	Deer	
	Bird	
	Untouchable	
	Mixed-birth tribal	
Wine-drinker	Worm	Donkey
	Insect	Mixed-birth tribal
	Moth	Musician/Magician
	Birds that eat excrement	
	Vicious creatures	
Thief	Spiders	Worm
	Snakes	Insect
	Lizards	Moth
	Aquatic animals	
	Vicious flesh-eating demons	

Defiler of the *guru*'s bed (wife)	Grass Shrub Creeper Carnivores Beasts with fangs Those doing cruel deeds[58]	Grass Shrub Creeper

Ludo Rocher notes the following differences between this system and the previous two: (1) it is more circumscribed; (2) within it the possible rebirths 'humans, animals, and plants appear side by side indiscriminately',[59] and (3) when the lists of *Manusmṛti* and *Yājñavalkya Smṛti* are compared, it appears that 'although the system as such was well established, the specific forms of rebirth were not'.[60]

Fourth System

This system, represented by *Manusmṛti* 12.61–69, focuses on stealing. This focus is also reflected in the *Yājñavalkya Smṛti* (3.213–15) and the *Viṣṇu Smṛti* (44.14–43), leading Ludo Rocher to remark that this:

> [...] confirms something we also know from other sources: classical India's preoccupation with theft; of all wrongdoings, theft is, in this kind of text, invariably given the most exhausting treatment. As a result, more than thirty types of theft are enumerated, each of them related to one single type of rebirth.[61]

It might be tedious to produce the list,[62] but Ludo Rocher notes that the two concluding stanzas in the sequence (*Manusmṛti* 12.68–69) deserve special consideration because:

> [...] the first seems to summarize the whole section by stating that whoever steals something from someone else becomes an animal. The second is interesting in that it specifically refers to the rebirth of women: women who are guilty of theft are reborn as the females of the animals listed in the preceding stanzas.[63]

Fifth System

In this system, the nature of one's rebirth is connected with the performance of one's *varṇa* duties. This system has both general and specific provisions. Ludo Rocher notes that in general, members of any *varṇa* who fall short of their specific duties, except in cases of emergency, 'migrate into despicable bodies' and 'will become the servants of the Dasyus.'[64] The specific results are more intimidating:

> Brāhmaṇa → Ulkāmukha Preta 'who feeds on what has been vomited'
> Kṣatriya → Kaṭapūtana (Preta) 'who eats impure substances and corpses'
> Vaiśya → Maitrākṣajyotika Preta 'who feeds on pus'
> Śūdra → Cāilāśaka (Preta) 'who feeds on moths' or 'body-lice'[65]

These severe outcomes are worth comparing with the apparently more reasonable provisions in 'Āpastamba (2.5.11.10–11) who lays down the general rule that the members of any *varṇa* "if they have fulfilled their duties" move up one *varṇa* in each future existence; on the contrary, "if they neglect their duties", they are each time reborn in the next lower *varṇa*.'[66] These analyses alert us to the fact that the *Manusmṛti* makes not only *literary* but also *didactic* use of the doctrine of karma.

VI

We turn now to the mechanics of karmic transmigration. One is struck by the paucity of *Dharmaśāstra* literature on this point. Thus we meet with the following statement in the *Manusmṛti* (12.12–14):

> [12] The one who makes this body act is called Kṣetrajña, 'the knower of the field'; the one who does the actions, on the other hand, the wise call Bhūtātman, 'the elemental self'. [13] Another inner self inmate to all embodied beings bears the name Jīva, 'the individual self', by whom are experienced all the pleasures and pains in succeeding births.
>
> [14] These two—Mahat, 'the Great', and Kṣetrajña, 'the knower of the field'—united with the elements, remain pervading the one who abides in creatures both great and small. [15] From his body innumerable forms stream forth, which constantly set in motion the creatures both great and small.[67]

These verses are not exactly clear, and perhaps because the actual mechanism was elaborated more in *Darśana* literature than in *Dharmaśāstra* literature, attempts to understand these verses draw heavily on that literature, as is obvious from the extended summary of such elucidatory speculation on these verses by the commentators offered by G. Bühler.[68]

The *Manusmṛti*, however, is relatively clear in dealing with purgatory:

> [16] When evil men die, another firm body is produced for them from the same five elemental particles, a body designed to suffer torments. [17] After experiencing there the torments of Yama with that body, they merge into those very elemental particles, each into its corresponding particle.
>
> [18] After paying for the sins resulting from attachment to sensory objects, sins that lead to misery, he is freed from taint and approaches the same two beings of great power. [19] Unwearied, these two jointly examine his merits and sins, linked to which one secures happiness or suffering here and in the hereafter.
>
> [20] If he acts righteously for the most part and unrighteously to a small degree, enveloped in those very elements, he enjoys happiness in heaven. [21] If, on the other hand, he acts unrighteously for the most part and righteously to a second degree, abandoned by those elements, he suffers the torments of Yama. [22] After enduring the torments of Yama, Jīva, 'the individual self', becomes freed from taint and enters those same five elements, each into its corresponding particle.
>
> [23] Seeing with his own intellect those transitions of this Jīva, 'the individual self', resulting from righteous and unrighteous conduct, let him always set his mind on righteous conduct.[69]

VII

The doctrine of karma and rebirth in Hinduism is sometimes considered as offering a fairly reasonable explanation of human destiny, especially when compared with the eschatological scenarios provided by Abrahamic religions. Critical philosophical investigation of the concept has, however, identified at least three aporias in relation to it: (1) When did karma begin? (2) What determines when a particular karma will fructify? and

(3) How do the karmas of various people interact? That is to say, if my wallet is stolen, is it because I am being punished for my karma, or is the thief committing fresh karma, or both? And so on. One may conclude this chapter with a consideration of any light the *Manusmṛti* might shed on these issues.

Out of these, the *Manusmṛti* seems to touch on the first of these in its very first chapter in the following verses (1.28–30):

> [28] As they are brought forth again and again, each creature follows on its own the very *activity assigned to it in the beginning by the lord.* [29] Violence or non-violence, gentleness or cruelty, righteousness (*dharma*) or unrighteousness (*adharma*), truthfulness or untruthfulness—whichever he *assigned to each at the time of creation*, it stuck automatically to that creature. [30] As at the change of seasons each season automatically adopts its own distinctive marks, so do embodied beings adopt their own distinctive acts.[70]

So, to the question 'What sets original karma in motion?', the *Manusmṛti* seems to suggest that God made an original karmic assignment. This view is somewhat unusual inasmuch as Hindu Vedantic thought in general avoids such a scenario, although it is easy to see how a strong commitment to theism may produce such a view.

13

The Doctrine of the *Yugas* in the *Manusmṛti*

I

The doctrine of the *yugas* is a distinguishing feature of classical Hinduism and is not found as such in Vedic Hinduism.[1] This doctrine of the *yugas* is, very briefly, the doctrine of the:

> [...] four periods or ages of the world's existence. These *yugas* comprise 1. *kṛta* or *satya*. 2. *tretā*. 3. *dvāpara*, the three periods which have already elapsed, and 4. *kali*, the present period. The duration of each is enumerated respectively as 1,728,000; 1,296,000; 864,000 and 432,000 years, the descending numbers successively reduced by one quarter, being supposed to represent a similar reduction in the physical and moral standards of each age. The four ages total 4,320,000 years and constitute a 'great *yuga*' (*mahā-yuga*).[2]

Reference to such vertiginous numbers is inescapable in dealing with this doctrine, but the reader need not feel lost in this numerical jungle. The four *yugas*, along with their succession, constitute the key element in the doctrine. Their names go back to the fact that in gambling:

> [...] like the European gamester the Indian employed a special terminology for the throws of dice: *kṛta* (cater, four), *tretā* (trey), *dvāpara* (deuce), and *kali* (ace). So important was gambling in the Indian scheme of things that these four terms were applied to the four periods (*yugas*) of the aeon.[3]

The *Manusmṛti* refers to this doctrine in two of its chapters, the first and the ninth. The first chapter deals with the origins of things, and the ninth one deals with the duties of kings.

II

The first chapter of the *Manusmṛti* refers to this doctrine in two sets of verses. The traditional cosmic chronology is spelled out in the first set (I.69–72) as follows:

> The Kṛta Age is said to last 4,000 years. It is preceded by a twilight lasting 400 years and followed by a twilight of the same length. For each of the three subsequent Ages, as also for the twilights that precede and follow them, the first number of the thousands and the hundreds is progressively diminished by one.[4] These four Ages, computed at the very beginning as lasting 12,000 years, are said to constitute a single Age of the gods. The sum total of 1,000 divine Ages should be regarded as a single day of Brahmā and his night as having the same duration.[5]

The computation here is given in terms of divine years, as indicated in the last line of the translation. According to this formulation, the lengths of the *yugas* are 'respectively 4,800; 3,600; 2,400; and 1,200 years of the gods, each of which equals 360 human years'.[6] This point is explained and expanded in the following verses (I.72–73):

> The sum total of 1,000 divine Ages should be considered a single day of Brahmā, and his night as having the same duration. Those who know

> the propitious day of Brahmā lasting 1,000 Ages, as also his night of the same duration—they are the people who truly know day and night.[7]

I shall presently turn to the human significance of this divine calculation. The other verses in the first chapter of the *Manusmṛti* which deal with the doctrine of the *yugas* describe the characteristic features of each Age and its implication for the state of *dharma* in that Age (I.81–86):

> In the Kṛta Age, the Law is whole, possessing all four feet; and so is truth. People never acquire any property through unlawful means. By acquiring such property, however, the Law is stripped of one foot in each of the subsequent Ages; through theft, falsehood, and fraud, the Law disappears a foot at a time.
>
> In the Kṛta Age, people are free from sickness, succeed in all their pursuits, and have a life span of 400 years. In the Tretā and each of the subsequent Ages, however, their life span is shortened by a quarter. The life span of mortals given in the Veda, the benefits of rites, and the power of embodied beings—they all come to fruition in the world in conformity with each Age.
>
> There is one set of Laws for men in the Kṛta Age, another in the Tretā, still another in the Dvāpara, and a different set in the Kali, in keeping with the progressive shortening taking place in each Age. Ascetic toil, they say, is supreme in the Kṛta Age; knowledge in Tretā; sacrifice in Dvāpara; and gift-giving alone in Kali.[8]

The first point to note is that the *Manusmṛti* is among the early texts that contain a reference to the doctrine of the *yugas*. Luis González-Reimann has explored the origin of the doctrine of the *yugas* in some detail and his conclusions on the point are worth sharing:

> [… We] discover that the yuga theory is conspicuously absent from Vedic literature and makes its first appearances in the *Mahābhārata* itself, in the *Yuga Purāṇa* (a chapter of the *Gārgīya Jyotiṣa*), and in the *Mānava Dharma Śāstra*, all of which are roughly contemporaneous and date from the last centuries BCE or the early centuries CE. These texts reflect differing versions of the yuga theory, as would be expected at a

> time when the system was still taking shape. Also from this period is the Buddhist Pali Canon, in which the terms *kali, dvāpara, tretā* and *kṛta* appear many times, but always with reference to the names of the dice throws or the negative or positive—*kali* or *kṛta*—qualities of something. They are not applied to the yugas. This indicates that it was more common at the time to associate these names with dice throws or with things deemed good or bad, than with yugas. The connection between the names of the dice throws and those of the yugas made it easy to incorporate the yuga theory into the *Mahābhārata* and, eventually, superimpose its cosmic-historical blueprint onto the epic story.[9]

The association of the names of the throws of dice with the *yugas* is an important issue, which will also surface later in the chapter.

Let us now revert to the discussion of the doctrine of the four *yugas* with two facts in mind: (1) the fact that the 'best we can do with the available evidence is to date' the *Manusmṛti* 'between the first century BCE and the second century CE';[10] (2) and the fact that according to Hindu chronology, as represented by the *yugas*, we are living at present in the Kali Yuga, which is said to have commenced with the Mahābhārata War.[11] From the perspective of the point about to be made, it is very important to bear this coincidence of the Mahābhārata War and the commencement of the Kali Yuga in mind, and to note that the Kali Yuga is supposed to end catastrophically. The following observations of Professor A.L. Basham help place these traditions of the Mahābhārata War and the end of the Kali Yuga in a historical perspective:

> The end of the Kali-yuga, according to many epic passages, is marked by confusion of classes, the overthrow of established standards, the cessation of all religious rites, and the rule of cruel and alien kings. Soon after this the world is destroyed by flood and fire. This view is propounded strongly in texts which date from about the beginning of the Christian era, when alien kings did in fact rule much of India, and established practices were shaken by heresies such as Buddhism and Jainism. An earlier tradition would place the Mahābhārata War c. 900 B.C., according to which the 1,200 years of the Kali-yuga, *if read as human years and not as 'years of the gods'*, would at this time be nearing their end. Evidently some pious Hindus thought that the dissolution

of the cosmos was imminent. Perhaps it is to the departure of this fear in later times that we must attribute the devising of the 'years of the gods', which made the dissolution of the world comfortably distant.[12]

The fact that the scheme of the *yugas* has been presented in divine years, or the 'years of the gods', in the *Manusmṛti* needs to be revisited in the light of these remarks,[13] for they seem to indicate that, by the time the text was composed, the fear of immediate collapse had receded, so that one could make 'the dissolution of the world comfortably distant'. This interpretation seems to find support in the historical evidence available to us about the events surrounding the centuries immediately preceding and succeeding the Christian era. While the difficulties, caused by the various foreign invasions of north India by the Indo-Greeks, the Indo-Parthians, the Indo-Scythians, and then the Yüeh-chih tribes, from second century BCE until the first century CE,[14] were still very much part of the legacy of the author of the *Manusmṛti*, the hope of a recovery also seems to have been present on the horizon. The Jūnāgaḍh inscription of Rudradāman, dated c. 150 CE, indicates that signs of an indigenous revival were discernible. This inscription is not only 'among the earliest dated records of ancient India',[15] it is also the 'earliest important inscription in correct Sanskrit'.[16] Thus signs of indigenous self-assertion were in the air, and the danger of an immediate national collapse in the face of foreign invasions may have receded sufficiently by the time of the *Manusmṛti* to convert the human into divine years, and to push the nightmare into the distant future.

That the *Manusmṛti* refers to 'divine years' thus seems to indicate that it was composed in a period of recovery from a bleak mood, in which the outlook had been so dismal that total collapse was felt to be imminent. Such would be the case if the *yuga* calculations involved *human* years, as explained by Professor Basham. This conclusion thus seems to have historical support.

The series of verses in the *Manusmṛti* which speak in terms of divine years or the 'years of the gods' also go on to describe the features of the four *yugas*. This description is widely shared in the tradition, but the way this description ends in the *Manusmṛti* is potentially of great significance. It is claimed towards the end of this description that 'religious duties of men are different'[17] in the various Ages. The actual word used in the text, which is translated as 'religious duties', is the potent if polysemic word *dharma* itself. *Dharma* is often described *sanātana* in many texts. The word *sanātana* may mean either 'eternal' or 'immemorial'. But both these meanings emphasize the continuity of *dharma*, while the verses of the *Manusmṛti* (I.85–86) emphasize not its continuity but its mutability.[18] It is an interesting fact that the terminal verses are also shared by many other texts. As P.V. Kane points out:

> The dharmas in each of the four yugas are different; *tapas* is the highest in Kṛta, philosophic knowledge in Tretā, sacrifice in Dvāpara and charity alone in Kali (Manu I.85–86 = Parāśara I.22–23 = Śānti 232.27–28). Manu I.85, Śānti 232.27 and 261.8, Parāśara I.22 all have the same verse stating that the dharmas prescribed for men in each yuga differ.[19]

The point to note here is that in the verse found in the *Manusmṛti*, the different *dharmas* prescribed for the various Ages are spiritual in nature. In fact, G. Bühler translates the word *dharma* itself as 'virtue', when he translates this verse (I.86) as follows: 'In the Kṛta Age the chief (virtue) is declared to be (the performance of) austerities, in the Tretā (divine) knowledge, in the Dvāpara (the performance of) sacrifices, in the Kali liberality alone.'[20] It seems, however, that the idea was gradually extended to include social practices as well. If *dharma* in Kali Yuga is different, then it could also be taken to mean that certain usages, which were prevalent in other *yugas,* need not be practised in Kali Yuga. Such an attitude may well have led to the emergence of the doctrine of *kalivarjya,* or the view that certain 'actions are forbidden in the Kali Age'.[21]

There is hardly any trace of this in the *Manusmṛti*, wherein the seed-idea is presented that different practices are appropriate for different ages. The main referent in the *Manusmṛti* of this variation seems to be spiritual practices. When *Manusmṛti* condemns *niyoga* (levirate), for instance, it does not disapprove of it on the ground that it is *kalivarjya* (as was done later) but on other grounds, such as the following stated in 9.64: 'Twice-born men should never appoint a widowed woman to another man, for in appointing her to another man, they assail the eternal Law.'[22]

The expression which corresponds to 'eternal Law' in the *Manusmṛti* is *sanātana dharma*. However, when *niyoga* practice is forbidden in many other texts, this is done on the opposite ground of the mutability of tradition: that it is forbidden in the Kali Yuga.[23] This paradox seems to have gone unnoticed so far.[24]

Thus the door may have been opened by the verse in the *Manusmṛti* for a development according to which the acceptance of variation in spiritual practices across the Ages, when connected with the idea of the Kali Yuga as a degenerate Age in which earlier practices may be discontinued, led to extension of the acceptance of variation in social practices as well. This application of the idea paved the way for a legal fiction whereby change could be accommodated, or even initiated.[25] This principle was subsequently applied both progressively and retrogressively[26] from the standpoint of modern liberal norms, but what it does for us is to help put paid to the Orientalist notion of the unchanging East.[27]

III

As mentioned earlier, the doctrine of the *yugas* is directly alluded to in two chapters of the *Manusmṛti*, the first and the ninth. The references to the doctrine in the first chapter and their implications, some far-reaching, were examined in the previous section. In this section we turn to an examination of the doctrine of the *yugas* as presented in the ninth chapter of the *Manusmṛti*. In this chapter, the crucial reference is contained in the following two verses (9.301–02):

> The various ways in which a king behaves (resemble) the Kṛta, Tretā, Dvāpara and Kali ages; hence the king is identified with the ages (of the world).
>
> Sleeping he represents Kali (or iron age), waking the Dvāpara (or brazen [sic]) age, ready to act the Tretā (or silver age), but moving (actively) the Kṛta (or golden age).[28]

In order to appreciate the connection of these verses to those of the previous section, and the transition they represent, one needs to revert to the description of the various Ages as they deteriorate and ask the question: what implication does this description have for the nature of political arrangements which will prevail in that Age, as symbolized by kingship. According to most accounts, people were so virtuous in the Kṛta Age that they were even innocent of the institution of kingship, but by the time we come to the Kali Yuga, even the rulers are going to be depraved.[29]

This gave rise to the following chicken-and-egg question in Hindu political thought: Are kings going to be bad because the Age is bad, or is the Age going to be bad because the kings are bad?

The question is posed in quite a dramatic way in the *Mahābhārata*. As is well-known, when the grandsire Bhīṣma fell in battle and awaited his death on a bed of arrows, the battle was suspended and the scions of the Kuru race surrounded him to hear his parting words of wisdom. One of the questions on which Yudhiṣṭhira sought Bhīṣma's response was the one posed above. Bhīṣma's response to Yudhiṣṭhira's question, as found in the *Śānti-parvan* of the *Mahābhārata*, was: 'Whether it is the king who makes the age or the age that makes the king is a question about which you should not entertain any doubt. The truth is that the king makes the age.'[30]

The identification of the king's behaviour with the four Ages takes on new life when understood in this background. There is also a teasing parallelism between God and the king in the *Manusmṛti*, wherein the king has been described as a great divinity (7.8–13). In chapter one of the *Manusmṛti*, the *cosmic* state of affairs is connected with God's waking and sleeping (in verse 74), and with day and night (in verse 68); in chapter nine the *political* state of affairs is connected with similar movements of the king.

It is worth remarking on the revolutionary shift in the paradigm involved here. According to the account found in chapter one of the *Manusmṛti*, read traditionally, kings are going to be bad because we live in a wretched age; according to the second account in chapter nine of the *Manusmṛti*, the age becomes a wretched one because the kings are bad rulers. It is easy to miss or overlook the significant shift in the paradigm involved. In the first paradigm, one is a victim of the inexorable unfolding of the *yugas*, as matters go from bad to worse, for 'the four ages are calculated as a descending arithmetical progression, marked by progressive physical and spiritual deterioration. Present history is taking place within the Kali Yuga, which explains the violence and evil of human history.'[31] In such a situation, one 'cannot save the social process from the decay and dissolution that is an inherent part of its structure, but he can save himself from within the process.'[32]

The new paradigm makes the Age depend on the ruler, so that decay and dissolution are no longer inherent parts of the structure. The ruler can initiate structural changes and reconfigure the *yugas*, and many kings claimed to have achieved precisely that, no doubt hyperbolically, in the epigraphic records of their reigns which they left behind.[33]

The historical pessimism of the description of the doctrine of the *yugas* was addressed at an *individual* level in the doctrine, elaborated in texts such as the *Purāṇas*, that although the world is in a bad way, personal emancipation (or *mokṣa*) from it in the Kali Yuga could be secured by the individual with relative ease because, in such an Age, ironically, even a little virtue went a long way, given the nature of the times. The *Manusmṛti* seems to reject such escapist individualist tendencies and affirms that scope for betterment also exists at the *collective* level, through the agency of the king. Its answer to historical pessimism is not individual escapism, but political activism. We find the Kṛta Yuga concept being used in a conceptual rather than a temporal way, not just in the *Manusmṛti* but in several other texts and contexts as well. For example, the 'interim rule of Bhīṣma while the Pāṇḍava and Kaurava princes were growing up is said to have been the Kṛta Yuga'.[34] Similarly, the Kṛta Yuga has been associated with both the Rāmas: Paraśurāma and Rāmacandra. Thus the condition of the world is said to be that of Kṛta Yuga 'after Rāma Jāmadagnya—known in later literature as Paraśurāma—had killed off the kṣatriyas 21 times'.[35] The association of Kṛta Yuga with Rāma is even more celebrated. Thus 'the Rāmāyaṇa of Vālmīki (1.1.73) compares Rāma's rule after he had rescued Sītā to the Kṛta Yuga. At that time, things were "like in the Kṛta Yuga", *yathā kṛtayuge tathā*.'[36]

The term Rāma-rājya stands for ideal rule in Hinduism, and this is how it achieved its valence in Gandhian thought. The point to note is that the Rāma-rājya does not chronologically fall in the best of *yugas*, the Kṛta Yuga, but even according to Indic calculations it falls in the next *yuga*, the Tretā Yuga. In fact, in the famous sixteenth century Hindi version of the *Rāmāyaṇa*, known as the *Rāmacaritamānas*, Tulsīdās is fully aware of this fact and credits Rāma with making Kṛta Yuga appear in Tretā Yuga.[37]

The *Manusmṛti* also provides an interesting test of the thesis, developed by Luis González-Reimann, that students of the *Mahābhārata* have sometimes indiscriminately attached the meaning of the word *yuga* or Age to the four terms: Kṛta, Tretā, Dvāpara and Kali, when they actually occur in the *Mahābhārata* in the sense of a throw of dice. The best example of this:

> [...] is probably Kṛṣṇa's admonition to Karṇa shortly before the war, when he repeatedly warns the hero that as soon as the war breaks out 'there will ... be no Tretā, no Kṛta and no Dvāpara', *na tadā bhavitā tretā na kṛtaṃ dvāparaṃ na ca*, in what seems an obvious reference to the dicing match won by the Kauravas that had sent the Pāṇḍavas into exile. Kṛṣṇa appears to be telling Karṇa that this time around the confrontation will not be settled by throwing dice (tretā, kṛta, dvāpara). Instead it will be resolved in real combat. It is noteworthy that although the word 'yuga' does not appear in this passage, *modern translators have routinely added it* thus turning Kṛṣṇa's words about the difference between a game of dice and a real life battle into an ominous announcement of the arrival of the terrible Kali Yuga.[38]

Could a similar fate have befallen the *Manusmṛti*, where references to the Kṛta, Tretā, Dvāpara and Kali may have been overinterpreted as *yugas*?

The question achieves added force when it is recognized that, according to scholars, the concerned passage in the *Manusmṛti* 'closely agrees with the fourth exhortation, addressed to Indra by Rohita, Aitareya-Brāhmaṇa VII.15.'[39] And this exhortation refers to the four terms Kṛta, Tretā, Dvāpara and Kali. Luis González-Reimann explains this allusion as follows:

> The *Aitareya* relates the story of Śunaḥśepa, and within the story it describes how a young boy named Rohita was instructed by the god Indra to wander in the forest and not return to his village. Once a year Rohita returned and, each time, was again admonished by Indra to keep wandering in the forest. This happens five times, and on each occasion Indra exhorts him with a verse. After the third and fourth years, the god pronounces the two verses that are of interest to us here. They can be quoted together, as they are clearly two expressions of the same idea:
>
> > The fortune (*bhaga*) of one who is sitting down, sits down; that of one who is standing, stands up. That of one who is lying down, lies down; the fortune of one who keeps moving, moves.
> >
> > Lying down one becomes Kali; getting up, Dvāpara. Standing, one becomes Tretā; by moving, one becomes Kṛta.[40]

However, while in the *Aitareya* text the meaning of the words *kṛta* etc. is limited to dice throws, *Manusmṛti* IX.301–02 clearly contains the word *yuga*. Thus the *Manusmṛti* absorbs the sentiment, and the words, of the *Aitareya* text but extends the symbolism. And what is even more important, the political version of the *yuga* may have been meant to counter the defeatism or the pessimism of the chronological version, for the reference to the king as being the maker of the Age, in the *Manusmṛti*, is sandwiched between passages which emphasize the activism of the king. Thus *Manusmṛti* 300 states: 'Indeed, he should embark on his operations repeatedly, though repeatedly exhausted, for Fortune devotes herself only to a man who embarks on operations.'[41]

The succeeding verses are even stronger (9.303–11):

> The King should follow the energetic activity of Indra, Sun, Wind, Yama, Varuṇa, Moon, Fire, and Earth. As Indra showers rain during the four months of the rainy season, so the king, following the Indra-vow, should shower delights upon his realm. As Sun extracts water through its rays during the eight months, so the king should constantly extract taxes from his realm; for this is the Sun-vow. As Wind moves about infiltrating all creatures, so the king should infiltrate with his mobile spies; for that is the Wind-vow. As Yama, when the time has come, holds friend and foe alike in his grip, so the king should hold his subjects in his grip; for that is the Yama-vow. As we see people bound with fetters by Varuṇa, so the king should capture criminals; for that is the Varuṇa-vow. When his subjects are as delighted in him as are people when they see the full moon, that king is observing the Moon-vow. When the king is always inflamed and ablaze against evil-doers and crushes evil rulers of border districts, tradition calls it the Fire-vow.[42]

IV

Both the versions of the doctrine of the *yugas*, as found in the first chapter and then in the ninth chapter of the *Manusmṛti*, possess an honourable pedigree.

The idea of a *kalpa*, which constitutes part of the constellation of concepts associated with the temporal doctrine of the *yugas*, can be traced back to Buddha's time in all probability.[43] The word is referred to in the Rock Edicts of Aśoka and so epigraphically seems to go back to at least the third century BCE. The doctrine of temporal *yugas* thereafter finds constant mention. It is also obvious that it 'must have gone through several stages in the course of its development. For example, Brahmagupta (Brahmasphuṭa-Siddhānta XI.10) states that the theory of yugas, manus and kalpas set out by Āryabhaṭa was not like that of the smṛtis.'[44] Albīrūnī, in the eleventh century, describes this doctrine in full-fledged detail in his book on India.[45]

The other version of the doctrine of *yugas*, which we may call the royal version as compared to the temporal one, also possesses a distinguished pedigree. The early if ambiguous parallel found in the *Aitareya Brāhmaṇa* VII.15 was noted earlier.[46] The *Arthaśāstra* does *not* allude to the temporal doctrine of *yugas*, which seems to suggest that Indian statecraft steered clear of the pessimism implied in the temporal doctrine of the *yugas*. When the doctrine did come in touch with the tradition of political thought in India, the latter was able to shape it in its own way. The process is also reflected in the *Mahābhārata* in which, at one point, the four *yugas* are directly related to the degree and extent to which a king is able to maintain law and order (*daṇḍa-nīti)*.[47] This does not quite happen in the *Manusmṛti*, but is quite consistent with the importance, attached in the *Manusmṛti*, to punitive justice (*daṇḍa*).[48]

This discussion of the doctrine of the *yugas* in the *Manusmṛti* thus seems to confirm the thesis of this book that the *Manusmṛti* reflects many strands from within the tradition, rather than one particular standpoint, and participates in the pluralism which characterizes the Hindu tradition in so many ways.

14

The Hermeneutics of Suspicion and the *Manusmṛti*

The 'hermeneutics of suspicion', which has emerged in recent times as a lens for examining historical texts, is a hermeneutic which involves a fundamental philosophical reorientation.[1] Consciousness, which was once considered to be perceptually transparent in a Cartesian manner and linguistically transparent in a Wittgensteinian way, is now considered to consist primarily of the relationship between the hidden and the shown, between what is concealed and what is revealed.[2] Consciousness therefore needs decoding, and so also the texts that embody it. This understanding of consciousness is the fundamental assumption underlying the 'hermeneutics of suspicion' as espoused by Paul Ricœur, who referred repeatedly to the three 'masters of suspicion': Friedrich Nietzsche, Karl Marx and Sigmund Freud.[3] While these three might appear 'seemingly mutually exclusive',[4] for all of them 'the fundamental category of consciousness is the relation of hidden-shown or, if you prefer, simulated-manifested'.[5] The basic hermeneutical implication of their thought points in the same direction—a text may not be taken at its face value; indeed the face of a text may be no more than a mask which conceals underlying socio-economic, political and psychological realities in such a way as to obscure them, or render them more palatable, if not more acceptable.

A hermeneutics of suspicion may be said to occupy a mediate horizon as distinguished from the immediate and the ultimate, where the immediate involves only a literal reading of the text and the ultimate a deeper meaning intended by the author. While the 'hermeneutics of suspicion' also seeks to determine a non-evident meaning, such a hermeneutics focuses on a meaning which is different from the author's intention, whether evident or hidden. Accordingly, the present chapter, which concerns the exegesis of Hindu texts, represents an important fork in the road in the application of the hermeneutics of suspicion as it is currently understood. Both the expression 'hermeneutics of suspicion' and the idea embodied in this expression have become accepted and may even be said to be commonplace, in Hindu Studies.[6]

I will, however, be proposing a rather unconventional use of this hermeneutics. To me, it seems unnecessary to assume that the hermeneutics of suspicion always discloses that which is negative behind a text. It will be my contention that if the rigorous scrutiny implied by the hermeneutics of suspicion can reveal the negative implications and realities which lie behind a text that on the surface appear to be positive, then it is equally possible that such a hermeneutics may also disclose the positive implications which might lie behind a text that on the surface appears to be negative. I shall develop this rather unconventional idea through an examination of a passage from Śaṅkara's commentary on the *Bṛhadāraṇyaka Upaniṣad* (6.4.17) and then follow it up with selected passages from the *Manusmṛti*.

I

The applicability of a hermeneutics of suspicion to the study of Hindu texts becomes readily apparent in the case of Śaṅkara, the famous Hindu scholiast sometimes compared to Thomas Aquinas. Around 800 CE, Śaṅkara wrote a commentary on the *Bṛhadāraṇyaka Upaniṣad* (ca. 800 BCE). As might be expected, Hinduism had undergone many transformations during the more than 1,000 years which intervene between the composition of the *Bṛhadāraṇyaka Upaniṣad* and Śaṅkara's commentary on it. His understanding of the text reflects these transformations. For instance, one major transformation is related to the fact that women, who not only had access to Vedic studies in Vedic times but even had Vedic hymns revealed to them, had been debarred from studying the Vedas in the interregnum.

Śaṅkara was apparently aware of this restriction and had to contend with it when commenting on *Bṛhadāraṇyaka Upaniṣad* 6.4.17.

This particular text recommends a ritual for securing the birth of a learned daughter and is followed by a ritual for securing the birth of a learned son. The word used for denoting 'learned' in both cases is the same: *paṇḍitā* in the feminine and *paṇḍita* in the masculine. However, while Śaṅkara interprets 'learned' in the straightforward sense in the case of the male, he points out that in the case of the female such learning is limited to domestic skills.[7] As modern scholars are quick to note, he glosses the text in this manner 'because his age held that women were ineligible for Vedic studies'.[8] Śaṅkara himself adds: *vede'nadhikārāt,* (because women are not entitled to Vedic study) while 'the Upaniṣad seems to grant the privilege of learning and scholarship to women'.[9]

We know this to be so because the very Upaniṣad he is commenting on, the *Bṛhadāraṇyaka*, contains accounts of two women, Gārgī and Maitreyī, who discoursed about *Brahman* or the ultimate reality as discussed in the Vedas.[10] How does Śaṅkara handle these cases? Suspiciously. He conveniently overlooks the difficulty they pose to his position and uses them as an example to illustrate his point that the acquisition of the knowledge of the ultimate reality, or *Brahman*, does not require ritual practices as a precondition. A rival school had insisted on the prior and coordinate necessity of ritual as a precondition for the attainment of such knowledge.[11] But Śaṅkara argues that although women are not eligible for the performance of Vedic ritual (in the Hinduism of his times), the fact that Yājñvalkya instructs his wife Maitreyī regarding the acquisition of knowledge of *Brahman* in this Upaniṣad proves his point that Vedic rituals are not a prerequisite for the attainment of such knowledge. Thus, he uses the example of women acquiring knowledge of *Brahman* in the Upaniṣads not to question the prevailing view that women cannot study the Vedas, as one might expect, but to substantiate another point of his own doctrine! This is real exegetical chutzpah! This is an example of what might be called a 'heads I win, tails you lose' exegesis.

II

The case of Śaṅkara and the two women, Gārgī and Maitreyī, demonstrates the applicability of the hermeneutics of suspicion in a Hindu context. I would now, however, like to argue that the assumption of negativity, which might be implied by the word 'suspicion', in the expression 'hermeneutics of suspicion', prevents the full potential of this hermeneutical concept from being realized. To me it seems unnecessary, and lacking in imagination, to assume that ancient texts and their commentators were simply prejudiced and even evil. I admit that such commentators and texts could well possess a less radiant dimension as we all do, but I would also maintain that this need not necessarily be the case. In other words, if what on the surface seems to be positive is on inspection revealed to be negative, then it is equally possible that what appears to be negative on the surface might on inspection harbour a rather positive implication. But before proceeding to a demonstration that will render this rather unconventional contention regarding the hermeneutics of suspicion more plausible, I will, for the sake of emphasis and contrast, share a case which demonstrates the more straightforward, conventional use of such hermeneutics.

The position of women as portrayed in the standard *Smṛtis* is normative for classical Hinduism, but widely regarded as inconsistent with contemporary norms. A text such as the *Manusmṛti*, for instance, is replete with passages involving the patriarchal subjugation of women, from the debarment of their participation in Vedic ritual (9.18) to the doctrine of their 'perpetual tutelage' (5.147–49; 9.2–3). Even those passages which seem to cast women in a favourable light, such as 3.55–62 and 9.26–28, are taken as largely associated with their reproductive function, which keeps their status, even in praise, firmly anchored in patriarchy.

In these same *Smṛtis*, however, the punishment for adultery is remarkably mild. P.V. Kane even asserts: 'The humane character of the legislation of Indian sages is seen by the fact that even for adultery they do not allow the husband to drive the wife out of the house and abandon her.'[12] The question arises as to whether such humane treatment is confined to adultery with men of one's own or higher castes, or whether it also covers cases of adultery involving men of lower castes. Both Kane[13] and Basham cite *Manusmṛti* 8.371 in this connection, which stipulates that for adultery with a man of low caste 'she is to be punished by the king by being devoured by dogs'.[14] The verse itself, however, does not refer to the caste of the adulterer, nor does it seem to suggest that this punishment is inflicted only for adultery. Rather, such punishment is inflicted when adultery is committed out of pride (*darpa*) in 'the greatness of her relatives or (her own) excellence'.[15]

It may be that other texts also prescribe such punishment, but as Kane himself notes elsewhere, 'even this was modified' later and only abandonment was allowed. Therefore, Kane's overall assessment seems to stand the test of liberality:

> A wife is to be abandoned only if she commits adultery with a *śūdra*; and further that the abandonment consists in not allowing her to participate in religious rites and conjugal matters, but she is not to be cast on the streets; she is to be kept apart, guarded in a room and given food and raiment.[16]

This seems to be particularly true as this punishment seems to apply to adultery in general, as laid down in *Manusmṛti* 9.17, with the penance being 'lighter or heavier according to the caste of the adulterer'.[17]

The application of a hermeneutics of suspicion to the liberality of this provision leads to the remarkable conclusion that the provision may indeed be based on the *negative* assessment of women's character typically found in the *Smṛtis*. The point is that, given a woman's supposedly natural lasciviousness, as depicted, for instance, in *Manusmṛti* 9.14–15 and in the literature in general, such lapses are to be expected.[18] The hermeneutics of suspicion thus enables us to distinguish between reason and fact. It is true that the punishment for adultery is mild. This is a fact. But this fact could well be based on a reason that is not at all complimentary to women. One would hesitate to be dogmatic about this point, as both a high and a low estimation of women in general could arguably account for the leniency. A hermeneutics of suspicion, however, reveals what might otherwise have remained concealed, namely, that the lenient provision for adultery could well reflect a poor assessment of female character.

This case exemplifies the kind of results which might be obtained by applying the hermeneutics of suspicion in its conventional sense. I will now, however, suggest that just as in this case what was positive on the surface was revealed to be possibly negative in terms of the underlying reality, so also it is possible that what appears to be negative on the surface might conceal a more positive underlying reality, and that this reality can be uncovered by vigorously pursuing a hermeneutics of suspicion. I will use the social relationship between the *brāhmaṇas* and the *śūdras*, two classes in the Hindu caste system referred to in the *Manusmṛti*, to illustrate my suggestion.

III

In its classical formulation the so-called caste system of Hinduism, whether regarded as essential, specific or contingent to it, divides Hindu society into four classes on the basis of birth: *brāhmaṇas* (or priests, etc.), *kṣatriyas* (warriors, etc.), *vaiśyas* (traders, etc.) and *śūdras* (servants, etc.). The order is hierarchical and reflects ritual purity. In the popular version of this scheme, the *brāhmaṇas* are the top dogs and the *śūdras* are the underdogs. The text cited most often regarding their respective privileges and liabilities is the *Manusmṛti*, usually ascribed to the second century.

I inaugurate my investigation with a statement based on this text, made by that dean of Indologists, A.L. Basham:

> According to the Brāhmanical textbooks the chief duty of the pure śūdra was to wait on the other three classes. He was to eat the remnants of his master's food, wear his cast-off clothing, and use his old furniture. Even when he had the opportunity of becoming wealthy he might not do so *for a śūdra who makes money is distressing to the brāhmaṇs.*[19]

The last statement—'for a śūdra who makes money is distressing to the brāhmans'—is a verbatim citation from the *Manusmṛti* (10.129). The matter is quite straightforward so far. What could be more offensive to a member of the highest class than that the lowest should usurp their position financially? Such brazenness would be unacceptable. This citation establishes the *brāhmaṇa* and the *śūdra* once again as representing the two opposite poles of the caste system.

Let us now probe this text. The question to ask is: Who is a *brāhmaṇa* and who is a *śūdra* according to this text? One immediately notices a distinction drawn in the *Manusmṛti* between authentic and inauthentic *brāhmaṇas*, just as a distinction is sometimes drawn between pure and impure *śūdras*. We now turn to the broader picture as depicted by Basham:

> Opinions differed as to whether a Brāhmaṇ engaged in a secular profession was worthy of the respect accorded to the practising member of the class, and no clear ruling is laid down. Manu, the most

> authoritative of the Smṛtis, is uncertain on this point, and in different parts of the text diametrically opposed views are given. As far as can be gathered from general literature the special rights of the Brāhmaṇ were usually only granted to those who lived by sacrifice and teaching.[20]

Basham concludes that according to the literature in general, the 'special rights of the brāhmaṇ [*sic*] were usually only granted to those who lived by sacrifice and teaching' although, according to him, the *Manusmṛti* is equivocal on the point. Basham refers to two verses in the *Manusmṛti* as evidence of such equivocation: one which stipulates that a *brāhmaṇa* who is a hypocrite should not even be offered water (4.192), and another which states that even if *brāhmaṇas* resort to all sorts of mean occupations, they should still be venerated (9.319).

It seems to me that the contradiction here is apparent rather than real, for a *brāhmaṇa* is allowed to adopt mean occupations in times of political and economic crisis, or in extremis. The term used for mean occupations—*aniṣṭa karma*—is clearly comparable to the various undesirable occupations a *brāhmaṇa* may resort to in times of crisis (*Manusmṛti* 10.81). Basham's oversight, that this latter statement in 9.319 pertains to *a time of crisis*,[21] is puzzling in light of the fact that he is fully aware of the existence of this category of *āpad-dharma*.[22] For he explicitly states that 'Smṛti literature contains special sections on "duty when in distress" (*āpad-dharma*), which carefully define what a man may legitimately do when he cannot earn a living by the profession normally followed by his class'[23] and when other departures from normative behaviour are permitted. The point is that the *brāhmaṇa* was to subsist by sacrifice and teaching; that this ensured his entitlement to general respect; that in a crisis he could avail himself of other clearly described and circumscribed vocational options; and further, that he should not thereby be regarded as deprived of his dignity because these options were resorted to under duress. The fact remains that the special privileges accorded to the *brāhmaṇa* derived from the practice of his vocation as it was defined in terms of sacrifice and teaching.

I would now like to focus on that part of Basham's statement which suggests that 'the special rights of the brāhmaṇ were usually only granted to those who lived by sacrifice and teaching' (see *Manusmṛti* 10.74–76). Basham fails to mention here that the *brāhmaṇa* was also discouraged from acquiring wealth (2.13) and that he lost his status if he taught the Vedas for a stipulated fee (3.156; 11.63), although voluntary gifts were a different matter (2.245–246; 3.95). A *brāhmaṇa* could, however, accept fees for performing sacrifices, that is, sacrificial fees. But, in turn, he also had to sacrifice and give money away. His economic vulnerability is dramatized in an early text, the *Aitareya Brāhmaṇa*, where he is described as one who could be expelled at will![24] Moreover, between teaching and sacrifice, the less remunerative teaching had greater value attached to it (10.80). Several verses in the *Manusmṛti* attest to the fact that a practising *brāhmaṇa* was also a poor *brāhmaṇa* (3.66; 4.7–8; 11–15; 207–22; 228–51).

Such poverty contrasts starkly with the probity the *brāhmaṇa* was supposed to observe and the charity of outlook enjoined on him. The *brāhmaṇa* could not retaliate if attacked,[25] he was to be a friend of all (*Manusmṛti* 4.87) and a 'think-tank' on two feet (12.108–16). Moreover, he had to be constantly engaged in the practise of Yoga: 'He must be well-versed in his grasp of the Absolute or Brahma (*Brahma-dhāraṇa*: [1.93]) and his observance of vows (*niyama-dhāraṇa*: [10.3]) and must cultivate universal love.'[26]

The strong association of poverty with the practising *brāhmaṇa* surfaces in a most unlikely place. In the sixth chapter of the *Bhagavadgītā*, a text usually assigned to the second century BCE, Arjuna asks the question: What happens to a person who dies while practising Yoga, but before it has been practised to perfection? Kṛṣṇa's response is that such an unsuccessful Yogin is either reborn in a family possessing untainted wealth or in a family of intelligent Yogins. Śaṅkara, in commenting on this verse, adds the adjective 'poor' to the word Yogin, that is to say, one is reborn into a family of intelligent and poor Yogins. The word 'poor' is totally absent in the text and yet Śaṅkara introduces it twice in the course of his brief gloss on 6.42.[27] Moreover, according to Śaṅkara, this birth into a family of poor, intelligent Yogins is said to be even harder to secure than birth into a rich family of the pure-minded! The crucial question to ask from the standpoint of a hermeneutics of suspicion is: Why should a poor *brāhmaṇa*, inured to austere poverty, resent the accumulation of wealth on the part of the *śūdra*, as Basham maintains on the basis of a reference in the *Manusmṛti*?

The verse cited by Basham (10.129) is not the only verse in the *Manusmṛti* which bears on this point. There are numerous other passages where the well-being of a *śūdra* is alluded to (2.24; 9.157–59,169; 10.99–100; 11.34), and in one the *brāhmaṇa*'s compassionate disposition is distinctly directed toward a *śūdra* (3.112). Moreover, the *Gautama Dharma Sūtra*, a text from an earlier period, states that a *śūdra*'s accumulation of wealth 'should be for the support and benefit of other *varṇas*'.[28] This text does not prohibit the accumulation of wealth on the part of the *śūdra*, but refers rather to the proper distribution of the accumulated wealth. Again, the *Arthaśāstra*, a text which in its present form may be judiciously attributed to the third century,[29] specifically describes *vārtā*, or production of wealth, as a function of the *śūdra*.[30] Given this textual background, the provision in the *Manusmṛti* cited by Basham is clearly problematic, rather than probative, on this point.

The crucial significance of this oversight of Basham becomes clear when we grasp that he overlooks the following fact: that the *Manusmṛti*'s statement—'the śūdra who makes money is distressing to the brāhmans'—appears in a section dealing with times of distress. Indeed, Manu lived precisely during such a time of distress. The economic and political condition of India in and around the second century CE (the date assigned to the *Manusmṛti*) was one of distressing upheavals brought about by foreign invasions. Tribes such as the Indo-Greeks and those of Central Asia overran northern India, tearing a gaping hole in its political, social and economic fabric. These foreign rulers were classed as *śūdras* in the *Manusmṛti*, which mandated that a Vedic student who had completed his studies should not dwell in the country of a *śūdra* ruler (IV.61):

> This apparently points to the existence of śūdra rulers during this period. But they do not seem to have arisen from the fourth varṇa, for contemporary political history does not know of such rulers. They probably refer to the Greek, Śaka, Parthian and Kuṣāṇa rulers who were affiliated to Buddhism or Vaiṣṇavism and whom Manu describes as degraded kṣatriyas reduced to śūdrahood on account of their failure to consult brāhmaṇas and to perform enjoined Vedic sacrifices.[31]

It seems that under the veneer of a casteist statement the text of the *Manusmṛti* is expressing resentment towards the self-aggrandizing conquest of the country by foreign invaders. The *Manusmṛti* did not have at its disposal the Marxist vocabulary of the proletariat and the bourgeoisie, of economic imperialism or colonial exploitation, and Manu was not a Marxist in the sense of being able to identify growing economic disparity in terms of exploitation by foreign rulers. He did, however, protest against the economic exploitation of his country by foreign occupants.

One important aspect of Manu's vocabulary is that it reflects transitions in meaning, and this may account for why he does not express his nationalist protest against *śakas* (or Indo-Scythians, an invading group) as *mlecchas* in more forthright, negative terms. By Manu's time, the *śakas* were beginning to be assimilated into the indigenous community, and in texts usually ascribed to this period the *śakas* still 'seem to be different from the *mleccha*, who were foreigners, outsiders in a more radical sense'.[32]

It seems to me that Manu was trying to make a statement which sounds hopelessly warped when viewed through the more egalitarian lens of our own times, but when viewed in its own cultural milieu it constitutes an orthodox Hindu parallel to Gandhi asking Indians not to buy British goods. In Manu's time the statement meant asking *brāhmaṇas* not to accept presents from a king who was not descended from the *kṣatriya* race (4.84). A *positive* hermeneutics of suspicion reveals that a historical protest is lodged deep within what is traditionally considered an ahistorical text, and this protest is couched in language which carries both traditional and historical meanings, fusing the two horizons. Hermeneutical suspicion may now be focused more sharply on some of the key words of the verse cited by Basham. The verse runs as follows:

> śaktenāpi hi śūdreṇa na kāryo dhanasañcayaḥ
> śūdro hi dhanamāsādya brāhmaṇāneva bādhate

G. Bühler[33] and Wendy Doniger[34] suggest that this verse be rendered in English as follows: 'a *śūdra* should not amass wealth even if he can; a *śūdra* upon amassing wealth oppresses the very *brāhmaṇas*.'

The *śūdra* in this verse is characterized by the word *śakta*, a word formed from the root *śak*. This immediately brings to mind a people called the Śakas. The Śakas make their appearance in Indian history at the beginning of the Christian era. They are the Scyths who attacked both the Parthians and the Greeks in India and then penetrated as far as Mathurā. The Śaka era dates from 78 CE and the earliest Śaka king known to have ruled in India was Maues (c. 80 BCE). The association of the Śaka era with a foreign dynasty is widely accepted. From our point of view, if the widely accepted dating of the *Manusmṛti* is correct, then the following facts are crucial:

> For a while, around the beginning of the 2nd century AD, the Śātavāhanas were driven from the N. W. Deccan by invading Śaka of the clan of Kṣaharāta ... But the Śātavāhanas, under the greatest of their rulers, Gautamīputra Śātakarṇin, recovered their lands about AD 130, and nothing more is heard of the Kṣaharāta.[35]

Further, in the second century CE the Śātavāhana ruler Gautamīputra Śātakarṇi (106–130 CE) 'claims that he restored order to the confusion of the four *varṇas* by conciliating the *brāhmaṇas* and the *śūdras* (*avaras*). This alignment of the *varṇas* was directed by the *brāhmaṇa* ruler against the *kṣatriyas*, who perhaps belonged to foreign ruling dynasties.'[36]

Another controversy surrounding the Śaka era further illuminates the matter.[37] Richard Salomon argues that the two standard Hindu eras, the Vikrama (56 BCE) and the Śaka (78 CE) both date from this period, prior to which no system of reckoning from a fixed point seems to have existed. The system of dating from a fixed point was first introduced by foreign rulers during this period and was subsequently Indianized. It is significant that in the Hindu tradition the founding of both of these eras is associated with the Śakas. Also, the names of the eras themselves seem to be of nonindigenous origin. Such evidence suggests the possibility of a pun involving the words *śakta* and *śaka*. Although the argument presented in this chapter does not rest on this connection but rather on the historical connection between the text and its historical context, its plausibility does, I think, strengthen my argument.

Besides, the possibility of a pun involving the words *śakta* and *śaka* is worth pursuing, because the *Manusmṛti* teems with wordplays. These can be classified into three types: a) conventional wordplays; b) explicit wordplays; and c) implicit wordplays. Wordplays, which are accepted from within the tradition without comment, may be referred to as conventional wordplays. For instance, according to *Manusmṛti* 2.58 and the commentary on it, the word *kāyatra* refers to that which is sacred to Prajāpati. This sense involves understanding the word *kaḥ* to signify Prajāpati, a tradition based on the refrain in *ṚgVeda* 10.121, where the word is taken to refer to Prajāpati. In fact, the word *kaḥ* in this instance appears to be an interrogative: 'What god with our oblation shall we worship?'[38] Similarly, the word *śvavṛtti* (4.6.6) literally means 'canine lifestyle' but is conventionally understood to refer to 'service'. Strictly speaking, however, these examples represent more of a play on meanings than on words.

Of greater interest to us are the strikingly explicit wordplays involving words such as *nārayāṇa* (1.10), *śarīra* (1.17), *atithi* (3.102), *māṃsa* (5.55), *jāyā* (9.8), *pṛthivī* (9.44), *putra* (9.138) and *pāraśava* (9.178). Of even greater interest are the implicit wordplays, such as those between *rūpya* and *rūpa* (4.230), *aśva* and *aśvins* (4.231) and, most significantly, *śriyaḥ* and *striyaḥ* (9.26), from which it is only a short step to *śaka* and *śakta*. This step is not taken in the text itself, but the philological and historical evidence seems to suggest a possible connection between the two words. The use of the verb *bādhate* in relation to the *brāhmaṇas* introduces a philological consideration which is less speculative than the proposed connection between *śakta* and *śaka*. English translations of the *Manusmṛti* typically render this verb as 'gives pain'[39] or 'annoys'.[40] It seems to me, however, that these English equivalents leave the verb *bādhate* undertranslated in the present context, since they are primarily limited to mental pain. The verb might have a sense closer to 'oppression' in English. This rendering would be more consistent with the verb's use in *Manusmṛti* 9.248, where a king is asked to punish a person of low caste with severe penalties because he offended a *brāhmaṇa*. In current translations these penalties are prescribed for one who 'gives pain'[41] or 'bothers'[42] a *brāhmaṇa*.

Although Bühler's translation is stronger than Doniger's, it is worth noting that the penalty involved is rather severe and consists of terrifying corporal punishment. Such corporal punishment is prescribed for defamation (8.270–72) and assault (8.179–284). The fact that the verb is used in relation to *brāhmaṇas* in both instances is worth noting, as is the fact that the Śaka invasion, according to indigenous accounts, was particularly devastating. According to the account found in the *Yuga Purāṇa* section of the *Gārgī Saṃhitā*, the Śaka conquest reduced the population 'by one half, 25 percent being killed and 25 percent being enslaved and carried away.'[43] We can now piece together a coherent picture. Manu's text speaks of *śūdra-rājya* or *śūdra* kingdoms. The *foreign* rulers qua *foreign* rulers were like *śūdras*, but qua *rulers* (although foreign) they were like *kṣatriyas*. We noticed earlier that Manu directs *brāhmaṇa* students not to:

> [...] accept presents from a king who is not descended from a *kṣatriya* race. All these rules [were] obviously meant to prevent the recognition of foreign rulers by brāhmaṇas. But gradually the open hostility gave way to tolerance and ultimate recognition of the alien rulers as *kṣatriyas*, though of an inferior kind.[44]

The initial identification of the foreign rulers with *śūdra*; the fact that this statement occurs in the 'time of crisis' (*āpad-dharma*) section, which reflected the historical state of affairs; and the resentment felt by the *brāhmaṇa* over this state of affairs—all seem to point in one direction. Thus, applying a hermeneutics of suspicion to this Hindu text enables us, in all probability, to excavate its historical moment. Whereas the surface meaning of the text implies the suppression of the *śūdras* by the *brāhmaṇas*, the text actually reveals the perceived threat foreign rulers posed to the *brāhmaṇa* legislators! Wendy Doniger perhaps does not recognize the full *historical* implication of her own statement when she writes: 'Manu is not so much a text on *dharma* as it is on *āpad dharma*—the principles of life led in a perpetual state of crisis.'[45] Perhaps if one changed *the wording* 'perpetual state of crisis' to 'historical state of crisis' one would be closer to the mark, but in order for the full picture to emerge we must clarify the relationship between the Śaka people and the caste system.

Three distinct stages are discernible in terms of their placement in this system:

1. The famous Sanskrit grammarian Patañjali (second century BCE) assigns the Śaka to the class of *anirvasita*, that is, pure or clean *śūdras*.[46]
2. Manu (second century?) regards the Śaka as *śūdra* but asserts that they have fallen to this condition although they were once *kṣatriyas* (10.43–44).
3. In 325 CE a Śaka (?) king, Candravarman, erected the famous Iron Pillar, 'regarded as a masterpiece of engineering, since re-erected at Mehrauli, Delhi'.[47]

The stages by which the Śakas became incorporated into the Hindu community are now reasonably clear. At the time of Manu we find them in a liminal phase, when they are rich but resented as foreign rulers. The evidence we have seems to suggest that this ambiguity reached its high point during the reign of satrap (*kṣatrapa*) Nahapāna (119–25 CE), who ruled over a sizable section of western India and struck his own silver and copper coins. Nahapāna was defeated and killed by the Śātavāhana king Gautīmiputra Śātakarṇi, a regular Hindu *kṣatriya* who restruck Nahapāna's coins in his own name. Ironically, this military defeat may have ended in social victory for the Śakas, for thereafter they graduated to regular *kṣatriya*hood. Nahapāna's accumulation of wealth, his earlier successes against regular Hindu kings, and his foreign origin, would explain Manu's resentment of *śūdras* who accumulated wealth, as well as his simultaneous acceptance of Śakas as *śūdras*, albeit as fallen *kṣātriyas*.

The problem Manu had to contend with was the same as that posed to Śaṅkara in the eighth/ninth century CE, when he saw the *varṇa* system in disarray. At that time Śaṅkara had to conclude, as he does in his commentary on *Brahmasūtra* I.3.33, that although in his time the *varṇa* order had become disorganized and unstable as to the *dharmas*, 'that was not the case in earlier ages, since otherwise the [scriptural injunctions] laying down regulations ... would have to be deemed purposeless or futile.'[48] The irony is that Śaṅkara might have identified this time of original ideal arrangement with the period of Manu, as he took it to be.

Śaṅkara, however, was a philosopher while Manu was a law-giver. For Manu, the problem may have been similar, but it was also more acute. In one part of his text we find, I think, a cryptic allusion to the problem he was trying to resolve. This occurs in 10.129, where he states that *brāhmaṇas* fear oppression at the hands of *śūdras* who become rich. Another text would be 10.44, where he proposes to solve the problem by simultaneously conferring on the Śakas the dignity of being *kṣātriyas,* while also claiming that they had become degraded to the status of *śūdras* by falling out of ritual relationship with *brāhmaṇas*. I offer this conclusion as an example of the results which may be achieved by applying a *positive* 'hermeneutics of suspicion', in contradistinction to the negative connotations usually associated with this hermeneutic.

IV

In fact, strange as it might appear, it seems that attempts were made to develop a *positive* hermeneutics of suspicion within the Hindu tradition itself. A striking example of this can be identified in an episode in the *Mahābhārata*, where Bhīma, one of the five Pāṇḍavas, falls into the clutches of a python. Yudhiṣṭhira is then called upon by the python to answer a series of questions in order to secure his brother's release. The questions are modelled somewhat on the more famous episode of Yudhiṣṭhira's interrogation by a Yakṣa. The python is none other than King Nahuṣa under a curse, and the questions he poses to Yudhiṣṭhira include the following:

> SNAKE: Now, who is a brahmin, king, and what may he know, Yudhiṣṭhira? Speak up, for from your words we gather that you are very wise!
>
> YUDHIṢṬHIRA: He is known as a brahmin, king of Snakes, in whom truthfulness, liberality, patience, deportment, mildness, self-control, and compassion are found. And he may gain knowledge of the supreme Brahman—
>
> SNAKE: Authority, truth, and the Brahman extend to all four classes: even śūdras may be truthful, liberal, tolerant, mild, nonviolent, and compassionate, Yudhiṣṭhira—
>
> YUDHIṢṬHIRA: The marks of the śūdra are not found in a brahmin; but a śūdra is not necessarily a śūdra, nor a brahmin a brahmin. In whomever the brahmin's marks are found, Snake, he is known as a brahmin; and in whom they are not found, him they designate as a śūdra—
>
> SNAKE: If you judge a brahmin by his conduct, king, then birth has no meaning, my dear sir, as long as no conduct is evident.
>
> YUDHIṢṬHIRA: I think, great and wise Serpent, that birth is hard to ascertain among humankind, because of the confusion of all classes when any man begets children on any woman: language, intercourse, birth, and death are the common lot of all men. The standard of the seers is expressed in the formula *ye yajāmahe*, 'We, such as we are, give worship.' Therefore those see the truth of it who know that conduct is the chief postulate. It is enjoined that the birth rite take place before the navel string is cut; the Sāvitrī formula is called the mother there, and the teacher the father. One is reckoned the same as a śūdra by conduct

> as long as one is not reborn in the Veda. In the difference of opinion on this Manu Svāyaṃbuhva has said decisively, 'Class is determined by observance of tasks. If no conduct is observed, there is judged to be overwhelming class mixture,' O Indra of Snakes.[49]

Note that an attempt is being made here in the *Mahābhārata* to deconstruct the caste system. The caste system comprises the concepts of *varṇa* and *jāti*, and Yudhiṣṭhira is arguing that if one uses *jāti*, or birth, as the basis of the caste system then 'language, intercourse, birth and death are the common lot of all men.' Thus, human beings cannot be set apart on the basis of birth. Moreover, they cannot be set apart on the basis of birth in terms of *varṇa* either, because of rampant intermarriage. The only remaining basis for distinguishing among the *varṇas* then is qualities and worth, not birth. This is an important theme in the *Mahābhārata*.[50] But, what is surprising here is the *attribution of this view to Manu*. The *Manusmṛti*, as we know it, insists on birth as the major if not the sole criterion in these matters. Yudhiṣṭhira seems to be applying a positive hermeneutics of suspicion when he implies that such correlations in the *Manusmṛti* which pair caste with worth (and not birth) are meant to be subversive of the whole structure of caste based on birth.

Two points are especially noteworthy. First, the verse attributed to Manu is not found in the *Manusmṛti* as such. There is, however, one verse in the *Manusmṛti* (10.40) that does bear semantic resemblance to the verse attributed to the *Manusmṛti* in the *Mahābhārata*. It is cited here in translation:

> These races (which originate) in a confusion (of the castes and) have been described according to their fathers and mothers, may be known by their occupation whether they conceal or openly show them.[51]

The *Manusmṛti* suggests here that caste is determined by nativity, and if natal recognition of caste is not possible on account of miscegenation, then occupation may be used to determine it. Yudhiṣṭhira turns this around to claim that since occupation is taken to determine caste in such cases, it follows that occupation determines caste. In terms of the *Manusmṛti* this is a non sequitur.

The second point involves Yudhiṣṭhira's claim that one is considered a *śūdra* only as long as one is not reborn in the Veda—that is, prior to being invested with the sacred thread. In this case the words in the dialogue correspond closely to the text of the *Manusmṛti*. Not only is Yudhiṣṭhira's claim clearly contained in verse 2.172, but its last segment (*yāvadvede na jāyate*) corresponds exactly with a part of the verse in the critical text of the *Mahābhārata* (3.177.30). Here again, however, one runs into the same difficulty. The *Manusmṛti* seems to say that the uninitiated *brāhmaṇa* is on a par with the *śūdra*. Yudhiṣṭhira takes this to mean that the *śūdra* is equal to the uninitiated *brāhmaṇa* and therefore to the *brāhmaṇa*. What is typically overlooked is the fact that according to *Manusmṛti* 10.4, the *śūdra* was not allowed to be initiated and to this extent the parallel is false, or at least misleading.

I think the fact that the *Mahābhārata* seeks to go beyond the *Manusmṛti* by referring to the *Manusmṛti* itself is highly significant in the history of Hinduism. At the same time, one is constrained to point out that such a positive hermeneutics of suspicion remains largely unsuccessful when viewed in the light of the actual text of the *Manusmṛti*. Still, the attempt, albeit abortive, does suggest that the application of the hermeneutics of suspicion to Hindu texts is not without promise.

One should note that the hermeneutical move here involves two interpretations of a text considered authoritative within a tradition. An egalitarian interpretation is being associated with the same text within which another inegalitarian interpretation is present and this by means of developing the underlying logic of the text along different lines. The element of negative 'suspicion' here consists of the possibility that major socio-economic and political changes were subverting the hierarchy. The positive element consists in the possibility that the very phenomenon of *varṇa-saṅkara*, or the admixture of castes, which was so unnerving for orthodox thinkers, may have provided the basis for the egalitarian reinterpretation, as the sexual instinct recognized in this context was believed to be common to humanity.

V

I would like to take leave of the reader with a clarification. I have employed the words 'negative' and 'positive' exegetically in relation to the hermeneutics of suspicion without defining them. In so doing I am following Paul Ricœur, who also seems to employ these terms in an intuitively obvious way, leaving them undefined.[52] The words obviously involve a normative evaluation and their connotation would naturally change if the norm were altered. The norm used here is the same as Ricœur's, which broadly corresponds to what would be considered 'liberal' in academic circles.

15

Conclusions

The time has come to bring matters to a conclusion, or rather conclusions, as a work of this kind is bound to yield many. Some of these have already been drawn in the preceding chapters. I shall therefore confine myself to drawing conclusions of an overarching nature in this chapter and shall do so in two parts: A and B.

Part A

I

It might be useful to compare the results achieved by this study with those already current in the field. One school dealing with the interpretation of the *Manusmṛti* focuses on its positive aspects in the context of Indic civilization and virtually bypasses those aspects of it which do not redound to its credit. Under this category fall works which just ignore what we might call the 'negative' aspects of the *Manusmṛti*, as compared to other works which acknowledge them in various degrees and try to provide a suitable explanation or justification for them. Many other books, on the other hand, overemphasize the negative dimension of the *Manusmṛti*, especially when viewed in the light of modern liberal norms, and dub the doctrines of the *Manusmṛti* as *Manuvāda* ('the [detestable] doctrines of

Manu'). The general trend among the more academic books also tends to conform to this tendency to focus on the negative dimensions of the *Manusmṛti*. There are then these three broad trends discernible in the study of the *Manusmṛti*: books which highlight its positive aspects, books which highlight its negative aspects, and books that accept both these dimensions of the text but try to offer a justification for its negative contents. These could be labelled the positive, the negative and the apologetic approaches to the study of the *Manusmṛti*.

These approaches need not necessarily be mutually exclusive, and the same author, at different times, could adopt them in various degrees, but it is analytically helpful to distinguish among them. Such approaches could be considered as being involved in advocacy of some kind and may be usefully distinguished from works which are more concerned with analysis as such, as opposed to advocacy. Academic books ideally fall in this category, although these distinctions, as pointed out earlier, cannot be considered watertight. Such books are not interested in imparting a negative or positive or apologetic spin to the text but are rather interested in studying it as a text that deals with political, social and other realities.

There are, however, many books which belong to this last category, hence the necessity to explain why we need one more book of this kind and what sets this book apart from existing books in the same genre.

Two features of the present book may be said to set it apart. One of them is its thesis that the *Manusmṛti* reflects the plural character of the Hindu religious tradition. What this means is that when we find dissonance among certain passages within the *Manusmṛti*, or encounter odd passages on their own, instead of treating it as a logical issue where contradictions are to be resolved, or as a textual issue where their outlier significance is to be assessed, one views these as data reflecting different strands within the Hindu religious tradition, like different currents within the same river. The divergent passages are not seen so much as a problem requiring logical or textual reconciliation, though this is certainly one aspect of the issue, but as reflecting divergent strands within the tradition itself. When viewed in this light, the *Manusmṛti* may be seen as reflecting the state of Hindu tradition at a point in time, even as it is making an argument at a given point in time. In other words, the text of the *Manusmṛti* is as much a picture as a template. This also highlights the eclectic character of the tradition, which typically offers a range of solutions on any issue.

One has to keep in mind here the fact that Hindu law, as it was actually practised, accorded much more importance to custom, that is, to the oral tradition rather than the written word.

The second major feature of this book is the importance it attaches to the historical background of the *Manusmṛti*. This is not the only book to do so; actually most books on Hindu *dharma* which discuss the *Manusmṛti* do try to relate it to its historical background. What sets this book apart in this respect is something more specific. It is the importance it attaches to two events in the history of India anterior to the present date assigned to the *Manusmṛti*: the culpability of Aśoka's policies in what happened after his reign; and the impact of the invasions from the north-west of India on Indian society and polity in the period immediately preceding the *Manusmṛti*. When we view these events from what might be called a Hindu perspective (for want of a better word), their significance takes on a character of its own, which is hopefully demonstrated in this work.

What do we mean by a Hindu perspective? First, we mean that the word has been used anachronistically, and second, it is being used to describe the perspective of the people who inhabited this land, now called India, at the time of the *Manusmṛti*—people who had not consciously abandoned the Vedic tradition for Buddhism, Jainism or Materialism. For these people, the developments associated with the fall of the Mauryan Empire, especially the foreign invasions involved, posed a serious existential challenge for which they had to find a solution. It requires a certain amount of historical imagination to understand the gravity of the situation from their point of view because it possesses an affective dimension and not just a cerebral one.

An example from Jewish history may be helpful here, especially for the Western reader. The destruction of the Second Temple of the Jews by the Romans in 70 CE is a fact in Roman history, but if we are to appreciate its significance for the Jewish people, then we will have to understand it also as a fact in Jewish history. For the Romans the destruction meant establishing order in a disturbed part of the empire, but for the Jews it represented a matter of life and death. Just as when the lion hunts the deer as prey, for the lion it is just a meal, but for the deer it is a matter of life and death.

It is the contention of this book that unless we understand the text of the *Manusmṛti* as a response to the existential crisis the 'Hindu' community faced at the time, we will not be able to fully understand the text, no more than we can understand the formulation of the Mishna without relating it to the existential crisis the Jewish community faced after the destruction of the Temple.

Perhaps the point could be clarified by drawing upon the distinction between the 'etic' and the 'emic' already alluded to in the introduction. We will recall that an etic approach represents the outsider's view; the view of, say, someone who has never experienced slavery. No matter how sympathetic such a person might be to the plight of slaves, his or her experience of the trauma of being enslaved is second-hand and cannot compare with that of someone who has experienced slavery or its repercussions first-hand. A person who has experienced slavery represents the 'emic' or the insider's approach to that historical event and brings a lived experience to bear on that history. The Holocaust provides an interesting example here. The way a Jewish person who was a victim of the Holocaust will experience that history will have a different quality to it than how someone who is not from the community might experience it. I cite the examples of slavery and Holocaust to emphasize the fact that the outsider needs to understand the traumatic nature of such events in order to assess the role of a text in that situation.

II

Not only the overall significance of the *Manusmṛti* but that of some other dimensions of it emerge in a new light when these are reviewed with the help of the two foci mentioned earlier, namely the plural and the deeply historical character of the *Manusmṛti*.

For instance, the concept of *dharma* is considered central to the *Manusmṛti*, and the concept of Vedic authority is generally considered central to that of *dharma*. It turns out, however, that the situation in relation to the sources of *dharma* in the *Manusmṛti* is far more pluralistic, and therefore fluid, than the impression conveyed by existing studies in the field. Similarly, when we move to the so-called 'caste system' in the *Manusmṛti*—that is, the system which, the received academic tradition argues, the *Manusmṛti* formally set in place—we find probable reasons for why such a step might have been undertaken, as well as an unexpected openness to doing away with the 'caste system' if necessary. Moreover, scholarship has taken an agonistic approach to the relationship among constituents of the *varṇa* system in the *Manusmṛti*, but we find historical evidence of a much more harmonious approach towards their relationships, to the extent that a word can even be identified for it in the text—namely *varṇa-saṅsarga*—which seems to act as a foil to the oft-repeated *varṇa-saṅkara*. Even the notoriously discriminatory provisions in relation to the 'lower' castes, the Dalits and women require some reassessment, especially if one realizes that in Hinduism the idea of equality is not divorced from that of diversity and complementarity so that the ethically operational term often tends to be equity and justice rather than equality.

The implications of this study in relation to the political dimension of the *Manusmṛti* should serve as an eye-opener especially in a modern context, for the way it posits the relationship between the *yugas* and kingship upends ideas of historical pessimism sometimes associated with the idea of the four *yugas*. Even the advent of the Kali Yuga takes on a rather progressive aspect, as an age in which profound changes can occur in traditional mores.

Thus, not only the general context of the *Manusmṛti*, but also specific doctrines within it may have to be revisited, if the evidence adduced and the arguments presented in this book possess merit. Perhaps the most challenging reassessment involves the idea that Hinduism is not a missionary religion. The point is obviously one of major significance and may even be described as radical, at the risk of some exaggeration.

III

Some other implications of the investigations carried out may not be radical but certainly call for a revised understanding of at least some verses of the *Manusmṛti*. We saw how the notorious verse which ostensibly denies independence to women (9.3) was specifically related to her *legal* status and was not meant to be taken literally or generally. In fact, according to Medhātithi, the well-known ninth-century commentator on the *Manusmṛti*, the verse enjoins the protection of women (*tato rakṣediti*) and means that they should not be left to fend for themselves. Here Manu may be accused of patriarchal oversolicitude but not of not caring for their safety. Indeed, if we take cognizance of fourteenth-century commentator Rāghavānanda, the word *svātantrya* means that women should not be left without a protector (*svātantryam rakṣitṛrahitvam*). In which case the line usually translated as a 'woman is not fit for independence' should be translated as: 'No woman should be left unprotected.' The other verses, which are considered 'a *cause célèbre* in anti-Manu rhetoric',[2] are *Manusmṛti* 5.147–148, which also involve the issue of a woman's independence.

Commentarial material from Kullūka Bhaṭṭa (c. 1250) and others makes it clear that when the protection of father, husband or son is not available, the king is supposed to take care of her, so that the issue again turns on protection. Patrick Olivelle notes regarding this cluster of verses—9.3–4 and 5.147–148—that 'other and more positive depictions of the role of women and their relationship to males, however, are often ignored by critics. The term *svatantra* ("independent") also has specifically legal connotations and is used with reference to a person who can act independently to enter a legally binding contract.'[3] If one looks closely at these verses, however, and filters them through the commentarial material of the kind indicated earlier, the word *svatantra* may have to be re-understood not just as 'independent' but also as 'left to fend for oneself ' or 'left to one's own devices' or 'left to make one's own arrangements'.[4] The English expression 'left to make one's own arrangements' can have both a positive and a negative implication. Positively speaking, it could mean that a person, who earlier on was not allowed to make one's own arrangements, because they were made for him or her on account of their dependence, may now do so on one's own. Negatively, it could mean that someone who should be cared for and protected is now left without that protective cover and has to fend for oneself. When independence is denied to women in this verse, what is meant is that they should not be left to fend for themselves. These verses must be read in the context of Manu's concern for the protection of women of all *varṇas* (*Manusmṛti* 8.364).[5] Similarly, the verses usually cited to refer to the allegedly degraded status of the *śūdra* need to be reinterpreted and be read in light of the *Manusmṛti's* concern for the life and longevity of the *śūdra*.

But beyond such considerations as a balanced accounting of the verses, there is the more central point to be considered, that both positive and negative images of women and *śūdras* are to be found within Hinduism, and both of these are reflected in the *Manusmṛti*, perhaps at times in the same verse, because Hinduism is a plural tradition. It may be pointed out that the same could hold for *brāhmaṇas* and *kṣatriyas*. *Brāhmaṇas* who do not fulfill the required qualifications of a *brāhmaṇa* are said to be so only in name and compared to toys of leather and wood (2.157–158) while *kṣatriyas* are depicted as prone to vices (7.45–53). Thus, again, elements of both a positive and a negative portrayal are present in the *Manusmṛti*.

But specific verses apart, what about the assessment of the *Manusmṛti* as a whole as hierarchical and regressive?

If hierarchy means 'the classification of a group according to ability or economic, social, or professional understanding',[6] then the *Manusmṛti* is certainly hierarchical as it classifies society into the four *varṇas* of *brāhmaṇa, kṣatriya, vaiśya* and *śūdra*. But such a clinical or factual statement does not do justice to the issue in the face of the general perception that there is a negative value attached to this classification in the *Manusmṛti,* for which it has been much criticized. The issue therefore needs to be examined carefully.

One may begin with the rather obvious but perhaps not trivial observation that hierarchy has so far proved inescapable in the context of any developed society, so what must be examined is its *basis* and *nature*. By basis I mean whether it is based on wealth, power, seniority, purity or any other such criteria or a combination of them, and whether it is temporary, permanent, contextual and so on in nature. When viewed from this angle it is striking that the hierarchy of the *varṇas* is *not* based on wealth or power. This point is important because hierarchy implies privilege in the West; the higher-ups enjoy more wealth and power. Thus hierarchy is indexed to the privileges of possessing wealth and power. This is *not* the case in the scheme of the *varṇas* because if hierarchy was indexed with power, then the *kṣatriyas* would have been first in the list of the four *varṇas.* Nor is it indexed to wealth, for then the *vaiśyas* would have been at the top. Nor to serving people either, for then the *śūdras* would have been at the top.

It seems that the scheme of *brāhmaṇa, kṣatriya, vaiśya* and *śūdra* is indexed to moral and ritual purity, for that is what distinguishes the *brāhmaṇa.* The point is important as this means that just because the *brāhmaṇa* is at the top, it does not mean that the *brāhmaṇa* is therefore the 'top dog', in the sense of being endowed with wealth and power. One is likely to form such an impression because, in the West, being on top implies having the lion's share of wealth and power. The *brāhmaṇa* certainly enjoys certain 'privileges' such as precedence in some contexts and comparative freedom from corporal punishment. But are these 'privileges'? They relate to the fact that *brāhmaṇas,* by the very nature of their calling, cannot protect themselves because they are expected to be non-violent (except where ritual killing might be involved), while the other *varṇas* can protect themselves. After all a *brāhmaṇa* is supposed to be 'a friend of everyone' (*Manusmṛti* 2.87).[7]

Similarly, the *brāhmaṇa* leads an abstemious life on account of the requirements of moral and ritual purity. The fact that the *brāhmaṇa* may pluck corn from a field is not unrelated to the fact that starvation was almost a professional hazard for him or her. The fewer preparations the *brāhmaṇas* made to provide for their future, the higher their status. Whatever status the *brāhmaṇas* enjoyed was in terms of moral and ritual authority because of their ascetic lifestyle. This *dissociation* of wealth and power from *status* needs to be recognized because the modern mind invariably associates the two and may therefore assume the *brāhmaṇa* would possess automatic access to wealth and power just because one was a *brāhmaṇa.* It is important to remember this as hierarchies in modern societies *are* based on wealth and power and not on moral and ritual purity (except in the context of the church).

The next point to examine, after having considered the basis of the hierarchy, is the nature of hierarchy. This may be the place to recognize the importance of the point that hierarchy is a feature of every known premodern and even modern contemporary society. So, it should not come as a surprise that society, as envisaged in the *Manusmṛti,* is also hierarchical. This fact has sometimes been used apologetically to justify the 'caste system' but it is being invoked here analytically to clarify its nature. The initial impression one forms is that hierarchies in modern societies are fluid, in the sense that access to wealth and power is open to all. That is to say, modern societies may be hierarchical but given the equality of opportunity in modern societies, wealth and power may be achieved by anyone. This sets modern society apart from premodern societies wherein hierarchies tended to be rigid, as in when they are based on birth, so one must ask: How rigid does the *Manusmṛti* intend its hierarchies to be in principle?

Two successive verses in the *Manusmṛti* are worth examining on this point. They occur in chapter nine (*Manusmṛti* 9.294–297) and relate to the seven elements which constitute the *state,* comparable to the four elements—the four *varṇas*—which constitute *society*. The seven *prakṛtis*, as the constituent elements of the state, are described in a way which corresponds to the way the four *varṇas* constitute society. The verses run as follows:

> [294] The king and his minister, his capital, his realm, his treasury, his army, and his ally are the seven constituent parts (of a kingdom); (hence) a kingdom is said to have seven limbs (aṅga).
>
> [295] But let him know (that) among these seven constituent parts of a kingdom (which have been enumerated) in due order, each earlier (named) is more important and (its destruction) the greater calamity.
>
> [296] Yet in a kingdom, containing seven constituent parts, which is upheld like the triple staff (of an ascetic), there is no (single part) more important (than the others), by reason of the importance of the qualities of each for the others.
>
> [297] For each part is particularly qualified for (the accomplishment of) certain objects, (and thus) each is declared to be the most important for that particular purpose which is affected by its means. [8]

The listing of the seven elements called *prakṛtis* is clearly hierarchical as 'each earlier (named) is more important and (its destruction) the greater calamity'.[9] Yet, as a second point, 'There is no (single part) more important (than the others), by reason of the qualities of each of the others.'[10] Then why is some element sometimes depicted as the more important one? Because, and this is the third point, 'each part is particularly qualified for (the accomplishment of) certain objects, (and thus) each is declared to be the most important for that particular purpose which is effected by its means.'[11]

I think these verses seem to hold the key to how hierarchies are meant to be understood within Hinduism in general. There is an order to the listing, but that order does not necessarily mean that other elements in the listing are less important, as each element in certain contexts may turn out to be the most important. Although the *Manusmṛti* does not spell this out so explicitly in the context of *varṇas* as it does in the case of the *prakṛtis*, I will argue that its approach here also provides the key to understanding the situation regarding the *varṇas* in the *Manusmṛti*. Thus, in the chapters in which the training of the students is described, the emphasis is on *brāhmaṇas* as they are the students par excellence; in the chapters having to do with rulership, the king, the *kṣatriya* par excellence, is celebrated.

The *vaiśyas* were among the main patrons of the Buddhists, whereas the emphasis in the *Manusmṛti* on the *śūdras* serving the three higher *varṇas* seems to stem from the need to prevent them from drifting away from the fourfold order when it was under stress. Hence a statement such as this (*Manusmṛti* 1.91): 'A *single* activity did the Lord allot to the Śūdra, however: the ungrudging service of those very social classes.'[12] The sentiment is reinforced in other verses but the following verses (10.99–100) may hold a clue to the situation:

> [99] When a Śūdra is unable to enter into the service of twice-born men and is faced with the loss of his sons and wife, he may earn a living by the activities of artisans— [100] that is, the activities of artisans and various kinds of crafts the practice of which best serves the twice-born.[13]

The point to note is that Kauṭilya does not restrict the *śūdra* to serving the higher *varṇas* and accepts the *śūdra*'s right to artisanship as a matter of course; indeed, he specifically accords Ārya status to the *śūdra*. The *Manusmṛti* allows this only as an option in distress, perhaps revealing an eagerness to align the *śūdra* directly with the *varṇas*.[14] The *vaiśyas* and the *śūdras* thus may not have been glorified like the *brāhmaṇas* and the *kṣatriyas*, but that could well be a reflection of the historical situation in which the *Manusmṛti* was formulated. Elsewhere, however, the *vaiśyas* and the *śūdras* are also given their due. The *vaiśyas* were numerically the most significant component of the four *varṇas* anyway and hardly needed to be lauded but when we shift our sight from the *Manusmṛti* to the Hindu tradition of which it is an important legal text we find that, like the other *varṇas*, the *śūdras* have *also* been lauded as the key *varṇa*, as in this Singaya-Nāyaka inscription of 1368:

> The three castes, viz. brahmanas and the next [i.e., kshatriyas and vaishyas], were produced from the face, the arms and the thighs of the lord; and for their support was born the fourth caste from his feet. *That the latter caste is purer than the former [three] is self-evident; for this caste was born along with the river Ganga [which also springs from*

> *his feet], the purifier of the three worlds.* The members of this caste are eagerly attentive to their duties, not wicked, pure-minded, and are devoid of passion and other such blemishes; they ably bear all the burden of the earth by helping those born in the kingly caste.[15]

I think we gain a better perspective of the hierarchical nature of the *Manusmṛti* if we keep these considerations in mind, as also when we realize that the same text may contain other mitigating hierarchies such as that of age for instance, which allows a *śūdra* to be respected on account of one's age (2.137, 155). There is also the distinction between equality and equity to be kept in mind: that extra rights may have been matched by extra responsibilities.

This still leaves the issue of differential punishments to be addressed specifically and we turn to it next. Certain aspects of it have already been discussed and what I would like to emphasize here is its historical nature in more than one sense. It represents, first of all, one phase in the legal history of India, namely, the classical phase from c. 400 BCE to c. 1200 CE in the main. But that it gained prominence during this phase may also have to do with the Aśokan interlude, and its possible association with Aśoka's attempt to introduce *daṇḍa-samatā* or legal equality; the negative assessment of Aśoka's rule in view of the invasions which followed the end of his dynasty and the alleged role of his pacifism in it; and therefore the eschewal of such an approach upon recovery after invasions because it had come to be negatively associated with him. Here I would also like to add a philosophical point for our consideration.

Legal egalitarianism is a vital principle in a secular society because law represents justice in such a society. Such a society does not believe in a Day of Judgement when justice will be meted out. Hence law stands in such a society for justice, and the prevalence of human rights discourse in a secular society confirms this. What then could be more unjust than inequality before the law? This is where the buck stops. In Hinduism, however, the ultimate principle which represents justice is not just law but the doctrine of karma, and the *Manusmṛti* accepts this doctrine.

If, however, karma is the ultimate guardian of justice and not just law, then the proper parallel to equality before the law in a secular frame of reference would be karma in a Hindu frame of reference, which the *Manusmṛti* represents. So, the relevant question to ask is:

Does the *Manusmṛti* provide for equality before karma as a counterpart to equality before the law. Are all human beings equal before karma in the *Manusmṛti?* It turns out that not only are all human beings equal before karma in the *Manusmṛti,* all sentient creatures too would perhaps be considered equal before karma in the *Manusmṛti,* and even the gods may not be beyond the range of its operation. This is not a light aside but a point of some moment. The modern egalitarian vision seems to extend only to all human beings but when such a vision emerges in Hinduism it typically extends to all creatures, the favourite expression for virtuous people being *sarva-bhūta-hite ratāḥ*—seeking the good of all creatures [and not just human beings]. The *Manusmṛti* has a remarkable line celebrating egalitarianism in its section on *sannyāsa* (6.44): 'A bowl, the foot of a tree, a ragged piece of cloth, a solitary life, and *equanimity towards all*—these are the marks of the renouncer.'[16] It is worth noting that the word which has been translated in the above passage as equanimity, namely *samatā*, is the word used for the English word equality in many Indian languages. Another verse in the same chapter refers to 'treating all creatures alike' as the true test for people in all stages of life. In a sense such ecological egalitarianism seems to be a feature of the Indic religious worldview, just as legal egalitarianism is of the secular worldview.

Such a perspective may appear 'regressive' from a modern point of view, which is more anthropocentric than that of the *Manusmṛti*. The application of terms such as equality before the law to the *Manusmṛti* compels one to take a closer look at them. Such terms as 'progressive' or 'regressive' often appear in a context in which 'modernity' is contrasted with 'tradition'. Two comments seem called for here. One is of course the need to distinguish between Westernization and modernization. To use them as synonyms is to confuse geography with history. But the second comment may be the more helpful one: that such a traditional text as the *Manusmṛti* concludes its second chapter with sentiments which sound rather modern, even liberal. For instance:

> [238] A man with faith should accept fine learning even from a low-caste man; the highest Law even from a man of the lowest caste; and a splendid woman even from a bad family. [239] One should take ambrosia even from poison; words of wisdom even from a child; a good example

> even from an enemy; and gold even from filth. [240] Women, gems, learning, Law, purification, and words of wisdom, as well as crafts of various kinds, may be accepted from anyone.[17]

The reader may wish to note that the Sanskrit words for 'knowledge, Law, and purification' tend to lose some of their semantic force in translation. No less than *vidyā* and *dharma*—and even rules of purity (*śauca*)—may be learnt from everywhere.

IV

An effort is also made in this book to bring the study of the *Manusmṛti* in line with some more recent methodological developments. This is most obvious in the chapter on the hermeneutics of suspicion. As a result of the patterns of thought associated with the names of Nietzsche, Marx and Freud, the three masters of suspicion according to Paul Ricœur, one major strand in the study of Hinduism tends to reduce the apparently 'religious' in Hinduism to what is political, social, psychological and/or economic and so on, with striking results. These three masters of suspicion belong to the West. Edward Said, has, however, directed his gaze of suspicion at the West itself, through what has come to be called Orientalism, thereby raising the possibility that Said may also have to be hailed one day as a master of suspicion, at least in the East.

Part B

I

Let us now examine and assess some of the common criticisms levelled against the *Manusmṛti* in a consolidated way, in the light of the facts and perspectives identified in the body of the book. For just because something is critical of the *Manusmṛti*, it does not mean that it is correct.

(i) That the *Manusmṛti* does not value the life of the *śūdra*.

This proposition is not supported by the evidence available in the *Manusmṛti*, as discussed in Chapter 5.

If this is so, then how did such an impression gain ground? The following factors seem to have been responsible: (1) the decontextualization of a relevant verse by James Mill; (2) the overinterpretation of another verse by a series of scholars; and (3) the preconception that Hindu texts *invariably* view the *śūdras* negatively.

The *śudra*, however, is not immune from capital punishment for certain crimes.

(ii) That the *Manusmṛti* does not accord legal rights to women.

This proposition is also not supported by the evidence available in the *Manusmṛti*, as discussed in Chapter 7.

So why did this impression gain ground? The following factors seem to be responsible: (1) A particular verse was decontextualized; (2) Another verse is ignored; and (3) The preconception that Hindu texts *invariably* view women negatively.

Women, however, did possess less legal independence and rights than men in the *Manusmṛti*.

A general point relevant to both these propositions is the failure to factor in the *plural* nature of Hinduism, which may have led to misleading conclusions.

(iii) That the *Manusmṛti* is casteist.

Yes and no. It is casteist in the sense that it employs the concepts of *varṇa* and *jāti* in the matter of *organizing* society, but it is not casteist in the sense that it used these concepts only to *divide* society. It is casteist in the sense that punishments varied according to *varṇa,* but it is not casteist in the sense that it *invariably* discriminated against the lower castes.

A point often overlooked in this context is that the higher *varṇas* had to pay higher penalties for theft. When it is not overlooked, it is not realized that this is also true of three other areas: (1) beating up a person, close to one; (2) depriving women of their rights; and (3) penance for sins. What is further overlooked is that theft is the *main* item of discussion in the matter of crimes in the *Dharmaśāstras*.

(iv) The *Manusmṛti* resulted in a closed Hindu society.

This proposition requires a nuanced response. By constructing the Hindu community primarily as a society, and in reconstructing society along the lines of *varṇa* and *jāti*, it did create what one might call a caste-bound society. However, two impressions which such a statement might create would be misleading: (1) that such a society could not change according to the *Manusmṛti*, and (2) that a closed society also involved a closed theology. Let us pursue these points in turn.

It should be clear from the discussion in the book that the appearance of the *varṇas*, which could be considered a *natural* phenomenon in the *Puruṣa Sūkta*, is reduced to a *conditional* phenomenon in the *Manusmṛti*. The *Manusmṛti* also provides for modification in, as well as the abandonment of, that structure, in the sense that it does not rule out such developments. The *Manusmṛti* bound the society in some way, but it did not make it hidebound. An interesting parallel suggests itself at this point. Pāṇini, the famous grammarian, usually placed in the fifth century BCE, is said to have moulded the Sanskrit language through his highly influential grammar in a way which holds good even today. The fact that Pāṇini influenced Sanskrit in this way, however, does not mean that Sanskrit did not continue to evolve after him or ceased to be a living language as a result of his influence; yet in some ways he did define Sanskrit language and certainly Sanskrit grammar. In the same way, the fact that the *Manusmṛti* left a deep impression on Hindu society does not mean that this society did not continue to evolve or that it ceased to develop as a result of this. What it does mean is that it left a profound impression on it and certainly on Hindu sociology. The fact that the *varṇa* and *jāti* continue to be diagnostic features of Hinduism is perhaps a legacy of Manu.

One could argue that the *Manusmṛti* (12.95) is reluctant to accept Buddhist and similar texts as authentic because it considers them outside the pale of the Vedas. *Within* the Hindu milieu, however, it proclaims religious tolerance in no uncertain terms (12.123): 'Some call him Fire, some Manu the Prajāpati, others Indra, still others Breath, and yet others the eternal Brahman.'

This verse apparently resonates with the well-known dictum of the *ṚgVeda* (1.164.46). Thus the 'closed' society of the *Manusmṛti* did not involve a closed theology to go with it.

II

Does this mean then that there are no good reasons for criticizing the *Manusmṛti?* No. There are.

One reason for which the *Manusmṛti* could be criticized is that it took the wrong path at a fork in the road. This calls for an explanation. It is a major assumption of this book that the *Manusmṛti* represents an effort to rebuild society (and polity) in the wake of devastating foreign invasions. At that point it was confronted with the two aforementioned courses open to it—either to orient this reconstruction around the male members of the three upper *varṇa*s, namely, the *brāhmaṇas,* the *kṣatriyas* and the *vaiśyas,* often referred to as *dvijas,* or to include everyone, that is to say, of not excluding *śūdras* and women. It chose the first option and oriented the reconstruction around the *dvijas.* That both these options were available to it is clear from the concluding *sūtras* of the *Āpastamba Dharma Sūtra,* which state clearly that issues regarding *dharma* should be decided either by consulting the *dvijas* or by consulting everyone, where all the *varṇas (sarvavarṇa)* and women, are clearly and specifically mentioned.

In doing so it followed the American Independence model. That is to say, Americans faced a similar situation after the end of British rule sometime after 1776. They had the option of orienting the future of their country and culture to include *all* Americans, such as members of the First Nations, Blacks and women, but they decided to orient it towards the WASPs—the White Anglo-Saxon Protestant males. They chose the WASP model just like Manu who chose the *dvija* model. What makes this comparison particularly intriguing is that the person who popularized the concept of WASP, sociologist E. Digby Baltzell, was a student of Hindu sociology.

Another interesting parallel is provided by another moment in world history: that of Indian Independence in 1947, which leads us to identify an Indian Independence model. With the end of British rule over India in 1947, Indians had the option, once again, of orienting the future of their country, their culture and even their civilization to include all Indians or to orient it towards the male members of the three upper *varṇas* (or even just to Hindus!), but they chose to include all Indians under the leadership of persons like Mahatma Gandhi and Dr. B.R. Ambedkar.

I think we are justified in criticizing Manu for having taken the lower moral road. One hesitates to say this too strongly, because Manu is not here to defend himself. Manu might urge that he had no choice in the face of the failure of the Aśokan model.

Another criticism that could be made of the *Manusmṛti* is that its political model did not envisage a politically united India, that it was built on the premise of numerous independent kingdoms, unlike the model in the *Arthaśāstra* which envisaged a *cakravartī*, who ruled over the whole of India. One might thus even hold the *Manusmṛti* guilty of having contributed to the legendary lack of political unity in Indian history.

III

The significance of the comparisons just made between what followed at the end of British rule in America and in India perhaps needs to be spelled out in more detail to be fully appreciated. Indians of the generation, who secured Indian independence from Britain, could well have concluded that the battle for independence was mainly fought by upper-caste Hindus, and was actively opposed by some sections of the Muslims and Christians and other communities, and that the role of the Dalits may have been mixed. Therefore, that generation could have felt morally justified in excluding such groups from its vision of a new India and accorded to them only a secondary role, or even only second-class citizenship. The parallel to this would be the conclusion which could have been reached by Manu in the second century CE that there were various segments of society which did not share his enthusiasm for a new vision, and therefore he was justified in according them lesser rights than those extended to the male members of the three upper *varṇas*. So far as women are concerned, they were probably not even viewed as major players in public life. One can thus see the plausibility of how a narrow vision of modern India's future could have been espoused by the generation which secured India's independence. But that generation, and its leaders, did not adopt such a course. With the benefit of hindsight, we can probably say that Manu adopted a narrower vision.

The same generation could also have concluded that the political unification of India brought about by the British and the establishment of a central government by them, as well as the establishment of the various administrative services including the fabled Indian Civil Service (ICS), was the work of 'evil Britishers' and therefore a legacy to be jettisoned on account of its association with past evil masters. It is significant that there was actually a move to abolish the ICS, the so-called steel frame of British India, on account of such emotions. We should not forget that almost all of the leading figures of the movement for Indian independence had been sentenced to imprisonment by members of the ICS at some point in their life. This was resisted successfully by Sardar Vallabhbhai Patel, who insisted on the formation of a successor service to the ICS, which is now known as the Indian Administrative Service or the IAS. Similarly, of the 565 states over which British paramountcy had lapsed at the time of Independence, Sardar Patel *integrated* all the states that chose to join India. He thus rejected the political model of the *Manusmṛti* which envisaged an India consisting of several independent states. One can again see how—on an emotional rather than a prudential consideration of the matter—the leaders of the time could have gone Manu's way by rejecting the idea of a politically united India with a firmly centralized administration, because this unity had been secured by the evil British and because the central administration undergirding it had been established by them.

Such a centralized system of imperial administration had actually been secured under the first ruler of the Mauryan dynasty, Candragupta Maurya, the grandfather of Aśoka. It was only a few centuries or so later that the Han dynasty established a similar system in China. The system survived until 1911 in China and was a major factor in securing the administrative and political unity of that country through the centuries.

Arguably, in India, this legacy was lost due to its association with Aśoka, who had become a *bête noire* for the Indians of the generation of the *Manusmṛti* because of the political disasters which followed Aśoka's reign. One can thus argue, again tentatively and with the benefit of hindsight, that the *Manusmṛti* was at least partly responsible for the lack of political unity in Indian history in later times.

Thus the final assessment about the *Manusmṛti*, in light of the conclusions drawn in this book and the historical comparisons just outlined, must be that it possesses both positive and negative dimensions. It set out to save Hindu society (and polity) at a time when it was in grave danger of going under. Given that a Hindu society with a Vedic orientation has survived into our own times means that the *Manusmṛti* may have succeeded in this task, which is no mean achievement. In doing so, however, the *Manusmṛti* gave Hindu culture a social rather than a political orientation. It saved the 'society' but perhaps not the 'polity'. Its failure to save the polity may have been due to its visceral dislike of the Aśokan experiment, which was characterized by political unity and a centralized administration. But in rejecting these, along with its rejection of Aśokan pacifism, did the *Manusmṛti* throw the baby out with the bath water?

APPENDICES

Appendix I

Dalits in the *Manusmṛti*

I

Dalit is a somewhat equivocal word which is sometimes used for all oppressed communities, whether former untouchables or other lower castes. In this appendix it will be primarily used as an appellation for the untouchables. Untouchability is also an equivocal word and could be used for people who prepared food that could not be partaken by some, or for people whose mere touch could be polluting. In this appendix, this word will be used primarily in the latter sense, to denote people whose physical touch, or the touching of objects touched by them, could pollute.

The *Manusmṛti* clearly refers to such pollution, for a verse mentions a people whose touch was supposed to contaminate.[1] It runs as follows (3.241): 'a pig spoils with its breath, a cock with the waft of its wings, a dog with its gaze, and a *low-caste man with his touch*.'[2] It is striking that the word *avara* is used here in the original for a person whose touch is polluting. The word occurs at only two places in the *Manusmṛti* (2.223 and 3.241). And the word is associated with pollution by touch in both the cases. Others who caused pollution by touch were: (1) *divākīrti*; (2) a menstruating woman (*udakyā*); (3) a fallen person (*patita*); (4) a woman who had just given birth (*sūtikā*); (5) a corpse (*śava*); and (6) one who had touched a corpse. The pollution was removed by a bath. Verse

5.85 introduces several interesting considerations. One of them is the phenomenon of temporary untouchability. Thus a menstruating woman and one who had just given birth is said to cause pollution by touch, but only so long as they were in that condition. They were not polluting per se. They could cease to be polluting. However, some persons, such as the *divākīrti* and the *patita*, could be considered to continue to be sources of pollution for a longer time.

To turn first to the *patita*, a *patita* is one guilty of these four crimes: killing a *brāhmaṇa*, drinking liquor, stealing and having sex with the *guru*'s wife (*Manusmṛti* 11.55, also see 11.181–82). After the performance of proper penance, however, such a sinner could be restored to society and cease to be a polluting agent. So the upshot of the present discussion is that women could be temporarily polluting, and men (and women?) who had committed the four sins could also remain so for a longer time—until they atoned for their sins. What is important to recognize is that none of them were permanent sources of pollution. That leaves us with the *divākīrti*. Who is the *divākīrti*? Patrick Olivelle glosses the word as follows:

> *Divākīrti*: the meaning of this term (literally 'calling or declaring during the day') is unclear. Most commentators take it to mean a Cāṇḍāla: see *MBh* 12.136.106, where its meaning is clearly a Cāṇḍāla (see also *MBh* 12.136.110). The term may refer to the fact that these individuals were expected to go about only during the day and to announce their presence.[3]

Most commentators gloss the word as *cāṇḍāla*. So the question arises: Who is the *cāṇḍāla*? The word appears several times in the *Manusmṛti* in the tenth chapter (verses 10, 26, 37, 38, 51 and so on) and is defined in the *Manusmṛti* (10.12) as a person of the *pratiloma* (hypogamous) caste sprung from a *śūdra* male and a *brahmāṇa* female. P.V. Kane points out that the *Vedavyāsa Smṛti* (I.9–10) uses the term for three kinds of people: (1) the offspring of a *śūdra* male from a *brāhmaṇa* woman; (2) the offspring of an unmarried woman; and (3) the offspring of union with a *sagotra* girl, or a consanguineous marriage.[4] It is used in the *Manusmṛti* in only the first sense; Kane makes the useful point that all the three types of *cāṇḍālas* are so by the fact of their birth.[5] *So this is the one source of pollution which is permanent—as it is based on birth.*

Two other points are significant here. One is that the word used for untouchables in many Indian languages, namely *aspṛśya* (literally untouchable), is not used in the *Manusmṛti*. The earliest occurrence of this word in this sense, as mentioned earlier, is found in the *Viṣṇu Dharma Sūtra* (5.104), assigned also to the second century. The other is that the *Manusmṛti* (10.51) assigns the *caṇḍāla*, along with the *śvapaca* (literally dog-eater), to a place outside the village, while it consigns another class, that of the *antyāvasāyin* (born of a *niṣāda* woman from a *caṇḍāla*) to the cemetery (10.39). This means that there might have been a category even below the *caṇḍāla*.

Another fact needs to be taken into consideration at this point. Although P.V. Kane clearly states that 'the only antyaja who was *aspṛśya* according to Manu was the cāṇḍāla',[6] yet 'it is strange that the twice-born men accepted meat from their hands (V.131)'.[7] The context in which this statement is made deserves being considered as a whole:

> [128] Water collected on the ground is pure if it is sufficient to slake the thirst of a cow, is uncontaminated with foul substances, and has the right odour, colour, and taste. [129] The hand of an artisan is always pure, as are goods displayed for sale; the almsfood received by a student is always ritually clean—that is the settled rule. [130] A woman's mouth is always pure; so is a bird when it makes a fruit to fall, a calf when it makes the milk to flow, and a dog when it catches a deer. [131] The meat of an animal that has been killed by a dog or some other predator, or by a Cāṇḍāla or some other lowlife, is pure—that is the judgment of Manu.[8]

It was mentioned earlier how untouchability could be of two kinds: one in which pollution resulted from touching the *person*, and the other in which pollution resulted from the consumption of *food* touched or prepared by an undesirable person. Here is a case where the touch of the *person* is polluting, but the *food* touched by the person is not. This also seems to be the right place to introduce the concept of *apapātra* found in the *Manusmṛti*. The word appears in *Manusmṛti* 10.51, wherein it is said of the *cāṇḍālas* and *śvapacas* that they should be made *apapātra*,[9] a term explained by Patrick Olivelle as follows:

Apapātras: it appears that this term in its early usage referred to certain individuals excluded from society because of some serious lapse. One interpretation of the term is that when an Apapātra eats food from someone in a vessel, that vessel should be thrown away. See also the mention of broken vessels in verses 52 and 54. Another interpretation is that the food should not be placed in vessels that they hold in their hands but either placed on the ground or held by someone else.[10]

V.S. Agrawal remarks of them that 'their utensils were untouchable (apapātrāḥ) and broken (bḥinnabhāṇḍa). It is likely that they correspond to the "niravasita" type of śūdras in Pāṇini (II.IV.10)'.[11] Since the *cāṇḍālas* are included in the *apapātra* category, could it be that it was kosher to accept *meat alone* from them?

II

It was important to devote an appendix to the Dalits in the *Manusmṛti* because it has sometimes even been maintained, tacitly at least, that there are no references to untouchability in the *Manusmṛti*.[12] One discovers that contrary to the standard version which equates untouchability only with physical contact of someone considered polluting, untouchablity in the *Manusmṛti* covers a wider phenomena. Untouchability includes untouchability brought about by temporary pollution as well as resulting from moral turpitude on the part of persons. It also includes the standard form of untouchability in the case of the *cāṇḍāla,* who is so by birth. Additionally, untouchability in the form of not touching the utensils or food of someone else is also a form of untouchability present in the *Manusmṛti*.

III

The condition of the untouchable, who dwelt on the margins of society, was far from enviable but the untouchable did enjoy two 'privileges': (1) the untouchable, like every Hindu, was entitled to liberation, and (2) what is even more startling, could guide others to liberation. This follows from an analysis of *Manusmṛti* 2.238c: *antyādapi param dharmam*.

> A man who has faith may receive good learning even from a man who is lower, *the ultimate law even from a man of the lowest (castes),* and a jewel of a woman even from a bad family.[13]

The controversy centres on *paraṃ dharmam*. G. Bühler translates the entire expression as 'the highest law even from the lowest'.[14] Law here has the sense of teaching, like the word Torah which means teaching but is rendered usually in English as Law.

The commentary of Kullūka Bhaṭṭa (c. 1250) on this verse is of great interest on this point. He expresses dissatisfaction with the way Medhātithi (c. 825–900) explains this part of the verse. According to Medhātithi it is to be understood as follows: If even an untouchable tells you 'Don't tarry here; do not bathe in these waters' you should heed those words. The *dharma* here pertains to mundane and *not* supramundane *dharma.*[15]

Kullūka offers a very different interpretation of his own. According to Kullūka, what is meant is that liberative knowledge may be acquired even from an untouchable. Now the question naturally arises as to how could an untouchable be in possession of liberative knowledge? Kullūka anticipates this question and explains that this is possible on account of the force of yogic accomplishment of a previous life, despite being reborn as an untouchable in this life as a result of residual negative karma that remains to be worked out.

The statement of Kullūka is reminiscent of Śaṅkara's gloss on *Vedāntasūtra* III.4.36 when he concedes that Vidura, Dharmavyādha and others were liberated beings, although *śūdras*, on account of the inevitable maturation of *jñāna* as a result of transformative knowledge acquired earlier.[16]

It is clear then, that it is possible in a metempsychotic way to attain liberation through *jñāna* even as a *śūdra* or worse.[17]

The story does not end here. That the untouchable could become enlightened or liberated is the clear implication of the verse itself, which further states that members of higher *varṇas, dvijas* (twice-born), could learn from him, that is, he could even stand in relation to them as a *guru.* Spirituality often turns out to be the one big loophole in the rigid social structures associated with such texts and that loophole ends up as a leaphole in this case. We know from *Manusmṛti* 3.156 that *śūdra gurus* were around, unless one interprets the verse as referring to *śūdra gurus* who only had *śūdra śiṣyas*.[18]

Another privilege, in relation to the untouchables, was that an untouchable could not be ridiculed or made to feel small for who he or she was, if the word *jātihīna* in *Manusmṛti* 4.141 is seen as referring to a class of people which includes the untouchables. The verse is translated by Patrick Olivelle as follows: 'He must not *ridicule* people who have too few or too many limbs, who are uneducated, who are very old, who lack beauty or wealth, or *who are of low birth*'.[19] Georg Bühler translates the verb *nākṣipet* more strongly: 'let him not insult [...] those who are of low birth',[20] and Wendy Doniger and Brian Smith follow his lead: 'He should not insult [...] those of [...] too low a birth'.[21]

Here *Manusmṛti* (4.141) anticipates a provision of the Scheduled Castes and Scheduled Tribes (Prevention of Atrocities) Act 1989. According to the provision number (X) under section L:

> [...] whoever not being a member of a Scheduled caste or Scheduled tribe...intentionally insults or intimidates with intent to humiliate a member of a SC or a ST in any place in public view ... shall be punishable with imprisonment for a term that shall not be less than six months but which may extend to five years.[22]

Appendix II

Clusters of Verses

It was emphasized in the body of the text that reading verses of the *Manusmṛti* in isolation is an invitation to misrepresentation. This appendix follows up this point by providing a cluster of verses which are best read together as an illustration of this point. It is proposed, for instance, that one should read:

1. 1.100 with 8.336–38
2. 1.85–86 with 9.301–02
3. 2.16 with 2.66
4. 9.3 with 8.28–29; 9.4; 91; 195.
5. 8.102 with 1.95
6. 11.132 with 8.104–05 and 11.67
7. 5.162 with 9.175
8. 4.211 with 4.253
9. 9.235 with 5.56
10. 9.46 with 3.155;181; 9.79; 175–76.
11. 1.92–101 with 2.162
12. 2.6 with 4.46
13. 5.154 with 9.79
14. 8.371 with 8.359 and 11.177
15. 9.88 with 9.89–91

16. 2.31(a) with 2.33
17. 3.25 and 351–54 with 8.204
18. 8.88 with 10.126
19. 1.91 with 10.99
20. 9.236 with 8.349

Appendix III

Is Hinduism Brahmanical?

It is true that Hinduism is regularly characterized in Western as well as Indian academia and media as Brahmanical, and the *Manusmṛti* is sometimes held responsible for making it so. But is Hinduism truly Brahmanical? How does this description measure up against the evidence?

I

To begin with Hindu myths: A major myth of Vedic Hinduism is that of Indra and Vṛtra, in which Indra slays Vṛtra. What are their respective *varṇas*? Indra is a *kṣatriya*, Vṛtra is a *brāhmaṇa*; so it is the *brāhmaṇa* who gets killed. Similarly, a major myth of classical Hinduism is that of the struggle between Rāma and Rāvaṇa, in which Rāma slays Rāvaṇa. What are their respective *varṇas*? Rāma is a *kṣatriya*, Rāvaṇa is a *brāhmaṇa*; so it is again the *brāhmaṇa* who gets killed. In both these myths the *brāhmaṇa* gets killed; this raises the question: Is Hinduism Brahmicidal or Brahmanical?

A major Hindu doctrine is that of incarnations (*avatāra*). In the traditional listing of the ten incarnations, Viṣṇu incarnates himself in only two of them as a *brāhmaṇa*, as Vāmana and as Parāsurāma, while his most popular incarnations remain those of Rāma and Kṛṣṇa. To describe this list as Brahmanical is also, therefore, a bit of a stretch.

A third point of interest is provided by the Hindu Trinity, which consists of Brahmā, Viṣṇu and Śiva. While Viṣṇu and Śiva are widely worshipped in Hinduism, the worship of Brahmā declined in India to such an extent that he is now worshipped in only a handful of places. This fact acquires significance in the present context because if any among the three gods may be said to have a special connection with *brāhmaṇas*, it is Brahmā. Once again it becomes problematic to describe Hinduism as Brahmanical in such a context.

II

Hinduism, however, could be considered Brahmanical in another sense. It is said that upon seeing a grave injustice being committed, the *brāhmaṇa* protests by saying: 'Stop; otherwise I will kill myself', while a *kṣatriya* protests by saying: 'Stop; otherwise I will kill you'. If Hinduism only adopted the first approach, so well honed by Mahatma Gandhi in our times, then one could argue that Hinduism is Brahmanical in this sense. Hinduism, however, does not confine itself to the first approach alone despite Mahatma Gandhi's heroic efforts to foreground it.

Could it then be considered Brahmanical in the sense that the *brāhmaṇas* enjoyed a privileged status within Hinduism? After all, they are often to be punished the least for various crimes, given precedence, supported by the king when in distress, and so on. Such a depiction however ignores certain elements of the situation: in case of theft they are punished the most (*Manusmṛti* 8.337–38); although they are to be shown preference by *others*, they *themselves* are instructed to recoil from such treatment (2.162) and the ruler and others are meant to support them because hunger was an occupational hazard with them (4.7–8,133–34; 11.21). And the so-called privileges are not only subject to limitations, the privileges are balanced by special responsibilities (for instance, 6.34). Moreover, there are periods in Indian history, such as the early Vedic period, during which such privileges had not yet been conferred on them or had been in the main abolished, as in the three *nibandhas* (medieval legal digests)—the *Smṛticandrikā* (c. 1200), the *Madanaratna* (c. 1400–1450) and *Sarasvatīvilāsa* (sixteenth century)—seem to indicate. These privileges have of course become obsolete in the modern period; these previously cited texts suggest that they were already considered obsolete in many parts of India in the medieval period itself. Furthermore, differential provisions are not invariably discriminatory provisions and even in the case of differential treatment for crimes in classical law, two *Smṛtis*, those of Kātyāyana and Vyāsa, *impose progressively higher punishments for the higher varṇas.*

III

Could Hinduism be considered Brahmanical because the *brāhmaṇas* bore the brunt of the attacks when the non-Hindu rulers of India chose to persecute the Hindus? It is well documented that Alexander had them gibbetted, Sikandar Lodi had one burnt alive, even Akbar forced some of them to convert on his own admission, and the British executed Nand Kumar by resorting to a legal ruse. This, however, would endow the *brāhmaṇas* with the halo of martyrdom. This would be inconsistent with the context in which Hinduism is often described as Brahmanical, in a pejorative manner. Moreover, it is clear from the history of Hindu resistance to foreign rule that not just *brāhmaṇas* but Hindus from all levels of society participated in its defense. They may have formed the vanguard of the struggle in this sense but the struggle, especially in its later stages under Mahatma Gandhi, was characterized by mass rather than class participation.

Could Hinduism be considered Brahmanical in a genetic sense, in the sense that all Hindus are derived from the *brāhmaṇas*? The suggestion may appear far-fetched but there is some textual basis for this. Some sacred texts state that originally there was only one *varṇa* or 'caste'. In some accounts these original people are called Haṃsa, but in other texts it is stated that originally in the 'golden age' as it were, there was only the *brāhmaṇa* class and the later *varṇas* arose from it when, for various reasons, the *brāhmaṇas* abandoned their original vocation and took to other means of livelihood. This carries the implication that the so-called 'caste system' is a product of cosmic degeneration so that if one wishes to restore the 'golden age', as the rulers are exhorted to do, then all caste and class distinctions need to be eliminated. But perhaps the implications of this view are too radical for those who like to describe Hinduism as Brahmanical, although the convergence of this perspective with some modern revolutionary ideas, which proclaim the need for a caste-free and class-free society, is hard to overlook. Moreover, the fact that the *brāhmaṇas* constitute the *centre* and not the *top* in this scheme may also not be welcomed by all.

IV

Could Hinduism be considered Brahmanical in yet another sense? Hinduism has been repeatedly characterized as Brahmanical in modern times when its social system was identified as the 'caste system' under British rule. This process gained momentum after the institution of the British census from 1871 onwards. The Indians on whom the British relied during this process were largely *brāhmaṇas*, as documented by Nicholas Dirks.[1] One could then say that, in this sense, the modern caste system is Brahmanical. It could also be considered Brahmanical during this period in another sense. Two parts of India where the popular sentiment against the *brāhmaṇas* is quite strong are Tamil Nadu and Maharashtra.[2] In these parts, it was the *brāhmaṇas* who first took to English education with alacrity as a source of employment under the British government and thereby came to dominate the lower echelons of British administration. People thus came in contact with them as employees of the British government and arguably came to resent the power they seemed to have over them. Such exposure on their part of the myrmidons of the law then either reinforced the traditional caste dominance, or the hostility felt by the people has been mistakenly attributed to religious factors. It is doubtful, however, that those who describe Hinduism as Brahmanical have such considerations in mind.

V

Could not modern Hinduism be considered Brahmanical in another sense? Hinduism is often represented as undergoing a renaissance during the modern period, which is frequently depicted as the outcome of the work of a series of Hindu reformers from Raja Ram Mohun Roy (d. 1833) to S. Radhakrishnan (d. 1975). Most of these reformers were of *brāhmaṇa* lineage, and modern Hinduism could be considered Brahmanical in this sense. There are notable exceptions to this in the figures of Keshab Chunder Sen, Swami Vivekananda, Mahatma Gandhi and Sri Aurobindo. Moreover, if we take a qualitative rather than a quantitative approach to the issue and ask 'Who are the most influential among these reformers?' Mahatma Gandhi would probably be considered the most influential. And if we asked for two of them to be named, then Swami Vivekananda would probably be included in this roll of honour. This consideration generates the paradox of an allegedly Brahmanical tradition being influenced by non-*brāhmaṇas* the most!

It could be argued that although these modern reformers were not *brāhmaṇas* themselves, what they were propagating was a religion shaped by *brāhmaṇas*, and that Hinduism is Brahmanical in this sense. And that this holds true for the whole history of Hinduism. This raises the question: Who shaped Hinduism? Vedic Hinduism was shaped by the *rshis* or seers, many of whom had origins sometimes unorthodox to the point of being unnatural, as in the case of Agastya and Kaṭha. There is also the danger of anachronism in viewing the social reality in terms of 'caste' distinctions during a period when the system may not be in place. Later, *kṣatriyas* appear as teachers in the Upaniṣads. Classical Hinduism was shaped in Tamil Nadu by, among others, the Āḷvārs and the Nāyanmārs who came from different social backgrounds, including the untouchables. The point may even cut deeper, that spiritual saints and not *brāhmaṇas* are the generating centres of Hinduism. Could it then not be claimed that Hinduism is Brahmanical because *brāhmaṇas* are its transmitters? Could it be that Hinduism may not be Brahmanical in terms of its mythology, theology, ethics or even history, but may be considered so because it was mainly transmitted by the *brāhmaṇas* over the centuries? Hence it should be described as Brahmanical.

If the *brāhmaṇas* transmitted the sacred texts of the Hindus, then it makes sense to ask: Who transmitted the texts of the early Buddhists and the Jainas? These texts were originally transmitted orally in the case of these two traditions as well, like the Vedas, so it is quite relevant a question to ask. According to a well-known study cited by A.L. Basham,[3] about 40 per cent of the monks in early Buddhism, whose origins can be ascertained, came from a *brāhmaṇa* background. Similarly the twelve *gaṇadharas*—who decoded and transmitted the teachings of the last Jaina Tīrthaṅkara, Mahāvīra—were all of *brāhmaṇa* lineage. So it turns out that the *brāhmaṇas* were involved in the transmission of the texts of all the three members of the classical Indic religious tradition: Hinduism, Buddhism and Jainism. So if Hinduism is Brahmanical, should the early

Buddhist and Jaina traditions also be so characterized, as *brāhmaṇas* seem to be involved in the oral transmission of all the three traditions?

VI

Perhaps one has been looking for the Brahmanical nature of Hinduism in the wrong places. Is it in its sociology that Hinduism is Brahmanical, for the *brāhmaṇas* are the first to be mentioned in the list of the four *varṇas*, which seems to spell out a hierarchy? These four *varṇas* are those of the: (1) *brāhmaṇas* (Vedic scholars, priests and so on) (2) *kṣatriya* (warriors, kings, bureaucrats and so on) (3) *vaiśyas* (traders, businessmen, agriculturists and so on) and (4) *śūdras* (servants and so on). What then, one might ask, is this hierarchy based on? Is it based on power? If that were the case, the *kṣatriyas* would be heading it. If based on wealth, the *vaiśyas* would be heading it; and if based on service, the *śūdras* would be heading it. It is obviously based on ritual and moral purity and scriptural learning, as these are associated with the *brāhmaṇas* who have been placed on top. This problematizes the point under discussion on account of the common perception that those at the apex of a social system tend to monopolize wealth and power. It is possible to argue that *brāhmaṇas*, as a class, may have cornered both in some parts of India or during certain periods of its history, but this is certainly not a feature of the scheme itself. The classical formulation of this scheme is usually located in the *Manusmṛti* (assigned by scholars to the second century).

The title of that text also seems to problematize the point further. The text is named after Manu, who was a *kṣatriya*! So it may be a Brahmanical text but it seems to appeal for its authority to a non-Brahmin. Incidentally, Manu is also considered a major legal authority in Burmese Buddhism. This could suggest that the *brāhmaṇas* and the rulers (the *kṣatriyas*) joined hands in exploiting the other classes. This could well be the case, but in that case Hinduism should not be described as Brahmanical but rather at 'Dvijaite' in character. This verbal oddity results from one's desire to couch the exploitation of the lower castes and classes by the three higher *varṇas* (*brāhmaṇas*, *kṣatriyas* and *vaiśyas*) together into traditional idiom in which all three are called *dvijas* or twice-born, on account of their right to wear the sacred thread, a right denied to the *śūdras* (and to women). This would correspond somewhat to the 'brahmin-bania conspiracy' in modern ideological name-calling; but then Hinduism will have to be considered as characterized by a Dvijaite rather than a Brahmanical conspiracy.

Support for this point comes from a surprising source. The concept of WASP, as you may remember, is short for White Anglo-Saxon Protestants, which refers to those who constitute the dominant component of American culture. This concept was apparently developed by E. Digby Baltzell, who taught at the University of Pennsylvania before he died in 1996. He was a sociologist as well as a student of Hinduism. If the category of WASP was developed by him on the prototype of the *dvijas* (the male members of the three higher *varṇas*) in Hindu sociology—as is generally accepted—then those who describe Hinduism as the hotbed of the 'brahmin-bania conspiracy' may be closer to the mark than those who describe it as a Brahmanical conspiracy. This has the support of the Hindu *Dharma Sūtras*, one of which, the *Āpastamba*, concludes by stating in the penultimate *sūtra* or aphorism that, in matters of *dharma*, the norms set by the twice-borns or *dvijas* should be considered authoritative. This seems to clinch the issue, but for the fact that the last aphorism of the same text also says: Others are of the opinion that in these matters the views of *all the varṇas and of women* should be taken into account.

VII

It is clear therefore that Hinduism contains two streams of thought within it. According to one, the male members of the three higher *varṇas* are meant to be arbiters of *dharma*. According to another school of thought, however, all the *varṇas*, and women as well, had to be part of the process. As Hinduism encompasses both these views it would be incorrect to claim that it is Brahmanical even if the term is used as a synecdoche and the *brāhmaṇas*, who constitute a part of the *dvija* category, are made to stand for the whole of it, which consists of *kṣatriyas* and *vaiśyas* as well. One could also identify such a 'Brahmanical Hinduism' in a neutral, a positive and a negative sense. A neutral version will be purely descriptive. The positive version would denote that version of Hinduism which the *dvija* or a narrower 'priestly class' may identify as the ideal version of Hinduism and wish for, favour or espouse. One could similarly think of a *kṣatriya* or a *vaiśya* or a *śūdra* (or a Dalit) version of Hinduism. In a negative sense it could denote how these or other groups may have manipulated or sought to manipulate Hinduism in their favour at the expense of its other constituents.

Thus it may be valid to say that there is a Brahmanical Hinduism but not to say that Hinduism is Brahmanical *as this statement misrepresents Hinduism.* The situation in this case is not very different from the one we encounter in the case of other religions. It seems valid to say that there is a jihadist Islam, but if one were to describe Islam itself as jihadist one would be overstating the case. Similarly, one could identify what one might call Christian imperialism, but to identify Christianity with imperialism would be equally misleading. The question remains: Did the *Manusmṛti* contribute to casteist Hinduism? The reader may wish to draw his or her own conclusions in the matter by taking two major factors into account—that on the one hand the *Manusmṛti* favours the *dvija* option for who determines what Hinduism is, and that on the other hand it also reflects the plural character of Hinduism.[4]

Bibliography

Agrawala, V.S. *India as Described by Manu.* Varanasi: Prithivi Prakashan, 1970.

Aiyar, C.P. Ramaswami. 'The Philosophical Basis of Indian Legal and Social Systems'. In *The Indian Mind: Essentials of Indian Philosophy and Culture*, edited by Charles A. Moore. Honolulu, HI: University of Hawaii Press, 1967.

Altekar, A.S. *The Position of Women in Hindu Civilization.* Delhi: Motilal Banarsidass, 1962.

Apte, V.M. 'Social and Economic Conditions'. In *The Vedic Age*, edited by R.C. Majumdar. Mumbai: Bharatiya Vidya Bhavan, 1967.

Apte, Vaman Shivram. *The Practical Sanskrit-English Dictionary.* Fourth revised and enlarged edition. New Delhi: Motilal Banarsidass, 1965.

Ayoub, Mahmoud M. 'The Islamic Tradition'. In *World Religions: Western Traditions*, edited by Willard G. Oxtoby. Toronto: Oxford University Press, 1996.

Bailey, Greg. '*Dharmarāja* in the *Mahābhārata*, *Dharmarāja* in early Buddhist Literature'. In *On Meaning and Mantras: Essays in Honor of Frits Staal*, edited by George Thompson and Richard A. Payne. Moraga, CA: Institute of Buddhist Studies and BDK America, Inc., 2016.

Basham, A.L. *The Wonder That Was India.* New York, NY: Grove Press Inc., 1954.

———. *The Wonder That Was India.* New Delhi: Rupa & Co., 1996 [1954].

———. *The Wonder That Was India*. New Delhi: Rupa & Co., 1999 [1967].

———. *Studies in Indian History and Culture.* Calcutta: Sambodhi Publications Private Ltd., 1964.

———. *Conference on the Date of Kaniṣka*. Leiden: E.J. Brill, 1968.

———. *The Origins and Development of Classical Hinduism*, edited and completed by Kenneth G. Zysk. Oxford: Oxford University Press, 1991.

Bhandarkar, D.R. 'Asoka and His Successors'. In *A Comprehensive History of India*, edited by K.A. Nilakanta Sastri. Bombay: Orient Longman, 1957.

Bose, Sugata and Ayesha Jalal. *Modern South Asia: History, Culture, Political Economy*. New Delhi: Oxford University Press, 1998.

Bose, Sugata. *His Majesty's Opponent: Subhash Chandra Bose and India's Struggle Against Empire.* Cambridge, MA: Belknap Press of Harvard University, 2011.

Boutin, Maurice. 'Réponses / Responses to John C. Roberston / 1'. *Studies in Religion* 8, no. 4 (1979): 379–88.

Bowes, Pratima. *The Hindu Religious Tradition: A Philosophical Approach.* London: Routledge and Kegan Paul, 1977.

Bronkhorst, Johannes. 'Brahmanism: Its Place in Ancient Indian Society'. *Contributions to Indian Sociology* 51, no. 3 (2017): 361–69.

Bühler, G., trans. *The Laws of Manu.* New Delhi: Motilal Banarsidas, 2001 [1886].

Campbell, Joseph, ed. *Heinrich Zimmer: Philosophies of India.* Princeton, NJ: Princeton University Press, 1969 [1951].

Ch'en, Kenneth K.S. *Buddhism: The Light of Asia.* New York, NY: Barron's Educational Series, 1968.

Coedes, G. *The Indianized States of Southeast Asia,* edited by Walter F. Vella. Honolulu, HI: East-West Center Press, 1968.

Dalrymple, William. *The Last Mughal: The Fall of a Dynasty, Delhi 1857.* New York, NY: Alfred A. Knof, 2008.

Dandekar, R.N. 'Dharma, the First End of Man'. In *Sources of Indian Tradition.* Second Edition, edited and revised by Ainslie T. Embree. New York, NY: Columbia University Press, 1988.

Davis, Donald R. 'Hinduism as a Legal Tradition'. *Journal of the American Academy of Religion* 75, no. 2 (2007): 241–67.

Daweewarn, Dawee. *Brāhmaṇism in South-East Asia: From the Earliest Times to 1445* AD. New Delhi: Sterling Publishers Private Limited, 1982.

Derrett, J. Duncan M. *Religion, Law and The State in India.* New York, NY: The Free Press, 1968.

Dirks, Nicholas B. *Castes of Mind: Colonialism and the Making of Modern India.* Princeton, NJ: Princeton University Press, 2001.

Doniger, Wendy and Brian K. Smith, trans. *The Laws of Manu.* Harmondsworth: Penguin Books, 1991.

Doniger, Wendy. *The Hindus: An Alternative History.* New York, NY: The Penguin Press, 2009.

Elst, Koenraad. *Indigenous Indians: Agastya to Ambedkar.* New Delhi: Voice of India, 1993.

———. 'Is the Term Dharma Untranslatable?' In *Probodhan II: Thoughts on Hindu Society,* edited by Saradindu Mukherjee. Gurugram, Haryana: World Hindu Foundation, 2018.

Embree, Ainslie T., ed. *Alberuni's India,* translated by *Edward C. Sachau.* New York, NY: W.W. Norton and Company, 1971.

———, ed. *Sources of Indian Tradition.* Second edition. New York, NY: Columbia University Press, 1988.

Gadamer, Hans-Georg. *Truth and Method.* Translation edited by Garrett Barden and John Cumming. New York, NY: Seabury Press, 1975.

Gandhi, M.K. *Hindu Dharma,* edited by Bharatan Kumarappa. Ahmedabad: Navajivan Trust, 1958.

———. *An Autobiography: The Story of My Experiments with Truth.* Boston: Beacon Press, 1993.

Gode, P.K. and C.G. Karve, eds. *Prin. Vaman Shivram Apte's The Practical Sanskrit-English Dictionary.* Poona: Prasad Prakashan, 1958.

González-Reimann, Luis. *The Mahābhārata and the Yugas: India's Great Epic Poem and the Hindu System of World Ages.* New York, NY: Peter Lang, 2002.

———. 'Time in the Mahābhārata and the Time of the Mahābhārata'. In *Epic and Argument in Sanskrit Literary History,* edited by Sheldon Pollock. New Delhi: Manohar, 2010.

Halbfass, Wilhelm. *India and Europe: An Essay in Understanding.* Albany, NY: State University of New York Press, 1988.

Hiltebeitel, Alf. *Dharma: Its Early History in Law, Religion, and Narrative.* New York, NY: Oxford University Press, 2011.

———. 'India's Second Urbanization, Forest Gleaners and the *Mahābhārata* Myth of the Unburdening of the Earth'. In *Questioning Paradigms,*

Constructing Histories: A Festschrift for Romila Thapar, edited by Kumkum Roy and Naina Dayal. New Delhi: Aleph Book Company, 2019.

Hiriyanna, M. *Indian Philosophical Studies*. Mysore: Kavyalaya Publishers, 1957.

———. *The Essentials of Indian Philosophy*. New Delhi: Motilal Banarsidas 2005 [1948].

Hume, Robert Ernest, trans. *The Thirteen Principal Upanishads*. London: Oxford University Press, 1968 [1877].

Isischei, Elizabeth. 'Some Ambiguities in the Academic Study of Religion'. *Religion* 23 (1993): 379–80.

Jacolliot, Louis. *La Bible Dans L'Inde*. Paris: Librairie Internationale, 1869.

Jaffrelot, Christophe. *Dr. Ambedkar and Untouchability: Fighting the Indian Caste System*. New York, NY: Columbia University Press, 2005.

Jaini, Padmanabh S. *The Jaina Path of Purification*. Berkeley, CA: University of California Press, 1979.

Jamison, Stephanie W. *Sacrificed Wife/Sacrifer's Wife: Women, Ritual, and Hospitality in Ancient India*. New York, NY: Oxford University Press, 1996.

Jamison, Stephanie and Joel Brereton, trans. *The Rigveda: The Earliest Religious Poetry of India*. New York, NY: Oxford University Press, 2014.

Jois, M. Rama. *Legal and Constitutional History of India*. Allahabad: Universal Law Publishing, 2004.

I-Tsing, *A Record of the Buddhist Religion as Practised in India and the Malay Archipelago (A.D. 671–695)*, translated by J. Takakusu. New Delhi: Munshiram Manoharlal, 1966; [1896]

Kale, M.R. *The Abhijñānaśākuntalam of Kālidāsa*. New Delhi: Motilal Banarsidass, 1980 [1969].

———. *The Pañcatantra of Viṣṇuśarmā*. Delhi: Motilal Banarsidass, 1986.

Kane, P.V. *History of Dharmaśāstra*. Poona: Bhandarkar Oriental Research Institute, 1974.

Kangle, R.P. *The Kauṭilīya Arthaśāstra*. Bombay: University of Bombay, 1963.

Klostermaier, Klaus K. *A Survey of Hinduism*. Second edition. Albany, NY: State University of New York Press, 1994.

Lahiri, Nayanjot. *Ashoka in Ancient India*. Cambridge, MA: Harvard University Press, 2015.

Larson, Gerald James. 'Karma as a "Sociology of Knowledge" or "Social Psychology" of Process/Praxis'. In *Karma and Rebirth in Classical Indian*

Traditions, edited by Wendy Doniger O'Flaherty. Berkeley: University of California Press, 1980.

Larus, Joel. *Culture and Political-Military Behavior: The Hindus in Pre-Modern India*. Calcutta: Minerva Associates, 1979.

Legge, J., trans. *A Record of Buddhist Kingdoms*. New York, NY: Dover Publications, 1965.

Lipner, Julius. *Hindus: Their Religious Beliefs and Practices*. London: Routledge, 1994.

Maddison, Angus. *The World Economy*. Paris: Development Centre of the Organisation for Economic Co-operation and Development, 2006.

Mahadevan, T.M.P. *Outlines of Hinduism*. Bombay: Chetana Publications, 1971 [1956].

Majumdar, R.C., ed. *The Age of Imperial Unity*. Bombay: Bharatiya Vidya Bhavan, 1951.

———. *Hindu Colonies in the Far East*. Calcutta: Firma K.L. Mukhopadhyay, 1963.

———, ed. *The Age of Imperial Kanauj*. Bombay: Bharatiya Vidya Bhavan, 1964.

———, ed. *The Age of Imperial Unity*. Bombay: Bharatiya Vidya Bhavan, 1968.

———, ed. *The Classical Age*. Bombay: Bharatiya Vidya Bhavan, 1970.

Mahābhārata, Critical Edition: Poona, Bhandarkar Oriental Research Institute, 1966.

McGovern, Nathan. *The Snake and the Mongoose: The Emergence of Identity in Early Indian Religion*. New York, NY: Oxford University Press, 2019.

Merriam-Webster's Collegiate Dictionary. Tenth edition. Springfield, MA: Merriam-Webster, Incorporated, 2002.

Mill, James. *The History of British India*. Vol. 1. New Delhi: Associated Publishing House, 1972 [1871].

———. *The History of British India*. Abridged, with an introduction by William Thomas. Chicago, IL: The University of Chicago Press, 1975.

Mitra, Kana. 'Human Rights in Hinduism'. In *Human Rights in Religious Traditions*, edited by Arlene Swidler. New York, NY: The Pilgrim Press, 1982.

Monier-Williams, Monier. *A Sanskrit-English Dictionary*. Oxford: Clarendon Press, 1964.

Motwani, Kewal. *Manu: A Study in Hindu Social Theory*. Madras: Ganesh and Co. 1984.

Muir, J. *Original Sanskrit Texts.* New Delhi: Oriental Publishers, 1972 [reprint].

Mukherji, Radha Kumud. 'Social Condition'. In *The Age of Imperial Unity,* edited by R.C. Majumdar. Bombay: Bharatiya Vidya Bhavan, 1951.

Murty, K. Satchidananda. *Revelation and Reason in Advaita Vedānta.* New York, NY: Columbia University Press, 1959.

———. *Vedic Hermeneutics.* New Delhi: Motilal Banarsidas, 1993.

Narayanan, Vasudha. 'The Hindu Tradition'. In *World Religions: Eastern Traditions,* edited by Willard G. Oxtoby. Toronto: Oxford University Press, 1996.

Olivelle, Patrick. *The Āśrama System: The History and Hermeneutics of a Religious Institution.* New York, NY: Oxford University Press, 1993.

———. *The Early Upaniṣads: Annotated Texts and Translation.* New York, NY: Oxford University Press, 1998.

———. *Dharmasūtras: The Law Codes of Āpastamba, Gautama, Baudhāyana, and Vasiṣṭha.* New York, NY: Oxford University Press, 1999.

———. *The Law Code of Manu.* New York, NY: Oxford University Press, 2004.

———. *King, Governance, and Law in Ancient India Kauṭilya's Arthaśāstra.* New York, NY: Oxford University Press, 2013.

Palmer, Richard E. *Hermeneutics: Interpretation Theory in Schleiermacher, Dilthey, Heidegger, and Gadamer.* Evanston, IL: Northwestern University Press, 1969.

Pande, G.C. *Dimensions of Ancient Indian Social History.* New Delhi: Books & Books, 1984.

Panikkar, K.M. *Hindu Society at Cross Roads.* Bombay: Asia Publishing House, 1961.

Panikkar, Raimundo and Arvind Sharma. *Human Rights as a Western Concept.* New Delhi: D.K. Printworld, 2007.

Pant, Apa. *A Moment in Time.* London: Hodder and Stoughton, 1974.

Pollock, Sheldon. '*Rāmāyaṇa* and Political Imagination in India'. *Journal of Asian Studies* 52. no. 2 (1993): 261–97.

Prabhu, Pandhari-Nath. *Hindu Social Organization: A Study in Social-Psychological and Ideological Foundations.* Bombay: Popular Book Depot, 1954 [1940].

Pusalkar, A.D. 'Aryan Settlements in India'. In *The Vedic Age,* edited by R.C. Majumdar. Bombay: Bharatiya Vidya Bhavan, 1965.

Radhakrishnan, S., ed. *The Principal Upaniṣads.* London: Allen & Unwin, 1953.

———, ed. *The Principal Upaniṣads.* Atlantic Heights, NJ: Humanities Press, 1992 [1953].

Rao, Velcheru N., David Schulman and Sanjay Subrahmanyam. *Symbols of Substance: Court and State in Nāyaka Period Tamilnadu.* New Delhi: Oxford University Press, 1992.

Rapson, E.J., ed. *Ancient India.* Cambridge: Cambridge University Press, 1922.

Raychaudhuri, H.C. 'Appendix: Note on the Date of *Artha-Śāstra*'. In *The Age of Imperial Unity,* edited by R.C. Majumdar. Bombay: Bharatiya Vidya Bhavan, 1951.

Raychaudhuri, Hemachandra. *Political History of Ancient India, Commentary by B.N. Mukherjee.* New Delhi: Oxford University Press, 1997.

Renou, Louis, ed. *Hinduism.* New York, NY: George Braziller, 1962.

Ricœur, Paul. *Freud and Philosophy: An Essay in Interpretation,* translated by Denis Savage. New Haven, CT: Yale University Press, 1970.

———. *The Conflict of Interpretations: Essays in Hermeneutics,* edited by Don Ihde. Evanston, IL: Northwestern University Press, 1974.

Rocher, Ludo. 'Karma and Rebirth in the Dharmaśāstras'. In *Karma and Rebirth in Classical Indian Traditions,* edited by Wendy Doniger O'Flaherty. Berkeley, CA: University of California Press, 1980.

Rodis-Lewis, Geneviève. *Descartes: His Life and Thought,* translated by Jane Marie Todd. Ithaca, NY: Cornell University Press, 1998.

Roy, Kumkum and Naina Dayal, eds. *Questioning Paradigms, Constructing Histories: A Festschrift for Romila Thapar.* New Delhi: Aleph Book Company, 2019.

Sadhle, G.S., ed. *The Bhagavad Gītā with Eleven Commentaries.* Bombay: The Gujarati Printing Press, 1935.

Sastri, K.A. Nilakanta, ed. *A Comprehensive History of India.* Bombay: Orient Longman, 1957.

———. *Development of Religion in South India.* New Delhi: Orient Longman, 1963.

———. *A History of South India from Prehistoric Times to the Fall of Vijayanagar.* Madras: Oxford University Press, 1976.

Sastry, Alladi Mahadeva, trans. *The Bhagavadgītā with the Commentary of Śrī Śaṅkarāchārya.* Chennai: Samata Books, 1985.

Scharfe, Hartmut. *The State in Indian Tradition.* Leiden: E.J. Brill, 1989.

Scheible, Kristin. 'Toward a Buddhist Policy of Tolerance: The Case of Ashoka'. In *Religious Tolerance in World Religions,* edited by Jacob Neusner and Bruce Chilton. West Conshohocken, PA: Templeton Foundation Press, 2008.

Sen, K.M. *Hinduism*. Harmondsworth: Penguin Books, 1961.

Sharan, Mahesh Kumar. *Studies in Sanskrit Inscriptions of Ancient Cambodia.* New Delhi: Abhinav Publications, 1974.

Sharma, Arvind. *Hinduism for Our Times.* New Delhi: Oxford University Press, 1996.

———. *Hinduism and its Sense of History.* New Delhi: Oxford University Press, 2003.

———. *Hindu Egalitarianism: Equality or Justice.* New Delhi: Rupa Co., 2006.

Sharma, Ram Sharan. *Śūdras in Ancient India.* New Delhi: Motilal Banarsidass, 1958.

———. *Śūdras in Ancient India.* New Delhi: Motilal Barnarsidass, 1980 [1958].

Shastri, J.L. ed. *Manusmṛti with the Sanskrit Commentary Manvartha-Muktāvalī of Kullūka Bhaṭṭa.* New Delhi: Motilal Banarsidass, 1983.

Shrivastava, Vijay Shankar. *Hinduism in South-East Asia.* New Delhi: Ramanand Vidya Bhavan, 1939.

Singh, Upinder. *Political Violence in Ancient India.* Cambridge, MA: Harvard University Press, 2017.

Sircar, D.C. 'The Śakas and the Pahlavas'. In *The Age of Imperial Unity*, edited by R.C. Majumdar. Bombay: Bharatiya Vidya Bhavan, 1951.

———. *Studies in the Society and Administration of Ancient and Medieval India.* Calcutta: K.L. Mukhopadhyay, 1967.

Smith, Donald Eugene. *India as a Secular State.* Princeton, NJ: Princeton University Press, 1963.

Smith, Huston. *The Religions of Man.* New York, NY: Harper and Brothers Publishers, 1958.

Spear, Percival, ed. *The Oxford History of India.* Oxford: Clarendon Press, 1958.

———. *India: A Modern History.* Ann Arbor, MI: The University of Michigan Press, 1972.

———, ed. *The Oxford History of India by the Late Vincent A. Smith, C.I.E.* Fourth edition. New Delhi: Oxford University Press, 1997.

Sternbach, Ludwik. *The Mānava Dharmaśāstra I-III and the Bhaviṣya Purāṇa.* Varanasi: All India Kashi Raj Trust, 1974.

Stutley, Margaret and James Stutley. *A Dictionary of Hinduism: Its Mythology, Folklore and Development 1500* BC–AD *1500*. London: Routledge and Kegan Paul, 1977.

Sudarshan, T.N. 'The Science and Nescience of Sastra'. In Śā*stra-s Through The Lens of Western Indology—A Response*, edited by K.S. Kannan. Reclaiming Sanskrit Studies Book 2. Chennai: Infinity Foundation India, 2018.

Sukthankar, Vishnu S., ed. *The Āraṇyakaparvan (Part 2)*. Poona: Bhandarkar Oriental Research Institute, 1924.

Sullivan, Bruce M. *The A to Z of Hinduism*. New Delhi: Vision Books, 2003.

The Complete Works of Swami Vivekananda. Mayavati Memorial Edition. Calcutta: Advaita Ashrama, 1986.

The Works of Śaṅkarācārya in Original Sanskrit. New Delhi: Motilal Banarsidass, 1987.

Tripathi, Ram Shankar. *History of Ancient India*. New Delhi: Motilal Banarsidass, 1967.

Tarkateertha Laxmanshastri. *Development of Indian Culture: Vedas to Gandhi*, translated by S.R. Nene. Wai, Satara: Prajna Pathsala Mandal, 2001.

van Buitenen, J.A.B., trans. *The Mahābhārata Vol 2*. Chicago, IL: The University of Chicago Press, 1975.

———, trans. *The Mahābhārata Vol 3*, Chicago, IL: The University of Chicago Press, 1978.

Vasudevamurthy, Rajath. 'Sastra: An Impediment to Progress?' In Śā*stra-s Through The Lens of Western Indology—A Response*, edited by K.S. Kannan. Reclaiming Sanskrit Studies Book 2. Chennai: Infinity Foundation India, 2018.

von Stietencron, Heinrich. 'Political Aspects of Indian Religious Art'. *Visible Religion, Annual for Religious Iconography* Vols. IV–V (1985/86): 16–36.

Walker, Benjamin. *The Hindu World*. New York, NY: Frederick A. Praeger, 1968.

Wells, H.G. *The Outline of History*. Toronto: Doubleday, Doran & Gundy Limited, 1929 [1920].

Williams, Rowan. 'The Suspicion of Suspicion: Wittgenstein and Bonhoeffer.' In *The Grammar of the Heart*, edited by Richard H. Bell. San Francisco, CA: Harper & Row Publishers, 1988.

Wilson, H.H., trans. *The Vishṇu Purāṇa*. Calcutta: Punthi Pastak, 1961 [1840].

Notes

Preface

1 See Patrick Olivelle, *The Law Code of Manu* (New York, NY: Oxford University Press, 2004), xvii–xviii.
2 Mohandas K. Gandhi, *An Autobiography: The Story of My Experiments with Truth* (Boston, MA: Beacon Press, 1993), 34.
3 See Sugata Bose, *His Majesty's Opponent: Subhash Chandra Bose and India's Struggle Against Empire* (Cambridge, MA: Belknap Press of Harvard University, 2011).
4 William Dalrymple, *The Last Mughal: The Fall of a Dynasty, Delhi 1857* (New York, NY: Alfred A. Knopf, 2008), 13.
5 Olivelle, *The Law Code of Manu*, 47.
6 Ibid, xvii.
7 Percival Spear, ed., *The Oxford History of India by the Late Vincent A. Smith, C.I.E.*, Fourth edition (New Delhi: Oxford University Press, 2015 [1958]), 70.
8 But see Alf Hiltebeitel, 'India's Second Urbanization, Forest Gleaners and the *Mahābhārata* Myth of the Unburdening of the Earth', in *Questioning Paradigms, Constructing Histories: A Festschrift for Romila Thapar*, eds. Kumkum Roy and Naina Dayal (New Delhi: Aleph Book Company, 2019).

9 See G.C. Pande, *Dimensions of Ancient Indian Social History,* Vol. I (New Delhi: Motilal Banarsidass, 1990 [1984]), 162.

10 P.V. Kane, *History of Dharmaśāstra,* Vol. III, second edition (Pune: Bhandarkar Oriental Research Institute, 1973), 38.

11 See Kane, *History of Dharmaśāstra*, Vol. II, Part I, 61.

12 See G.C. Pande, *Life and Thought of Śaṅkarācārya* (New Delhi: Motilal Banarsidass, 1994), 63–64.

13 See Vasudha Narayanan, 'The Hindu Tradition', in *World Religions: Eastern Traditions*, ed. Willard G. Oxtoby (Toronto: Oxford University Press, 1996), 114.

14 E.J. Rapson, ed., *Ancient India* (Cambridge: Cambridge University Press, 1922), 293.

15 M. Rama Jois, *Legal and Constitutional History of India* (Allahabad: Universal Law Publishing, 2004), 31–32.

16 Chart from www.visualcapitalist.com.

17 Angus Maddison, *The World Economy* (Paris: Development Centre of the Organisation for Economic Co-operation and Development, 2006), *passim.*

18 T.N. Sudarshan, 'The Science and Nescience of Sastra', in Śā*stra-s Through The Lens of Western Indology—A Response*, Reclaiming Sanskrit Studies Book 2, ed. K.S. Kannan (Chennai: Infinity Foundation India, 2018), 185, note 1:

> The terms were coined in 1954 by linguist Kenneth Pike, who argued that the tools developed for describing linguistic behaviours could be adapted to the description of any human social behavior. *Emic* and *etic* are derived from the linguistic terms *phonemic* and *phonetic* respectively, which was in turn derived from Greek roots. The possibility of a truly objective description was discounted by Pike himself in his original work; he proposed the *emic/etic* dichotomy in anthropology as a way of getting around philosophical issues about the very nature of objectivity.

19 A.L. Basham, *The Wonder That Was India* (New Delhi: Rupa & Company, 1996 [1967]), 148.

20 Olivelle, *The Law Code of Manu*, 47.

21 James Mill, *The History of British India,* Vol. 1 (New Delhi: Associated Publishing House, 1972 [1871]), 283–84.

22 Tarkateertha Laxmanshastri, *Development of Indian Culture: Vedas to Gandhi*, trans. S.R. Nene (Wai, Satara: Prajna Pathsala Mandal, 2001), 222.

23 It has even been claimed that 'This distinction between *Śruti* and *Smṛti* of the separation of the eternal principles and time-space dependant social

norms, is unique to Hinduism; and it is this feature that enables Hinduism to constantly adapt to changing circumstances and be a living tradition continuously.' (Rajath Vasudevamurthy, 'Sastra: An Impediment to Progress?', in *Śāstra-s Through The Lens of Western Indology—A Response*, K.S. Kannan, ed., 126).

24 T.M.P. Mahadevan, *Outlines of Hinduism* (Bombay: Chetana Limited, 1971), 31.

25 *The Complete Works of Swami Vivekananda*, Mayavati Memorial Edition, Vol. VII (Calcutta: Advaita Ashrama, 1986), 176.

26 See M.K. Gandhi, *Hindu Dharma*, ed. Bharatan Kumarappa (Ahmedabad: Navajivan Trust, 1958), 384.

27 Olivelle, *The Law Code of Manu*, 130.

28 James Mill, *The History of British India*, abridged, with an introduction by William Thomas (Chicago, IL: The University of Chicago Press, 1975), 105.

I: Introduction

1 *Mahābhārata*, Critical Edition (Poona: Bhandarkar Oriental Research Institute, 1966), 1.67.9; 1.111.31; 3.177.30; 5.37.1; 12.21.12; 12.37.6; 12.96.14; 12.259.35; 13.116.12.

2 See M.R. Kale, *The Pañcatantra of Viṣṇuśarman* (New Delhi: Motilal Banarsidass, 1986), 227.

3 See Kane, *History of Dharmaśāstra*, Vol. II, Part I, 579; also see note 1353 (ibid.) for Sanskrit text.

4 Ibid., Vol. I, Part I, 317.

5 Hartmut Scharfe, *The State in Indian Tradition* (Leiden: E.J. Brill, 1989), 222.

6 See Spear, ed., *The Oxford History of India*, 70:

> The early Sanskritists unduly exalted the authority of the *Laws of Manu*, which they regarded as veritable laws instead of mere rulings of a textbook writer, and that they actually are. The fuller knowledge of the present day sees the book in true perspective, but the old errors still exert a baneful influence in many directions.

7 Also see Christophe Jaffrelot, *Dr. Ambedkar and Untouchability: Fighting the Indian Caste System* (New York, NY: Columbia University Press, 2005), 48.

8 See Oliville; *The Law Code of Manu*, xxii, xxiii.

9 Ibid., 155.
10 Ibid., 169.
11 Kane, *History of Dharmaśāstra,* Vol II, Part I, 367.
12 A.S. Altekar, *The Position of Women in Hindu Civilization* (New Delhi: Motilal Banarsidass, 1962), 239.
13 Ibid., 240.
14 See Basham, *The Wonder That Was India,* 240–241; Wendy Doniger, *The Hindus: An Alternative History* (New York, NY: The Penguin Press, 2009), 116–19.
15 Olivelle, *The Law Code of Manu,* 177–78, emphasis added.
16 G. Bühler, trans., *The Laws of Manu* (New Delhi: Motilal Banarsidass 2001 [1886]), 399.
17 Olivelle, *The Law Code of Manu,* 283.
18 Wendy Doniger and Brian K. Smith, trans., *The Laws of Manu* (Harmondsworth: Penguin Books, 1991), 231, note 321.
19 Patrick Olivelle, *The Early Upaniṣads: Annotated Text and Translation* (New York, NY: Oxford University Press, 1998), 50–51. The main point for which this passage is being cited emerges even more clearly in its earlier translation by Robert Ernest Hume (*The Thirteen Principal Upanishads* [London: Oxford University Press, 1968 (1877)]), 84–85:

> 11. Verily, in the beginning this world was Brahma, one only. Being one, he was not developed. He created still further a superior form, the Kshatrahood, even those who are Kshatras (rulers) among the gods: Indra, Varuṇa, Soma, Rudra, Parjanya, Yama, Mṛityu, Īśāna. Therefore there is nothing higher than Kshatra. Therefore at the Rājasūya ceremony the Brahman sits below the Kshatriya. Upon Kshatrahood alone does he confer this honor. This same thing, namely Brahmanhood (brahma), is the source of Kshatrahood. Therefore, even if the king attains supremacy, he rests finally upon Brahmanhood as his own source. So whoever injures him [i.e. a Brahman] attacks his own source. He fares worse in proportion as he injures one who is better. 12. He was not yet developed. He created the Viś (the commonality), those kinds of gods that are mentioned in numbers: the Vasus, the Rudras, the Ādityas, the Viśvadevas, the Maruts. 13. He was not yet developed. He created the Śūdra caste (*varṇa*), Pūshan. Verily, this [earth] is Pūshan, for she nourishes everything that is. 14. He was not yet developed. He created still further a better form, Law (*dharma*). This is the power (*kṣatra*) of the Kshatriya class (*kṣatra*), viz. Law. Therefore there is nothing higher than Law. So a weak man controls a strong

man by Law, just as if by a king. Verily, that which is Law is truth. Therefore they say of a man who speaks the truth 'He speaks the Law,' or of a man who speaks the Law, 'He speaks the truth.' Verily, both these are the same thing. 15. So that Brahma [appeared as] Kshatra, Viś, and Śūdra. So among the gods Brahma appeared by means of Agni, among men as a Brahman, as a Kshatriya by means of the [divine] Kshatriya, as a Vaiśya by means of the [divine] Vaiśya, as a Śūdra by means of the [divine] Śūdra. Therefore people desire a place among the gods in Agni, among men in a Brahman, for by these two forms [pre-eminently] Brahma appeared.

20 Louis Renou, ed., *Hinduism* (New York, NY: George Braziller, 1962), 142.
21 Olivelle, *The Law Code of Manu*, 24.
22 Vaman Shivram Apte, *The Sanskrit-English Dictionary* (New Delhi: Motilal Banarsidass, 1965), 13.
23 Olivelle, *The Law Code of Manu*, 23.
24 Ibid., 24.
25 Ibid., 77.
26 Ibid., 40.
27 But also see Donald R. Davis, 'Hinduism as a Legal Tradition,' *Journal of the American Academy of Religion* 75, no. 2 (2007): 241–67.
28 Kane, *History of Dharmaśāstra*, Vol. V, Part II, 1270.
29 Olivelle, *The Law Code of Manu*, 40.
30 For this connection see 12.88, etc.
31 See chapter 297 in Vishnu S. Sukthankar, ed., *The Āraṇyakaparvan (Part 2)* (Poona: Bhandarkar Oriental Research Institute, 1924), 1025.
32 Kane, *History of Dharmaśāstra*, Vol. V, Part II, 1271, with some modifications.
33 For a discussion of this point see Arvind Sharma, *Hinduism for Our Times*, 19–21.
34 Patrick Olivelle, Dharmasūtras*: The Law Codes of Āpastamba, Gautama, Baudhāyana, and Vasiṣṭha* (New York, NY: Oxford University Press, 1999), 72–73.
35 Ibid.
36 Ibid., 73.

2: *Manusmṛti*: The Historical Context

1 Olivelle, *The Law Code of Manu*, xxiii.
2 Ibid.
3 Basham, *The Wonder That Was India*, 50

4 Ibid.
5 Ibid.
6 Olivelle, *The Law Code of Manu.*, xlii.
7 The following remarks of Upinder Singh (*Political Violence in Ancient India* [Cambridge, MA: Harvard University Press, 2017], 363) become relevant here:

> An interesting aspect of the Indian attitude toward war throughout the twelve hundred years we have surveyed are the scant details of the many invasions from the northwest. Early Orientalists remarked with incredulity on the absence of reference in Indian sources to the invasion of Alexander of Macedon. The reason may be that the invasion was a brief episode that barely grazed the fringes of the sub-continent, one that was considered more significant by the Greeks than the Indians. But what about other invasions, for instance, those that occurred between circa 200 BCE and 200 CE? We do not get any detailed accounts of these events in the Indian sources; the accounts come from elsewhere. The narratives usually have to be painfully pieced together from the epigraphic, numismatic, and archaeological data, or from much later Indian textual or foreign sources. There are a few epigraphic references. Kharavela claims to have defeated the Yavana king Dimita. Gautamiputra Satakarni states that he had destroyed the Shakas, Yavanas, Pahlavas, and Kshaharatas. The lists of victories do not seem to distinguish between 'indigenous' and 'foreign' foes. Among the many invaders who surged into the subcontinent during the period we have surveyed, it is the Hunas, who seem to have left the longest and most powerful imprint in Indian texts and inscriptions, although, like other invaders, they were swiftly assimilated into the Indian cultural matrix.

8 Ram Sharan Sharma, *Śūdras in Ancient India* (New Delhi: Motilal Banarsidass, 1958), 219.
9 Hemachandra Raychaudhuri, *Political History of Ancient India, Commentary by B.N. Mukerjee* (Delhi: Oxford University Press, 1997), 434.
10 Sharma, *Śūdras in Ancient India*, 198, 218.
11 Olivelle, *The Law Code of Manu*, xx.
12 Ibid.
13 Ibid.
14 Ibid.

15 Ibid.
16 Ibid.
17 H.G. Wells, *The Outline of History* (Toronto: Doubleday, Doran and Gundy, Limited, 1929 [1920]) 369.
18 Ibid., 371.
19 R.C. Majumdar, ed., *The Age of Imperial Unity* (Mumbai: Bharatiya Vidya Bhavan, 1951), 92.
20 Benjamin Walker, *The Hindu World*, Vol. 1 (New York, NY: Frederick A. Praeger, 1968), 82–83. The statement about the erasure of Aśoka from Hindu history has been questioned in Nayanjot Lahiri, *Ashoka in Ancient India* (Cambridge, MA: Harvard University Press, 2015), 301–305.
21 Olivelle, *The Law Code of Manu*, xlii.
22 Ibid.
23 Ibid., xliii.
24 Ibid.
25 Raychaudhuri, *Political History of Ancient India,* 309.
26 Altekar, *The Position of Women in Hindu Civilization,* 350.
27 Ibid.
28 Sharma, *Śūdras in Ancient India,* 241.
29 Raychaudhuri, *Political History of Ancient India*, 324, note 3.
30 Ibid. See Vaman Shivram Apte, *The Practical Sanskrit-English Dictionary*, Revised and enlarged edition, Third edition (New Delhi: Motilal Banarsidass, 1965), 510: '*Devānāmpriyaḥ:* an irregular compound meaning 1. a goat 2. a fool, idiot like a brute beast.' Two interesting facts relating to this point are that Aśoka is called a fool in the context of his personal life in the *Mahāvaṃsa* of Śrī Laṅkā, and his successor, Daśaratha, also used the same title (Lahiri, *Ashoka in Ancient India,* 281, 292).
31 Ram Shankar Tripathi, *History of Ancient India* (New Delhi: Motilal Banarsidass, 1967), 240, emphasis added.
32 Singh, *Political Violence in Ancient India,* 267–68.
33 Olivelle, *The Law Code of Manu*, xxi.
34 Ibid., xxvi.
35 Patrick Olivelle also connects Aśoka with the *Manusmṛti* but in a manner very different from the one canvassed here. Upinder Singh judiciously summarizes Olivelle's position as follows (*Political Violence in Ancient India,* 56):

> Patrick Olivelle has suggested that the Buddha took over the concept of dharma with its strong royal associations (along with other royal symbols) from the Brahmanical tradition and gave it

new ethical content, also using it to refer to his doctrine. Then, Ashoka came along and talked extensively about dhamma in his edicts. It was his appropriation of the word and his injection of new ethical content into it that transformed it into a central cultural concept, which the Brahmanas were forced to take note of by inventing the disciple of Dharmashastra. For the Buddhists, dhamma stood for the word and the teaching of the Buddha, who was its authoritative source. The Brahmanas had to scramble about and come up with their own version of dharma and to identify its source. They did this by creating an enormous authoritative corpus of texts that dealt specifically with the subject—Dharmashastra.

Compelling as this hypothesis is, it depends to a great extent on the chronology of individuals, events, and texts. If the Buddha is placed in the sixth and fifth centuries BCE and if the composition of the earliest Dharmashastra texts also goes back to this period, and Ashoka appears on the scene afterward, the hypothesis collapses. However, there is no doubt that in the long run, the 'classical' Indian understanding of dharma emerged out of an intense cultural conversation between different religious, philosophical, and intellectual traditions. As an influential participant in this conversation, Ashoka played a significant role in the evolution of the idea, especially through his public propagation of the idea of a strong connection between kingship, the soteriological goals of the individual, and social ethics.

36 Sharma, *Śūdras in Ancient India*, 218.
37 Ibid., 198, also see 219.
38 Raychaudhuri, *Political History of Ancient India*, 740.
39 Nathan McGovern, *The Snake and the Mongoose: The Emergence of Identity in Early Indian Religion* (New York, NY: Oxford University Press, 2019), 17.
40 Ibid., 19–20.
41 Sugata Bose and Ayesha Jalal, *Modern South Asia: History, Culture, Political Economy* (New Delhi: Oxford University Press, 1998), 33.
42 Sheldon Pollock, '*Rāmāyaṇa* and Political Imagination in India', *Journal of Asian Studies* 52, no. 2 (1993), 261–97.
43 K.M. Panikkar, *Hindu Society at Cross Roads* (Mumbai: Asia Publishing House, 1961), 117.
44 Sharma, *Hinduism and its Sense of History, passim.*
45 Basham, *The Wonder That Was India,* 371.

46 Raychaudhuri, *Political History of Ancient India*, 165.
47 Heinrich von Stietencron, 'Political Aspects of Indian Religious Art', *Visible Religion, Annual for Religious Iconography*, Vols. IV–V (1985/86), 21.
48 Ibid.
49 Ibid.

3: Sources of Dharma in the *Manusmṛti*

1 Olivelle, *The Law Code of Manu.*, 23.
2 Olivelle, *The Law Code of Manu*, 24.
3 This scheme finds an interesting parallel in Islamic law, see Mahmoud M. Ayoub, 'The Islamic Tradition', in *World Religions: Western Traditions*, ed. Willard G. Oxtoby (Toronto: Oxford University Press, 1996), 409:

> Islamic law as it was developed in the legal schools is based on four sources. Two of these, the *Qur'ān* and *sunnah* of the Prophet and his generation, are its material and primary sources. The other two are formal sources representing human endeavour and acceptance. These two are personal reasoning (*ijtihād*) of the scholars, involving analogy (*qiyās*), and the general consensus (*ijmā'*) of the community. The schools of Islamic law differed, among other things, in the degree of emphasis or acceptance that they gave to each of these.

4 Ibid., 218.
5 Ibid., 219.
6 Ibid., 41.
7 Bühler, trans., *The Laws of Manu,* 73; Doniger and Smith, trans., *The Laws of Manu,* 42.
8 Olivelle, *The Law Code of Manu*, 217–18.
9 K. Satchidananda Murty, *Vedic Hermeneutics* (New Delhi: Motilal Banarsidass, 1993), 46, emphasis added.
10 Olivelle, *The Law Code of Manu*, 40.
11 Doniger and Smith, trans., *The Laws of Manu,* 40, note. Doniger and Smith here connect the Sanskrit text as cited above with the example set by women and *śūdras*. I take it independently.
12 Olivelle, *The Law Code of Manu*, 18.
13 Ibid., 236.
14 Ibid., 19.
15 Murty, *Vedic Hermeneutics*, 63, footnote.
16 Ibid., 63.

17 Ibid.
18 Ibid., 63–64.
19 Ibid., 105.
20 Bühler, trans., *The Laws of Manu,* 30.
21 The issue has an interesting parallel in Islamic Law, see Ayoub, 'The Islamic Tradition', in *World Religions*, ed. Oxtoby, 409.
22 Altekar, *The Position of Women in Hindu Civilization,* 153. He also notes:

> Medhātithi's view that the verse of Parāśara refers to a woman seeking service for her maintenance and not to her contracting a fresh marriage is rendered altogether untenable by the inclusion of impotency as one of the causes of her doing so. The verse does contemplate a second marriage.

23 Olivelle, *The Law Code of Manu,* 24. The following explanation is helpful here (Ibid., 237):

> When two vedic injunctions contradict each other, both are authoritative; such a contradiction gives rise to an option. An example of such an option is given in verse 15. Some vedic passages prescribe the morning fire offering (*agnihotra*) to be performed just before sunrise, and others after sunrise. One has, therefore, the option to follow either rule. A contradiction, however, gives rise to an option only when the two injunctions are of equal force (see *GDh I.4*). If one of them is weaker (e.g. a traditional text) and the other stronger (e.g. an explicit vedic text), then the stronger prevails.

24 Mahadevan, *Outlines of Hinduism,* 32. See *Vākyapadīya* 1.136 with commentary, 224.
25 Olivelle, *The Law Code of Manu,* 159.
26 Ibid.
27 Ibid., 278.
28 Altekar, *The Position of Women in Hindu Civilization,* 146–47.
29 Kane, *History of Dharmaśāstra*, Vol. II, Part I, Second edition, 602–03.
30 Ibid., 603.
31 Ibid., 602.
32 Ibid., 603.
33 Ibid., 604–05.
34 J.L. Shastri, ed., *Manusmṛti with the Sanskrit Commentary Manvartha-Muktāvalī of Kullūka Bhaṭṭa* (New Delhi: Motilal Banarsidass, 1983), 33.
35 Olivelle, *The Law Code of Manu,* 187.
36 Ibid., 285, with some modification.

37 M.R. Kale, *The Abhijñānaśākuntalam of Kālidāsa* (New Delhi: Motilal Banarsidass, 1980 [1969]), 31.
38 Ibid., 41.
39 Ibid.
40 Olivelle, *The Early Upaniṣads*, 297.
41 Ibid., 130–31. Bühler clarifies that 'The Kūṣmāṇḍa texts are found, Taittirīya Ār. X, 3-5; the verses addressed to Varuṇa, Rig-Veda I, 24, 15; and the verses addressed to the Waters X, 9, 1–3' (Bühler, trans., *The Laws of Manu*, 272, note 106).
42 Shastri, ed., *Manusmṛti with the Sanskrit Commentary*, 33.
43 Olivelle, *The Law Code of Manu*, 41.
44 Doniger and Smith, trans., *The Laws of* Manu, 41.
45 Bühler, trans., *The Laws of Manu*, 72–73.
46 See *Manusmṛti* 8.385.
47 Shastri, ed., *Manusmṛti with the Sanskrit Commentary*, 75.
48 Kane, *History of Dharmaśāstra*, Vol. V, Part II, 921, note 1468a.
49 Stephanie W. Jamison, *Sacrificed Wife/Sacrifer's Wife: Women, Ritual, and Hospitality in Ancient India* (New York, NY: Oxford University Press, 1996), 249–50, emphasis added.
50 Murty, *Vedic Hermeneutics*, 62.
51 This is the English translation of the opening verse of the second chapter of the *Manusmṛti*.
52 Ibid., 62–63. This is how Patrick Olivelle translates this verse which is strikingly eloquent in Sanskrit: 'Learn the Law always adhered to by the people who are erudite, virtuous, and free from love and hate, the Law assented to by the heart' (*The Law Code of Manu*, 23).
53 Olivelle, *The Law Code of Manu*, 40.
54 Ibid.
55 Doniger and Smith, trans., *The Laws of Manu*, 40.
56 Bühler, trans., *The Laws of Manu*, 70.
57 M. Hiriyanna, *Indian Philosophical Studies* (Mysuru: Kavyalaya Publishers, 1957), 69.

4: The Doctrine of *Varṇas* in the *Manusmṛti*

1 Renou, ed., *Hinduism*, 64–65. I also include here a more recent translation of the hymn by Stephanie W. Jamison and Joel P. Brereton, trans., *The Rigveda: The Earliest Religious Poetry of India*, Vol. 3 (New York, NY: Oxford University Press, 2014), 1539–40:

1. The Man has a thousand heads, a thousand eyes, and a thousand feet. Having covered the earth on all sides, he extended ten fingers' breadth beyond.
2. The Man alone is this whole (world): what has come into being and what is to be. Moreover, he is master of immortality when he climbs beyond (this world) through food.
3. So much is his greatness, but the Man is more than this: a quarter of him is all living beings; three quarters are the immortal in heaven.
4. With his three quarters the Man went upward, but a quarter of him came to be here again.
5. From there he strode out in different directions toward what eats and what does not eat. From him the Virāj was born; from the Virāj the Man. Upon his birth, he reached beyond the earth from behind and also from in front.
6. When, with the Man as the offering, the gods extended the sacrifice, spring was its melted butter, summer its firewood, autumn its offering.
7. On the ritual grass they consecrated that sacrifice, the Man, born at the beginning.With him the gods sacrificed, (also) the Sādhyas and those who were seers.
8. From that sacrifice, when it was offered in full, the clotted-butter mixture was collected.It [=the sacrifice] was made into the animals; those of the air (and both) those that belong to the wilderness and those that belong to the village.
9. From this sacrifice, when it was offered in full, the verses and chants were born.Meters were born from it. The sacrificial formula—from it that was born.
10. From it horses were born and whatever animals have teeth in both jaws. Cows were born from it. From it were born goats and sheep.
11. When they apportioned the Man, into how many parts did they arrange him? What was his mouth? What his two arms? What are said to be his two thighs, his two feet?
12. The brahmin was his mouth. The ruler was made his two arms. As to his thighs—that is what the freeman was. From his two feet the servant was born.
13. The moon was born from his mind. From his eye the sun was born. From his mouth Indra and Agni, from his breath Vāyu was born.

14. From his navel was the midspace. From his head the heaven developed. From his two feet the earth, and the directions from his ear. Thus they arranged the worlds.
15. Its enclosing sticks were seven; the kindling sticks were made three times seven,when the gods, extending the sacrifice, bound the Man as the (sacrificial) animal.
16. With the sacrifice the gods performed the sacrifice for themselves: these were the first foundations. These, its greatness, accompanied (it) to heaven's vault, where the ancient Sādhyas and the gods are.

The comments of the translators are helpful here. They identify this hymn as 'one of the best-known and most influential hymns of the ṚgVeda' (Ibid., 1537) and offer the following remarks on verse 12, which is central to our concerns (Ibid. 1538):

> The parts of the sacrifice also became the three upper *varṇas* … His mouth the brahmins, masters of knowledge and speech; his arms the rulers, the possessors of power and his thighs the freemen or clansmen, who are the productive support of society. These three classes form parts of the sacrifice because they can participate in the sacrifice. The śūdras or 'servants' are not part of the sacrifice but rather emerge from the feet of the man, a symbol of their low social status and their exclusion from the sacrifice.

The statement about the śūdras could be anachronistic.

2 Pandhari-Nath Prabhu, *Hindu Social Organization: A Study in Social-Psychological and Ideological Foundations* (Bombay: Popular Book Depot, 1954 [1940]), 291.

3 Jamison and Brereton, trans., *The Rigveda,* 7–9.

4 Prabhu, *Hindu Social Organization,* 291. Jamison and Brereton translate the relevant verse (1.113.6) somewhat differently as follows: '(she has awakened) one for dominion, another for fame, another to seek greatness, another to go to whatever his goal. Living being [sic] are not alike in what they have in view. – dawn has awakened all the creatures.' (Jamison and Brereton, trans., *The RigVeda,* Vol. I, 264.)

5 J. Muir, *Original Sanskrit Texts*, Part I (New Delhi: Oriental Publishers, 1972), 17.

6 Ibid., 18.

7 Ibid., 159.

8 Olivelle, *The Early Upaniṣads,* 49–50.

9 Olivelle, *The Law Code of Manu,* 15.

10 Ibid., 19.
11 Ibid.
12 Prabhu, *Hindu Social Organization*, 292.
13 Olivelle, *The Law Code of Manu*, 183.
14 Ibid., 177–78.
15 Ibid., 283.
16 Ibid., 24.
17 Ibid., 292.
18 'Instead of referring to a vertical, hierarchical order, we may also try to visualize this scheme of social and xenological thinking as a sequence of concentric circles, which surround the center of ritual purity and perfection.' (Wilhelm Halbfass, *India and Europe: An Essay in Understanding* [Albany, NY: State University of New York Press, 1988], 180).
19 Kane, *History of Dharmaśāstra*, Vol. II, Part I, Second edition, 43.
20 Ibid.
21 Ibid., 45–46.
22 Ibid., 49.
23 Ibid., 47.
24 Ibid., 55.
25 Ibid.
26 Ibid.
27 Olivelle, *The Law Code of Manu*, xxiii.
28 Ibid.
29 Halbfass, *India and Europe*, 332.
30 The *Puruṣa Sūkta* is also quite capable of being interpreted in an egalitarian manner, see Prabhu, *Hindu Social Organization*, 292.
31 Olivelle, *The Law Code of Manu*, 184.
32 *Sūtasaṃhitā* 1.12.51. I am indebted to Dr. Sanjay Kumar for this reference.
33 Olivelle, *The Law Code of Manu*, 181. Their occupations, residence and dress are also spelled out (Ibid., 183):

> [46] The 'low-born' among the twice-born, as well as those that tradition calls 'delinquent-born', should live by occupations despised by the twice-born— [47] to Sūtas, management of horses and chariots; to Ambaṣṭhas, medicine; to Vaidehakas, taking care of women; to Māgadhas, trade; [48] to Niṣādas, fishing; to Ayogavas, carpentry to Medas, Andras, Cuñcus, and Madgus, hunting wild animals; [49] to Kṣattṛs, Ugras, and Pulkasas, trapping and killing

animals living in burrows; to Dhigvaṇas, working in leather; and to Veṇas, playing drums. [50] These should live by memorial trees and in cemeteries, hills, and groves, well-recognizable and living by the occupations specific to them.

34 Kane, *History of Dharmaśāstra*, Vol. II, Part I, Second edition, 47.
35 Olivelle, *The Law Code of Manu*, 130.
36 Ibid., 54–56.
37 Panikkar, *Hindu Society at Crossroads*, 117.
38 J. Duncan M. Derrett, *Religion, Law and State in India* (New York, NY: The Free Press, 1968), 175–76.
39 Bose and Jalal, *Modern South Asia*, 33.
40 Kane, *History of Dharmaśāstra*, Vol. II, Part I, Second edition, 33.
41 Bühler, trans., *The Laws of Manu*, 13–14.
42 Ibid., 24.
43 Olivelle, *The Law Code of Manu*, 77.
44 Bühler, trans., *The Laws of Manu*, 56.
45 Raychaudhuri, *Political History of Ancient India*, 627.
46 Klaus K. Klostermaier, *A Survey of Hinduism* (Albany, NY: State University of New York Press, 1989), 46–50; Koenraad Elst, 'Is the Term Dharma Untranslatable?' in Saradindu Mukherjee, ed., *Probodhan II: Thoughts on Hindu Society* (Gurugram: World Hindu Foundation, 2018), 219–33.
47 Doniger and Smith, trans., *The Laws of Manu*, 90.
48 Klostermaier, *A Survey of Hinduism*, 49.
49 Kane, *History of Dharmaśāstra*, Vol. V, Part II, Second edition, 1270.
50 Kane, *History of Dharmaśāstra*, Vol. II, Part I, Second edition, 61.
51 Julius Lipner, *Hindus: Their Religious Beliefs and Practices* (London: Routledge, 1994), 12.

5: The Position of the *Śūdras* in the *Manusmṛti*

1 Olivelle, *The Law Code of Manu*, 133.
2 Basham, *The Wonder That Was India*, 144.
3 Ibid., 524.
4 Kane, *History of Dharmaśāstra*, Vol. II, Part I, Second edition, 163–64. Although the number differs the same verse is referred to. The word *cāṣa* is usually translated as 'blue jay' (and *pracalāka* as a snake) (Bühler, trans., *The Laws of Manu*, 457).
5 Sharma, *Śūdras in Ancient India*, 123–24.

6 Kane, *History of Dharmaśāstra*, Vol. II, Part I, Second edition, 164, note 384.
7 Sharma, *Śūdras in Ancient India*, 124, note 2.
8 Olivelle, *The Law Code of Manu,* 199–200, emphasis added.
9 Shastri, ed., *Manusmṛti with the Sanskrit Commentary,* 449–50.
10 Bühler, trans., *The Laws of Manu*, 457, note 132.
11 Olivelle, *The Law Code of Manu,* 194.
12 Bühler, trans., *The Laws of Manu*, 272.
13 Ram Sharan Sharma does note the verses but the passage is read as enhancing the value of the life of the *brāhmaṇa*. He writes in *Śūdras in Ancient India* (214):

> Curiously enough, in one provision of Manu's rules regarding murder there is no trace of varṇa distinctions. If the case involves the death of a member of any varṇa, a falsehood may be spoken and the sin arising therefrom may be expiated by making offering to the Sarasvatī. Manu also declared that slaying women, śūdras, vaiśyas and kṣatriyas is a minor offence, causing loss of caste. But this rule is probably merely meant to emphasise the importance of the life of a brāhmāṇa.

14 Mill, *The History of British India,* 105.
15 Kane, *History of Dharma*śāstra, Vol. II, Part I, Second edition, 154–64.
16 Bühler, trans., *The Laws of Manu*, 141.
17 Kane, *The Laws of Manu,* Vol. II, Part 1, Second edition, 156, emphasis added.
18 Bühler, trans., *The Laws of Manu*, 402, emphasis added.
19 Ibid., note 2. This verse, however, could also be interpreted in a very different way and taken to mean that the *brāhmaṇa* should instruct the others only in matters pertaining to the means of subsistence. That Medhātithi does not do so is striking.
20 Olivelle, *The Law Code of Manu*, 188–89.
21 Bühler, trans., *The Laws of Manu*, 429. This incidentally is a good example of *sadācāra* serving virtually as an independent source of *dharma.*
22 See Kane, *History of Dharmaśāstra*, Vol. II, Part I, Second edition, 157.
23 Bühler, trans., *The Laws of Manu*, 429.
24 Olivelle, *The Laws of Manu,* 188.
25 Ibid., 285.
26 Kane, *History of Dharmaśāstra,* Vol. II, Part I, Second edition, 159.
27 Ibid.
28 Ibid., 160.

29 Ibid.
30 Ibid.
31 Sharma, *Śūdras in Ancient India,* 242.
32 Olivelle, *The Law Code of Manu,* 147–48.
33 Ibid., 145.
34 Ibid., 188.
35 Kane, *History of Dharmaśāstra,* Vol. V, Part I, Second edition, 161.
36 Kane, *History of Dharmaśāstra,* Vol. II, Part I, Second edition, 112, note 239.
37 Olivelle, *The Law Code of Manu,* 83.
38 Ibid.
39 Ibid., 187.
40 Sharma, *Śūdras in Ancient India,* 240.
41 Kane, *History of Dharmaśāstra,* Vol. II, Part I, Second edition, 161.
42 Ibid., 163.
43 Sharma, *Śūdras in Ancient India,* 202.
44 Ibid.
45 Ibid.
46 Ibid., 202–03.
47 Olivelle, *The Law Code of Manu,* 78, emphasis added.
48 Kane, *History of Dharmaśāstra,* Vol. II, Part I, Second edition, 164.
49 Sharma, *Śūdras in Ancient India,* 130.
50 Ibid., 222.
51 Kane, *History of Dharmaśāstra,* Vol. II, Part I, Second edition, 168.
52 Ibid. The word *niravasita* means excluded and *aniravasita* non-excluded and we might say in a general way that the untouchables belonged to the former category.
53 Ibid., 172, emphasis added. *Antyaja* are those born or residing on the periphery. P.V. Kane seems to omit including *śvapāka* here.
54 Ibid., 173–74, emphasis added.
55 Ibid., 170–71.
56 Ibid., 171.
57 Ibid., 81.
58 Ibid., 171.
59 The origin is variously explained but again the ascription is natal (ibid., 97).
60 Olivelle, *The Law Code of Manu,* 183.
61 Sharma, *Śūdras in Ancient India,* 229.
62 Ibid.
63 *Manusmṛti* 3.13; 9, 137.

64 V.S. Agrawala, *India as Described by Manu* (Varanasi: Prithivi Prakashan, 1970), 21, 54.
65 Kane, *History of Dharmaśāstra*, Vol II, Part I, 163.
66 Olivelle, *The Law Code of Manu*, 83.
67 Ibid., 70.
68 Ibid., 180.
69 Kane, *History of Dharmaśāstra*, Vol. II, Part I, 159, emphasis added.
70 Olivelle, *The Law Code of Manu*, 143.
71 Ibid., 274.
72 See Velcheru Narayana Rao, David Schulman and Sanjay Subrahmanyam, *Symbols of Substance: Court and State in Nāyaka Period Tamilnadu* (New Delhi: Oxford University Press, 1992), 74–75.
73 Ibid., 75.
74 Ibid.
75 Ibid.
76 Ibid., 76; also see footnote 33 on the same page.

6: The Doctrine of *Āśramas* in the *Manusmṛti*

1 Kane, *History of Dharmaśāstra*, Vol. 2, Part 1, 423.
2 Ibid., where the praise bestowed on it by Deussen is cited.
3 Mahadevan, *Outlines of Hinduism*, 75.
4 Olivelle, *The Law Code of Manu*, 105.
5 Kane, *History of Dharmaśāstra*, Vol. 2, Part 1, 416 ff.
6 Patrick Olivelle, *The Āśrama System: The History and Hermeneutics of a Religious Institution* (New York, NY: Oxford University Press, 1993).
7 Olivelle, *The Law Code of Manu*, 43. emphasis added.
8 Buhler, *The Laws of Manu*, 215.
9 Gandhi, *Hindu Dharma*, 206.
10 Kane, *History of Dharmaśāstra*, Vol.1, Part 1, 424.
11 Ibid.
12 Ibid.
13 Ibid.
14 Ibid., 425
15 Olivelle, *The Law Code of Manu*, 105.
16 Kane, *History of Dharmaśāstra*, Vol. 2, Part 1, 426.
17 Basham, *The Wonder That Was India*, 159.

18 McGovern. *The Snake and the Mongoose*, *passim*.
19 Ibid., 3.
20 Ibid., 217.
21 Ibid., 218.
22 Ibid., 213.
23 Ibid., 163.
24 Ibid, 154.

7: Women in the *Manusmṛti*

1 Arvind Sharma, *Hindu Egalitarianism: Equality or Justice* (New Delhi: Rupa Co., 2006), 101.
2 Olivelle, *The Law Code of Manu*, 155.
3 Ibid.
4 Ibid., 96.
5 Ibid., 258.
6 Ibid., 258.
7 See Altekar, *The Position of Women in Hindu Civilization*, 219, ff.
8 Ibid.
9 Olivelle, *The Law Code of Manu*, 169.
10 Ibid., 161 emphasis added. Kane's comments (*History of Dharmaśāstra*, Vol. II, Part I, Second edition, 442):

> But it is clear that no blame attached to the girl married after puberty or to the husband; the idea, however, had arisen even then that the father or guardian incurred blame or sin by not getting a girl married before puberty. Manu (IX.89–90) goes so far as to say, 'A maiden may rather stay in her father's house even till her death, though she may have attained puberty; but the father should never give her to one who is devoid of good qualities. A maiden after attaining puberty may wait for three years (to see if she is given away by her father or brother &c.) but after this period she should seek a husband who is similar to her.' Anuśāsanaparva 45.16 is to the same effect. Baud. Dh. S. IV.1.14 and Vas. Dh. S. 17.67–68 give the same rule as in Manu Ix. 90. But both add (Vas. 17.70–71 and Baud. Dh. S. IV.1.12) that the father or guardian incurs the sin of destroying an embryo at each appearance of menses as long as the girl is unmarried. Yāj. I.64 and Nārada (strīpuṁsa, verses 25–27) state the same rule.

11 The translations are by the author from the critical edition of the *Māhābharata* III.277, ff.
12 Kale, *The Pañcatantra of Viṣṇuśarmā*, 475.
13 Ibid., 227.
14 Kane, *History of Dharmaśāstra*, Vol. II, Part I, Second edition, 577.
15 Olivelle, *The Law Code of Manu*, 39.
16 Ibid., 156. Patrick Olivelle provides the following note on 9.17 (Ibid., 276): 'Note the close parallel between this verse and the assigning of various duties to different classes at 1.87–91.'
17 Ibid.
18 Kane, *History of Dharmaśāstra*, Vol. II, Part I, Second edition, 581.
19 Ibid.
20 Olivelle, *The Law Code of Manu*, 33.
21 Ibid.
22 Ibid., 78.
23 Ibid., 169, 170.
24 Ibid., 54.
25 Ibid., 34. A.S. Altekar is puzzling on this point, when he says that 'there are passages who place the father and the preceptor higher than the mother' and cites (Manu 2, 145–46) in support.
26 Olivelle, *The Law Code of Manu*, 241.
27 Kane, *History of Dharmaśāstra*, Vol. II, Part I, Second edition, 580.
28 Olivelle, *The Law Code of Manu*, 41.
29 Ibid., 162.
30 Ibid., 278.
31 Altekar, *The Position of Women in Hindu Civilization*, 101.
32 Kane, *History of Dharmaśāstra*, Vol. II, Part I, Second edition, 580.
33 Olivelle, *The Law Code of Manu*, 78.
34 Doniger and Smith, trans., *The Laws of Manu*, 91.
35 Bühler, trans., *The Laws of Manu*, 158.
36 *Manusmṛti's* determined opposition to the 'selling of children' is perhaps to be seen in the following background (Panikkar, *Hindu Society at Cross Roads*, 57):

> Yāska's Nirukta (11–4 Anandasharama edition, pp. 208) declares: 'They give away to others the female children. There exist *dāna*, *vikraya* and *atisarga* of the female but not of the male.' *Dāna* means gifts, *vikraya* means sale, and *atisarga* means abandonment. Durgacharya, the commentator explains these three methods of the disposal of daughters as in giving away in marriage (*dāna*),

an acceptance of payment for marriage (*vikraya*) and freedom to choose (*atisarga*).

37 Olivelle, *The Law Code of Manu,* 47.

38 Ibid., 162.

39 Ibid., 279.

40 Ibid., 154.

41 Altekar, *The Position of Women in Hindu Civilization*, 235, note 1, emphasis added.

42 Olivelle, *The Law Code of Manu,* 164.

43 Ibid., 158.

44 Ibid., 47–48.

45 Ibid., 156–157.

46 Ibid., 52, emphasis added.

47 Ibid., 78.

48 Ibid., 161.

49 Ibid., 162.

50 Ibid., 160–161.

51 Ibid., 145, emphasis added.

52 See *Manusmṛti* 8.336–38.

53 Kane, *History of Dharmaśāstra*, Vol. I, Part I, Second edition, 596.

54 Alf Hiltebeitel, *Dharma: Its Early History in Law, Religion, and Narrative* (New York, NY: Oxford University Press, 2011), 224.

55 Bühler, trans., *The Laws of Manu*, 416.

56 Olivelle, *The Law Code of Manu,* 97.

57 Hiltebeitel, *Dharma: Its Early History*, 224–25.

58 Altekar, *The Position of Women in Hindu Civilization*, 313.

59 Ibid.

60 'According to Manu XI.60 adultery is an *upapātaka* and the ordinary penance for it is *govrata* or *cāndrāyaṇa*' (Kane, *History of Dharmaśāstra*, Part II, Vol I, Second edition, 572, note 1331).

61 Kane, *History of Dharmaśāstra*, Part II, Vol. I, Second edition, 572–73.

62 Olivelle, *The Law Code of Manu,* 150.

63 Ibid.

64 Ibid., 276.

65 Kane, *History of Dharmaśāstra*, Vol. II, Part I, Second edition, 575.

66 Ibid., 593–94.

67 Ibid., 575, note 1340.

68 Olivelle, *Dharmasūtras: The Law Codes,* 306.

69 Bühler, trans., *The Laws of Manu*, 318–19.

70 Olivelle, *The Law Code of Manu*, 96–97.
71 Kane, *History of Dharmaśāstra*, Vol. I, Part II, 595.
72 Ibid., 596.
73 Olivelle, *The Law Code of Manu*, 203, emphasis added.
74 Kane, *History of Dharmaśāstra*, Vol I, Part I, 596.
75 Ibid.
76 Olivelle, *The Law Code of Manu*, 40.

8: Legal Discrimination in the Manusmṛti

1 The term, it seems, is used broadly to include rape, seduction, fornication and so on.
2 Kane, *History of Dharmaśāstra*, Vol. III, 398, note 634.
3 Doniger and Smith, trans., *The Laws of Manu*, 165.
4 Bühler, trans., *The Laws of Manu*, 301–06.
5 Kane, *History of Dharmaśāstra*, Vol. III, 535.
6 Olivelle, *The Law Code of Manu*, 149–51.
7 Bühler, trans., *The Laws of Manu*, 278.
8 Ibid., 382.
9 Bühler translated 8.338 (d) as '(each of them) knowing the nature of the offence' seems to be unclear and may even be incorrect. The expression seems to explain why the *brāhmaṇa* is penalized so heavily; 'for he knew about virtues and vices' (Doniger and Smith, trans., *The Laws of Manu*, 188). Olivelle comments (*The Law Code of Manu*, 275):

> The penalty is calculated on the basis of the value of the stolen goods. In general, the principle is that lighter penalties are assessed for people of higher classes. But here a different principle is enunciated, more in keeping with the penances, where the severity of the penance for the same offence increases for those of higher classes.

10 Sharma, *Śūdras in Ancient India*, 194. For more on the Kali Yuga on its sense of imminence in the post-Mauryan period see Basham, *The Wonder That Was India*, 321.
11 R.N. Dandekar, 'Dharma, the First End of Man', in Ainslie T. Embree, ed., *Sources of Indian Tradition*, Vol. I, Second edition (New York, NY: Columbia University Press, 1988), 232, note 8.
12 Kane, *History of Dharmaśāstra*, Vol. II, Part I, Second edition, 146.
13 Ibid., 153–54. See *Manusmṛti* 8.341.

14 Bühler, trans., *The Laws of Manu*, 436.
15 Ibid., 265.
16 Sharma, *Śūdras in Ancient India*, 189.
17 Kana Mitra, 'Human Rights in Hinduism', in *Human Rights in Religious Traditions*, ed. Arlene Swidler (New York, NY: The Pilgrim Press, 1982), 79 note 8.
18 Embree, ed., *Sources of Indian Tradition*, Vol. II, 162.
19 Kane, *History of Dharmaśāstra*, Vol. III, 398, note 634.
20 Ibid., Vol. I, Part II, 737–41.
21 Ibid., 804–09.
22 Ibid., Vol. III, 512. Also see note 924 for proof texts.
23 Ibid., 398, note 634; but also see Derrett, *Religion, Law and the State in India*, 452.
24 Prabhu, *Hindu Social Organization*, 285.
25 V.M. Apte, 'Social and Economic Condition', in *The Vedic Age*, ed. R.C. Majumdar, 391–92.
26 Sharma, *Śūdras in Ancient India*, 16.
27 Kane, *History of Dharmaśāstra*, Vol. II, Part I, Second edition, 25.
28 Murty, *Vedic Hermeneutics*, 14.
29 Sharma, *Śūdras in Ancient India*, 107.
30 The passage in *Majjhima Nikāya* (ii.68) is clear and unambiguous: *evaṃ sante eme cattāro vaṇṇā samasamā honti.*
31 Sharma, *Śūdras in Ancient India*, 148, note 1.
32 Ibid., 198.
33 Ibid., 219.
34 Scharfe, *The State in Indian Tradition*, 221–22.
35 Kane, *History of Dharmaśāstra*, Vol. II, Part I, 142–43.
36 Raychaudhuri, *Political History of Ancient India*, 318–19.
37 Basham, *The Wonder That Was India*, 120. But see Hemachandra Raychaudhuri, *Political History of Ancient India*, 306, 318–19. Upinder Singh (*Political Violence in Ancient India*, 52) offers an explanation similar to the one offered by Basham:

> The main point emphasized in this edict is that the *rājūkas* should discharge their duties vis-à-vis the handing out of rewards and punishments fairly and fearlessly, and they should ensure impartiality (*samatā)* in judicial proceedings and punishment. It should be noted that justice and impartiality are important aspects of the idea of the righteous king (*dhammiko dhammarāja*) in early Buddhism.

38 'So far as the operation of criminal laws is concerned, a passage from the *Majjhima Nikāya* [ii.88] shows that in cases of adultery and theft the same punishment applied to the offender, irrespective of his varṇa' (Sharma, *Śūdras in Ancient India*, 121). The choice of the offences mentioned here is significant, as from the point of view of the *varṇas,* the punishment for adultery involves negative discrimination (the higher the *varṇa* the lower the punishment) and that for theft involves positive discrimination (the higher the *varṇa* the higher the punishment). Thus *both* kinds of discriminatory punishments are absent in the passage from the *Majjhima Nikāya.*
39 Sharma, *Śūdras in Ancient India*, 207–08.
40 Bühler, trans., *The Laws of Manu*, 313.
41 Kane, *History of Dharmaśāstra*, Vol. III, 395.
42 Ibid., note 630, emphasis added.
43 Sharma, *Śūdras in Ancient India*, 193, emphasis added.
44 Ibid., 107.
45 Ibid., 194, emphasis added.
46 Bühler, trans., *The Laws of Manu*, 436.
47 Doniger and Smith, trans., *The Laws of Manu*, 260–61. The following note is also relevant (ibid., 260, note 101):

> The club is carried to the king by the thief, as we learn from 8.314–16. The commentators are quite troubled by this verse, which seems to allow for the possibility that the king may kill a priest. They argue variously that the corporal or capital punishment (*vadha*) is merely a blow, not fatal, or that the text distinguishes between the thief whom the king may kill, who is not in fact a priest, and the thief who is purified by mere inner heat, who is a priest. This latter interpretation is supported by some manuscripts that read 'or' in place of 'but' ('or a priest may purify himself by inner heat').

48 Kane, *History of Dharmaśāstra*, Vol. II, Part I, Second edition, 110–11.
49 Ludo Rocher, 'Karma and Rebirth in the Dharmaśāstras', in Wendy Doniger O'Flaherty, ed., *Karma and Rebirth in Classical Indian Traditions* (Berkeley, CA: University of California Press, 1980), 69.

9: The Political System of the *Manusmṛti*

1 Kane, *History of Dharmaśāstra*,Vol III, Second edition, 66, note 96.
2 Scharfe, *The State in Indian Tradition*, 12.

3 Ibid.
4 Ibid.
5 Ibid.
6 Ibid.
7 Ibid.
8 Olivelle, *Dharmasūtras: The Law Codes*, 25.
9 Ibid.
10 K.A. Nilakanta Sastri, *Development of Religion in South India* (New Delhi: Orient Longman, 1963), 16–17.
11 Ibid.
12 Ibid.
13 Upinder Singh makes the interesting point that: 'While the idea of Aryavarta suggests a potential spatial incorporation of the forest people into an expanding Brahmanical universe, the idea of the *mleccha* (often translated as barbarian) indicates their cultural segregation … there were *mlecchas* within Aryavarta as well' (*Political Violence in Ancient India*, 376–77).
14 Hiltebeitel, *Dharma: Its Early History in Law, Religion, and Narrative*, 191.
15 Cited, ibid.
16 Cited, ibid.
17 Kane, *History of Dharmaśāstra*, Vol. III, Second edition, 9.
18 Scharfe, *The State in Indian Tradition*, 22.
19 Ibid., 23–24.
20 Kane, *History of Dharmaśāstra*, Vol, III, Second edition, 9.
21 Kane, *History of Dharmaśāstra*, Vol. V Part II, Second edition, 1629.
22 Embree, ed., *Sources of Indian Tradition*, 211.
23 R.P. Kangle, *The Kauṭilīya Arthaśāstra*, Part II (Mumbai: University of Bombay, 1963), 15.
24 Kane, *History of Dharmaśāstra*, Vol. III, Second edition, 9. Various commentators disapprove of it though (ibid., 9–10).
25 Ibid., 10.
26 Olivelle, *The Law Code of Manu*, 174.
27 Basham, *The Wonder That Was India*, 125.
28 Kangle, *The Kauṭilīya Arthaśāstra*, Part III, 259–60. Kangle also notes Basham's oversight on this point.
29 Olivelle, *The Law Code of Manu*, 112–13.
30 Kangle, *The Kauṭilīya Arthaśāstra*, Part III, 83.
31 Ibid., 82.
32 Cited, ibid.

33 Ibid., 81. It is worth noting that 'the gods and Brahmins are those local to those territories. "Exemptions" refer to tax holidays of varying lengths granted to brahmins and other significant individuals of the conquered lands' (Olivelle, *The Law Code of Manu*, 267).
34 Bühler, trans., *The Laws of Manu*, 395.
35 Ibid.
36 Kane, *History of Dharmaśāstra*, Vol. III, Second edition, 21.
37 Olivelle, *The Law Code of Manu*, 107.
38 Kane, *History of Dharmaśāstra*, Vol. III, Second edition, 22.
39 Ibid., 32
40 Ibid., 125.
41 Olivelle, *The Law Code of Manu*, 107.
42 Ibid.
43 Ibid., 262.
44 Ibid., 176.
45 Ibid., 282.
46 Kane, *History of Dharmaśāstra*, Vol. III, Second edition, 23.
47 Ibid., 107.
48 Olivelle, *The Law Code of Manu*, 114.
49 Ibid., 107.
50 Kane, *History of Dharmaśāstra*, Vol III, Second edition, 52.
51 Ibid., 25.
52 Ibid.
53 Greg Bailey, '*Dharmarāja* in the *Mahābhārata, Dharmarāja* in early Buddhist Literature', in *On Meaning and Mantras: Essays in Honor of Frits Stal*, eds. George Thompson and Richard A. Payne (Moraga, California: Institute of Buddhist Studies and BDK America, Inc., 2016), 3–27.
54 D.R. Bhandarkar, 'Asoka and His Successors', in *A Comprehensive History of India*, Vol. II, ed. K.A. Nilakanta Sastri (Mumbai: Orient Longman, 1957), 40.
55 Ibid., 41. Also see Singh, *Political Violence in Ancient India*, 35.
56 Lahiri, *Ashoka in Ancient India*, 68. Also see 85–86 and 250.
57 Bhandarkar, 'Asoka and His Successors', in *A Comprehensive History of India*, ed. K.A. Nilakanta Sastri, 41.
58 Ibid. The author concludes the passage with the comment: 'Nevertheless, she has doubtless gained in cosmopolitanism and humanitarianism which have now become the basic principles of Hindu society.'
59 Olivelle, *The Law Code of Manu*, 147.
60 Ibid., 275.

10: Foreign Policy in the *Manusmṛti*

1 Kangle, *The Kauṭilīya Arthaśāstra*, Part III, 248.

2 Scharfe, *The State in Indian Tradition*, 205. Scharfe calls it a soldier's expression.

3 Ibid., Scharfe calls it a legal term.

4 Joseph Campbell, ed., *Heinrich Zimmer: Philosophies of India* (Princeton, NJ: Princeton University Press, 1969 [1951]), 115. Heinrich Zimmer's explanation of the diagram is helpful although he tends to depict the state in the centre as hemmed in by the *rear*, whereas the standard model depicts it as aggressive and ready to move forward (Ibid., 114–115, emphasis added):

> The principal Hindu formula for the arrangement of foreign alliances and coalitions is based on a pattern of concentric rings of natural enemies and allies. Each king is to regard his own realm as located at the center of a kind of target, surrounded by 'rings' (*maṇḍalas*) which represent, alternately, his natural enemies and his natural allies. The enemies are represented by the first surrounding ring; these are his immediate neighbors, all alert to pounce. The second ring then is that of his natural friends, i.e., the kings just to the rear of his neighbors, who threaten them in turn through the very fact of being neighbors. Then beyond is a ring of remoter danger, interesting primarily as supplying reinforcement to the enemies directly at hand. Furthermore, within each ring are subdivisions signifying mutual natural animosities; for since each kingdom has its own maṇḍala, an exceedingly complicated set of stresses and cross-stresses must be understood to exist. Such a plan of mutual encirclement is to be cast, carefully weighed, and then used as a basis for action. It delineates and brings into manifestation a certain balance and tension of natural powers, as well as touching off periodic, terrific outbursts of widely spreading conflict. *Taken for granted as a universal social principle is the propensity of neighbors to be unfriendly, jealous, and aggressive, each biding his hour of surprise and treacherous assault.*

5 Kangle, *The Kauṭilīya Arthaśāstra*, Part III, 249.

6 Ibid.

7 Ibid.

8 Ibid.

9 Kane, *History of Dharmaśāstra*, Vol. III, 17.

10 Ibid.
11 Kangle, *The Kauṭilīya Arthaśāstra*, Part III, 250.
12 Ibid., 248.
13 Ibid., 251.
14 Scharfe, *The State in Indian Tradition*, 206.
15 Ibid. KN = *Kāmandakīya-nītisāra.*
16 Ibid.
17 Ibid., 206–07.
18 Kangle, *The Kauṭilīya Arthaśāstra*, 255.
19 Scharfe, *The State in Indian Tradition*, 209.
20 Kangle, *The Kauṭilīya Arthaśāstra*, 255.
21 Scharfe, *The State in Indian Tradition*, 209–10.
22 Kangle, *The Kauṭilīya Arthaśāstra*, 255; śāmana=śāma.
23 Ibid.
24 Scharfe, *The State in Indian Tradition*, 210.
25 Campbell, ed., *Heinrich Zimmer: Philosophies of India*, 123.
26 Patrick Olivelle, *King, Governance, and Law in Ancient India Kauṭilya's Arthaśāstra* (New York, NY: Oxford University Press, 2013), 350.
27 Ibid.
28 Olivelle, *The Law Code of Manu*, 267.
29 Olivelle, *King, Governance, and Law in Ancient India*, 394.
30 Scharfe, *The State in Indian Tradition*, 219.
31 Ibid.
32 Ibid.
33 Ibid. For more on the distinction between Buddhist *dhamma* and the *dhamma* of the *dhamma-vijaya* see Kristin Scheible, 'Toward a Buddhist Policy of Tolerance: The Case of Ashoka', in *Religious Tolerance in World Religions*, eds. Jacob Neusner and Bruce Chilton (West Conshohocken, PA: Templeton Foundation Press, 2008), 317–30.
34 Raychaudhuri, *Political History of Ancient India.*, 632.
35 Ibid., 272. He also notes (290, note 1):

> The Aśokan conception of dhammavijaya was similar to that described in the *chakravatti sihanāda sutta*, 'conquest not by the scourge, not by the sword, but by righteousness' (*Dialogues of the Buddha*, Part III, p. 59). It was different from the Hindu conception explained and illustrated by the *Mahābhārata* (XII.59.38–39), the *Harivaṃśa* (I.14.21), The *Kauṭilya* (p. 382) and the *Raghuvaṃśa* (IV.43).

36 S. Radhakrishnan, ed., *The Principal Upaniṣads* (Atlantic Heights, NJ: Humanities Press, 1992 [1953]), 797.

37 See *Mahābhārata* 3.88.7; 3.107.1; 3.188.91; 12.27.10; 13.14.133; 13.14.137; 13.75.26; 13.151.42; 14.4.23. I am indebted to Sanjay Kumar for these references.

38 Upinder Singh presents interesting pictures of the *vijigīṣu*. At one point she says: 'The *vijigīṣu* of the Arthashastra is not just an ambitious king who wants to achieve military success; he is a king endowed with positive personal qualities, the constituents of whose state are in excellent condition, and who rules through the means of good policy.' (*Political Violence in Ancient India*, 308) At another point she explains: 'The *rāja-maṇḍala* theory is obviously a theoretical construct based on some basic insights into interstate relations. Its goal is to overcome and destroy the circle and reduce it to one element—the *vijigīṣu* himself.' (Ibid., 309) When that happens the *vijigīṣu* becomes the *cakravartī*.

39 Kane, *History of Dharmaśāstra*, Vol. III, 66.

40 Ibid.

41 Scharfe, *The State in Indian Tradition*, 52.

42 Ibid., 52–53.

43 Ibid., 51–55.

44 Campbell, ed., *Heinrich Zimmer: Philosophies of India*, 127–28.

45 Ibid., 129–30.

46 Scharfe, *The State in Indian Tradition*, 218.

47 Ibid., 219–20.

48 Raychaudhuri, *Political History of Ancient India*, 640, note 31.

49 Lahiri, *Ashoka in Ancient India*, 197–98.

50 Raychaudhuri, *Political History of Ancient India*, 291.

51 Ibid., 325. CHI = Corpus Inscription Indicarum.

52 Ibid., 321

53 Scharfe, *The State in Indian Tradition*, 223–24. KA = Kauṭilīya *Arthaśāstra*.

54 Olivelle, *The Law Code of Manu*, xliii.

55 Ibid.

56 Raychaudhuri, *Political History of Ancient India*, 630.

57 Campbell, ed., *Heinrich Zimmer: Philosophies of India*, 135.

58 Scharfe, *The State in Indian Tradition*, 226.

59 Ibid., parentheses removed.

60 Ibid., note 175. For more on the association of Aśoka with the concept of the *cakravartin* see Nathan McGovern, (*The Snake and the Mongoose*, 48–49):

This can be seen most clearly in the *Cakkavatti-sīhanāda Sutta* ('The *Sūtra* on the Lion's Roar of the *Cakravartin*'), in which the Buddha describes *cakravartin* monarchs of the distant past and future. The very fact that this and other early Buddhist texts would describe a monarch who is more than an ordinary king (*rājā*) by virtue of having conquered the known world (lit. 'conqueror of the four quarters': *cāturanto vijitāvi*) suggests a context in which such monarchs exist. The earliest such monarchs are the Nandas, who immediately preceded the Mauryas in the 4th century BCE, conquering much of North India from their base in Magadha, and the Mauryas themselves, who in the late 4th century and 3rd century BCE expanded the Magadha-based empire to an even greater extent, reaching its apogee, during the reign of Aśoka. Indeed, an empire of the extent first achieved by Aśoka would seem to be implied by the description of the *cakravartin* in the *Cakkavatti-sīhanāda Sutta*. The area conquered by the *cakravartin* is here described as 'this earth bound by the ocean' (*imaṃ pathaviṃ sāgarapariyantaṃ*); Aśoka was the first Indian monarch, and indeed one of the few throughout history, to establish an empire that covered most of the Indian subcontinent. Moreover, the entire ideology of kingship espoused by the *Cakkavatti-sīhanāda Sutta* seems suspiciously similar to that expressed by Aśoka himself in his edicts. The *cakravartin* in this *sutta* does not conquer by force of arms, but rather by the *dhamma*, which is physically represented by a wheel that precedes his armies as he proceeds throughout the four quarters and various peoples submit to him without a fight. Of course, in real life Aśoka did conquer by force of arms, but he explicitly expresses regret for this and, like the Buddhist *cakravartin*, repeatedly refers to his desire to rule through *dhamma* rather than force, as well as making use of the symbolism of the wheel. These close similarities between the Buddhist concept of the *cakravartin* and Aśoka's known ideology of kingship all suggest that the concept of the *cakravartin* arose during the reign of Aśoka himself, or perhaps afterward as his model of peaceful *dhamma*-based kingship fell apart.

61 See Kane, *History of Dharmaśāstra*, Vol. III, Second edition, 71:

Kauṭilya (VII.16) prescribes that the conqueror should not covet the territory, wealth, sons and wives of the slain (in battle), that he should re-instate the late king's kinsmen in their proper places (or positions), that he should install the son of the deceased king on the throne of the father and adds that the emperor who kills or imprisons the kings that submit and covets their lands, wealth, sons or wives provokes the maṇḍala (the circle of States) and makes it rise against himself.

62 Olivelle *The Law Code of Manu*, 121.

63 Kane, *History of Dharmaśāstra*, Vol. III, Second edition, 66–67.

64 Olivelle, *King, Governance, and Law in Ancient India*, 675.

65 Ibid.

66 Upinder Singh offers these helpful remarks on *dharma-vijaya* in the *Arthaśāstra* (*Political Violence in Ancient India*, 318):

> Suprisingly, in an analysis dominated by the calculation of profit and loss, there is also an evaluation in terms of levels of righteousness. Kautilya declares that a battle in which the place and time for fighting are indicated (this corresponds to open war) is the most righteous (*dharmiṣṭha*). Honor and righteousness are also part of Kautilya's enumeration of the three types of attacking kings. The 'righteous victor' (*dharma-vijayin*) is satisfied with submission. The weak king is advised to submit to him, as well as when there is danger from others. The 'greedy victor' (*lobha-vijayin*) is satisfied with the seizure of land and goods. The weak king is advised to surrender his wealth to him. The 'demonic victor' (*asura-vijayin*) is satisfied only with the seizure of the enemy's land, goods, sons, wives, and life. If attacked by him, the weaker king should take countermeasures and remain out of reach. The three types of victors can be distinguished by the degree and nature of violence that they inflict on the enemy. The *vijigīṣu* is not directly exhorted here to be a *dharma-vijayin*. However, if we connect this section with Kautilya's injunctions elsewhere that the *vijigīṣu* should not covet the land, property, sons, or wives of the slain king, he seems to be suggesting that the king should behave like a righteous victor.

67 Olivelle, *The Law Code of Manu*, 147.

68 Ibid., 275.

69 Ibid., 135.

70 Ibid., 272.

71 Basham, *The Wonder That Was India*, 146.

72 Sastri, ed., *A Comprehensive History of India*, Vol II, 312.

73 Ibid.

74 Ibid.
75 Raychaudhuri, *Political History of Ancient India*, 365–66.
76 Ibid., 435–36.

11: The *Manusmṛti* on Hinduism as a Missionary Religion

1 Donald Eugene Smith, *India as a Secular State* (Princeton, NJ: Princeton University Press, 1963), 163; Ainslie T. Embree, ed., *Alberuni's India*, translated by *Edward C. Sachau* (New York, NY: W.W. Norton and Company, 1971), 20, 100, 163; Percival Spear, *India: A Modern History* (Ann Arbor, MI: The University of Michigan Press, 1972), 41; Pratima Bowes, *The Hindu Religious Tradition: A Philosophical Approach* (London: Routledge & Kegan Paul, 1977), 129, note 7; etc.
2 Renou, ed., *Hinduism*, 16, 48; Joel Larus, *Culture and Political-Military Behavior: The Hindus in Pre-Modern India* (Calcutta: Minerva Associates, 1979), 172, ff.; G. Coedes, *The Indianized States of Southeast Asia*, ed. Walter F. Vella (Honolulu, HI: East-West Center Press, 1968) *passim*.
3 Larus, *Culture and Political-Military Behavior*, 173; R.C. Majumdar, *Hindu Colonies in the Far East* (Calcutta: Firma K.L. Mukhopadhyay, 1963), 8–9; Dawee Daweewarn, *Brāhmaṇism in South-East Asia: From the Earliest Times to 1445* AD, (New Delhi: Sterling Publishers Private Limited, 1982), 198 ff.
4 Basham, *The Wonder That Was India*, vii.
5 Ibid., 127, 145–46. Also see P.K. Gode and C.G. Karve, eds., *Prin. Vaman Shivram Apte's The Practical Sanskrit-English Dictionary*, Vol. II (Poona: Prasad Prakashan, 1958), 1296.
6 Larus, *Culture and Political-Military Behavior*, 180, 181.
7 Ibid., 180.
8 Ibid., 181.
9 Ibid., 181–82.
10 Ibid., 182.
11 Ibid., 183.
12 A.L. Basham, *Studies in Indian History and Culture* (Calcutta: Sambodhi Publications Private Ltd., 1964), 149.
13 Monier Monier-Williams, *A Sanskrit—English Dictionary* (Oxford: Clarendon Press, 1964), 1282.
14 The use of the word Hindu here is anachronistic but seems to be more appropriate than any other such as Aryan, Vaidika, Sanātana, etc. which

may be suggested, as their semantic field has varied over time in such a way as to render them misleading.

15 Kane, *History of Dharmaśāstra*, Vol. I, Part I, 306.

16 Mahesh Kumar Sharan, *Studies in Sanskrit Inscriptions of Ancient Cambodia* (New Delhi: Abhinav Publications, 1974), 165; R.C. Majumdar, *Political History of Ancient India*, 209.

17 Renou, ed., *Hinduism*, 47.

18 Spear, ed., *The Oxford History of India*, 70.

19 Mahmoud M. Ayoub, 'The Islamic Tradition' in Willard Oxtoby, ed., *World Religions. Western Traditions* (Toronto: Oxford University Press, 2021), p. 342.

20 Ibid., pp. 387–388.

21 A.L. Basham, *The Wonder That Was India* (New Delhi: Rupa and Co. 1976 [1954]), pp. 145–146.

22 Bühler, trans., *The Laws of Manu*, 411.

23 Shastri, ed., *Manusmṛti with the Sanskrit Commentary*, 411.

24 Bühler, trans., *The Laws of Manu*, 32–33.

25 Ludwik Sternbach, *The Mānava Dharmaśāstra I–III and the Bhaviṣya Purāṇa* (Varanasi: All India Kashi Raj Trust, 1974), 12.

26 See Percival Spear, ed., *The Oxford History of India*, 42, note 1.

27 H.H. Wilson, trans., *The Vishṇu Purāṇa* (Calcutta: Punthi Pastak, 1961 [1840]), 267–68.

28 Bühler, trans., *The Laws of Manu*, 412. Also see D.C. Sircar, *Studies in the Society and Administration of Ancient and Medieval India*, Vol. I (Calcutta: K.L. Mukhopadhyay, 1967), 49.

29 Muir, *Original Sanskrit Texts*, Part I, 483.

30 Ibid., 484.

31 Bühler, trans., *The Laws of Manu*, 36–37.

32 It seems one of the reasons why this point has hitherto been overlooked is that the *Manusmṛti* is more explicit about negative provisions or statements relating to the *vrātyas* (see *Manusmṛti* 2.39(d); 8.373; 10.20–23; 11.63 and 198). These have held the attention of scholars, leading them to overlook *naitairapūtair vidhivat* in 2.40(a). It is glossed by Kullūka as *yathāvidhiprāyaścittam* (Shastri, ed., *Manusmṛti with the Sanskrit Commentary*, 39). The actual penance involved is described in *Manusmṛti* 11.212 and 213. At this point a question might arise: How is the *varṇa* of a *vrātya* to be determined if *vārṇika* identity has been lost due to prolonged exclusion? Such exclusion is a common factor in all the three categories of (1) *vrātya* (2) *mleccha* and (3) *dasyu* vide *Manusmṛti* 2.23 and 39; 10.20

and 45, each implying a progressively greater measure of deviation from the original *varṇa*. The answer is provided by *Manusmṛti* 10.57, namely that when *varṇa* cannot be determined by birth, as in this case, it should be determined on the basis of actions.

33 Ibid., 406–07.

34 A.D. Pusalkar, 'Aryan Settlements in India', in *The Vedic Age*, ed. R.C. Majumdar, 248, emphasis added.

35 An interesting point pertains to the distinction between *Bramāvarta* and *Brahmarṣideśa*. The verse which defines *Brahmarṣideśa* comes after the verse which defines *Brahmāvarta* in the *Manusmṛti* (2.18–19). And the verse which says that the *brāhmaṇas* of *this* region would be global norm-setters follows it. This raises the question: The *brāhmaṇas* of which region are referred to here? As the verse immediately follows the one which defines *Braharṣideśa,* so it is clear that this region is meant. The question which arises is: Are *brāhmaṇas* of *only* this region intended, or are the *brāhmaṇas* of *Brahmāvarta* included therein or not? The commentaries are not clear on this point. One could argue that the people of *Brahmāvarta* alone define what ideal conduct is in general, and the *brāhmaṇas* of *Brahmarṣideśa* set the ideals in terms of the whole world. In other words, we have two distinct ideal types here. One group defined ideals in general and the other upholds it for the world to follow. It seems, however, that *brāhmaṇas* of *both* the regions are meant to be beacons for humanity, although those of only one region are so specified. P.V. Kane certainly takes it to be so when he writes: 'Manu (II.20) manifests great pride in and love for the holy countries of Brahmāvarta, Kurukṣetra, Matsya, Pañcāla and Śūrasena by glorifying the *brāhmaṇas* of these countries as those from whom all men on this broad earth should learn the actions and usages appropriate to them' (*History of Dharmaśāstra*, Vol. III [second edition], 137).

36 Majumdar, ed., *The Vedic Age*, 177.

37 Larus, *Culture and Political-Military Behavior*.

38 Majumdar, ed., *The Vedic Age*, 180.

39 Kane, *History of Dharmaśāstra*, Vol. II, Part I, 61, 63.

40 Majumdar, ed., *The Vedic Age*, 177.

41 Sharan, *Studies in Sanskrit Inscriptions of Ancient Cambodia*, 149.

42 Sircar, *Studies in Society and Administration*, Chapter III.

43 Kane, *History of Dharmaśāstra*, 16.

44 Ibid., 61.

45 Wilson, trans., *The Vishṇu Purāṇa*, 267–68.
46 K. Satchidananda Murty, *Revelation and Reason in Advaita Vedānta* (New York, NY: Columbia University Press, 1959), 8, emphasis added.
47 Alladi Mahadeva Sastry, trans., *The Bhagavadgītā with the Commentary of Śrī Śaṅkarāchārya* (Madras: Samata Books, 1985), 3.
48 Ibid., 3.
49 Ibid.
50 R.C. Majumdar, ed., *The Age of Imperial Kanauj* (Bombay: Bharatiya Vidya Bhavan, 1964), 443.
51 Ibid., 443.
52 'It is stated in a contemporary record that he learnt the Śāstras (sacred scriptures) from Bhagavat Śaṅkara, who is undoubtedly the famous Śaṅkarācārya' (Ibid., 438). Also see K.A. Nilakanta Sastri, *A History of South India from Prehistoric Times to the Fall of Vijayanagar* (Chennai: Oxford University Press, 1976), 428; Mahesh Kumar Sharan, *Studies in Sanskrit Inscriptions of Ancient Cambodia*, 284; etc.
53 See R.C. Majumdar, ed., *The Classical Age* (Bombay: Bharatiya Vidya Bhavan, 1970), 652–53; Majumdar, ed., *The Age of Imperial Unity*, 655; Majumdar, ed., *The Age of Imperial Kanauj*, 418, 420, 425; Vijay Shankar Shrivastava, *Hinduism in South-East Asia* (New Delhi: Ramanand Vidya Bhavan, 1939); and Daweewarn, *Brāhmaṇism in South-East Asia*, *passim*; among others.
54 Dawee Daweewarn, *Brāhmaṇism in South-East Asia*, 202.
55 Majumdar, *The Age of Imperial Kanauj*, 180.
56 Even here there are some interesting exceptions. Faxian describes Java (c. 414 CE) as a place 'where various forms of error and Brahmanism are flourishing, while Buddhism in it is not worth speaking of', (James Legge, trans., *A Record of Buddhist Kingdoms* (New York, NY: Dover Publications, 1965, [1886], 113). The text is cited as 'Heretic Brahmans flourish there, and Buddha-dharma hardly deserves mentioning' by J. Takakusu, in I-Tsing, *A Record of the Buddhist Religion as Practised in India and the Malay Archipelago (AD. 671–695)*, trans. J. Takakusu (New Delhi: Munshiram Manoharlal, 1966; [1896]), xlviii. Some scholars distinguish between heresy and Brāhmaṇism, see Daweewarn, *Brāhmaṇism in South-East Asia*, 264. I-Tsing's account includes evidence about people who 'seem to have embraced *Buddhism* for some time; and there are several points which show that they were of *Hindoo origin*' (Ibid., xliv)

57 Huston Smith, *The Religions of Man* (New York, NY: Harper and Brothers Publishers, 1958), 223.

12: Karma and Rebirth in the Manusmṛti

1 Olivelle. *The Law Code of Manu*, 77.

2 Bühler, trans., *The Laws of Manu*, 155, note 172. P.V. Kane considers a similar case from the *Mahābhārata* as an *arthavāda* or exaggeration (*History of Dharmasāstra*, Vol. V, Part II, Second edition, 1598): 'The Mahābhārata contains interesting verses on the transference of the effects of *karma* to one's descendents. The Adiparva states: "If the consequences of sin are not seen as affecting the perpetrator, they will surely be seen in the sons and grandsons." This again is an *arthavāda*.' The following account by Apa Pant in his work *A Moment in Time* (London: Hodder and Stoughton, 1974, 25–26) may be of interest in this context:

> By 1818 the last war of the Marathas with the British had ended with the absorption of their first homeland by the British Presidency of Bombay, except for Satara, Kolhapur and some smaller States that were allowed to remain as they were. In 1848, however, Satara was annexed by the British, who offered to pay well if my great-grandfather would leave Karad and let them have the surrounding area on a twenty-year lease. The treaty was drawn up in the English language, which my great-grandfather did not know. An interpreter called Gokhale was paid by the British to translate the treaty into Marathi, which he did without disclosing that in the English version, which naturally was the binding one, the lease was agreed to in perpetuity. To this day the family of Gokhale, who played false with my great-grandfather has had no male heirs, and in three generations the heirs who were adopted were murdered.

3 Olivelle, *The Law Code of Manu*, 251.

4 Ibid., 186.

5 Kane, *History of Dharmasāstra*, Vol. V, Part II, Second edition, 1638, note 2620.

6 Olivelle, *The Law Code of Manu*, 145–46.

7 Ibid., 146.

8 Ibid.

9 Ibid., 50–51.

10 Ibid., 97.
11 Ibid., 246.
12 Kane, *History of Dharmasāstra*, Vol. V, Part II, Second edition, 1577.
13 Ibid.
14 Olivelle, *The Law Code of Manu*, 146.
15 Kane, *History of Dharmasāstra*, Vol. V, Part II, Second edition, 1598.
16 Olivelle, *The Law Code of Manu*, 124.
17 Ibid., 88.
18 Ibid., 254. P.V. Kane provides the following helpful note here (*History of Dharmasāstra*, Vol V, Part II, Second edition, 1533–34):

> The same idea is set forth as to flesh-eating in Manu and Viṣṇu-dharmasūtra, which state 'that being whose flesh I eat here would eat me in the next world, the wise declare this to be the origin of the word 'māṁsa'.' The Śat. Br. in another passage refers to a strange legend. Bhṛgu, who had become vain on account of his learning and thought himself more learned than his father Varuṇa, was asked by his father to go to the four quarters from east to north and report what he would see there. Horrible sights met him in all directions e.g. in the east he saw men dismembering men, hewing off their limbs one by one and saying 'this to you, this to me.' He said 'this is horrible.' They replied 'these indeed dealt with us in yonder world and so we now deal with them in return.' Then in the north he saw that men crying aloud were being eaten by men crying aloud. When he said 'horrible &c.'; they replied 'these indeed dealt with us…in return'. This is a long story and it is not necessary to set out the whole. This story probably gives expression to the popular notion of 'tit for tat'. But one thing is clear that the Śat. Br. indicates by this story that a belief had then arisen that one who does evil in one life has to suffer for it in a later life from that being whom he treated badly.

19 Consider the following remarks by Ludo Rocher ('Karma and Rebirth in the Dharmaśāstras', in Doniger O'Flaherty, ed. *Karma and Rebirth*, 69):

> Does this mean anything for the particular relation between stealing object A and being reborn as animal B? There is no easy answer to this question. We might understand why a thief of grain will be reborn as a rat, or someone who steals meat, as a vulture. We may be able to appreciate, for very different reasons, why the thief of a cow (*go*) is reborn as an iguana (*go-dhā*), or the thief of

molasses (*guḍa*) as 'a flying-fox' (*vāgguda*). We can even imagine why a thief of drinking water is reborn as 'a black-white cuckoo,' for this bird is said to subsist on raindrops. But, in general, names of animals in Sanskrit are often uncertain, and so is their relation to the objects stolen.

20 Kane, *History of Dharmasāstra*, Vol. V, Part II, Second edition, 1591.
21 Gerald James Larson, 'Karma as a "Sociology of Knowledge" or "Social Psychology" of Process/Praxis', in Doniger O'Flaherty, ed., *Karma and Rebirth*, 303–04.
22 Ibid.
23 Ibid., 304.
24 Ibid., 305.
25 Ibid., 306.
26 Ibid.
27 Ibid.
28 Ibid., 312.
29 Ibid.
30 Ibid., 314.
31 Ibid., 316.
32 Olivelle, *The Law Code of Manu*, 82–83.
33 Bruce M. Sullivan, *The A to Z of Hinduism* (New Delhi: Vision Books, 2003), 209. For a detailed discussion of the rite, see Kane, *History of Dharmasāstra*, Vol. IV, Second edition, section III.
34 Ibid., 334.
35 Kane, *History of Dharmasāstra*, Vol. V, Part II, Second edition, 1598.
36 Padmanabh S. Jaini, *The Jaina Path of Purification* (Berkeley, CA: University of California Press, 1979) 302–04.
37 Kane, *History of Dharmasāstra*, Vol. V, Part II, Second edition, 1598.
38 Ibid., Vol. IV, 338.
39 M. Hiriyanna, *The Essentials of Indian Philosophy* (New Delhi: Motilal Banarsidas 2005 [1948]), 49.
40 Kane, *History of Dharmasāstra*, Vol. IV, 335–36.
41 Ibid., 335–36.
42 Ibid., 337.
43 Ibid., 340.
44 Ibid., 339, 340.
45 Olivelle, *The Law Code of Manu*, 64.
46 Ibid., 57.

47 Rocher, 'Karma and Rebirth in the Dharmaśāstras', in Doniger O'Flaherty, ed., *Karma and Rebirth*, 77.
48 Ibid., 62.
49 Ibid., 62–63.
50 Ibid.
51 Ibid.
52 Ibid., 66.
53 Ibid., 65.
54 Ibid., 68. Patrick Olivelle translated these as 'killing a Brahmin, drinking liquor, stealing and having sex with an elder's wife—they call these 'grievous sins causing loss of caste' (*The Law Code of Manu*, 194). He also provides an interesting note (Ibid., 286): 'it appears that drinking liquor becomes a grievous sin only when done by Brahmins … stealing is also a grievous sin when it involves the gold of Brahmins.'
55 Olivelle, *The Law Code of Manu*, 194.
56 Rocher, 'Karma and Rebirth in the Dharmaśāstras', in Doniger O'Flaherty, ed., *Karma and Rebirth*, 68.
57 Olivelle, *The Law Code of Manu*, 214–15.
58 Rocher, 'Karma and Rebirth in the Dharmaśāstras', in Doniger O'Flaherty, ed., *Karma and Rebirth*, 70. He also provides parallels from Yā*jñavalkya Smṛti*.
59 Ibid., 68.
60 Ibid.
61 Ibid., 69.
62 Ibid., 72ff.
63 Ibid., 69.
64 Ibid.
65 Ibid.
66 Ibid., 71, 76.
67 Olivelle, *The Law Code of Manu*, 212.
68 Bühler, trans., *The Laws of Manu*, 485–87.
69 Olivelle, *The Law Code of Manu*, 212.
70 Ibid., 14–15.

Chapter 13: The Doctrine of the *Yugas* in the *Manusmṛti*

1 'The ṚgVeda does not contain the names of all the four well-known yugas viz. Kṛta, Tretā, Dvāpara and Kali. The word "Kṛta" when used in

the Ṛg Veda appears to mean "the best throw of dice or of the seeds of vibhītaka in gambling (X.34.6, X.43.5)".' (Kane, *History of Dharmasāstra*, Vol. III, 886). He also notes that 'Kali as a throw of dice does not occur in the ṚgVeda. In the Atharva Veda VII.114.1, Kali means a throw of dice' (Ibid., 887).

2 Margaret Stutley and James Stutley, *A Dictionary of Hinduism: Its Mythology, Folklore and Development 1500* BC–AD *1500* (London: Routledge & Kegan Paul, 1977), 351. For a more elaborate account see Basham, *Studies in Indian History and Culture*, 320–21.

3 Ibid., 207. This also explains why sometimes the Ages are described as the Winning Age, the Age of Trey, the Age of the Deuce, and the Losing Age (see Doniger and Smith, trans., *The Laws of Manu*, 329, 355, 315 and 326. Also see Luis González-Reimann, *The Mahābhārata and the Yugas: India's Great Epic Poem and the Hindu System of World Ages* (New York, NY: Peter Lang, 2002), 7–8.

4 '*For each…by one*: Tretā: 3,000 years with twilights of 300 years each; Dvāpara: 2,000 years, with twilights of 200 years each; Kali: 1,000 years, with twilights of 100 years each. The total of all four Ages thus comes to 12,000 years' (Olivelle, *The Law Code of Manu*, 236).

5 Ibid., 17–18, without the superscripts.

6 Basham, *Studies in Indian History and Culture*, 321.

7 Olivelle, *The Law Code of Manu*, 18, without the superscripts.

8 Ibid., 18–19, without the superscripts.

9 Luis González-Reimann, 'Time in the *Mahābhārata* and the Time of the *Mahābhārata*', in Sheldon Pollock, ed., *Epic and Argument in Sanskrit Literary History* (New Delhi: Manohar, 2010), 65.

10 Olivelle, *The Law Code of Manu*, xxiii.

11 Basham, *Studies in Indian History and Culture*, 321.

12 Ibid. Emphasis added. Other traditions place Mahābhārata War in the third or fourth millennium BCE, see P.V. Kane, *History of Dharmaśāstra*, Vol. III, 896 ff.

13 Luis González-Reimann writes ('Time in the *Mahābhārata*', in Sheldon Pollock, ed., *Epic and Argument*, 16, note 9): '[A]s in *Mahābhārata* 3.186.18–23 and *Mānava Dharma Śāstra* I.64–74 where it is never said that the duration of the *yugas* is to be understood as given in divine years.' This could involve an oversight in relation to the *Mānava Dharma Śāstra*, as the Manusmṛti (1.71) clearly employs the expression *devānāṃ yugam*, which has been translated as such: by Bühler as 'one age of the gods' (*The Laws of Manu*, 20); by Doniger and Smith, trans., as 'an Age of the gods'

(*The Laws of Manu*, 11); and by Patrick Olivelle as 'a single Age of the gods' (*The Law Code of Manu*, 18).

14 Basham, *Studies in Indian History and Culture*, 62.

15 Ibid.

16 Ibid.

17 Doniger, trans., with Smith, *The Laws of Manu*, 12.

18 This did pose a hermeneutical problem for the exegesis of the tradition: Is *dharma* one or many? Thus the famous ninth-century commentator on the *Manusmṛti*, Medhātithi maintained (González-Reimann, 'Time in the *Mahābhārata*', in Sheldon Pollock, ed., *Epic and Argument*, 173):

> [...] that *dharma* itself did not change as the yugas advanced. One should rather understand that due to the decreasing capacity of men in each yuga they are less able to follow it correctly. According to him, dharma, in these passages, means the different ways of acquiring merit that are not easily attainable according to the yuga. Whether Medhātithi's interpretation of Manu's words is correct or not, the implication is still that things are done differently in each yuga, and the way to attain, or obtain, merit will vary accordingly.

19 Kane, *History of Dharmaśāstra*, Vol. III, 892.

20 Bühler, *The Laws of Manu*, 24.

21 Kane, *History of Dharmaśāstra*, Vol. III, 885.

22 Olivelle, *The Law Code of Manu*, 159.

23 Kane, *History of Dharmaśāstra*, Vol. II, Part I, 603.

24 'It is clear from Medhātithi's Bhāsya on Manu (IX.112) that long before his time (9th century AD) there were writers who had condemned Govadha (in Madhuparka etc.), *niyoga* and the giving of a larger share to the eldest son and expressed the view that those practices were only allowed in bygone ages' (Kane, *History of Dharmaśāstra*, Vol. V, Part II, Second edition, 1267).

25 Kane, *History of Dharmaśāstra*, Vol. V, Part II, Second edition, 1269–70:

> According to Pūrvamīmāṁsā Veda is eternal, self-existent and of absolute authority; one fails to understand how sages could have authority at the beginning of the Kali-yuga to prohibit what the Veda enjoined or permitted. This seems to be a fiction invented to accommodate as Dharma the changes in people's ideas and practices that had occurred. It would have been honest and straightforward if the writers on Dharmaśāstra had said that changed circumstances required that the words of the Veda or

of the old smṛtis should not be followed. And there is nothing novel or revolutionary in saying this. Both Manu and Yājñavalkya prescribe that one should not observe but give up, what was (once) deemed to be dharma, if it had become hateful to the people and if it would end in unhappiness and not lead to the attainment of heaven. Even the Mitākṣarā follows this precept of the two smṛtis and expressly says that unequal distribution (at partition) of ancestral wealth, though found in the Śāstras, should not be followed because people had come to hate it. It may be noted that the word used by Yāj. and others is 'lokavidviṣṭa' or 'lokavikruṣṭa' (hated or reviled by the people) and not 'siṣṭa-vidviṣṭa', the idea being that even if orthodox learned *pandits* insist that people must follow what the Veda and smṛtis declare to be Dharma, common people may give up practices condemned by them or hateful to them. This attitude recognizes the historical facts that practices change in the course of centuries and common people are entitled to ignore the dicta even of the Veda (much more of the smṛtis).

The *Manusmṛti* also adopts this approach at places, see 4.176.

26 Ibid., Vol. II, Part II, 1311

27 Ibid., Vol. III, 967:

The chapter on Kalivarjyas can be employed as a very effective answer to those who trot out the theory of the 'unchanging East'. Social ideas and practices undergo substantial changes even in the most static societies. Many of the practices, that had the authority of the Veda (which was supposed to be self-existent and eternal) and of such ancient smṛtis as those of Āp., Manu and Yāj., had either come to be given up or had become obnoxious to popular sentiment. This fiction of great men meeting together and laying down conventions for the Kali age was the method that was hit upon to admit changes in religious practices and ideas of morality. The Kalivarjya texts are also a complete answer to those who hold fast to the notion that dharma (particularly ācāradharma) is immutable and unchangeable (*aparivartanīya*). This chapter on Kalivarjya unmistakably shows how the most authoritative dicta of the Veda and of ancient sages and law-givers were set aside and held to be of no binding authority because they ran counter to prevailing notions and furnishes a powerful weapon in the hands of those who want to introduce reforms in the incidents of marriage, inheritance and other matters touching modern Hindu society. One can further see how some practices still persist in spite of the prohibitions in the Kalivarjya texts viz. marriage with one's maternal uncle's daughter, sannyāsa, agnihotra and even śrauta animal sacrifices (rarely).

28 Bühler, trans., *The Laws of Manu*, 396.

29 Kane, *History of Dharmaśāstra*, Vol. III, Second edition, 40. Also see Embree, ed., *Alberuni's India*, 382: 'Śūdras will be kings, and will be like rapacious wolves, robbing the others of all that pleases them […].' The *Mahābhārata* (12.70.23) states that kings will be cruel in Kali Yuga.

30 C.P. Ramaswami Aiyar, 'The Philosophical Basis of Indian Legal and Social Systems', in Charles A. Moore, ed., *The Indian Mind: Essentials of Indian Philosophy and Culture* (Honolulu, HI: University of Hawaii Press, 1967), 250. See *Mahābhārata* 12.70.6; also see 5.130.15.

31 Embree, ed., *The Hindu Tradition*, 221.

32 Ibid.

33 Kane, *History of Dharmaśāstra*, Vol. III, 890.

34 González-Reimann, 'Time in the *Mahābhārata*', in Sheldon Pollock, ed., *Epic and Argument*, 68.

35 Ibid., 71, note 24.

36 Ibid., 71, note 28

37 González-Reimann, *The Mahābhārata and the Yugas*, 136, note 40.

38 Ibid. Also see, González-Reimann, 'Time in the *Mahābhārata*', in Sheldon Pollock, ed., *Epic and Argument*, 64. Emphasis added.

39 Bühler, trans., *The Laws of Manu*, 396, footnote.

40 González-Reimann, *The Mahābhārata and the Yugas*, 61–62.

41 Olivelle, *The Law Code of Manu*, 176.

42 Ibid., 176–77, without the superscripts.

43 Kenneth K.S. Ch'en, *Buddhism: The Light of Asia* (New York, NY: Barron's Educational Series, 1968), 42.

44 Kane, *History of Dharmaśāstra*, Vol. III, Second edition, 890. Also see González-Reimann, *The Mahābhārata and the Yugas* (198, note 98): [Āryabhaṭa] 'considered the four yugas to be of equal length, thus ignoring the 4-3-2-1 sequence established by the names of the dice throws.'

45 Embree, ed., *The Hindu Tradition*, Part I, 379–82.

46 Bühler, trans., *The Laws of Manu*, 396 footnote.

47 J.A.B. van Buitenen, trans., *The Mahābhārata*, Vol. 3 (Chicago, IL: The University of Chicago Press, 1978), 430:

> Bhārata, a king acquires a quarter of the merit of the Law that his subjects practice when well protected by their king. When a

king practices his Law, he is worthy of divinity: when he practices lawlessness, he only goes to hell. Strict government applied by a ruler according to his own Law constrains the four-class order and restrains the people from breaking the Law. When a king pursues strict government perfectly and completely, then the best of eras begins, the Kṛta Age. Have no doubt whether the time causes the king, or the king causes the time: it is the king who is the cause of the times. The king is the creator of the Kṛta Age, of the Tretā and the Dvāpara, and the king is the cause of the fourth Age. By causing the Kṛta, a king enjoys heaven beyond measure, by causing the Tretā a king enjoys heaven, though not beyond measure. By setting in motion the Dvāpara he enjoys it but moderately. A wicked king dwells in hell for years without end; for the world is touched by a king's flaws, and the king by the world's.

48 *Manusmṛti* 6.14–31.

14: The Hermeneutics of Suspicion and the *Manusmṛti*

1 See Richard E. Palmer, *Hermeneutics: Interpretation Theory in Schleiermacher, Dilthey, Heidegger, and Gadamer* (Evanston, IL: Northwestern University Press, 1969); Paul Ricœur, *The Conflict of Interpretations: Essays in Hermeneutics,* ed. Don Ihde (Evanston, IL: Northwestern University Press, 1974); Hans-Georg Gadamer, *Truth and Method*, translation edited by Garrett Barden and John Cumming (New York, NY: Seabury Press, 1975).

2 Rowan Williams, 'The Suspicion of Suspicion: Wittgenstein and Bonhoeffer', in *The Grammar of the Heart,* ed. Richard H. Bell (San Francisco, CA: Harper & Row Publishers, 1988), 36–53.

3 Paul Ricœur, *Freud and Philosophy: An Essay in Interpretation*, trans. Denis Savage (New Haven, CT: Yale University Press, 1970), 32.

4 Ibid.

5 Ibid., 33–34. I leave it to the reader to decide whether Michel Foucault and Edward Said should now be included in this list. The case for René Descartes is less clear. See Geneviève Rodis-Lewis, *Descartes: His Life and Thought,* trans. Jane Marie Todd (Ithaca, NY: Cornell University Press, 1998), 79–81.

6 Elizabeth Isischei, 'Some Ambiguities in the Academic Study of Religion', *Religion* 23 (1993): 379–80. See also Doniger and Smith, trans., *The Laws*

of Manu, lxvii, note 83. For the hermeneutics of suspicion as an integral part of the appropriation of meaning, see Maurice Boutin, 'Réponses / Responses to John C. Roberston', *Studies in Religion* 8, no. 4 (1979): 380, note 2.

7 *The Works of Śaṅkarācārya in Original Sanskrit*, I (New Delhi: Motilal Banarsidass, 1987), 1008.

8 Altekar, *The Position of Women in Hindu Civilization*, 3, note 2.

9 Radhakrishnan, ed., *The Principal Upaniṣads*, 326.

10 Ibid., 222–24, 230–34.

11 Murty, *Revelation and Reason in Advaita Vedānta*, 103–4.

12 Kane, *History of Dharmaśāstra*, Vol. 2, Part 1, 571.

13 Ibid., 572.

14 Basham, *The Wonder That Was India*, 172.

15 Bühler, trans., *The Laws of Manu*, 318.

16 Kane, *History of Dharmaśāstra*, Vol. II, Part 1, 575, note 1750.

17 Ibid., 572, note 1331.

18 Ibid., 576–78.

19 Basham, *The Wonder That Was India*, 143–144, emphasis added.

20 Ibid., 140.

21 Doniger, and Smith, trans., *The Laws of Manu*, 250.

22 Ibid., lii–liv.

23 Basham, *The Wonder That Was India*, 140.

24 Ibid.

25 Kane, *History of Dharmaśāstra*, Vol. 2, Part 1, 121.

26 Radha Kumud Mukherji, 'Social Condition', in *The Age of Imperial Unity*, ed. R.C. Majumdar, 543.

27 *The Bhagavad Gītā with Eleven Commentaries*, ed. G S. Sadhle (Bombay: The Gujarati Printing Press, 1935), 583.

28 Kane, *History of Dharmaśāstra*, Vol. 2, Part 1, 121.

29 H.C. Raychaudhuri, 'Appendix: Note on the Date of Artha-Śāstra', in *The Age of Imperial Unity*, ed. R.C. Majumdar, 286. See also Scharfe, *The State in Indian Tradition*, 21.

30 Mukherji, 'Social Condition', in *The Age of Imperial Unity*, ed. R.C. Majumdar, 543. As the word *brahma* could also mean the Veda, the expression *brahma-dhāraṇa* could well refer to its memorization, as the word *dhāraṇa* is also used in this sense.

31 Sharma, *Śūdras in Ancient India*, 208.

32 Halbfass, *India and Europe*, 176. He also notes: 'In a curious and conspicuous statement, Patañjali's *Mahābhāsya* (second century BCE)

on Pāṇini 11, 4, 10 (śūdrāṇām aniravasitānām) presents the *yavana*, together with the śaka, as "śūdras who are not excluded" (*aniravasita*). The chronological implications of this reference have been the subject of much debate.'

33 Bühler, trans., *The Laws of Manu*, 430.
34 Doniger, and Smith, trans., *The Laws of Manu*, 250.
35 Basham, *The Wonder That Was India*, 61.
36 Sharma, *Śūdras in Ancient India*, 219.
37 See A.L. Basham, *Conference on the Date of Kaniṣka* (Leiden: E. J. Brill, 1968).
38 Renou, ed., *Hinduism*, 66.
39 Bühler, trans., *The Laws of Manu*, 386.
40 Doniger and Smith, trans., *The Laws of Manu*, 224.
41 Bühler, trans., *The Laws of Manu*, 386.
42 Doniger and Smith, trans., *The Laws of Manu*, 250.
43 Altekar, *The Position of Women in Hindu Civilization*, 350. For Sanskrit text see note 1.
44 Sharma, *Śūdras in Ancient India*, 208.
45 Doniger and Smith, trans., *The Laws of Manu*, xl.
46 D.C. Sircar, 'The Śakas and the Pahlavas', in *The Age of Imperial Unity*, ed. R.C. Majumdar, 121–22.
47 Stutley and Stutley, *A Dictionary of Hinduism*, 258. The claim that Candravarman was a Śaka king has been contested, see Hemchandra Raychaudhuri, *Political History of Ancient India*, 425–26, 738, 768–69. The rise of Śakas to political power, however, which this claim is supposed to support, is generally accepted (Ibid., 446, 691, 737, 751).
48 Kane, *History of Dharmaśāstra*, Vol. 2, Part 1, 61.
49 J.A.B. van Buitenen, trans., *The Mahābhārata*, Vol. 2 (Chicago, IL: The University of Chicago Press, 1975), 564.
50 K.M. Sen, *Hinduism* (Harmondsworth: Penguin Books, 1961), 29–31; Pande, *Dimensions of Ancient Indian Social History*, 162.
51 Bühler, trans., *The Laws of Manu*, 411.
52 Ricœur, *Freud and Philosophy*, 32, 35.

15: Conclusions

1 Louis Jacolliot, *La Bible Dans L'Inde* (Paris: Librairie Internationale, 1869), 33–37; Kewal Motwani, *Manu: A Study in Hindu Social Theory* (Chennai: Ganesh and Co. 1984).

2 Olivelle, *The Law Code of Manu*, 258.
3 Ibid.
4 Apte, *The Practical Sanskrit English Dictionary*, 1019.
5 The following description, however, attributed to Mrs Terry Brown, probably describes the positive dimension too enthusiastically:

> In Hinduism, a woman is looked after not because she is inferior or incapable, but on the contrary, because she is treasured. She is the pride and power of society. Just as the crown jewels should not be left unguarded, neither should a woman be left unprotected. If there are costly jewels, we do not throw them here or there like brass vessels. Costly material is protected.

Regrettably the weblink containing this quotation is no longer available.
6 *Merriam-Webster's Collegiate Dictionary*, Tenth edition (Springfield, MA: Merriam-Webster, Incorporated, 2002), 545.
7 But also see Olivelle, *The Law Code of Manu*, 240.
8 Bühler, trans., *The Laws of Manu*, 395.
9 Ibid.
10 Ibid.
11 Ibid.
12 Olivelle, *The Law Code of Manu*, 19, emphasis added.
13 Ibid., 187.
14 Basham, *Conference on the Date of Kaniṣka*, 143, 144.
15 Koenraad Elst, *Indigenous Indians: Agastya to Ambedkar* (New Delhi: Voice of India, 1993), 384–85, emphasis added.
16 Olivelle, *The Law Code of Manu*, 101, emphasis added.
17 Ibid., p. 41.

Appendix I: Dalits in the *Manusmṛti*

1 Agrawala, *India as Described by Manu* 21.
2 Olivelle, *The Law Code of Manu*, 61, emphasis added.
3 Ibid., 256. P.V. Kane notes that, according to the *Amarakośa* 'both cāṇḍāla and nāpita are called Divākīrti' (*History of Dharmaśāstra*, Vol. II, Part I, 84).
4 Ibid., 81.
5 Ibid.
6 Kane, *History of Dharmaśāstra*, Vol. II, Part I, 172.
7 Agrawala, *India as Described by Manu*, 17.

8 Olivelle, *The Law Code of Manu*, 94, emphasis added.
9 Ibid., 183.
10 Ibid., 284.
11 Agrawala, *India as Described by Manu*, 17.
12 Raimundo Panikkar and Arvind Sharma, *Human Rights as a Western Concept* (New Delhi: D.K. Printworld, 2007), 63, note 24.
13 Doniger and Smith, trans., *The Laws of Manu*, 41–42, emphasis added.
14 Bühler, trans., *The Laws of Manu*, 72–73.
15 Shastri, ed., *Manusmṛti with the Sanskrit Commentary*, 75.
16 Kane, *History of Dharmaśāstra*, Vol. V, Part II, 921, note 1468a.
17 See Embree, ed., *Alberuni's India*, Part 1, 104.
18 Agrawala, *India as Described by Manu*, 21.
19 Olivelle, *The Law Code of Manu*, 75, emphasis added.
20 Bühler, trans., *The Laws of Manu*, 151.
21 Doniger and Smith, trans., *The Laws of Manu*, 87.
22 For the bracketing of Scheduled Castes and Scheduled Tribes in the *Manusmṛti* see Agrawala, *India as Described by Manu*, 16–17.

Appendix III: Is Hinduism Brahmanical?

1 Nicholas B. Dirks, *Castes of Mind: Colonialism and the Making of Modern India* (Princeton, NJ: Princeton University Press, 2001), 225–26.
2 Ibid., 204.
3 A.L. Basham, *The Origins and Development of Classical Hinduism*, edited and completed by Kenneth G. Zysk (Oxford: Oxford University Press, 1991), 130.
4 The reader may also wish to consult Johannes Bronkhorst, 'Brahmanism: Its Place in Ancient Indian Society', *Contributions to Indian Sociology* 51, no. 3 (2017): 361–69.

Index

Abhijñānaśākuntalam, Kālidāsa, 47, 50
Ādityas, 8, 210–211
adultery, 81, 123–125, 127, 129–130, 136, 139, 142, 144, 201–202, 236–237; punishment for, 124, 130, 136, 142, 236–237
Agni Purāṇa, 210
Agrawala, V.S., 91
agriculture, 9, 59
Aitareya Brāhmaṇa, 63, 67, 231–232, 240
Ākranda, 164
Albīrūnī, 232
Alexander, invasion of India, 15
Altekar, A.S., 20, 44, 116, 123–124
Ambedkar, B.R., xvii, 27, 266; burning *Manusmṛti*, 4
America, 196, 267
American Council of Learned Societies, 204
antyādapi paraṃ dharmam, 49
Āpastamba Dharma Sūtra, 13, 38, 74, 103, 122, 266
Apte, V.M., 141
Aquinas, Thomas, 234
Arabs, xiii, 29
ari, 163–165
Arjuna, xxiv, 194, 240
artha, 17, 71, 154–155, 158
Arthaśāstra, Kauṭilya, 15–17, 83, 86, 98, 150, 153–59, 166–68, 170–71, 176–78, 232, 241, 267; Basham on, 157
Āryabhaṭa, 232
Āryans, 58, 68, 113, 141, 152–153, 186, 189–190
Āryāvarta, 150–153, 176, 185, 187, 193
asceticism, 19, 39, 95, 97–99, 101, 259; sexual life and, 99
Aśoka, Emperor, 15–16, 18–19, 21, 24–25, 28, 70, 162, 168–169,

172–178, 261, 268; Aramaic inscriptions of, 70; as Buddhist, 144; *dhamma*, 172; dispensation, 144; experiment, 269; Hindu view of, 22; inscriptions, 70; pacifism, 21, 145, 267, 269; patronage of Buddhism, 98; policies, 18, 20, 175, 253; Raychaudhuri on, 20; Rock Edicts of, 232
Aśokan pillar, 21
Āśramas, 68, 72, 84, 91–92, 95–101, 103, 194; Basham on, 102; system of, 97–98, 101; theory of, 95
āsura-vijaya, 168
aśvamedha, 145, 176
Atharva Veda, 61, 141
ātma-tuṣṭi, 35–36, 39, 47, 50, 53–54
Attlee, x

bādha, 98–100
Basham, A.L., xv, 29–30, 74, 76, 101–102, 144, 157, 179, 182, 224–225, 236, 238–242
battle of Plassey, 25
Baudhāyana Dharmasūtra, 74, 151
Bhagavadgītā, 159, 194–195, 240
Bhāgavata Purāṇa, 79, 170
Bhakti movement, xiii
Bhandarkar, D.R., 162
Bharatas, 109, 191
Bhaṭṭa, Devaṇṇa, 139
Bhaṭṭa, Kullūka, 46, 49, 53, 75
Bhaviṣyapurāṇa, 46
Bhīmeśvarapurāṇa, 94
bhiṣak or physician, 61
Bhṛgu, 23
Biardeau, Madeleine, 24
Bimbisāra, 173
Bose, Netaji Subhas Chandra, ix–x
Bose, Sugata, 26
braharṣi-deśa, 150–151, 191
brahmacarya, 99–100, 114
Brāhmaṇas/Brahmans, 6–7, 22–27, 60–61, 64–66, 68–69, 103, 136–137, 152, 183–185, 188–195, 211, 237–239, 242–246, 257–258, 260; accepting food, 83–84; as *agrajanmā* or first-born, 10; of Āryāvarta, 187; of *Brahmarṣi-deśa,* 187; priestly power, 8; sex with *śūdra* woman, 126; woman, 90
brāhmaṇatva, 194–195
Brāhmanic: institutions, 189
Brahmanism, 103
Brahma Purāṇa, 209
Brahmarṣideśa, 152, 194
Brahmasūtra, xi, 246
Brahminhood, 102–3
Brahmins, 7–10, 19, 36–37, 48, 58–60, 66–68, 80, 82–83, 92–93, 109, 118–119, 126, 151–152, 174, 183–184; homage to Kṣatriya, 8; kills Kṣatriya, 75; kills Vaiśya, 75; murdering, 201
Bṛhadāraṇyaka Upaniṣad, 7, 58–61, 65–66, 234–235
Bṛhaddevatā, 170
Bṛhaspati 154
bride-price, 117
British rule, xii, xvii, 25–27, 266–267
Bronkhorst, Johannes, 25
Brothers, xxiv, 106–108, 115–117, 121, 127, 156
Buddha, 25, 173, 232; 'Enlightened One,' 171; as incarnation of Viṣṇu, 100

Buddhism, xv–xvi, *xxiv,* 19, 22, 25, 64, 96–102, 169, 175–176, 178, 183, 188, 190, 196; propagation of, 15
Buddhists, 19, 99, 144, 162, 169, 172, 174–175, 194, 260, 265; movements, xiii; tradition in Burma, xi
Būhler, G., 7, 42, 49, 53, 70, 76, 79, 219, 226, 242, 244
van Buitenen, J.A.B., 30

cakra, 170
cakravartī, 169, 177, 267; Hindu concept of, 176
cakravartin, 170–172, 174–178
Cāṇakya, 15–16
caṇḍāla, 46, 67, 87–90, 193; as polluting, 88; woman, 125
Candragupta, 15–16
Candravarman, 245
capital punishment, xxii, 135, 147; and *sudra,* 264
carmamna or tanner, 61
caste (*jāti*) system, xi–xiii, xv–xvi, 6, 9, 68, 72, 141, 238, 245, 248, 254, 258; lower, xi, 4, 65–66, 72, 236, 255, 264; upper, xiii
celibates, 122, 128, *see also sannyāsa*
Cēmakuura Veṇkaṭakvai, 93
Cevvappa, 94
Chakravarti, Uma, 25
Christianity, xvii, 185–186, 196
Christians, 196, 267
Cīnas (Chinese Yüeh-chih tribes), 64, 68, 189
class system, 179
Coedes, G., 182
cosmic ages, 39
creator, 23, 159
Criminal Procedure Code of India, 143
criminals, 231; execution of, 123

Dalits, 255, 267
daṇḍa, 159–161, 165–166, 171, 174, 232
daṇḍa-nīti (law and order), 232
daṇḍa-samatā, 261
Dandekar, R.N., 137
Daradas, 68, 177, 189
Dasyus, 59, 68, 185–186, 189
daughter (*putrikā*), x, 6, 77, 85, 89, 106–107, 109–110, 112–114, 116–118; unmarried, 121–122, 129–130
Davids, Rhys, 19
Day of Judgement, 261
defamation, 133, 146, 244
Demetrius, 20
Derrett, J. Duncan M., 68
dhamma-vijaya, 162, 169, 172, 174, *see also dharma-vijaya*
dharma, xv, 11; concept of, 169, 254; as Law, 70; and *pramāṇa,* 54; sources of, 11–12, 35–37, 39–42, 46–47, 49, 51–54, 71–72, 254
dharmarāja, 161–162, 169, 172, 174, 178, *see also* kings
Dharmaśāstra, 17, 98, 118, 123, 143, 146, 149, 153–156, 159, 204, 211–212, 218–219
Dharma Sūtras, xviii, 81, 83, 142, 153
dharma-vijaya, 168–69, 172, 176–177
Dharmavyadha, 50
Digby Baltzell, E., 266

dig-vijaya, 168–169
Doniger, Wendy, 7, 49, 71, 242, 245
Dravidas/Dravidians, 65, 67, 183; Larus on conversion of, 184
Droṇasimha, King of Valabhī, 4, 143
Dṛṣadvatī, 9, 150, 187
Duḥṣanta, 50–51
Duṣyanta, 47, 50
Dvāpara age, 39–40, 221–224, 226–27, 229–230
dvijas, 13, 39, 80, 87, 266
dvijātis, 45, 91, 136

Egalitarianism, 144, 261–262
emic approach, xiii–xiv, xvi, 206, 254
equality, 138–140, 143–145, 148, 255, 258, 261–262
etic approach, xiii–xvi, 254
evil diseases, 120, 128, 201–202
evil-doers, 160, 231
execution, 48, 123, 126; lie and, xxi

falsehood xxii, 9, 76–77, 223
false testimony, xxi, 48
'female-son': putrikā, Jolly on 118
Fideism, xxiii
Fitzgerald, James, 24
foreign: invasions, 15–16, 19–20, 25–26, 64, 96, 98, 102, 225, 253, 261, 266; policy, 163, 165–166; rule, xiii, 19, 25–26
Freud, Sigmund, 233, 263

Gāndharva marriage, 50
Gandhi, Mahatma, ix, xx, 27, 97, 167, 266
Gaṅgā, 93–94
Gārgīsaṃhitā, 21, 244
Gārgīya Jyotiṣa, 223
Gautama, 123, 125, 146
Gautama Dharma Sūtra, 81, 124, 241
Ghaznivids, xiii
Ghose, Aurobindo, 27
gods, 8–9, 56–58, 78, 83, 85, 92, 109–110, 119–120, 160, 222, 224–225
Gokhale, Gopal Krishna, 27
González-Reimann, Luis, 223, 229–230
good woman, 111, 120, 122, 127–128
Great Boar, Basham on, 29
gṛhastha (householder), 84, 91, 95–97, 99–100, 102–103, 119–120, 148
guardian deities, 119; Olivelle on, 160
guests, 83, 121–122, 130, 201
Guptan sculptures, 29
Guptas, 16, 24, 28, 161, 175
guru, xxiv, 49, 89, 115, 195
gurudroha, xxiv

Hariṣeṇa, Jaina, 21
hermeneutics of suspicion, 233–235, 237, 240, 242, 246, 263
hierarchy, 11, 60–61, 66, 146, 249, 257–259
Hiltebeitel, Alf, 24, 122–123, 153
Hindu ethics, xxii–xxiii
Hinduism, xiii, xv–xvi, xviii–xx, xxiii–xxiv, 3–4, 6, 98–102, 140, 182, 184–185, 194–196, 209–210, 234–235, 255–256, 261–265; Brahminical, 102; classical, 95, 104, 184–186, 195, 221, 236; expansion of, 183; modern, xx, 27
Hinduization, 192

Hindu law, xvi–xvii, 107, 138, 142, 253
Hindus, xiv–xv, xvii–xix, xxi, 3, 6, 22, 25, 27–30, 139, 180, 182–183, 185–186, 252–253; political thought, 163
'Hindu' state system, 68
Hindu tradition, xx, 7, 100, 158, 207, 232, 243, 246, 252, 260
Hiraṇyadama, 195
The History of British India, Mill, 76
human rights, xxiii, 261
husband, 5, 42, 44–45, 86, 105–113, 116, 118–121, 123–125, 127–130, 201–202, 236; death of, 43–44, 122, 128

Indian Culture, 18
Indian Independence, 266, 268
Indian National Army (INA), ix
Indo-Bactrians, xiii
Indo-Greeks, 225, 241
Indo-Parthians, xiii, 225
Indo-Scythians, 225, 242
inheritance, law of, 85, 137
inscriptions, 15, 30–31, 152, 176, 192, 195; Junāgarh rock, 23; Kuruattur Viṣṇu Temple, 4; Nasik cave, 24, 142; of Rudradāman, Jūnāgaḍh, 225; Singaya-Nāyaka, 260
Institutes of Hindu Law, xvi
intermarriage, 66–67, 141, 192, 248
intertextuality, 5, 9, 11
Iron Pillar, Delhi, 245

Jainas, xiii, 99
Jainism, xv–xvi, 64, 70, 96–99, 101–102, 183, 209, 224, 253
Jalal, Ayesha, 26
Jamison, Stephanie, 50
jātībhraṃśa, 190
jātis, xv–xvi, 63–65, 67, 193, 248, 264–265
jātyutkarṣa, 193
Jayavarman II, 195
Jews, 28, 253–254; destruction of the Temple of, 253; Law of, 140
jñāna (knowledge), 50, 207, 235, 247, 263; liberative, 50, 277; source of 54
judges, appointment of, 135

Kākatīya Dynasty, 94
Kali, 19, 39–40, 144, 180, 223–224, 226–230, 255
Kalinga, 168–170; war of, 20, 169, 173
kalivarjya, 226
kali yuga, 19, 144–145, 221–222, 224, 226–229, 255
kalpa, 231
kāma, 11, 71
Kāmasūtra, 154
Kāmbojas, 67, 177
Kane, P.V., 12–13, 44–45, 62, 67, 69, 71, 74, 76–78, 80, 84, 86–89, 98, 113–116, 124–126, 129–130, 136, 139, 202–203, 209–211, 236–237; on *dharmas* in *yugas*, 226
Kangle, R.P., 157–158
Kant, xxiii
Kaṇvas, 24
karma, xv, 199–204, 206–212, 218–220, 261–262; as indigenous conceptual system, 204–207; Kane on birth and, 203; and rebirth, 199, 202, 209–211; Rocher on, 212–218

karmāra or *kārmāra* (ironsmith), 61—62
Karṇa, 230
Kauṇḍinya, 192–193, 196
Kauravas, 229–230
Kauṭilya, 15–16, 83, 150, 154–155, 166–167, 177, 260
Ketkar, S.V., 85
Khāravela, 169–170
Khaśas, 68
kings, xxii, 30, 89–90, 109–110, 123, 125–126, 135, 137–140, 142, 144–147, 153–154, 156, 158–168, 170–174, 177–180, 191–192, 200–202, 227–229, 231–232, 244–245, *see also dharmarāja*
kingship, 153, 158–161, 178, 227–228
kirātas, 68, 177, 189, 193
Kishwar, Madhu, xxi
Krishnamurti, Jiddu, 27
Kṛṣṇa, 161, 194, 230
Kṛta Age, 39–40, 221–224, 226–227, 229–231
Kshaharāta dynasty, 180, 243
Kshatriyas, 7–9, 23–24, 47, 57, 76, 140–141, 180, 260; 47–49, 57–61, 66–69, 81, 86, 110, 135–137, 146–147, 181, 189–190, 193, 242–246, 257, 260; killing, 76; Olivelle on, 7; towards Brahmins, 7
Kullūka Bhaṭṭa, 49, 50, 87–89, 186, 256
Kumārila, xi, xxiv
Kuṇḍina, 191–192
Kurukṣetra, 9, 151–152
Kushāṇas, xiii, 15, 19, 21, 70, 188, 241
Kūṣmāṇḍa formulas, xxi

Lahiri, Nayanjot, 162
Lakṣmīdevī, xii
land, ix, 10, 30, 150–153, 156, 168, 183, 185, 187, 243, 253; of *āryāvarta*, 177; creation of, 9
Larson, Gerald James, 204–207
Larus, Joel, 183–184, 195
law, books, xix, xxiv, 109, 146, 184–185; as *dharma*, 8, 11; of Manu, xi; right to take, 138–145; of women, 128
life, stages of, 95–96, 101, 103, 262, see also *āśramas*
Lingat, R., 153
livelihood, 9, 80, 92
lobha-vijaya, 168
loka as the 'world,' Kane on, 12
low birth (*jātihīna*), 92, 94
'low born' (*avaraja*), 12, 38–39, 53, 67, 126, 130, 203

Madanaratnapradīpa or *Madanaratnadīpa*, 139
Maddison, Angus, xii–xiv
Madhvācārya, 38
madhyama, 163–164
Magadha, 20, 98, 162, 173
Mahābharata, 3, 7, 9, 12, 38, 40–41, 46–47, 50, 78–79, 108, 112, 122, 124, 161, 223–224, 228–230, 232, 247–249; Basham on Kali Yuga in, 224
Mahadevan, T.M.P., xix, 95
mahājana, 13
mahārāja, 161, 175
Maitrī Upaniṣad, 170
Majjhima Nikāya, 142, 144

Majumdar, R.C., 18
Mānava Dharma Śāstra, xix, 154, 223
Mānava Dharma Sūtra, 3
maṇḍala, 24, 55, 57, 163, 165–166, 170
Manu, xi–xii, xix–xx, 3–4, 17, 22–23, 44–45, 80–81, 83–85, 87–89, 98–100, 105–107, 121–126, 153–155, 188–190, 192–195, 202–204, 241–242, 244–246, 248, 265–268; denier of rights to women, 6; as *kṣatriya*, 23; as lawgiver, xi; name of, xi, 4
Manusmṛti: as casteist, 264; for closed Hindu society, 265; intertextuality of, 5–6; as *Manuvāda*, 251–252; Satchidananda Murty on, 40
Mārkaṇḍeya Purāṇa, 109–111, 211
marriage, x, 45, 50–51, 86, 98, 107–110, 117, 120, 127, 129–130, 190, 192–193, 195; consecration, 127; law of, 137, *see also* intermarriage
Marriott, McKim, 204
Maruts, 8
Marx, Karl, 233, 263
mātsya-nyāya, 159, 167
Matsya Purāṇa, 191, 210
Matsyas, 9, 151, 187
Mauritian Hindus, 72
Maurya, Chandragupta/ Candragupta, 15, 20, 30, 268
Mauryas, 14–16, 18–20, 22, 24–25, 28, 64–65, 145, 172–173, 175, 177, 253
McGovern, Nathan, 102–104
Medhātithi, 49, 75, 78–80, 84, 88–89, 91–92, 152, 193, 255
Menander, 20
Mill, James, xvii–xviii, xxii, 76, 264
Milton, 178
Mīmāṁsā, 45, 187
Mishnah, 28
Mitākṣarā, xii
Mitamiśra, 161
mitra, 163–165
Mitra, Kana, 139
mlecchas, 65–66, 68, 152–153, 177, 182–183, 189–190, 193, 242
modernity, xii, xx, 144, 262
mokṣa, 78, 82, 84, 91–92, 204, 208, 210, 229
monasticism, 97–98, 100; cenobitic, 97–98, 100; eremitic, 98
morality, xxi, xxiii, 46–47, 172
mother, x, 77, 85, 89, 106, 108–109, 113–116, 141, 208, 210, 248
Mudrārākṣasa, Viśākhadatta, 30
Muir, J., 141, 189
Mukherjee, B.N., 172
Mūlavarman, 152
Muslim rule, xiii, 26–28
Muslims, 26, 68, 185, 267
Mutiny 1857–58, ix, xvii, 27

Nahapāna, 246
Nandas, 25
Narayana Guru, Sree, 27
Nāyaka, 93–94
neo-Brahmans, 103
Netaji, ix–x
Nibandhas, xviii–xix, 140
Nietzsche, 263
Nilakanta Sastri, K.A., 151
Nirukta, 6, 63
nirvāṇa, 169
nivṛtti, 100, 205

niyoga (levirate), 12, 43–45, 226
Nrisinghacharya, 26

Oḍras, 65, 67
Olivelle, Patrick, xi, 16–17, 19–20, 22, 39–40, 46–49, 59–60, 80, 93, 105–106, 115–117, 151, 160, 162, 179, 202–203
oppression, xi, 31, 244
ordinance, xxii, 77
Orientalism, xvii, xxii, 227, 263

pakṣas, 98, 100
Pañcālas, 9, 151, 187
Pañcatantra, 3, 112
Pāṇḍavas, 45, 229–230, 247
Panikkar, K.M., 19, 27–28
Pāṇini, 63, 192, 265
pāparoga, Olivelle on, 202
Pāradas, 68, 177, 189
Paramahaṃsa, Rāmakṛṣṇa, 27
paraṃ dharmam, 49
Parāśara, xix, 124, 226
Paraśurāma, 7, 24, 180, 229
pārṣṇi-grāha, 164–165
Parthians (Pahlavas), 15–16, 20, 64, 68, 177, 181, 189, 241–242
Patañjali, 87–88, 103, 245
Patel, Sardar, 268
patriarchal, 128–129, 236, 255
Patrick, 117
Pauṇḍrakas, 65, 67, 189
perjury, xxii, 77, 135, 137, 147
Phule, Jyotirao, 27
pollution, 88–89, 182, 204
Potter, Karl H., 205–206
Prahbu, Pandhari-Nath, 59
Prajāpati, 113, 119, 127, 243, 265
prakṛtis, 165–166, 259
Pratāparudra, King, 143
pratiloma castes, 88, 129
pravṛtti, 100, 205
proselytization, 27, 187
punarjanma, 209–210
punishment, 121, 125–127, 130, 133, 136, 139, 144, 148, 156, 160, 172, 236–237; for *brāhmaṇa*, 142; corporal, 81, 135, 137, 244, 258; for defamation, 135–136; of male offender, 123; for *śūdras*, 123; for theft, 82, 136; for women, 123
purification, 37, 48, 129, 192, 263
pūrtadharma, 79
Puruṣa Sūkta, 6–7, 10, 55–59, 65–66, 69, 93, 265
Puruṣottama, 68
Pūrvamīmāṅsā-sūtra, Jaimini, 62
Pusalkar, A.D., 191

Qur'ān, 186

Radhakrishnan, S., xx, 27
rājamaṇḍala, 163–165, 170
Rājanītiprakāśa, Mitamiśra, 161
Rajashekhara, King of Mahodaya Pura, 4
Rājātaranginī, 173
rākṣasas, 65, 161
Rāma-rājya, 159, 229
Rāma/Rāmacandra, 26, 180, 229
Rāmāyaṇa, as *Rāmacaritamānas*, 229
Rāmāyaṇa of Vālmīki, 229
Ranade, Mahadev Govind, 27
Ranga Swami Aiyangar, K.V., 85
rathakāra (chariot maker), 61–62
rationalism, xxiii
Raychaudhuri, H.C., 20, 29–30, 173
rebirth, 199, 202–203, 210–212, 219

Renou, Louis, 55
renunciation, 96–98, 103
ṚgVeda, 6, 55–57, 60–61, 69–70, 140–141, 191, 243, 265
Ricœur, Paul, 233, 250, 263
rivers: as Brahmāvarta, 9, 150–151, 187, 191; Sarasvatī, 150–151
Rocher, Ludo, 149, 211–212
Roy, Rammohun, xx, 27
Rudradāman, 16, 23, 225
Rudras, 8, 210–211
Śabaras, 63, 114
sacrifices, 40, 43, 56, 58–60, 145, 151, 193–194, 201, 223, 226, 239–241
sadācāra, 35, 39, 42, 46–47, 49, 53–54
Said, Edward, 263
Śakas (Scythians), xiii, 15–16, 21, 23, 64, 68, 177, 180–181, 188–189, 241–246
śakti, 167
Śakuntalā, 47, 50–51
Salomon, Richard, 243
Sāmānya or *sādhāraṇa dharmas*, xxiii, 139
Sāmavidhāna Brāhmaṇa, 74, 170
Śaṁkarācārya, 72
Saṃnyāsa, 84, 91–92, 96, 99–101, 262
Samprati, 98
samuccaya, 98–100
Samudragupta, 16, 21–22, 31, 175–176
sanātana dharma, xxiv, 226
Śaṅkara, xi, xxiv, 72, 188, 194, 234–235, 240, 246; enunciation of, 194; on *Vedāntasūtra*, 50
Śaṅkarācārya, 78, 99
Sāṅkhya system, 207
Saṃnyāsa, 84, 91–92, 96, 99–101, 252
Sanskrit, 13, 16, 31, 70, 115, 196, 265
Śāntiparva, 84, 91, 124
Sarasvatī, 150, 187; Dayānanda, 27
Sarasvatīvilāsa, 139, 143
Sarvajña-Nārāyaṇa, 100
sarvataḥ, 37, 48; Olivelle on, 47
Śātakarṇi, Guautamīputra/ Gautīmiputra, 16, 24, 142, 180, 243, 246
Śatapatha Brāhmaṇa, 7, 57–58, 60
Śātavāhanas, 24, 243
Satchidananda Murty, K., 40, 52
Satī, 111–112
satya age, 221
Satyavān, 110–111
Savarkar, V.D., 27
Sāvitrī, 108–111, 190
Scharfe, Hartmut, 142, 151, 154, 166, 170, 173, 176
Scheduled Castes and Scheduled Tribes (Prevention of Atrocities) Act of 1989, 92
Sen, Keshub Chunder, 27
servants, 59, 68, 79–80, 82, 111, 119, 121, 238
sharecropper (*ardhasītika*), 83, 92
Sharma, Ram Sharan, 24, 74, 76, 85–86, 142, 146
Sikhism, xv–xvi
Singh, Upinder, 22
śiṣṭācāra, 49
śiṣṭas or 'cultured' twice-borns, 53
sisters, x, 77, 85–86, 90, 94, 113–116, 121
śiśya (disciple), xx, 79
Smith, Brian K., 7, 49, 71
Smṛticandrikā, of Devaṇṇa Bhaṭṭa, 139

Smṛtis, xviii–xxi, 3–4, 39–40, 42–43, 45, 47–48, 127, 129, 140, 142, 146, 149, 236–237, 239
social classes, 9, 38, 56, 59, 87, 160, 179, 260
śrāddha, 68, 84, 91, 115, 208, 210–211; Sullivan on, 209
śramaṇas, 103
Śruti, 42–43, 45–48, 54, 155
strī-dhana, 107–108
Sudās, 191
śūdrāhatyāvratam, 75
śūdras, xxi–xxii, 6–9, 19, 48–50, 57–62, 66–69, 73–88, 90–94, 122–125, 127, 135–137, 141–142, 146–147, 192, 200, 237–238, 240–246, 249, 256–257, 260–261; and artisanship, 260; *āśrama* and, 84; Basham on, 74, 238; creation of, 59; and *dharma*, 82; from feet of Puruṣa, 56; and food to *brāhmaṇa*, 83–84; and gifts to *brāhmaṇa*, 83; killing, 75–76; *Manusmrti* and life of, 263–264; and offences, 81–82; offspring of Brahmin from women of, 66; as once-born man, 93; as Pūṣan, 8; and sacraments, 80–81; sex with a Brahmin woman, 126; as sharecropper, 83; Sharma on, 74; son of *brāhmaṇa*, 137; and studying Vedas, 78–79; treatment of, 73–74; value of life, 85–87; and Vedic sacrifices, 79–80
Śukranītī, 161
Sullivan, Bruce M., 209
Śunaḥśepa, 230
Śuṅga, Puṣyamitra, 16
Śuṅgas, 16, 24
Śūrasenakas, 9, 151, 187
sūta, bard or, 61–62
śvapacas, 90
svatantra, 106, 256

Tagore, Devendranath, 27
Tagore, Rabindranath, 27
Taittirīya Upaniṣad, 42, 48
taṣṭā, maker of chariots, 61
Tilak, Bal Gangadhar, 27
Tirrukōneri Dāsyai, xi
Trader-Merchant hypothesis, 183
Tretā Yuga, 39–40, 221–224, 226–227, 229–230
Tripathi, Rama Shanker, 21
truth, xx–xxii, 8, 13, 48, 76–77, 141, 160, 223, 228
Tulsīdās, 229
twice-born, 23, 39, 44, 86, 93, 125, 147–148, 181, 211, 226, 260
tyaṣṭā (carpenter) 61

udāsīna, 163–164
Udayagiri, Manchapuri cave at, 28–29, 169
Udayana, xi
uniform justice, 145
untouchability (*asprśya*), 6, 49–50, 82, 84, 87–91, 122
Upaniṣads, xii, 70, 235
Uśanas, 154

vaiśyas, 7–9, 48–49, 56–58, 60–61, 67, 69, 81, 85–86, 136–137, 140–141, 146–147, 257, 260; killing, 76
Vājasaneyī Saṃhitā, 193
vānaprastha, 97, 99–100

vaptā (barber), 61, 83, 92
varṇas, 6, 24, 49, 55, 57–69, 92, 135–135, 140, 148–149, 180–181, 185–186, 192–193, 243, 248, 257–260, 264–266; categories within categories, 62; classes or, 61; origin of, 7, 10, 57–59, 66; scheme, 23, 57, 65–66, 70–72, 146, 186; scheme of, 58; system, xv–xvi, 6, 57, 65, 69–70, 177, 186, 189, 193, 246, 254; theory of, 95
varṇa-saṃsarga, 179–180
varṇa-saṅkara, 249, 255
varṇāśrāma dharma, xv, xxiii, 104, 177, 194–195, 204, 207
Vasiṣṭha, 191
Vaṣiṣtha Dharma Sūtra, 126
Vāśiṣṭhīputra Pulumāvi, 142
Vasus, 8, 211
Vāyu Purāṇa, 191, 193, 211
Veda, xviii–xix, 11–13, 36–43, 47–48, 52, 58–59, 66, 68, 71–72, 78–79, 94, 194, 210, 234–235, 248–249; is root of *all dharma*, 37; root of Law, 35; teaching, 37, 52
Vedāṅgas, 63
Vedāntasūtra, 194; Śaṅkara in, 91–92
Vedic Age, 22, 58, 63–65, 68, 140, 142
Vidura, 50, 78
vijigīṣu, 24, 163–165, 170
Vijñāneśvara, xii
vikalpa, 98–100
virtue, xxiii, 90, 93, 110, 121, 127, 226
Viśākhadatta, 29–30
Viśeṣa dharmas or *pṛthag dharmas*, xxiii
Viṣṇu, 24, 100; incarnation as boar, 28–29
Viṣṇu Dharma Sūtra, 88, 129, 155
Viṣṇu Purāṇa, 145, 190
Viśvāmitra, 46, 63, 191
Viśvarūpa, 45, 62, 125
Vivekananda, Swami, xx, 27
von Stietencron, Heinrich, 30
vrātya, 125, 190
vyūhas, 168

Walker, Benjamin, 19
warfare, 18, 31, 158, 167
WASPs—the White Anglo-Saxon Protestant males, 266
Weber, Max, 207
welfare, 11–12, 38, 53, 130
well-being, material, 155
Wells, H.G., 18
Wertgesichtspunkt/Wertbeziehung, Weber, 208
Western ethics, xxiii
widow (*vidhavā*), 43–45, 116; and *Satī*, 112
wife, 43, 82, 85–86, 89, 109–110, 112, 114–116, 118–120, 126, 128–129, 148, 201–202, 236–237; abandonment of, 124; beating of, 121; childless, 43; loss of husband, 42
Wilson, President, 20
Winternitz, 158
women, x–xii, xxiv, 5, 37–39, 47–48, 88, 105, 107–108, 113–115, 117–118, 124–130, 136, 255–256, 262–263, 266; attitude towards, 77; depiction of, 114–115; feminine qualities,

123, 125; Kane on, 121; killing , 76; Manu and treatment of, xvii, 264; person of , xxiv; pregnancy, 121–122, 130; protection of, 129, 255–256; as revered, x; and sex, 123, 125; status/position of, xvii, 5–6, 73, 77, 105–106, 123, 128, 236; *śūdra*, 81, 147; treatment of, xvii, 73

yajña, 152, 194
Yājñavalkya, xii, xix, 124, 235
Yājñavalkya Smṛti, xii, 45, 62, 80, 89, 121, 124, 126, 156, 203
YajurVeda, 56–57, 61
Yama, 8, 111, 160–161, 219, 231
Yavanas (Greeks), xiii, 15–16, 20, 64, 68, 70, 174–175, 177, 180–181, 189, 241–242
yuddha (battle), 25, 157, 167, 191, 228, 267
Yudhiṣṭhira, xi, xxiv, 12–13, 178, 228, 247–249
Yüeh-chih (Kuṣāṇas), 15, 225
Yuga Purāṇa, 21, 223, 244; *Gārgīsaṃhitā* of, 21
yugas, 6, 39–40, 221–232, 255; doctrine of, 221; theory, 223–224, 232

ben Zakkai, Johanan, 28
Zimmer, Heinrich, 166, 171, 175

About the Author

Formerly of the Indian Administrative Service (IAS), Arvind Sharma is the Birks Professor of Comparative Religion in the School of Religious Studies at McGill University in Montreal, Canada. He has taught in universities in Australia (Queensland, Sydney), the United States (Northeastern, Temple, Boston, Harvard) and India (Nalanda). He has also published extensively in the fields of Indology and comparative religion and was instrumental, through three global conferences (2006, 2011, 2016), in facilitating the adoption of a Universal Declaration of Human Rights by the World's Religions.

Books authored by him include *Gandhi: A Spiritual Biography*, *Hinduism and Its Sense of History*, *Religious Tolerance: A History* and *The Ruler's Gaze: A Study of British Rule over India from a Saidian Perspective*. He is contributing editor of *Our Religions: The Seven World Religions Introduced by Preeminent Scholars from Each Tradition*, and series editor of the *Encyclopedia of Indian Religions*.

By the Same Author

Religion has become a vital element in identity politics globally after the terror attacks of 11 September 2001 in the United States of America. And so the question of how religious tolerance may be secured in the modern world can no longer be avoided. Can religious tolerance be placed on a firmer footing by finding grounds for it within the different faiths themselves? This book addresses that question. In *Religious Tolerance: A History*, Arvind Sharma examines Judaism, Christianity, Islam, Hinduism, Buddhism, Jainism, Sikhism, Confucianism, Daoism and Shinto—whose followers together cover over two-thirds of the globe—to identify instances of tolerance in the history of each of these to help the discussion proceed on the basis of historical facts. This is a timely book—the first of its kind in scope and ambition.

Edward Said's *Orientalism* (1978) is a seminal work in the field of postcolonial culture studies. It critiqued Western scholarship about the Eastern world for its patronizing attitude and tendency to view it as exotic, backward and uncivilized. Arvind Sharma, longstanding professor of comparative religion at McGill University in Montreal, Canada, now takes up the Palestinian academic's groundbreaking ideas—originally put forth predominantly in a Middle Eastern context—and tests them against Indian material. He explores in an Indian context Said's contention that the relationship between knowledge and power is central to the way the West depicts the non-West.

Scholarly and accessible, *The Ruler's Gaze* throws fresh light on Indian colonial history through a Saidian lens.

HarperCollins *Publishers* India

At HarperCollins India, we believe in telling the best stories and finding the widest readership for our books in every format possible. We started publishing in 1992; a great deal has changed since then, but what has remained constant is the passion with which our authors write their books, the love with which readers receive them, and the sheer joy and excitement that we as publishers feel in being a part of the publishing process.

Over the years, we've had the pleasure of publishing some of the finest writing from the subcontinent and around the world, including several award-winning titles and some of the biggest bestsellers in India's publishing history. But nothing has meant more to us than the fact that millions of people have read the books we published, and that somewhere, a book of ours might have made a difference.

As we look to the future, we go back to that one word—a word which has been a driving force for us all these years.

Read.